48756

AF697331

Divisia Monetary Aggregates

Divisia Monetary Aggregates

Theory and Practice

Edited by

Michael T. Belongia
Hearin-Hess Professor of Economics and Finance
University of Mississippi, USA

and

Jane M. Binner
Senior Lecturer in Finance
Department of Finance and Business Information Systems
Nottingham Business School, UK

palgrave

Selection and editorial matter © Michael T. Belongia and Jane M. Binner 2000
Introduction and Chapter 13 © Michael T. Belongia 2000
Chapter 3 © Leigh Drake, K. Alec Chrystal and Jane M. Binner 2000
Chapters 1, 2, 4–12 © Palgrave Publishers Ltd 2000

All rights reserved. No reproduction, copy or transmission of this publication may be made without written permission.

No paragraph of this publication may be reproduced, copied or transmitted save with written permission or in accordance with the provisions of the Copyright, Designs and Patents Act 1988, or under the terms of any licence permitting limited copying issued by the Copyright Licensing Agency, 90 Tottenham Court Road, London W1P 0LP.

Any person who does any unauthorised act in relation to this publication may be liable to criminal prosecution and civil claims for damages.

The authors have asserted their rights to be identified as the authors of this work in accordance with the Copyright, Designs and Patents Act 1988.

First published 2000 by
PALGRAVE
Houndmills, Basingstoke, Hampshire RG21 6XS and
175 Fifth Avenue, New York, N. Y. 10010
Companies and representatives throughout the world

PALGRAVE is the new global academic imprint of St. Martin's Press LLC Scholarly and Reference Division and Palgrave Publishers Ltd (formerly Macmillan Press Ltd).

Outside North America
ISBN 0–333–64744–0

In North America
ISBN 0–312–22300–5

This book is printed on paper suitable for recycling and made from fully managed and sustained forest sources.

A catalogue record for this book is available from the British Library.

Library of Congress Cataloging-in-Publication Data
Divisia monetary aggregates : theory and practice / edited by Michael T. Belongia and Jane M. Binner.
p. cm.
Includes bibliographical references and index.
ISBN 0–312–22300–5 (cloth)
1. Money supply—Mathematical models—Congresses. I. Belongia, Michael T. II. Binner, Jane M., 1961–

HG226.3 .D58 2000
332.4'6—dc21

99–054660

10 9 8 7 6 5 4 3 2 1
09 08 07 06 05 04 03 02 01 00

Printed and bound in Great Britain by
Antony Rowe Ltd, Chippenham, Wiltshire

Contents

List of Figures

List of Tables

Notes on the Contributors

Joseph Atta-Mensah is a senior analyst at the Bank of Canada. He gained his PhD in Financial Economics from Simon Fraser University, Vancouver, Canada. His research interests include: monetary policy issues, information extraction from financial assets, valuation of financial instruments and economic forecasting models.

William A. Barnett is the originator of Divisia monetary aggregates. He derived the formula for the monetary services' user cost, which he used in establishing the relevancy of aggregation and index number theory to monetary economics. He is editor of the Cambridge University Press journal, *Macroeconomic Dynamics* and the Cambridge University Press monograph series, International Symposia in Economic Theory and Econometrics, and is a fellow of the American Statistical Association.

Michael T. Belongia is Hearin-Hess Professor of Economics and Finance at the University of Mississippi. Prior to this appointment he served as economist and economic advisor at the Federal Reserve Bank of St Louis. He has also served as consultant or visiting scholar at several central banks in Europe.

Jane M. Binner is a Senior Lecturer in Finance at the Nottingham Business School. Previous positions include senior lecturer in Statistics at the University of Derby and Business Analyst with the Experian Group. Jane gained her PhD in Multivariate Time Series Analysis from the University of Leeds in 1990. Her research comprises a diverse range of areas including artificial intelligence applications, game theory modelling in the health and retail sectors, application of advanced time series analysis techniques in the area of contract law, and the evaluation of the econometric performance of Divisia monetary aggregates across Europe as European Monetary Union gets under way.

K. Alec Chrystal is a Research Adviser to the Bank of England within the Monetary Analysis Division. His previous appointment was as the National Westminster Bank Professor of Monetary Economics within the Department of Banking and Finance at the City University Business School, London. He is author of *Controversies in Macroeconomics* (Prentice-Hall) and co-author (with R.G. Lipsey) of *An Introduction to Positive Economics* and *Economics for Business and Management* (both Open University Press).

Robert E. Dorsey is Associate Professor of Economics and Finance at the University of Mississippi. His primary research interests are econometrics of non-linear systems, artificial intelligence and experimental economics. Prior to taking up a post at the University of Mississippi, Robert was head of the Department of Risk Management at the University of Arizona.

Leigh Drake is a Professor in the Economics Department at Loughborough University and Deputy Director of the Loughborough University Banking Centre. He has published widely in the area of Monetary Economics and Banking. Recent journal publications include: *Economic Journal* (1996); *Oxford Economic Papers* (1997); and the *Review of Economics and Statistics* (1997). Leigh Drake is author of *The Building Society Industry in Transition* (Macmillan, 1989).

Martin M.G. Fase is the Deputy Director of the Nederlandsche Bank and manager of the Bank's Econometric Research and Special Studies Department. He is Professor of Monetary Economics at the University of Amsterdam. He has published extensively on statistics, monetary economics and the history of economic thought, and is a member of the Royal Dutch Academy of Arts and Sciences.

Robert Fluri is Deputy Head of the Statistics Section of the Swiss National Bank in Zurich. He has a Masters degree in Economics from the University of Bern.

Jeong Ho Hahm is Deputy General Manager of the Cheongju branch of the Bank of Korea. Previous positions include Chief Economist at the Institute for Monetary and Economic Research at the Bank of Korea, and visiting research fellow at the Kiel Institute of World Economics in Germany. Jeong gained his PhD in Economics at the University of Texas, USA.

Heinz Herrmann is a Senior Economist in the Research Department at the Deutsche Bundesbank, Frankfurt am Main. He is author of the book, *Problems of Monetary Policy Considering Reactions of Commercial Banks* (1977).

Kazuhiko Ishida is Chief Manager and Senior Economist in the Institute for Monetary and Economic Studies, Bank of Japan. His previous positions include Senior Economist at the Research and Statistics Department, Bank of Japan and Economist in the Economic and Statistic Department at OECD, Paris.

Norbert G.J. Janssen has been an analyst in the Bank of England's Monetary Assessment and Strategy Division since 1995. Prior to this, he was a lecturer at Maastricht University, the Netherlands, where he wrote his PhD thesis, 'The

Definition and Policy Relevence of Monetary Aggregates in the Netherlands'. Norbert's work has been published in the *Bank of England's Quarterly Bulletins*, the *Economic Journal*, and the *Swiss Journal of Economics and Statistic.*

Jun Tae Kim joined the Bank of Korea in 1991 as a junior economist in the Institute for Monetary & Economic Research. Currently, Jun Tae Kim is working as an Economist at the Chongju Branch of the Bank of Korea.

Clemens J.M. Kool is the Professor of Money, Banking and European Financial Markets at the University of Maastricht in the Netherlands. Clemens obtained his PhD from Erasmus University, Rotterdam, the Netherlands in 1989. Previous positions held include senior adviser at the Netherlands central bank and visiting professor at both the Federal Reserve Bank of St Louis and the School of Business at Indiana University. Clemens has published widely in journals such as *European Economic Review, Journal of Business and Statistics* and the *Journal of International Money and Finance.*

G.C. Lim is an Associate Professor of Economics in the Economics Department at the University of Melbourne. Previous positions include Director of the Monetary and Financial Economics Program at the University of Melbourne, and President of the Victorian Branch of the Economics Society. His main areas of interest include Monetary Economics, exchange rate modelling and non-linear dynamics.

Yi Liu is an Assistant Professor of Economics at the University of South Alabama and obtained his PhD from Washington University in St Louis in 1995. He has published work with William Barnett and Mark Jenson in the journal *Macroeconomic Dynamics* (1997).

David Longworth is currently the Chief in the Bank of Canada's Research Department. Prior appointments include Chief in the Department of Monetary and Financial Analysis, and Deputy Chief in the International Department at the Bank of Canada. He joined the Bank of Canada in 1974 and gained a PhD from Massachusetts Institute of Technology in 1979.

Vance L. Martin is Reader of Economics in the Economics Department at the University of Melbourne. He has edited two books on non-linear models in economics with John Creedy, and his main areas of interest include monetary economics, exchange rate modelling and non-linear dynamics.

Koji Nakamura is an analyst in the Policy Planning Office at the Bank of Japan. He has an MA degree in Economics and an MBA degree from Boston University.

Hans-Eggert Reimers is a Professor in the Economics Department of the Fachhochschule Wismar. From 1991 to 1994 he worked in the Research Department of the Deutsche Bundesbank. He gained his PhD in Economics at the University of Kiel in 1991 and is the author of *Analysis of Cointegrated Variables with Vector Autoregressive Models* (1991).

Yen Chrystal Shih is currently Director General of the Economic Research Department at the Central Bank of China, Taiwan, which she joined in 1988. She served as an Adjunct Associate Professor in the Department of Banking at the National Chengchi University of Taiwan from 1991 to 1994. She gained her PhD in Economics at Ohio State University in 1987.

Erich Spoerndli is currently the Director of the Monetary Operations Division of the Swiss National Bank. Previous positions include, Head of the Economic Studies Section at the Swiss National Bank and Head of the Macro-Forecasting Unit at the Swiss Federal Institute of Technology in Zurich. Erich gained his PhD in Economics at Zurich University in 1971 and his main research interests include monetary economics and the statistical and methodological aspects of business cycle indicators.

Karl-Heinz Toedter is a Senior Economist in the Research Department at the Deutsche Bundesbank, Frankfurt am Main. He is author of *The Specification Problem in Econometrics* (Frankfurt, 1980).

Introductory Comments, Definitions, and Research on Indexes of Monetary Services

Michael T. Belongia

With apologies to Mark Twain, reporting practices of modern central banks beg the expression, 'Lies, damned lies, *and monetary data.*' Although demonstrably wrong in their construction, simple-sum measures of the money stock continue to be the official data published by central banks and are used to guide policy decisions if monetary quantity variables are part of that process. Moreover, whether by tradition or ease of access, academic research also persists in using simple-sum monetary aggregates to test hypotheses about the effects of money on economic activity.

In fairness to all involved, however, the conventional wisdom changes slowly. Indeed, less than thirty years have passed since Milton Friedman and Anna Schwartz, in *Monetary Statistics of the United States* (1970) ended their discussion of the potential usefulness of weighted aggregates by concluding that, 'So far there is only the barest beginning of an answer [of how to do it properly]' p. 152. Indeed, just prior to the publication of Friedman and Schwartz's book, two papers in the *Federal Reserve Bank of St Louis Review* were dramatic in that they called attention to money at all – the now-famous study by Leonall Andersen and Jerry Jordan (1968) reporting a primary linkage between money and nominal spending (*and* the ineffectiveness of fiscal actions), and Karl Brunner's (1968) introduction of the term 'monetarism', with a summary of its main principles. In some senses, these papers also marked the mid-point of a sweeping change in orthodox economics. Only nine years earlier, a paper by Brunner and Anatol B. Balbach presented evidence on money and economic activity that, in many ways, was more compelling than that of the Andersen–Jordan study. Disregarded by attendees of the Western Economic Association meetings of 1959, this paper is virtually unknown today. By 1979, however, arguments and evidence that could have been drawn directly from Brunner and Balbach were the basis of a fundamentally new focus for monetary policy: Most of the world's major central banks adopted monetary aggregate targeting in their efforts to control an accelerating rate of inflation. In view of this history, it is perhaps not surprising that superlative indexes of the money stock are going through a typical gestation period prior to their broad acceptance.

And, while new ideas are accepted slowly, it can also be said that no debate in economics is really 'new'. From the first discussions of the Equation of Exchange, economists knew that finding a measure for 'M' was of central importance to empirical work. Schumpeter's (1954) *History of Economic Analysis*, for example, cites numerous views on the definition of money from both European and American perspectives over the period 1870–1911. Still, by the early 1930s, Lauchlin Currie was compelled to create his own money supply data to test the hypothesis that restrictive money growth caused the Great Depression. Why? As he put it at the time:

> It is a rather startling conclusion that the growth of money under the Federal Reserve System has been largely a matter of accident or, at best, an incidental by-product of the system's other policies. In this connection it is highly significant that while an enormous mass of statistical data is available on the composition of member bank assets, there does not exist in any of the system's publications, so far as I am aware, a series of money.[1]

It was not until 1948 however, that monetary data for the USA were published by the Federal Reserve Board. It also is notable that those initial data were not revised and improved at the Board, but rather were guided by work by William Abbott under the direction of Homer Jones at St Louis.

To many, all this *Sturm und Drang* produced one of the greater ironies in the history of economic thought: after two decades of effort to get the data reported, to convince people that money mattered, and to push central banks towards the adoption of monetary aggregates as intermediate targets – everything went wrong. Previously stable velocity functions shifted quickly and erratically. The strong connection between money growth and inflation all but disappeared. Wildly alarmist warnings of a resurgent inflation were embarrassingly wrong. The role of a quantity variable in implementing monetary policy was discredited.

Some observers have interpreted the events since 1980 as a clear repudiation of using monetary quantity variables for the conduct of policy. Others have remained steadfast in their belief that money has potent effects on economic activity, but admit that the published quantity data are erroneous indicators of what the central bank is doing. Still another group has focused on the possibility that fundamental problems of measurement may be responsible for the recent monetary turmoil. This volume is directed to providing empirical evidence on this last proposition.

Progress on monetary measurement since 1970

After Friedman and Schwartz concluded that weighted monetary aggregates had intuitive appeal but were, as yet, not well defined in theory, a solution to the problem developed rather quickly. Using Erwin Diewert's (1976, 1978) results on aggregation and index number theory, William Barnett (1978) derived a measure of 'prices' (user costs) for the flow of monetary services from a stock of monetary assets. With these prices and the readily-available quantity data for monetary asset stocks, Barnett (1980) then applied an index from Diewert's class of superlative indexes – the Divisia – to create weighted monetary aggregates for the USA.[2] The principles behind his new measures and a step-by-step guide to their construction were discussed at greater length in Barnett (1982). Although alternative superlative indexes could serve the same purpose, Barnett's careful and thorough examination of the Divisia index led to its adoption in most applications of weighted monetary aggregates.[3]

Definitions of common concepts

To avoid redundancies across papers in this book, some common definitions are provided here for general reference. Unless specifically noted otherwise in an individual chapter, the expressions below are those employed in each study. For greater detail on technical issues associated with adjusting data to match these general expressions, the reader is referred to Farr and Johnson (1985), Dietrich and Kliesen (1992), and the country-specific documentation in the individual chapters.

A Divisia index of monetary service flows is expressed as: $\Delta \ln DivM_t = \sum_{i=1}^{k} 0.5^*(s_{it} + s_{i,t-1})^* \Delta \ln q_{it}$, where s_{it} is the share of total expenditures on monetary services allocated to the ith asset at time t and q_{it} is the quantity of balances in the ith asset category. The expenditure shares are defined as: $s_{it} = (u^*_{it} q_{it} / \sum_{i=1}^{k} (u^*_{it} q_{it})$, where u_{it} is the user cost (rental price) of the ith asset. Nominal user costs are determined as $u_{it} = \{(R_t - r_{it})\} \;/\; (1 + R_t)\}^* \, P_t$, where R_t is the rate of return on a benchmark asset, r_{it} is the own-rate of return to the ith asset and P_t is a cost-of-living index. The marginal tax rate also is included in Barnett's (1978) original derivation but, in the absence of a consistent time series for this concept (at least in the USA), it has been omitted in most subsequent studies.[4]

With the r_{it} and q_{it} readily-observable from market data and the use of the CPI or the GDP Deflator as a proxy for P_t, treatment of R_t has been the major consideration of many researchers attempting to construct Divisia indexes.[5] Indeed, of the three most frequent criticisms of Divisia monetary aggregates, discussions of the benchmark return have been among the most persistent.[6] As the return on a completely illiquid asset (one that is incapable of producing any monetary services), R_t should be something akin to the rate of return on human capital in a world without slavery. Without a measure for this, the search for an empirical proxy has focused on identifying some asset where $R_t \geq r_{it} \forall_{it}$. Early studies chose the return on B-grade bonds for this purpose until disinflation and an inverted yield curve produced negative user costs from this formulation. Some addressed this problem by adding an arbitrary constant to their chosen value for R_t such that user costs always would be positive. The practice was justified by arguing that the constant captured the effects of service fees, minimum balance requirements and other factors not reflected explicitly in own-rates of return. But, while solving the practical problem, it was widely recognised for the arbitrary choice it was.

A better solution to this problem has been offered, however, and it has become the predominant approach to measuring the benchmark return. Viewing R_t as the maximum-available holding-period yield at each point in time and recognising that expenditures on monetary services are part of lifetime utility-maximization problem, consumers will adjust their portfolios of money and goods in every period as they face new vectors of relative prices. In this context, it is possible (if not likely) that different assets will occupy the role of the benchmark asset at different moments in time. This strategy is both consistent with the more general consumer choice problem behind Divisia aggregation, and solves the practical problem of assuring that all values for user costs are non-negative.[7] Some chapters in this book have addressed the benchmark rate in different ways, however, and these exceptions are noted in the text.

Other issues

The general expressions given above describe how a Divisia aggregate can be constructed and this book evaluates the empirical properties of such an index for a variety of countries. At least one other issue is worth noting, however, before examining this evidence. For the non-specialist, the expression for a Divisia aggregate merely notes summation across k monetary assets. In most applications, including many in this volume, Divisia aggregates are constructed from the same asset collections used to determine the simple-sum aggregates reported by central banks. Thus, for example, Divisia M3 is evaluated for Germany and Divisia M2 + CDs is evaluated for Japan. Although Barnett's (1982) survey paper expressly notes that a choice criterion should be applied to determine which asset bundles are candidates for aggregation, much work, including some of his own, relies on asset collections identified by *ad hoc* criteria of central banks. The reason for doing so is related to the discussion in Note 5: with first-order gains from the use of a superlative index, an error in the choice of the best asset collection has been regarded as one of second-order importance. This thinking is amplified by the logic that, unlike simple-sum measures, Divisia aggregation will give a smaller weight to this type of mistake.

The last chapter in this book, however, suggests that the consequences of such choices may be larger than has previously been believed. By testing the weak separability condition required for aggregation, Belongia finds that some official aggregates fail this test, often because they include one or more time deposit categories. Some of the chapters in this book also test for weak separability as a preliminary step to aggregation. Others accept official central bank definitions and construct Divisia measures of them. In either case, most of the authors indicate that the choice of an asset bundle is a question worth addressing, as results generally do vary across broad and narrow measures. An area of research in need of attention encompasses the development of better tests for weak separability and the application of them to monetary data for a variety of countries.

Future research on superlative indexes of money

In a tribute to Homer Jones on his retirement as Director of Research at the Federal Reserve Bank of St Louis, Milton Friedman, his former student and teacher, stated that regular publication of data on the money supply and the price level by the St Louis 'Fed' probably contributed more than any other factor towards changing the profession's view of money. To repeat an earlier theme, however, it should be noted that twenty-two years (almost to the day!) separated Jones's appointment as Director of Research at St Louis and the Fed's adoption (at least in words) on 6 October 1979 of M1 as its primary intermediate target variable. The professional acceptance of Divisia aggregates appears to be moving at a parallel pace. But, if Friedman's interpretation of events still applies, measures of the money supply published by central banks will be changed when a sufficiently large and persuasive body of empirical evidence requires that it is to be done. Unfortunately, like the physicist who cannot predict which additional grain of sand will cause the existing pile to cascade, it is not clear when superlative indexes of money will be used more widely. It is clear, however, that more and better evidence will be needed to force this change.

It is a long leap from Francis Walker's (1878) homily, 'Money is that money does', to the very hard work exemplified by the contributors to this volume. Fortunately, economic theory and index number theory have been linked to provide guideposts for careful measurement of the money stock. Theory also provides arguments against the use of simple-sum measures of money. When some perspective is given to the range of issues facing macroeconomists, it seems clear that more attention must be directed to basic measurement problems before the profession can be engaged in informed discussion of important questions. In fact, much of the evidence in this book suggests that several key 'problems' in monetary economics might well disappear if data measurement were to be grounded better in economic theory.

Notes

1. See Lauchlin Currie, *The Supply and Control of Money in the United States* (1935), p. 54. This classic work, and the large body of his related writings in the *Journal of Political*

Economy and the *Quarterly Journal of Economics* in the early 1930s, are largely overlooked as a consequence of accusations in 1948 that he had supplied information to Soviet spies while working in the Roosevelt Administration. Although the FBI was never able to substantiate any of the charges brought against him, Currie stated that, 'You never live down guilt by association'. He emigrated to Bogota, Colombia in 1950 and attained Colombian citizenship in 1958. He remained there until his death at the age of 91 on 23 December 1993.

2. Naturally, even these developments are not entirely new. The name for the Divisia index (and its capitalisation) comes from the index number work of French statistician François Divisia (1925). Moreover, the fundamental problems with simple-sum aggregation were discussed in detail by Irving Fisher (1922). John Maynard Keynes (1930) also recognised the problems of simple-sum indexes.
3. The primary alternative has been the Fisher Ideal index, which is the geometric average of the Paasche and Laspeyres indexes. It can be expressed as:

$$(FI_t/FI_{t-1}) = \sum_{i=1}^{k} s_{i,t-1}\,(q_{it}/q_{i,t-1})\}/\{\sum_{i=1}^{k} S_{it}(q_{i,t-1}/q_{it})\}]^{0.5}$$

where quantities (q_{it}), user costs (u_{it}), and expenditure shares (s_{it}) are as defined in the text. Because this index is expressed in levels, it has often been used to connect periods when new assets are introduced to a Divisia aggregate. This need arises because a Divisia index, which is expressed in growth rates, is undefined at these points. Other work has simply constructed Fisher Ideal indexes and then taken their growth rates for empirical applications.
4. Hahm and Kim (Chapter 9 in this volume) address this issue by using after-tax own-rates of return.
5. This, however, has not been the only concern. As discussed by Longworth and Atta-Mensah (Chapter 12 in this volume), for example, legitimate questions can be raised about the effects of minimum balance requirements, service fees and cross-subsidisation of accounts by banks on the observed own-rates of return. Moreover, when aggregating across assets with different maturities, yield curve adjustments must be made so that all own-rates of return are expressed on a common basis. But while these are legitimate issues and should not be dismissed out of hand, it clearly is not correct to use them as a primary defence for the continued publication and use of simple-sum aggregates. The reason is simply one of order of magnitudes. While comparisons of Divisia and simple-sum aggregates show first-order effects from the choice of alternative index numbers (see, for example, Belongia, 1996), the impact of the points noted above on own-rates of return (some of which are off-setting) occurs at a much smaller order of magnitude. For example, studies of the robustness of measurement to choice of alternative values for the benchmark return, R_t, all indicate that its effects are quite small. See, for example, Barnett (1991) and Hahm and Kim (Chapter 9 in this volume).
6. See, for example, comments by Issing (1992) and the response by Belongia (1995). The other two ongoing criticisms are, first, that the empirical differences of Divisia and simple-sum aggregates of the same asset collections are small. The second is that, even if a Divisia aggregate were a better indicator variable, it could not be used as an intermediate target because endogenous interest rates in the Divisia expenditure share weights would eliminate the central bank's ability to control its behaviour. The first objection is strongly rejected by the evidence in this volume and the growing empirical literature in the journals. The second, however, is merely an

unsubstantiated assertion. In fact, in one of the few cases where this issue has been investigated, Belongia and Chalfant (1989) find that Divisia aggregates are *more controllable* by the Fed than their simple-sum counterparts. This is seen in the data by plotting the growth rate of a money multiplier derived as: $\Delta\ln m_t = \Delta\ln DivM_t - \Delta\ln AMB_t$, where *AMB* is the adjusted monetary base. One explanation for lower variance in a Divisia aggregate's multiplier would be a strong negative covariance between portfolio substitutions of the public and the banking system in response to a given change in interest rates.

7. See Barnett *et al.* (1992), p. 2108, for more discussion of this topic.

References

Abbott, William J. (1960) 'A New Measure of the Money Supply', *Federal Reserve Bulletin*, October, pp. 1102–23.

Abbott, William J. (1962) 'Revision of Money Supply Series', *Federal Reserve Bulletin* August, pp. 941–51.

Andersen, Leonall C. and Jerry L. Jordan (1968) 'Monetary and Fiscal Actions: A Test of Their Relative Importance in Economic Stabilization', *Federal Reserve Bank of St Louis Review*, November, pp. 11–23.

Barnett, William A. (1978) 'The User Cost of Money', *Economics Letters*, vol. 1, no. 2, pp. 145–49.

Barnett, William A. (1980) 'Economic Monetary Aggregates: An Application of Index Number and Aggregation Theory', *Journal of Econometrics*, September, pp. 11–48.

Barnett, William A. (1982) 'The Optimal Level of Monetary Aggregation', *Journal of Money, Credit, and Banking*, pt 2, November, pp. 687–710.

Barnett, William A. (1991) 'A Reply to Julio J. Rotemberg', in, M. T. Belongia (ed.), *Monetary Policy on the 75th Anniversary of the Federal Reserve System* (Norwell, Mass: Kluwer).

Barnett, William A., Douglas Fisher and Apostolos Serletis (1992) 'Consumer Theory and the Demand for Money', *Journal of Economic Literature*, December, pp. 2086–119.

Belongia, Michael T. (1995) 'Weighted Monetary Aggregates: A Historical Survey', *Journal of International and Comparative Economics*, pp. 87–114.

Belongia, Michael T. (1996) 'Measurement Matters: Some Recent Results in Monetary Economics Re-examined', *Journal of Political Economy*, October, pp. 1065–83.

Belongia, Michael T. (1999) 'Consequences of Money Stock Mismeasurement: Evidence from Three Countries', Ch. 13, this volume.

Belongia, Michael T. and James A. Chalfant (1989) 'The Changing Empirical Definition of Money', *Journal of Political Economy*, April, pp. 387–98.

Brunner, Karl (1968) 'The Role of Money and Monetary Policy', *Federal Reserve Bank of St Louis Review*, vol. 50, no. 7, pp. 9–24.

Brunner, Karl and Anatol B. Balbach (1959) 'An Evaluation of Two Types of Monetary Theories' in *Proceedings of the Thirty-Fourth Annual Conference of the Western Economics Association*, September 2–4 (Santa Barbara, Calif.), pp. 78–84.

Burns, Arthur and Wesley C. Mitchell (1946) *Measuring Business Cycles*, National Bureau of Economic Research, Studies in Business Cycles, no. 2 (New York: Columbia University Press)

Currie, Lauchlin (1935) *The Supply and Control of Money in the United States* (Cambridge, Mass.: Harvard University Press).

Dietrich, Lynn D. and Kevin L. Kliesen (1992) 'Appendix to Thornton and Yue', *Federal Reserve Bank of St Louis Review*, November/December, pp. 46–52.

Diewert, W. Erwin (1976) 'Exact and Superlative Index Numbers', *Journal of Econometrics*, May, pp. 115–45.
Diewert, W. Erwin (1978) 'Superlative Index Numbers and Consistency in Aggregation', *Econometrica*, July, pp. 883–900.
Divisia, François (1925) 'L'indice monetaire et la theorie de la monnaie', *Revue d'economie politique*, pp. 980–1008.
Farr, Helen and D. Johnson (1985) 'Revisions in the Monetary Services (Divisia) Indexes of Monetary Aggregates', Special Studies Paper No. 59 (Washington, DC: Board of Governors of the Federal Reserve System).
Fisher, Irving (1922) *The Making of Index Numbers* (Cambridge, Mass.: Houghton Mifflin).
Friedman, Milton (1976) 'Homer Jones: A Personal Reminiscence', *Journal of Monetary Economics* November, pp. 433–36.
Friedman, Milton and Anna J. Schwartz (1970) *Monetary Statistics of the United States* (New York: Columbia University Press).
Issing, Otmar (1992) 'Theoretical and Empirical Foundations of the Deutsche Bundesbank's Monetary Targeting', *Intereconomics*, November/December, pp. 289–300.
Keynes, J. M. (1930) *A Treatise on Money*, vol. 2 (London: Harcourt Brace & Company).
Schumpeter, Joseph A. (1954) *History of Economic Analysis* (New York: Oxford University Press).
Thornton, Daniel L. and Piyu Yue (1992) 'An Extended Series of Divisia Monetary Aggregates', *Federal Reserve of St Louis Review*, November/December, pp. 35–46.
Walker, Francis A. (1878) *Money* (New York: Henry Holt & Company).

Part 1
New Results in Theory and Practice

1

Beyond the Risk-neutral Utility Function

William A. Barnett and Yi Liu

> The economic statistics that the government issues every week should come with a warning sticker: user beware. In the midst of the greatest information explosion in history, the government is pumping out a stream of statistics that are nothing but myths and misinformation. (Michael J. Mandel, 'The Real Truth about the Economy: Are Government Statistics So Much Pulp Fiction? Take a Look', *Business Week*, cover story, 7 November 1994, pp. 110–18.)

1.1 Introduction

In the case of perfect certainty, it is well known that the Divisia index exactly tracks any aggregator function. This follows from the fact that the Divisia line integral is directly derivable from the first-order conditions for optimising behaviour. For example, in the case of consumer behaviour, the Divisia index is derived directly from the total differential of the demand function after substitution of the first-order conditions for maximising utility, subject to a budget constraint. See, for example, Barnett (1982a, 1983, 1997). However, the exact tracking property of the Divisia index also applies to demand for monetary services by firms and supply of produced monetary services by financial intermediaries. See Barnett (1987); Barnett and Hahm (1994); Barnett, Hinich and Weber (1986); Barnett and Zhou (1994a, 1994b); Drake and Chrystal (1994); Hancock (1987, 1991); and Barnett, Kirova and Pasupathy (1995).

Risk aversion is another story. The first-order conditions in the case of risk aversion are Euler equations. Since those are not the first-order conditions used in deriving the Divisia index under perfect certainty, the tracking ability of the unadjusted Divisia index is compromised. The degree to which the tracking ability degrades is a function of the degree of risk aversion and of risk. Much earlier work has had as its objective the investigation of the degree of compromise in tracking ability under risk aversion. See, for example, Barnett,

Hinich and Yue (1991); and Barnett, Kirova and Pasupathy (1995). In these papers, the utility or production functions were estimated by generalised method of moments estimation of the parameters of the Euler equations, and the resultings values of the nested monetary aggregator function were produced. The Divisia index path was then compared with that of the estimated exact rational expectations monetary aggregate. This procedure is in accordance with the one widely advocated as the solution to the Lucas Critique, and to what Chrystal and MacDonald (1994, p. 76) have recently called the Barnett Critique. The hope was that the compromise in tracking ability resulting from using the uncorrected Divisia index, despite the existence of risk aversion, would be small, and indeed the tracking error has been found to be small in all such explorations so far.

Nevertheless, we cannot rule out the possibility that monetary assets in the monetary aggregates for some country may one day include very risky assets that might produce a non-negligible loss in tracking ability of the ordinary Divisia monetary aggregate. Indeed, there is at the time of writing increasing interest in the possibility of the inclusion of common stock mutual funds and long-term bond mutual funds as components of monetary aggregates in the USA. See, for example, Barnett and Zhou (1995). Furthermore, the existing results on the effects of risk on the ordinary Divisia monetary aggregates are all based on research with US data. We have not investigated the riskiness of the assets included in the monetary aggregates of other countries and the potential degradation of the Divisia index's tracking ability for other countries as a result of that risk in component assets rates of return. However, a corrected Divisia index, derived directly from the Euler equations under risk, has just been discovered by Barnett, Liu and Jensen (1997). Although there does not yet exist any significant degree of applied experience in the use of that extended Divisia index, its availability needs to be known and understood. Index number theory is no longer necessarily compromised by the existence of risk, since Barnett, Liu and Jensen's new extended Divisia index tracks exactly correctly, regardless of the degree of risk or of risk aversion. In this chapter, we describe the potential use of this little-known new discovery.

Barnet, Liu and Jensen's generalised Divisia index has a direct connection with the capital asset pricing model (CAPM) in finance. In a sense, Barnett, Liu and Jensen's theory is a generalisation of CAPM and of the Divisia index, since their theory contains both as nested special cases. In particular, CAPM deals with a two-dimensional trade-off between mean return and risk, while the Divisia index deals with the two-dimensional trade-off between investment return and liquidity. Barnett and Liu's generalised theory includes the three-dimensional trade-off between mean return, risk and liquidity.

For a unified development of the theory of monetary aggregation, with or without risk, see Barnett and Serletis (1999).

1.2 The Lucas critique

According to the Lucas critique, private-sector parameters and the parameters of central bank policy rules are confounded together within the demand and supply solution functions that are typically estimated in macroeconometric models. When modelled dynamically, these demand and supply functions are the feedback rules or contingency plans that comprise the solution functions to dynamic programming or optimal control decisions of consumers and firms. However, the central bank's policy process is among the laws of motion serving as constraints in the private sector's dynamic decision. Hence the feedback rules that solve the private sector's decision depend on the parameters of those processes as well of the private sector's own taste and technology parameters. Shifts in the parameters of the central bank's policy process will shift the private sector's solution feedback rules.

The source of this confounding is the solution of the first-order conditions (Euler equations) of the private sector's decision, since that solution cannot be acquired without augmenting the private sector's Euler equations with the government's policy rules. In particular, the central bank's policy rule, interest rate processes, and other governmentally influenced stochastic processes for variables that are in the private agent's decision, but are not under the control of that private decision-maker, must be augmented to the private decision-maker's Euler equations, before the solution for the feedback rules (demand and supply functions) can be found. But if the Euler equations of the private sector are estimated directly, the confounding problem is avoided. Hence, in macroeconomics in general, there is wide acceptance of the idea that Euler equations should be estimated, rather than the demand and supply functions that are the solution to the augmented system. In addition, generalised method of moments (GMM) estimation has made the estimation of Euler equations practical.

Despite the influence of Euler equation estimation, and the Lucas Critique in macroeconomics in general, a substantial portion of the literature on monetary economics has continued to base its conclusions on estimates of money demand and money supply functions, which are vulnerable to the Lucas critique. An exception is Poterba and Rotemberg (1987), who have proposed and applied an approach to Euler equation estimation applicable to consumer decisions in money markets. Surprisingly, the Lucas critique seems to have had little influence on monetary policy at any of the world's central banks, since to our knowledge none of the central banks uses a macroeconometric model in which the deep parameters of Euler equations have been estimated. Instead, conventional structural parameterisations are used. But it is the deep parameters of the Euler equations and not the parameters of conventional structural equations that are invariant to policy changes, and hence the macroeconomic models used by most central banks for policy simulations remain vulnerable to the Lucas critique; see Barnett, Kirova and

Pasupathy (1995). In short, it would not be unfair to conclude that the Lucas critique, although mathematically correct, is being ignored by the world's central banks.

However, there is another related critique of macroeconomic modelling which is not being ignored by central banks, as is evident from this volume and the conference that produced the papers reproduced in it. The next section relates to that subject.

1.3 The Barnett critique

According to the Barnett critique, as defined by Chrystal and MacDonald (1994, p. 76), an internal inconsistency exists between the microeconomics used to model private-sector structure and the aggregator functions used to produce the monetary data supplied by central banks. For a systematic statement of that critique and its implications for macroeconomics, see Barnett (194). The result can do considerable damage to inferences about private-sector behaviour, when central bank monetary aggregate data are used. Chrystal and MacDonald (1994, p. 76) have observed the following regarding 'the problems with tests of money in the economy in recent years .... Rather than a problem associated with the Lucas Critique, it could instead be a problem stemming from the "Barnett Critique"'. In fact, Barnett Critique issues have been used to cast doubt upon many widely-held views in monetary economics, as emphasised recently by Barnett, Fisher and Serletis (1992), Belongia and Chalfant (1989), Belongia (1996), and Chrystal and MacDonald (1994). Based on this rapidly-growing line of research, Chrystal and MacDonald (1994, p. 108) conclude – in our opinion correctly – that: 'Rejections of the role of money based upon flawed money measures are themselves easy to reject.'

The Poterba and Rotemberg approach to inference about consumer behaviour in the monetary sector circumvents the Barnett critique by nesting the monetary aggregator function within the consumer's utility function and estimating the aggregator function jointly with the other parameters of the consumer's decision. Hence, Poterba and Rotemberg have extended Barnett's (1980, 1987) perfect certainty theory to the case of risk. Subsequently, Barnett, Hinich and Yue (1991), Barnett and Zhou (1994a), and Barnett, Kirova and Pasupathy (1995) have investigated the tracking abilities of various nonparametric statistical index numbers, such as the Divisia, to the Poterba and Rotemberg estimated aggregator function under risk, and to the analogous weakly separable aggregator functions in the case of demand for financial services by manufacturing firms, or the supply of financial services by financial firms, where the aggregator function is estimated from generalised method of moments estimation of the Euler equations. But these papers, after having determined the magnitude of the tracking error produced by risk aversion, did not derive a closed form solution for the risk correction needed to eliminate that error. Only more recently did Barnett, Liu and Jensen (1997) succeed in deriving that risk correction. This chapter explains how, in practice, that correction can be used to produce an extended Divisia monetary aggregate that is not compromised by risk aversion.

1.4 Consumer demand for monetary assets

The consumer's decision

This line of research in monetary economics began with Barnett (1980) in the perfect certainty case, and Poterba and Rotemberg (1987) in the case of risk. Both papers were produced from models of consumer behaviour. In this chapter we shall describe newer results, but again we shall present results derived from consumer behaviour, despite the fact that analogous results are available for firms.

In this section we formulate a representative consumer's stochastic decision problem over consumer goods and monetary assets. The consumer's decisions are made in discrete time over an infinite planning horizon for the time intervals, $t, t+1, ..., s, ...,$ where t is the current time period and $t+T$ is the terminal planning period. The variables used in defining the consumer's decision are as follows:

$\mathbf{x}_s$ = n dimensional vector of real consumption of goods and services during period s;
$\mathbf{p}_s$ = n dimensional vector of goods and services prices and of durable goods rental prices during period s;
$\mathbf{a}_s$ = k dimensional vector of real balances of monetary assets during period s;
ρ_s = k dimensional vector of nominal holding period yields of monetary assets;
A_s = holdings of the benchmark asset during period s;
R_s = the one-period holding yield on the benchmark asset during period s;
I_s = the sum of all other sources of income during period s; and
p_s^* = $p_s^*(\mathbf{p}_s)$ = the true cost-of-living index.

Define Y to be a compact subset of the $n+k+2$-dimensional non-negative orthant. The consumer's consumption possibility set, $S(s)$ for $s \in \{t, ..., t+T\}$ is:

$$S(s) = \{(\mathbf{a}_s, \mathbf{x}_{s,}, A_s) \in Y : \sum_{i=1}^{n} p_{is}x_{is} = + \sum_{i=1}^{k}[(1+\rho_{i,s-1})p_{s-1}^* a_i, s-1 - p_s^* a_{is}] + (1+R_{s-1})p_{s-1}^* A_{s-1} - p_s^* A_s + I_s\} \quad (1.1)$$

Under the assumption of rational expectations, the distribution of random variables is known to the consumer. Since current period interest rates are not paid until the end of the period, they may be contemporaneously unknown to the consumer. The benchmark asset A_s provides no services other than its yield R_s. As a result, the benchmark asset does not enter the consumer's contemporaneous utility function. In a finite planning horizon context, the benchmark asset would enter the intertemporal utility function only in the terminal period, but since we are using an infinite planning horizon model, the benchmark asset never enters the utility function and appears only in constraints as an investment that can be used for saving across periods.

Given the price and interest rate processes, the consumer selects the deterministic point $(\mathbf{a}_t, \mathbf{x}_t, A_t)$ and the stochastic processes $(\mathbf{a}_s, \mathbf{x}_s, A_s)$, $s = t+1$, ..., to maximise the expected value of utility over the planning horizon, subject to the sequence of choice set constraints.[1] Formally, the consumer's decision problem is as follows.

Problem 1 Choose the deterministic point $(\mathbf{a}_t, \mathbf{x}_t, \mathbf{A}_t)$ and the stochastic process $(\mathbf{a}_s, \mathbf{x}_s, \mathbf{A}_s)$, $s = t + 1, ..., \infty$, to maximise:

$$u(\mathbf{a}_t, \mathbf{x}_t) + E_t[\sum_{s=t+1}^{\infty} (\frac{1}{1+\xi})^{s-t} u(\mathbf{a}_{s,} \mathbf{x}_s)] \tag{1.2}$$

subject to $(\mathbf{a}_s, \mathbf{x}_s, A_s) \in S(s)$ for $s \geq t$, and also subject to:

$$\lim_{s\to\infty} E_t(\frac{1}{1+\xi})^{s-t} A_s = 0$$

The latter constraint rules out perpetual borrowing at the benchmark rate of return, R_t. The subjective rate of time discount, ξ, is assumed to be constant.

Existence of a monetary aggregate for the consumer

In order to assure the existence of a monetary aggregate for the consumer, we partition the vector of monetary asset quantities $\mathbf{a}_s$, such that $\mathbf{a}_s = (\mathbf{m}_s, \mathbf{h}_s)$. We correspondingly partition the vector of interest rates of those assets, ρ_s, such that $\rho_s = (\mathbf{r}_s, \mathbf{i}_s)$. We then assume that the utility function, u, is blockwise weakly separable in $\mathbf{m}_s$ and in $\mathbf{x}_s$ for some such partition of $\mathbf{a}_s$.[2] Hence there exists a monetary aggregator ('category utility') function, M, and consumer goods aggregator function, X, and a utility function, u^*, such that:

$$u(\mathbf{a}_s, \mathbf{x}_s) = u^*(M(\mathbf{m}_s)\mathbf{h}_s, X(\mathbf{x}_s)) \tag{1.3}$$

Then it follows that the exact monetary aggregate, measuring the welfare acquired from consuming the services of $\mathbf{m}_s$, is:

$$M_s = M(\mathbf{m}_s) \tag{1.4}$$

We define the dimension of $\mathbf{m}_s$ to be k_1, and the dimension $\mathbf{h}_s$ to be k_2, so that $k = k_1 + k_2$.

It is clear that Equation (1.4) does define the exact monetary aggregate in the welfare sense, since M_s measures the consumer's subjective evaluation of the services received from holding $\mathbf{m}_s$. However, it also can be shown that Equation (1.4) defines the exact monetary aggregate in the aggregation theoretic sense. In particular, the stochastic process M_s, $s \geq t$, contains all of the information about $\mathbf{m}_s$ that is needed by the consumer to solve the rest of the decision problem. For the proof, see Barnett, Liu and Jensen (1997).

The Euler equations that will be of the most use to us below are those for monetary assets. Replacing $X(\mathbf{x}_t)$ by c_t in u, and letting $\rho = \frac{1}{1+\xi}$, the Euler equations for monetary assets become:

$$E_t\left[\frac{\partial u}{\partial m_{it}} - \rho\frac{p_t^*(R_t - r_{it})}{P_{t+1}^*}\frac{\partial u}{\partial c_{t+1}}\right] = 0 \tag{1.5a}$$

for $i = 1, ..., k_1$, where $c_t = X(\mathbf{x}_t)$ is the exact quantity aggregate over $\mathbf{x}_t$ and p_t^* is its dual exact price aggregate.[3] Similarly, we can acquire the Euler equation for the consumer goods aggregate c_t, rather than for each of its components. The resulting Euler equation for c_t is:

$$E_t\left[\frac{\partial u}{\partial c_t} - \rho\frac{p_t^*(1 + R_t)}{p_{t+1}^*}\frac{\partial u}{\partial c_{t+1}}\right] = 0 \tag{1.5b}$$

See Barnett, Kirova and Pasupathy (1995) for more details regarding the derivation of the Euler equations.

The perfect certainty case

In the perfect certainty case, nonparametric index number theory is highly developed and is applicable to monetary aggregation. In the perfect certainty case, Barnett (1978, 1980) proved that the nominal user cost of the services of m_{it} is π_{it}, where:

$$\pi_{it} = p_t^*\frac{R_t - r_{it}}{1 + R_t} \tag{1.6}$$

The corresponding real user cost is π_{it}/p^*. In the risk-neutral case, the user cost formulae are the same as in the perfect certainty case, but with the interest rates replaced by their expected values – see Barnett (1995b). It can be shown that the solution value of the exact monetary aggregate $M(\mathbf{m}_t)$ can be tracked without error in continuous time (see, for example Barnett, 1983) by the Divisia index:

$$d\log M_t = \sum_{i=1}^{k_1} s_{it}d\log m_{it} \tag{1.7}$$

where the user cost evaluated expenditure shares are $s_{it} = \pi_{it}m_{it}/\sum_{j=1}^{k_1}\pi_{jt}m_{jt}$. The flawless tracking ability of the index in the risk neutral case holds regardless of the form of the unknown aggregator function, M. However, under risk aversion the ability of Equation (1.7) to track $M(\mathbf{m}_t)$ is potentially compromised.

An initial extension

The fact that the Divisia index tracts exactly under perfect certainty or risk neutrality is well known. However, we show in this section that neither perfect certainty nor risk neutrality is needed for exact tracking of the Divisia index. Only contemporaneous prices and interest rates need be known. Future interest rates and prices need not be known, and risk-averse behaviour relative to those stochastic processes need not be excluded. The proof is as follows.

Assume that R_t, p_t^*, and $\mathbf{r}_t$ are known at time t, although their future values are stochastic.

Then the Euler Equations (4.5a) for $\mathbf{m}_t$ are:

$$\frac{\partial u}{\partial m_{it}} - \rho p_t^*(R_t - r_{it})E_t\left[\frac{1}{P_{t+1}^*}\frac{\partial u}{\partial c_{t+1}}\right] = 0 \tag{1.8}$$

for $i = 1, \ldots, k_1$. Similarly the Euler Equation (1.5b) for aggregate consumption of goods, c_t, becomes:

$$\frac{\partial u}{\partial c_t} - \rho p_t^*(1 + R_t)E_t\left[\frac{1}{p_{t+1}^*}\frac{\partial u}{\partial c_{t+1}}\right] = 0 \tag{1.9}$$

Eliminating $E_t\left[\frac{1}{p_{t+1}^*}\frac{\partial u}{\partial c_{t+1}}\right]$ between Equations (1.8) and (1.9), we acquire:

$$\frac{\partial u}{\partial m_{it}} = \frac{R_t - r_{it}}{1 + R_t}\frac{\partial u}{\partial c_t} \tag{1.10}$$

But, by the assumption of weak separability of u in $\mathbf{m}_t$, we have:

$$\frac{\partial u}{\partial m_{it}} = \frac{\partial u}{\partial M_t}\frac{\partial M}{\partial m_{it}} \tag{1.11}$$

Where $M_t = M(\mathbf{m}_t)$ is the exact monetary aggregate we seek to track.

Substituting Equations (1.10) into Equation (1.11) and using Equation (1.6), we find that:

$$\frac{\partial M}{\partial m_{it}} = \pi_{it}\frac{\partial u/\partial c_t}{\partial u/\partial M_t} \tag{1.12}$$

Now substitute Equation (4.12) into the total differential of M to acquire:

$$dM(\mathbf{m}_t) = \frac{\partial u/\partial c_t}{\partial u/\partial M_t}\sum_{i=1}^{k_1}\pi_{it}dm_{it} \tag{1.13}$$

but since M is assumed to be linearly homogeneous, we have Euler's equation for linearly homogeneous functions. Substituting Equation (4.12) into Euler's equation, we have:

$$M(\mathbf{m}_t) = \frac{\partial u/\partial c_t}{\partial u/\partial M_t}\sum_{j=1}^{k_1}\pi_{jt}m_{jt} \tag{1.14}$$

Dividing Equation (1.13) by Equation (1.14), we produce Equation (1.7), which is the Divisia index. Hence the exact tracking property of the Divisia index is not compromised by uncertainty regarding future interest rates and prices, or by risk aversion. Nevertheless, this assumption is not trivial, as emphasised by Poterba and Rotemberg (1987), since current period interest rates are not paid until the end of the current period.[4] In fact, current period interest rates are not assumed to be contemporaneously known in our Euler Equations (1.5a) and (1.5b).

1.5 The extended Divisia index

As shown in the above sections, the tracking ability of the ordinary Divisia index is not exact when risk aversion exists relative to the risk of contemporaneous interest rates that are not known with certainty until the end of the current period, even though risk regarding unknown future period interest rates does not compromise the Divisia index's tracking ability. However, Barnett, Liu and Jensen (1997) have recently derived a generalised Divisia index, which is exact even when risk aversion exists. Their generalised Divisia index reduces to the ordinary Divisia index under perfect certainty. The form of the new extended Divisia index is identical to that of the ordinary Divisia index, but the user cost prices in the share weights are adjusted by a CAPM risk adjustment depending on the covariance between the own rates of return of the assets and the consumption stream of consumer goods. The risk of unknown contemporaneous yields has no effect on the consumer, if those yields are uncorrelated with the consumer's consumption of goods, since it is the consumer goods that enter the consumer's utility function and are the final objects of consumer preferences.

However, risk relative to the current period interest yields on components of existing monetary assets is low, and contributes very little to household consumption risk. In short, the covariance between those interest rates and consumption of goods during the same period is very low, and hence we should expect that the CAPM adjustment of the user costs in the Divisia index is so small as to be negligible. As in the risk neutral case, all that is needed to deal with risk is to replace the interest rates in the Divisia index by their expectations.

Nevertheless, there is increasing interest in the possibility of including much riskier assets in monetary aggregates. See, for example, Barnett and Zhou (1995) regarding the possible relevance of common stock and bond mutual funds as monetary aggregate components. If this research trend continues in the US or elsewhere, the CAPM adjustment of the user costs in the Divisia monetary aggregates may become entirely non-trivial. For that reason, we explain below the CAPM adjustment needed to apply Barnett, Liu and Jensen's (1997) result in practice.

The user cost of money under risk aversion

For notational convenience, we sometimes convert the nominal rates of return, r_{it} and R_t, to real total rates of return, $1 + r_{it}^*$ and $1 + R_t^*$, such that:

$$1 + r_{it}^* = \frac{p_t^*(1 + r_{it})}{p_{t+1}^*} \text{ and } 1 + R_t^* = \frac{p_t^*(1 + R_t)}{p_{t+1}^*} \tag{1.15}$$

where r_{it}^* and R_t^* defined in that manner are called the real rates of excess return. Also, let $\rho = \frac{1}{1+\xi}$, where ξ is the subjective rate of time discount defined in Equation (4.2) above. Further, to simplify the discussion below, consider the case of aggregation over all the monetary assets in the utility function, so that all monetary assets are assumed to be weakly separable within that utility function. Then there exist utility functions V and F, and monetary aggregator function M, such that $V(\mathbf{m}_s, c_s) = F(M(\mathbf{m}_s), c_s)$, where aggregate consumption of goods is defined by $c_s = X(\mathbf{x}_s)$.

As proved by Barnett, Liu and Jensen (1997), the risk adjusted user cost of the services of monetary asset i under risk is $\Pi_{it} = \pi_{it} + \Psi_{it}$, where:

$$\pi_{it} = \frac{E_t R_t - E_t r_{it}}{1 + E_t R_t} \tag{1.16}$$

and

$$\Psi_{it} = \rho(1 - \pi_{it}) \frac{\text{Cov}(R_t^*, \frac{\partial V}{\partial c_{t+1}})}{\frac{\partial V}{\partial c_t}} - \rho \frac{\text{Cov}(r_{it}^*, \frac{\partial V}{\partial c_{t+1}})}{\frac{\partial V}{\partial c_t}} \tag{1.17}$$

When the covariances in Equation (1.17) are zero, we are back to the risk neutral case in which the user costs are as Equation (1.16).

As we have observed, those covariances are indeed very small with the current components of the Federal Reserve's monetary aggregates. However, if riskier assets were to be considered as possible components of future monetary aggregates, we would need the ability to compute Equation (1.17). In its current form, Equation (1.17) depends on the form of the utility function V. In CAPM theory, it is well known that dramatic simplifications are possible by assuming quadratic utility or Gaussian processes for random variables. Either assumption produces the same result. Barnett, Liu and Jensen (1997) have proved that under either of those conventional CAPM assumptions, Equation (1.17) simplifies to:

$$\Psi_{it} = \frac{1}{1 + R_t^*} H_{t+1} \text{Cov}(r_{it}^*, c_{t+1}) \tag{1.18}$$

where $H_{t+1} = H(M_{t+1}, c_{t+1})$ is the well-known Arrow–Pratt measure of absolute risk aversion:

$$H(M_{t+1}, c_{t+1}) = \frac{-E_t[V'']}{E_t[V']} \tag{1.19}$$

where $V' = \partial V(\mathbf{m}_{t+1}, c_{t+1})$ and $V'' = \partial^2 V(\mathbf{m}_{t+1}, c_{t+1})/\partial c_{t+1}^2$. In this definition, risk aversion is measured relative to consumption risk, conditionally on the level of monetary services produced by $M_{t+1} = M(\mathbf{m}_t)$. Under risk aversion, H_{t+1} is positive and increases as the degree of absolute risk aversion increases.

To apply this formula to any country, the first step would be to compute the covariances $\mathrm{Cov}(r_{it}^*, c_{t+1})$ from data on aggregate consumption of goods and on the excess rates of return r_{it}^* on the component assets. If there is a component asset i, having sufficiently risky rate of return so that the covariance $\mathrm{Cov}(r_{it}^*, c_{t+1})$ is not negligible, it becomes worthwhile to compute the adjustment – Equation (1.18). Otherwise the ordinary Divisia index with the risk neutral user costs in Equation (1.16) are adequate. However, if the covariances $\mathrm{Cov}(r_{it}^*, c_{t+1})$ are found to be non-negligible for at least one asset i, it becomes necessary to acquire an estimate of the Arrow–Pratt measure of absolute risk aversion, H_{t+1}. For most countries, a large number of papers have been published containing estimates of that degree of risk aversion, and it makes sense to use an existing estimate. At that point, the computed values of Equations (1.18) and (1.16) can be substituted into $\Pi_{it} = \pi_{it} + \Psi_{it}$, which is then the correct user cost to substitute into the Divisia index formula, Equation (1.7). Clearly, the resulting generalised user cost reduces to the usual one only if $\Psi_{it} = 0$, so that $\Pi_{it} = \pi_{it}$.

An alternative, although mathematically equivalent form, exists for that adjusted user cost formula. Define $Z_t = H_{t+1}\, c_t$, where Z_t is a modified (time-shifted) Arrow–Pratt relative risk aversion measure. Barnett, Liu and Jensen (1997) have proved that:

$$\Pi_{it} = \frac{E_t R_t^* - (E_t r_{it}^* - \phi_{it})}{1 + E_t R_t^*} \tag{1.20}$$

where

$$\phi_{it} = Z_t \mathrm{Cov}\left(r_{it}^*, \frac{c_{t+1}}{c_t} \right) \tag{1.21}$$

As is evident from Equation (1.20), the function ϕ_{it} is a clear risk adjustment to the unadjusted expected excess rate of return $E_t \mathrm{r}_{it}^*$.

There is no such risk adjustment to the benchmark rate of return, since, in CAPM theory, it is conventional to treat the benchmark rate as a risk-free rate. So in applications of Equation (1.20), the benchmark rate must be computed from rates that have already been risk adjusted. We advocate the use of an envelope rate of the form $E_t R_t^* = \max\, \{E_t r_{it}^* - \phi_{it}\colon i = 1, k\}$, where the $k = k_1 + k_2$ risk-adjusted rates on the $\mathbf{a}_t = (\mathbf{m}_t, \mathbf{h}_t)$ assets within the envelope should include those of all of the k_1 components assets, $\mathbf{m}_t$, in the Divisia index – Equation (1.7) – along with the k_2 rates on the unused assets $\mathbf{h}_t$. Assuming data are available on enough assets $\mathbf{h}_t$, there should rarely, if ever, be a case in which any user cost is zero, and so long as all the k_1 assets in $\mathbf{m}_t$ are included within the envelope, a negative value for a user cost is impossible.

Even if a zero user cost is encountered occasionally, the resulting zero weight in the Divisia index applies temporarily only at the margin for the corresponding component asset's growth rate and does not mean that the level of the asset has no weight in the level of the aggregate. Also observe that the asset that is on the upper surface of the envelope is not likely to be the same asset throughout a single time period. The upper envelope is a proxy for the expected risk-adjusted benchmark asset, and not a direct measurement of that asset. In principle, the benchmark asset is one that has so little liquidity that its expected rate of return contains no liquidity premium. Such a pure investment asset cannot have a market of sufficient quality to produce regular data on its rate of return. In theory, the benchmark asset is often viewed as being the rate of return on human capital in a world without slavery. The adjusted rate of return on such an asset should be higher than that of the envelope rate, which always tracks the expected adjusted excess rate of return on an actual market asset, so we should not be concerned that no market asset can produce the benchmark rate. We should be more concerned with the fact that any market asset can ever equal that rate of return. The best way to raise the envelope towards the unmeasurable benchmark rate is to broaden the scope of the assets included in $\mathbf{h}_t$ and thereby included in the envelope but not in the aggregate.

The adjustment formula in Equation (1.21) has a very revealing and useful form. Observe that the covariance now is between a rate of return and a measure of the growth rate of consumption, rather than with the level of consumption, as in the earlier formula, Equation (1.18). Also observe from Equations (1.20) and (1.21) that a positive covariance results in a subtraction of a risk premium from the unadjusted expected rate of return. The reason is that positive correlation between an asset's rate of return and the consumption growth rate represents an increase in consumption risk from holding the asset. So the asset contributes positively to the consumer's risk, and hence a positive risk premium must be subtracted from the expected rate of return to get the risk-adjusted rate of return. Also observe that the size of that risk premium adjustment depends not only on the size of the covariance, but also on the degree of risk aversion.

With very risky assets, especially those having substantial principal risk, such as common stock and bond mutual funds, we should expect that the covariance will be positive, since such assets are likely to contribute positively to household consumption risk. But many of the currently existing assets within monetary aggregates contribute only very slightly to contemporaneous household consumption risk. With such assets, after aggregating over all the consumers in the country, it would not be surprising to find a small negative covariance between the asset's rate of return and the representative consumer's consumption growth. In theory, such assets can be viewed as 'diversifying' household risk, and hence holding such assets tends to decrease consumption risk. In such cases, the negative covariance results in an addition to the unadjusted rate of return on that asset. Since the benchmark rate is an envelope rate, a risk adjustment increasing a component rate of return cannot result in a negative user cost, since the rates of return within the envelope have already been risk adjusted, either positively or negatively.

While small negative covariances for low-risk assets are likely to be common, the word 'small' should be understood here to mean 'very small'. In short, we do not expect such positive risk adjustments ever to be more than tiny for any asset, since substantial household risk diversification by holding low-risk, liquid monetary assets seems very unlikely.

In the finance literature the well-known consumption-based beta of CCAPM theory is defined by:

$$\beta_{ic} = \frac{\mathrm{Cov}(r_{it}, c_{t+1})}{\mathrm{Var}(c_{t+1})}$$

The subscript c in β_{ic} designates 'consumption-based' beta, and the lack of a time subscript in the notation β_{ic} results from the assumption of stationarity of the interest rate and consumption bivariate process in most of that literature. Clearly, the risk adjustment needed to get the Divisia monetary aggregates to track exactly under risk aversion can be interpreted in terms of that beta.

1.6 Conclusions

We conclude that the Barnett critique can be circumvented by using Divisia monetary aggregates rather than simple-sum aggregates. Under perfect certainty, the ordinary Divisia index tracks exactly correctly under perfect certainty. Under risk neutrality, the exact tracking ability of the Divisia index still holds, so long as the rates of return in the user cost formulas are replaced be their expectations. Under risk aversion, the expected rates of return must be risk adjusted in accordance with the formula derived by Barnett, Liu and Jensen (1997). As explained in this chapter, that risk adjustment is easily computed and used, but is likely to be negligible for most, it not all, of the assets contained within current monetary aggregates. But if the trend continues towards absorbing increasingly risky assets into monetary aggregates, soon perhaps even including assets having substantial principal risk, such as stock and bond mutual funds, the risk adjustment method described in this chapter may become necessary.

As we have observed, central banks throughout the world appear to be ignoring the Lucas critique, since no central bank is using a macroeconometric model produced from estimating the deep parameters of the Euler equations.[5] Yet the Lucas critique would suggest that only deep parameters are invariant to policy changes, and hence conventional models based on structural parameters, rather than deep parameters, cannot be used for policy simulations. We do not know why it is that the world's central banks are ignoring the Lucas critique. But it is clear that they are not ignoring the Barnett critique, which concludes that an internal inconsistency exists in the use of models including monetary aggregates produced in a manner that is not consistent with the theory from which the models were produced. The seriousness with which the Barnett critique is being taken at central banks is evident from this book and the many papers published by central bank economists using theory-coherent monetary aggregator functions, or using the Divisia index that can track any of those aggregators under perfect certainty.

While the influence of the Barnett critique among central bankers has far exceeded that of the Lucas critique, we are asked not infrequently why theory-coherent monetary aggregates are not even more widely used in central-bank research. It is our impression that the issue of theory coherence under risk aversion has been the most commonly mentioned hindrance. In this chapter, we conclude that, with the availability of the new results in Barnett, Liu and Jensen (1997), this hindrance no longer exists.

We wish we could provide a new result that would encourage greater use of the Euler equations approach to modelling at central banks, since we consider the Lucas critique to be correct. But when asked why it is that central banks are not using deep parameter estimation in generating models for policy simulations, we must answer that we simply don't know.

For an empirical applications of this chapter's extension of Divisia monetary aggregation to risk, see the original source (Barnett, Liu, and Jensen, 1997), and the applied papers, Barnett and Xu (1996, 1998). Also see the unified development of the field in Barnett and Serletis (1999).

Notes

1. As is well known in general equilibrium theory, a derived utility function containing money exists, so long as money has positive value in equilibrium. See, for example, Feenstra (1986); Arrow and Hahn (1971); Sidrauski (1967); and Philips and Spinnewyn (1982). We assume that money has positive value in equilibrium and use the resulting derived utility function. The inverse mapping from the derived utility function back to the explicit motive for holding money is not unique, and hence the derived utility function cannot be used to reveal the explicit motive. But we have no reason to seek to determine that explicit motive, and the non-uniqueness of the inverse mapping proves that putting money into the utility function produces a generalisation over any model based on an explicit motive, such as a cash-in-advance constraint.
2. A wide literature exists on testing that weak separability assumption. See, for example, Barnett (1982b); Barnett and Choi (1989); Belongia and Chalfant (1989); and Swofford and Whitney (1987).
3. Assuming that X is linearly homogeneous, the exact price aggregator function is the unit cost function.

4. Also see Rotemberg, Driscoll and Poterba (1994).
5. For examples of such models, see Leeper and Sims (1994), and Barnett, Kirova, Pasupathy and Yue (1995).

References

Arrow, K. J. and F. Hahn (1971) *General Competitive Analysis* (San Francisco: Holden-Day).

Barnett, William A. (1978) 'The User Cost of Money', *Economics Letters*, vol. 1, pp. 145–9.

Barnett, William A. (1980) 'Economic Monetary Aggregates: An Application of Index Number and Aggregation Theory', *Journal of Econometrics*, vol. 14, pp. 11–48.

Barnett, William A. (1982a) 'Divisia Indices', in Samuel Kotz and Norman Johnson (eds), *Encyclopedia of Statistical Sciences*, vol. 2, pp. 412–15.

Barnett, William A. (1982b) 'The Optimal Level of Monetary Aggregation', *Journal of Money, Credit and Banking*, pt 2, vol. 14, no. 4, November, pp. 687–710.

Barnett, William A. (1983) 'Understanding the New Divisia Monetary Aggregates', *Review of Public Data Use*, vol. 11, December, pp. 349–55.

Barnett, William A. (1987) 'The Microeconomic Theory of Monetary Aggregation', in Barnett, William A. and Kenneth J. Singleton (eds), *New Approaches to Monetary Economics* (Cambridge University Press).

Barnett, William A. (1994) 'Perspective on the Current State of Macroeconomic Theory', *International Journal of Systems Science*, vol. 25, no. 5, pp. 839–48.

Barnett, William A. (1995) 'Exact Aggregation under Risk', in William A. Barnett, Herve Moulin, Maurice Salles and Norman Schofield (eds), *Social Choice, Welfare and Ethics* (Cambridge University Press), pp. 353–74.

Barnett, William A. (1997) 'The Divisia Monetary Aggregates', in David Glasner (ed.), *Encyclopedia of Business Cycles, Panics, Crises and Depressions* (Garland) pp. 173–7.

Barnett, William A. and Seungmook Choi (1989) 'A Monte Carlo Study of Tests of Blockwise Weak Separability', *Journal of Business and Economic Statistics*, vol. 7, no. 3, (July) pp. 363–77.

Barnett, William, Yi Liu and Mark Jensen (1997) 'CAPM Risk Adjustment for Aggregation over Financial Assets', *Macroeconomic Dynamics*, vol. 1, no. 2, pp. 485–512.

Barnett, William A. and Apostolos Serletis (1999) *The Theory of Monetary Aggregation* (North Amsterdam: Holland).

Barnett, William and Haiyang Xu (1996) 'An Investigation of Recent Empirical Paradoxes in Monetary Economics', *International Review of Comparative Public Policy*, vol. 8, pp. 130–55.

Barnett, William and Haiyang Xu (1998) 'Stochastic Volatility in Interest Rates and Nonlinearity in Velocity', *International Journal of Systems Science*, vol. 29, no. 11, pp. 1189–201.

Barnett, William A. and Ge Zhou (1994a) 'Financial Firm's Production and Supply-Side Monetary Aggregation Under Dynamic Uncertainty', *Federal Reserve Bank of St Louis Review*, vol. 76 (March/April) pp. 133–65.

Barnett, William A. and Ge Zhou (1994b) 'Response to Brainard's Commentary', *Federal Reserve Bank's Review*, pp. 169–74.

Barnett, William A. and Ge Zhou (1995) 'Mutual Funds and Monetary Aggregates: Commentary', *Federal Reserve Bank of St Louis Review*, special edition containing proceedings of the 'Symposium on Mutual Funds and Monetary Aggregates', vol. 76, November/December 1994, no. 6, pp. 53–62.

Barnett, William A., Douglas Fisher and Apostolos Serletis (1992), 'Consumer Theory and the Demand for Money', *Journal of Economic Literature*, vol. 92, pp. 2086–119.

Barnett, William A. and Jeong Ho Hahm (1994) 'Financial-Firm Production of Monetary Services: A Generalized Symmetric Barnett Variable-Profit-Function Approach', *Journal of Business and Economic Statistics*, vol. 12 (January).
Barnett, William A., Melvin Hinich and Warren Weber (1986) 'The Regulatory Wedge between the Demand-Side and Supply-Side Aggregation-Theoretic Monetary Aggregates', *Journal of Econometrics*, vol. 33, pp. 165–85.
Barnett, William A., Melvin Hinich and Piyu Yue (1991) 'Monitoring Monetary Aggregates under Risk Aversion', in Michael T. Belongia (ed.) *Monetary Policy on the 75th Anniversary of the Federal Reserve System*, Proceedings of the Fourteenth Annual Economic Policy Conference of the Federal Reserve Bank of St Louis (Boston, Mass.: Kluwer), pp. 189–222.
Barnett, William, Milka Kirova and Meenakshi Pasupathy (1995) 'Estimating Policy-Invariant Deep Parameters in the Financial Sector, when Risk and Growth Matter', *Journal of Money, Credit and Banking*, proceedings volume of Cleveland Federal Reserve Bank Conference on 'Liquidity, Monetary Policy, and Financial Intermediation', vol. 27, part 2, pp. 1402–30.
Belongia, Michael T. (1996) 'Measurement Matters: Recent Results from Monetary Economics Re-examined', *Journal of Political Economy*, vol. 104, pp. 1065–83.
Belongia, Michael and James Chalfant (1989) 'The Changing Empirical Definition of Money: Some Estimates from a Model of the Demand for Money Substitutes', *Journal of Political Economy*, vol. 97 (April) pp. 387–98.
Chrystal, K. Alec and Ronald MacDonald (1994) 'Empirical Evidence on the Recent Behavior and Usefulness of Simple-Sum and Weighted Measures of the Money Stock', *Federal Reserve Bank of St. Louis Review* (March/April), pp. 73–109.
Diewert, W. E. (1980) 'Recent Developments in the Economic Theory of Index Numbers: Capital and the Theory of Productivity Measurement', *American Economic Review* (May).
Drake, Leigh and Alec Chrystal (1994) 'Company-Sector Money Demand: New Evidence on the Existence of a Stable Long-run Relationship for the United Kingdom', *Journal of Money, Credit and Banking*, pt 1 (August) pp. 412–38.
Feenstra, Robert C. (1986) 'Functional Equivalence Between Liquidity Costs and the Utility of Money', *Journal of Monetary Economics* (March), pp. 271–91.
Hancock, Diana (1987) 'Aggregation of Monetary Goods: A Production Model', in William A. Barnett and Kenneth J. Singleton (eds), *New Approaches to Monetary Economics* (Cambridge University Press).
Hancock, Diana (1991) *A Theory of Production for the Financial Firm* (Boston, Mass.: Kluwer).
Leeper, Eric M. and Christopher A. Sims (1994) 'Towards a Modern Macroeconomic Model Usable for Policy Analysis', in Stanley Fischer and Julio J. Rotemberg (eds), *NBER Macroeconomics Annual*, (Cambridge, Mass.: MIT Press), pp. 81–118.
Philips, Louis and Frans Spinnewyn (1982) 'Rationality versus Myopia in Dynamic Demand Systems', in R. L. Basmann and G. F. Rhodes (eds), *Advances in Econometrics* (Greenwich, CN: JAI Press), pp. 3–33.
Poterba, James M. and Julio J. Rotemberg (1987) 'Money in the Utility Function: An Empirical Implementation', in William A. Barnett and Kenneth J. Singleton (eds), *New Approaches to Monetary Economics* (Cambridge University Press), pp. 219–40.
Rotemberg, Julio J., John C. Dirscoll and James M. Poterba (1995) 'Money, Output, and Prices: Evidence from a New Monetary Aggregate', *Journal of Business and Economic Statistics*, vol. 13, pp. 67–83.

Sargent, Thomas J. (1987) *Dynamic Macroeconomic Theory* (London and Cambridge, Mass.: Harvard University Press).
Sidrauski, Miguel (1967) 'Rational Choice and Patterns of Growth in a Monetary Economy', *American Economic Review*, vol. 57, no. 2 (May), pp. 534–44.
Swofford, James L. and Gerald A. Whitney (1987) 'Nonparametric Test of Utility Maximization and Weak Separability for Consumption, Leisure, and Money', *Review of Economics and Statistics*, vol. 69, no. 3 (August), pp. 458–64.

2

Neural Networks with Divisia Money: Better Forecasts of Future Inflation*

Robert E. Dorsey

If macroeconomists agree on anything, the most likely candidate would be the long-run relationship between the aggregate price level and the quantity of money or, alternatively, the long-run rates of money growth and inflation. But even this relationship is clouded. Even the relatively close relationships in the 1960s and 1970s, were disturbed occasionally by large shocks to the relative prices of energy and other primary commodities that had disproportionate effects on the price level (see, for example, Tatom, 1981). By the 1980s, however, some as-yet-unknown influence caused the trend rate of velocity to deviate sharply from the nearly constant 3 per cent rate it had exhibited over the previous thirty-five years and undermined virtually all attempts to 'fix' the aggregate price equation with further empirical efforts along these traditional lines. As such, the growth rate of the M1 aggregate in the USA (and similar measures abroad) became a very poor indicator of future inflation and led to some large overpredictions of inflation until at least the middle of the decade.

As to what caused the breakdown of the tight link between past money growth and inflation, opinions vary widely. To some, it was the sweeping financial innovations that, by increasing the substitutability among alternative bank and non-bank liabilities, made velocity more unpredictable and thus inevitably increased the range for errors of inflation forecasts. A specific variation of this theme (Rasche, 1993) is that the early 1980s witnessed an unprecedented switch in public credibility regarding a change in monetary policy and, hence, an unprecedented one-time decline in velocity as well. To others, the sharp decline in velocity growth was largely a measurement problem. Specifically, this hypothesis holds that the simple-sum monetary aggregates published by all central banks always have been and remain irreparably flawed index numbers that give misleading indications of the degree of monetary restraint or ease in place and, hence, the extent of future monetary pressures on the price level (Belongia, 1996). In this case, the

* I would like to acknowledge and express my appreciation for the substantial assistance and guidance provided by Mike Belongia in the development of this chapter.

financial innovations of the 1980s merely exposed just how badly those indexes could deviate from superlative indexes of the same monetary aggregate. Finally, some have argued that even the close link between money and prices in the 1960s and 1970s was a statistical fact associated with a very strong, but spurious, relationship in the 1960s alone.[1]

Apart from the purely scientific question of one day identifying why the relationship between money growth and inflation changed so suddenly and sharply in the 1980s, a more practical and immediate concern is of importance to nearly everyone: is there something that can be done to improve the accuracy of inflation forecasts now? This chapter begins an exploration of this question and presents a preliminary 'yes' answer by exploring the relative information content of Divisia money measures using a new econometric tool, the artificial neural network, in a standardised and quite simple forecasting experiment. After holding all other things constant, the advantage of the fixed neural network is that it can, in principle, 'learn' the process generating the actual data. To turn temporarily from the 'horserace' terminology that is offensive to some in an experiment of this type, the question might be phrased better as: is the process generating one set of data more stable, and can it be used more readily for forecasting than the others? In this particular case, because we *know* simple-sum numbers are a-theoretic index values, whereas Divisia measures are derived from the optimisation problem of a representative consumer, our null hypothesis is that the two are the same and is tested against a one-sided alternative preferring the Divisia's information content. This approach is applied to series of money and prices for Germany and the USA. Before discussing these matters in greater detail, however, it is worth taking time to review the data series and some of the problems experienced in recent empirical work on the money – inflation link.

2.1 Money growth and inflation

Annual rates of inflation for the world's two largest economies and the associated growth rates of their most widely discussed measures of money illustrate some of the properties that would be expected from two series sharing a common long-run relationship; these series also illustrate a number of periods where money and inflation seem to be completely unrelated. The most well-known episode is the very large gap between money and inflation in the USA between 1974–7 and 1981–2.

There are similar cases in the other countries as well. For example, by 1987, the M0 measure of the German money supply and German inflation appear to share few, if any, common properties that had justified targeting central bank money up to that point.[2] M3 was then adopted, only to be shocked by the considerable uncertainty about what effect the absorption of large quantities of implied Ost Marks would have on the overall German money supply. Even though the Bundesbank, in this case, was able to identify the causes of this sharp break from past relationships and responded quickly with an apparently prudent change in policy, current figures on the M3-price relationships are beginning to suggest more need for future research. Thus, rather than paying short-run costs in terms of output and employment, would it not be desirable to have a tool that could 'learn' the underlying cause of these breaks and utilise this learned structure in future forecasts?

With this as a backdrop, what strategies have been pursued by academics and central bankers to find a stable model of the long-run relationship between money and inflation? An enormous amount of work has been done on this question, and no attempt will be made here to include all or discuss each at length. Instead, it may be illustrative to look how the evolution of new data and new statistical techniques give rise to new empirical strategies designed to repair errors or to quiet uneasiness with available options.

Prior to 1980, it is fair to say that a long distributed lag of money growth explained 80 per cent or more of the variation in inflation in most OLS regressions if augmented with one or more dummy variables to account for the turbulent years of the first oil shock and price controls (see, for example Tatom, 1981). Although many economists have a bias or two when dummy variables are introduced to explain a large deviation by data from the estimated mode, this seemed to be a case where reasonable people would agree that the use of dummy variables was appropriate for the events of that time. By 1985, however, the collapse of velocity in the USA was well known, and attempts to fix the type of model just described with still more dummy variables began to elicit louder charges of *ad hoc*-ery.[3]

Seeing this path as generally leading nowhere, economists tried new approaches to the problem. Granger causality tests were implemented in some studies of money and inflation but their statistics did not distinguish well between the direction of an association between money growth and inflation and the uncertainty, strength or stability of that relationship. Others involved the use of a Dickey–Fuller test for stationarity of time series data. Although the test had been available for a number of years, its importance prior to 1987 had been directed primarily to evaluations of how many times a given series had to be differenced to induced stationarity; doing so was necessary to avoid the 'spurious regressions' criticism of Plosser and Schwert (1978). In early 1987, however, Engle and Granger published a paper which not only outlined their approach to cointegration but, by chance, its chosen illustration rejected the existence of a long-run relationship between money and inflation.[4]

Since that time, cointegration has been the tool most frequently used to investigate money's long-run relationships with other variables. And, up until quite recently, some economists had embraced it as the tool designed precisely to handle these types of question (Laidler, 1990). But there have been many problems with this approach as well. First, Dickey–Fuller tests on logs of quantity theory variables across countries consistently indicate that log money and log output are integrated of order one, while the log price series is integrated of order two. This result has many consequences, the first of which is that tests of cointegration must be performed on series integrated of identical orders. To finesse this problem, many economists have argued that, because the equation of exchange identity implies that all variables in it must be integrated of the same order, the ADF statistic for the price level should be played down in this type of situation; to buttress this logic, this approach generally argues that the *t*-statistic was also near its critical value and the ADF test has low power.

Even if this statistical requirement could in some way be avoided, however, results in the existing literature still present a formidable economic challenge. To state it precisely, if the problem were one of merely differencing each data series a sufficient number of times to make each stationery (even if different orders), the present results suggest that the growth rate of money is related to *changes* in the growth rate of the price level (that is, acceleration of the inflation rate). Statistical results aside, economic theory does not support this relationship between money and prices, and this is just one more illustration of why unit root tests and cointegration have generally added so little to our knowledge about the inflation process.

The usefulness of cointegration for testing the long-run link between money and prices was (perhaps) dealt a fatal blow by an insight from McCallum (1993). Specifically, he shows that there is no reason to expect that money and prices will share a cointegrating relationship if technology in the payments system has a trend. If technology in the payments system does have an upward trend, a researcher might well not find a cointegrating relationship, but that is only because a measure of the value of improved technologies is not available as an additional variable that would account for this phenomenon. If this point is accepted as valid, the dozens (or hundreds) of studies using cointegration to investigate whether money growth and inflation move together in the long run have not provided evidence – on either side – that is useful to framing an answer.

2.2 The past forecast record

The historical record for inflation forecasts based on past rates of money growth has been summarised in a number of literature reviews. Unfortunately, most, if not all, of the individual studies included are not directly comparable because of differences among sample periods, measurement of inflation, the test criterion for comparisons and, in particular for this chapter, measures of money. Nonetheless, a review of the existing literature can establish rough orders of magnitude for inflation forecast errors.[5]

Tables 2.1 and 2.2 present information on inflation forecast errors from several recent overviews of the topic. The top section of the table, for example, is taken from a paper by Meltzer (1991) evaluating the quality of Federal Reserve System forecasts.[6] While finding that its forecasts were neither significantly better nor worse than those of other forecasters, Meltzer emphasised the degree of imprecision in these numbers to buttress his case

Table 2.1 Inflation forecast errors, 1970–82

Year		*Mean absolute error*	*RMSE*
1970–3	Current quarter	1.2	1.4
	Next quarter	1.6	1.9
	Four quarters	4.0	4.8
1973–82	Current quarter	1.4	1.9
	Next quarter	1.7	2.3
	Four quarters	1.6	2.0

Note: For 1973–82 the Four quarters error is for the full four quarters; but for 1970–3 it is for a particular quarter.

Table 2.2 Mean absolute CPI forecast errors, 1986Q1–1991Q3 (early quarter)

Forecaster	*Forecast horizon (quarters)*							
	Q1	*Q2*	*Q3*	*Q4*	*Q5*	*Q6*	*Q7*	*Q8*
DRI	0.9	0.9	0.8	0.7	0.6	0.5	0.4	0.3
GSU	1.0	0.9	0.8	0.6	0.5	0.4	0.2	0.2
LHMA	0.8	0.9	0.8	0.7	0.5	0.5	0.4	0.4
RSQE	1.2	1.1	1.0	0.8	0.8	0.7	0.6	1.3
WEFA	1.0	1.0	0.9	0.8	0.6	0.5	0.4	0.3

Source: McNees (1992).

against discretionary policies aimed at fine-tuning economic activity. In particular, the forecast root-mean-squared-errors were large relative to the mean inflation rate of the period (8.1 per cent). Moreover, with the mean error being more closely related to the (positive) mean absolute error than to zero, the table indicates that the Fed tends to underestimate inflation when it is rising and overestimate it when it is falling.

The second portion of the table is from McNees (1992). It shows a more recent review of forecasts made by large economic forecasting enterprises. The sample period is somewhat longer than above and the CPI rather than the deflator is used as the basis for measured inflation. Although the MAEs are similar in magnitude to those of the first case, the bias noted in the Fed forecasts is often not evident. Thus, while the private sector has errors of comparable magnitude, its forecasts seem to be better in line with the course of future activity.

2.3 The neural network

At this point, the paper has come to three conclusions: first, the link between money and prices has been far weaker since 1981 relative to the two previous decades. Second, a review of the recent literature on errors in inflation forecasts indicated that the RMSE around a forecast was large relative to the inflation rate and that, in some cases, it also exhibited substantial bias. Third, although the precise cause still is not known, the 1980s have revealed to many of the developed economies that sharp and unexpected shifts in historical relationships among data series can have significant effects on economic activity and the outcome of particular policy actions. Thus, new efforts to forecast inflation could improve on existing models if they were able to reduce the error band around the mean forecast and/or diminish the degree of bias. Achieving these two goals alone, however, will not be sufficient if central banks also seek greater lead time in identifying the kind of dramatic shift in velocity that caught them completely off-guard in the early 1980s. Instead, this type of problem will require a model of completely flexible form that not only can 'learn' the properties of the data, but through this learning also predict structural shifts such as the great velocity puzzle of the 1980s.

Attempts to develop models that will forecast inflation accurately face significant barriers. Among these are the obvious problems encountered in most empirical work: the absence of a consensus model that accurately describes the mechanisms that drive measured inflation, equally fractious disputes about the variables that must necessarily be included in any model of inflation, and well-recognised problems in data measurement.[7] In this chapter we look at a tool that may be useful in helping researchers to address these barriers.

We use an artificial neural network (ANN) to explore the explanatory power of a variety of measures of a single variable that is certainly related to inflation and money. Artificial neural networks were developed as highly simplified models of the brain. Kolmogorov's theorem and recent improvements and extensions by Irie and Miyake (1988), Funahashi (1989), and Hornik *et al.* (1989) have shown that the ANN can approximate any Borel measurable function to any degree of desired accuracy given a sufficient number of hidden nodes. In other words, the artificial neural network can provide a completely flexible mapping that can approximate highly non-linear functions to any degree of desired accuracy as long as a sufficient number of hidden nodes are included in the ANN. This ability to approximate any unknown mapping provides researchers with a powerful tool that may enable them better to understand the interrelationships of explanatory variables.

Any evaluation of the explanatory power of a candidate variable using standard econometric methodology will be constrained by the specific functional form of the model being estimated. In the case of the relationship between money and inflation, any particular specified functional relationship will be arbitrary, and any conclusion made will be subject to the arbitrary model specification. Since the variables are not known, we use the ANN to look at a more basic issue. We examine the issue of how the variables are measured and explore whether the ANN can be useful in determining an appropriate measure of a variable.[8]

We explore the explanatory power of various measures of money by identifying a specific structure of the ANN that allows for a great deal of flexibility. Dorsey *et al.* (1994) have shown, for example, that an ANN with four input nodes and five hidden layer nodes is able to approximate a Mackey–Glass AR(5) chaotic series function with a high degree of accuracy. We therefore use a fixed-structure ANN to forecast inflation with a variety of measures of money. The same methodology is used for all the estimates. Therefore, since the ANN provides a great deal of flexibility of the functional form, the primary cause of any improvement in forecast accuracy should be directly attributable to the explanatory variable.

2.4. Methodology

To evaluate the degree to which limited data on money provides information for explaining inflation, two simple models were estimated. Throughout the following, it should be noted that a simple and constant design was chosen so that the information content of the monetary variables could be evaluated on an equal footing. Conversely, it is virtually certain in this context that the specific inflation errors of each model would be reduced by the adoption of more complex specifications.

The first model simply says that inflation in the current quarter is a function of the four most recent quarterly measures of money growth:

$$\pi_t = F(M_{t-1}, M_{t-2}, M_{t-3}, M_{t-4})$$

The second model expands the first model to include an AR(1) term for inflation:

$$\pi_t = G(M_{t-1}, M_{t-2}, M_{t-3}, M_{t-4}, \pi_{t-1})$$

Both of these models used simple-sum and Divisia measures of M1 and M2 for the USA, and simple-sum and Divisia M3 for Germany. A fixed-structure artificial neural network was used for all data sets. Specifically, the artificial neural network consisted of either four (model 1) or five (model 2) input nodes, six hidden nodes and one output node. Figure 2.1 shows a diagram of the structure of the neural network used with model 1.

Each observation is input to the ANN at the input layer. The values for the input variables are multiplied by weights corresponding to each of the connecting lines in the figure. Thus, the input to each of the hidden nodes is the weighted sum of the inputs:

$$h_{mi} = \sum_{j=i}^{4} \omega_{mj} X_{ji} - \omega_{m5}$$

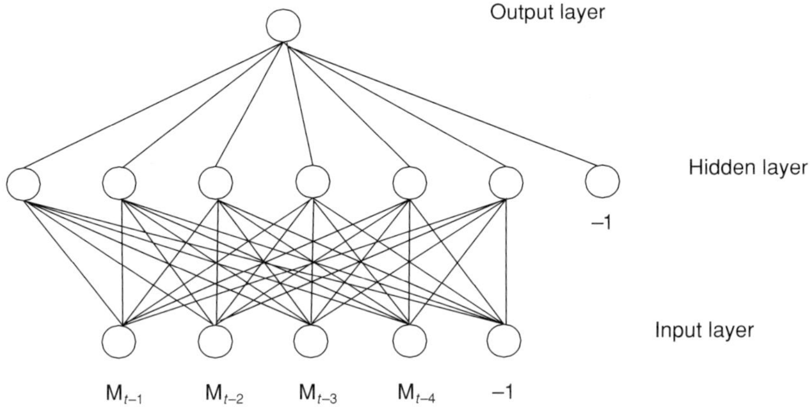

Figure 2.1 Artificial neural network used for Model 1

The weighted sum of the inputs then is passed through the non-linear function (the hidden node):

$$H_{mi} = \frac{1}{1 - e^{-h_{mi}}}$$

and the weighted sum of the outputs from the hidden nodes is the output of the network for that observation:

$$O_i = \sum_{m=1}^{6} \gamma_m H_{mi} - \gamma_7$$

The parameters of the model (ωs and γs) are selected to minimise the sum of squared errors (as in most problems of this type). The complexity of the error surface and the tendency of hill-climbing techniques to become trapped in local optima, motivated the use of a genetic algorithm adapted by Dorsey *et al.* (1994) to optimise the ANN.[9]

The genetic algorithm was first proposed by Holland (1976). In general, it works in a manner similar to natural selection. Each potential solution to the problem (a vector of the ωs and γs) is randomly selected from the parameter space. A population of these vectors – or strings, as they are commonly called – comprises a generation. In this analysis, a generation consisted of twenty vectors. Each vector of randomly-chosen values was used with the data to compute the sum of squared errors. A fitness value was then computed for each string, where the fitness value is inversely related to the sum of squared errors.

A new generation is then selected, with replacement from the current generation. The probability of any string being selected for the new generation increases with its fitness. Once a new generation has been selected, the strings are randomly paired. A corresponding point along each pair of vectors is randomly selected and they are broken at that point and the residual fragments are swapped. This is referred to as the crossover operation. Finally, each component of each new vector has a small probability of being selected for mutation. Should a component be mutated, then that element is replaced with a new value randomly drawn from the parameter space.

Each of the new strings is then used with the data to compute the sum of squared errors, and the process repeats. This process continues for a large number of generations until the solution converges. Dorsey and Mayer (1994) compared the genetic algorithm to a number of other global search algorithms on a wide variety of optimisation problems and found that it consistently dominated all the other algorithms in its ability to obtain the global solution.

For this study, the initial estimation of the model, with twelve hold-out values excluded from the data, consisted of 140,000 generations. This set of parameters was then used as the starting point for each of the subsequent optimisations as additional data was added to the model. Each of the subsequent optimisations was run for 30,000 generations. The US data consisted of historical data series provided by the FRED data base of the Federal Reserve Bank of St Louis; the German simple-sum series were also obtained from this source, whereas St Louis staff specially constructed the German Divisia M3 series. Inflation rates were computed as year-over-year rates change in the CPI.

2.5 Results

For each data set the model was estimated thirteen times. The initial estimation used the available data minus the last twelve quarters. Subsequent re-estimations of the model incrementally included each of the previously-excluded data. The in-sample root mean square errors, along with the out-of-sample errors for each of the 156 estimations, are available from the author and are summarised in Table 2.3.

The root mean squared error for the in-sample forecasts for the M1 data range from a low of 0.007692 to a high of 0.008419. The Divisia M1 data generate root mean squared errors of the estimates approximately 20 per cent smaller than the other thirteen models corresponding. They range from a low of 0.005518 to a high of 0.006772. Ordinary least squares estimates on the same data generate root mean squared errors three to five times larger than those generated with the ANN.

This pattern continues throughout all the estimates. *In every case,* the effect of using a Divisia measure reduces the size of the root mean squared error. Table 2.3 shows the relative size of the root mean squared errors across all models estimated.

Table 2.3 Root mean squared errors of in-sample forecasts

Data	*Normal*	*Divisia*
M1	8.172E-3	5.829E-3
M2	8.148E-3	7.246E-3
M1 AR	4.838E-3	4.583E-3
M2 AR	4.669E-3	4.574E-3
German M3	4.038E-3	3.359E-3
German M3 AR	3.314E-3	3.048E-3

The Divisia models of both M1 and M2 incorporating an autoregressive term (model 2), provide the greatest degree of explanatory power for the US inflation rate, with the M2 AR model providing only a small improvement in fit over the M1 AR model; this is despite the fact that the Divisia M2 data apparently does not contain as much information as the Divisia M1 data. Specifically, without the autoregressive term (model 1), the M1 data provided the least explanatory ability of the four data sets. The M2 data improved the fit only slightly. The Divisia M2 data, however, reduced the root mean squared error of the estimates by approximately 11 per cent relative to the simple-sum M2 data. The Divisia M1 data proved to be even better at explaining the inflation and was able to reduce the simple-sum M1 data root mean squared error by approximately 29 per cent.

When the autoregressive term was added to the models (model 2), the in-sample forecasts from all four data sets were improved. In all cases, the Divisia data generated the greatest improvements. The extent of the improvement provided by the Divisia data, however, was not nearly as large with model 2 as with model 1. For the M1 data, for example, the Divisia data reduced the root mean squared error by slightly over 5 per cent relative to the simple-sum measure, and for the M2 data the improvement was approximately 2 per cent. Similar results were obtained with the German M3 data in both models 1 and 2, resulting in improvements of 16.8 per cent and 8 per cent respectively.

Although the purpose of this research was to evaluate the information content of money measures as a precursor to developing a neural network model of inflation, and not to claim any credibility for such a simple model, it still is tempting to examine out-of-sample forecasts to evaluate the degree to which the model is stable beyond the estimation period. The out-of-sample forecast errors for each model are summarised in Table 2.4. Clearly, all the models deteriorate substantially out-of-sample, with the possible exception of the Divisia M1 models, which maintain a mean absolute forecast error of between 1 per cent and 1.5 per cent for the *three-year* out-of-sample period! Given the simplicity of the models, it is surprising that their accuracy is able to be maintained much beyond the first quarter, let alone to the horizons of the Fed and private forecasters shown in Table 2.1. The M2 AR and Divisia M2 AR

Table 2.4 Out-of-sample forecast errors

Model	*Mean Absolute Error*											
	1 (N = 12)	2 (N = 11)	3 (N = 10)	4 (N = 9)	5 (N = 8)	6 (N = 7)	7 (N = 6)	8 (N = 5)	9 (N = 4)	10 (N = 3)	11 (N = 2)	12 (N = 1)
M1	0.005013	0.006804	0.008857	0.012190	0.014949	0.019583	0.025383	0.028060	0.030230	0.046367	0.039350	0.042800
DM1	0.010865	0.013502	0.012245	0.013064	0.013064	0.013746	0.014580	0.014982	0.015700	0.015917	0.014985	0.012140
M2	0.012749	0.014956	0.017808	0.021026	0.020306	0.023400	0.026754	0.027920	0.037775	0.042967	0.046200	0.045600
DM2	0.011606	0.014131	0.016420	0.019011	0.021253	0.023331	0.025628	0.027746	0.030245	0.032880	0.034435	0.035030
M1 AR	0.004353	0.006084	0.008106	0.010771	0.013063	0.016357	0.019462	0.023018	0.019808	0.025320	0.029910	0.034500
DM1 AR	0.004769	0.006538	0.010290	0.014567	0.017010	0.020452	0.027310	0.027310	0.038935	0.043857	0.050250	0.055720
M2 AR	0.003049	0.003710	0.004492	0.005442	0.006529	0.007791	0.009383	0.011752	0.014153	0.016983	0.019285	0.018890
DM2 AR	0.003951	0.004400	0.004063	0.007618	0.007245	0.008411	0.013052	0.016050	0.019018	0.020537	0.021975	0.024660
G M3	0.014248	0.026543	0.024537	0.055459	0.044304	0.047781	0.044123	0.054014	0.038775	0.083623	0.155375	0.227500
G DM3	0.017657	0.042425	0.032212	0.072550	0.080664	0.086953	0.122752	0.098462	0.095105	0.116490	0.056945	0.134700
G M3 AR	0.006325	0.009717	0.012432	0.018843	0.023764	0.026152	0.032486	0.054994	0.079043	0.119343	0.222650	0.370400
G DM3 AR	0.006967	0.008991	0.018918	0.014626	0.019764	0.021237	0.023041	0.025313	0.026502	0.071623	0.137230	0.209800

models also are able to achieve mean absolute forecast errors of less than 1 per cent for more than six quarters out-of-sample. Examples of some of the better-performing models are illustrated in Figures 2.2 to 2.5.

2.6 Summary

The artificial neural network has the ability to approximate any continuous mapping to any degree of desired accuracy. Therefore, when the functional form is unknown, an artificial neural network can provide insight for the researcher as to the functional relationship and the informational content of potential explanatory variables. In this context, the artificial neural network is used to examine the ability of a range of monetary measures to explain inflation. Divisia measures of M1 and M2 for the USA and M3 for Germany are compared with their simple-sum counterparts using a simple, fixed structure, artificial neural network optimised with a genetic algorithm. The Divisia measure consistently dominates the simple-sum measure in explaining inflation across all models. In addition, the model appears to be somewhat stable, in that out-of-sample forecasts do not deteriorate rapidly despite the fact that only money is used in the model. In particular, the Federal Reserve's current horizon for 'precise' inflation forecasts might well be extended if a Divisia measure of money were to be combined with an artificial neural network to produce inflation forecasts.

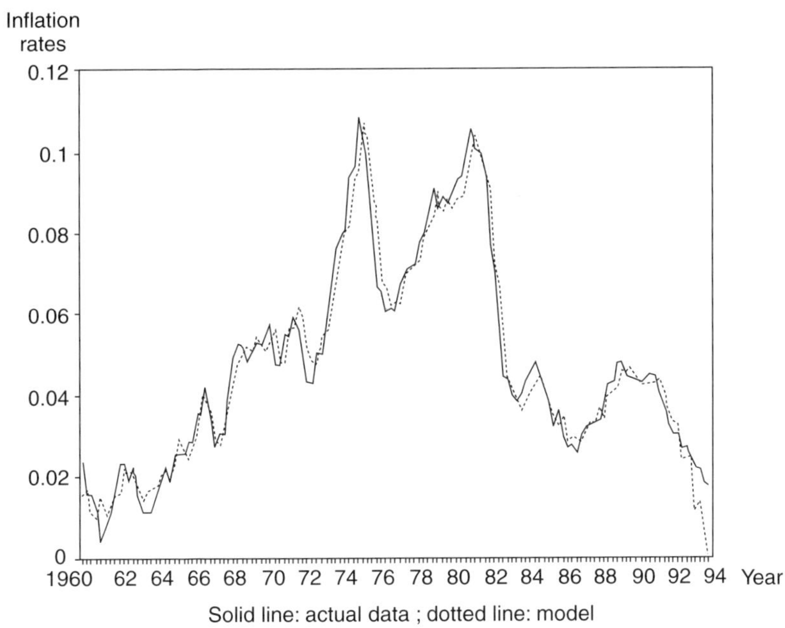

Figure 2.2 M1 AR model forecast (92Q1 to 94Q1 out-of-sample)

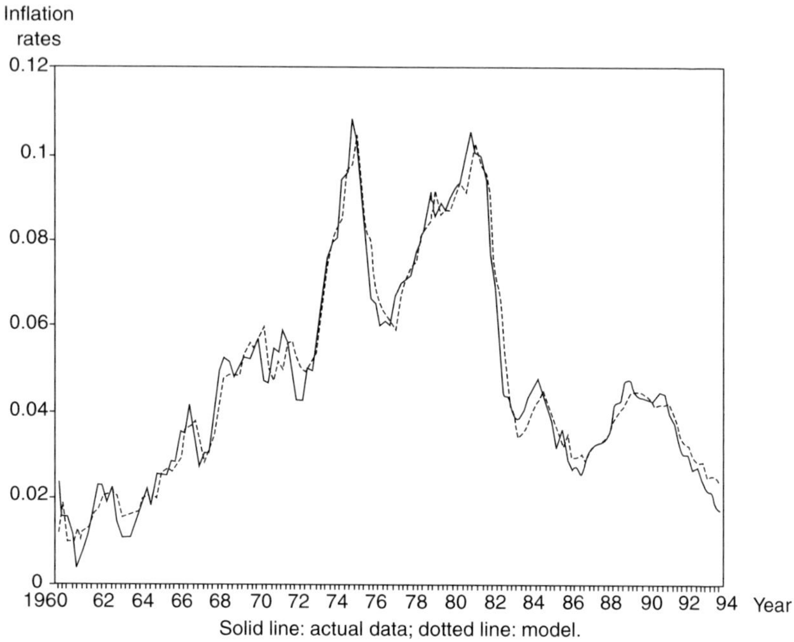

Figure 2.3 M2 AR model forecast (92Q1 to 94Q1 out-of-sample)

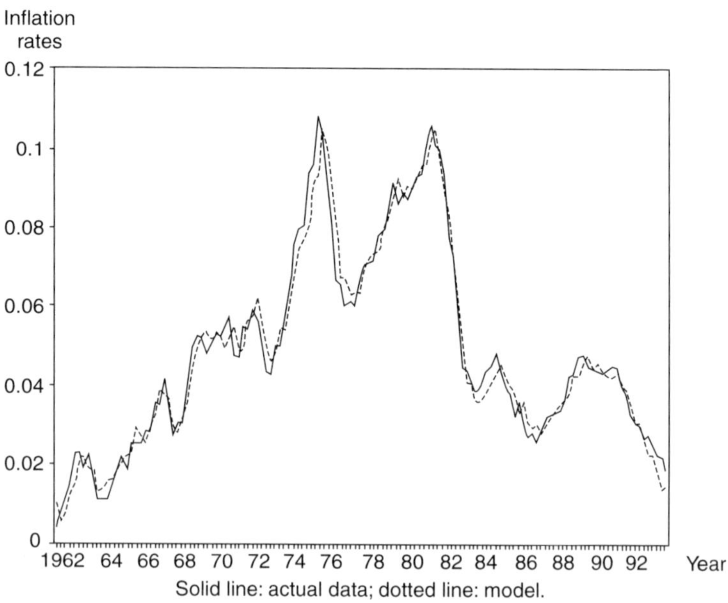

Figure 2.4 Divisia M1 AR model forecast (92Q1 to 93Q4 out-of-sample)

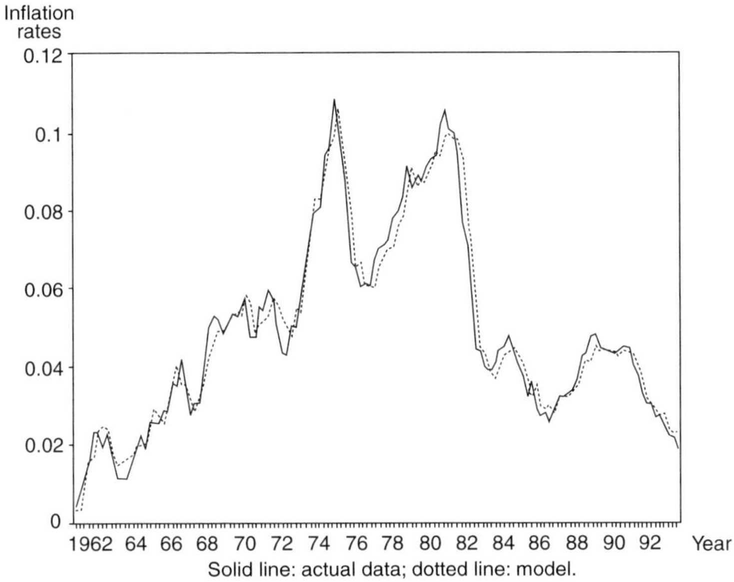

Figure 2.5 Divisia M2 AR model forecast (92Q1 to 93Q4 out-of-sample)

In sum, the combination of Divisia measures of money, along with the artificial neural network, offers a promising starting point for the development of an improved model of inflation. The incorporation of other standard data components of inflation models can only serve to improve the forecasting ability of the model and achieve a model that can 'learn' about changes in the structure of the economy over time, so that 'stable' and 'traditional' relationships never become anything less than that.

Notes

1. For a discussion of the first line of reasoning see, among others, Rasche (1993). On the second and third points, see Belongia (1996), and Friedman and Kuttner (1992).
2. See Toedter *et al.* (1993) for an application of the P-star model to German data and its ability to use M3 data in a policy dedicated to price stability.
3. One exception is Rasche (1993), who argues that an abrupt shift in inflation expectations in the early 1980s – working empirically in much the same practical manner as a dummy variable – revives the essential qualitative pre-1980 relationships between money and prices.
4. This curious result occurred because they ignored the 3 per cent trend rate of velocity growth in their analysis.
5. Because our focus in this chapter is limited to the marginal informational content of one approach to forecasting inflation relative to alternatives, it is not necessary to know the particular structures of the forecasting models or the role money plays in them.

6. Meltzer extracted these data from an earlier paper by Karmouzis and Lombra (1989).
7. These measurement problems extended well beyond the monetary focus of the papers in this volume. With respect to the price level, for example, issues of quality improvement have been a persistent issue. More recently, the treatment of the capital stock in the aggregate price level also has been suggested as a source of breaks in 'traditional' regularities.
8. If the necessary variables to be used in a model are known and are appropriately measured, then the ANN should be useful in approximating the relationship among the variables. The ANN has the ability to approximate complex non-linear interactions among variables to a high degree of accuracy and, as Caporaletti *et al.* (1994) have recently shown, the ANN works well for approximating simultaneous equation systems.
9. See Dorsey and Mayer (1994) for a detailed discussion of the application of the genetic algorithm for optimising the neural network.

References

Belongia, Michael T. (1996) 'Measurement Matters: Recent Results in Monetary Economics Re-Examined', *Journal of Political Economy*, October, pp. 1065–83.

Caporaletti, Louis E., Robert E. Dorsey, John D. Johnson and William A. Powell (1994) 'A Decision Support System for In Sample Simultaneous Equation Systems Forecasting using Artificial Neural Systems', *Decision Support Systems*, vol. 11, pp. 481–95.

Dorsey, Robert E. and Walter J. Mayer (1994) 'Optimization Using Genetic Algorithms', in John Johnson and Andrew Whinston (eds), *Advances in Artificial Intelligence in Economics, Finance and Management*, vol. 1 (Greenwich, CA: JAI Press), pp. 69–91.

Dorsey, Robert E. and Walter J. Mayer (1994) 'Genetic Algorithms for Estimation Problems with Multiple Optima, Non-Differentiability, and Other Irregular Features', *Journal of Business and Economic Statistics*, vol. 13, no. 1, pp. 53–66.

Dorsey, Robert E., John D. Johnson and Walter J. Mayer (1994) 'An Alternative Algorithm for Training of Multi-layered Feed Forward Neural Nets Utilizing Alternative Objective Functions', in *Advances in Artificial Intelligence in Economies, Finance and Management* (Greenwich, CN : JAI Press), pp. 93–111.

Engle, R. F. and C. W. J. Granger (1987) 'Co-integration and Error Correction: Representation, Estimation and Testing', *Econometrica*, vol. 55, pp. 251–76.

Friedman, Benjamin M. and Kenneth N. Kuttner (1992) 'Money, Income, Prices and Interest Rates', *American Economic Review*, vol. 82, no. 3, pp. 472–92.

Funahashi, K. (1989) 'On the Approximate Realization of Continuous Mappings by Neural Networks', *Neural Networks*, vol. 2, pp. 183–92.

Holland, J. (1975) *Adaptation in Natural and Artificial Systems* (Ann Arbor, Mich.: University of Michigan Press).

Hornik, K., M. Stinchcombe and H. White (1989) 'Multilayer Feedforward Networks are Universal Approximators', *Neural Networks*, vol 2, pp. 359–66.

Irie, B. and S. Miyake (1988) 'Capabilities of Three Layer Perceptions', *IEEE Second International Conference on Neural Networks*, vol. I, pp. 641–8.

Kolmogorov, A. N. (1957) 'On the Representation of Continuous Functions of Many Variables by Superposition of Continuous Functions of One Variable and Addition', *Dokladly Akadamie Nauk USSR*, vol. 114, pp. 953–6.

Laidler, David (1990) *Taking Money Seriously and Other Essays* (Cambridge, Mass. MIT Press).

McCallum, Bennett T. (1993) 'Unit Roots in Macroeconomic Time Series: Some Critical Issues', *Federal Reserve Bank of Richmond Economic Quarterly*, vol. 79, no. 2 (Spring).

McNees, Stephan K. (1992) 'How Large are Economic Forecast Errors?' *New England Economic Review* (July/August), pp. 25–42.

Meltzer, Alan H. (1991) 'The Fed at Seventy Five' in Michael T. Belongia (ed.), *Monetary Policy on the 75th Anniversary of the Federal Reserve System*, ed. (Boston, Mass.: Kluwer).

Plosser, Charles I. and William G. Schwert (1978) 'Money, Income, and Sunspots: Measuring Economic Relationships and the Effects of Differencing', *Journal of Monetary Economics*, vol. 4, pp. 637–60.

Rasche, Robert H. (1993) 'Monetary Aggregates, Monetary Policy and Economic Activity', *Federal Reserve Bank of St Louis Review*, vol. 75, March/April, no. 2, pp. 1–35.

Tatom, John, A. (1981) 'Energy Prices and Short-Run Economic Performance', *Federal Reserve Bank of St Louise Review*, vol. 63, January, no. 1, pp. 3–17.

Toedter, Karl-Heinz, and Hans-Eggert Reimers (1994) 'P-Star as a Link Between Money and Prices in Germany', *Weltwirtschaftliches Archiv*, Bd. 130, pp. 273–89.

Part II

Evidence from European Economies and the Planned EMU Area

3
Weighted Monetary Aggregates for the UK*

Leigh Drake, K. Alec Chrystal and Jane M. Binner

At the conference in Oxford, Mississippi, it was tempting to locate the theme of the conference in the work of Oxford's greatest son, and, indeed, one of the greatest literary figures of the twentieth century. William Faulkner. It is clear that Faulkner was a student of the economies of inflation ... Why else would he have written a book on 'Soldiers' Pay'? It could also be that he anticipated the demise of monetarism in 'As I Lay Dying', though this more likely to be an allusion to the Keynesian medium term (since we know what happens to Keynesians in the long run!). No doubt he had Divisia in mind as the 'Intruder in the Dust'. As far as this chapter is concerned, we shall anticipate the comments of our discussants by suggesting the potential parallel between this and 'The Sound and the Fury'. This is a story told through the eyes of several different characters, one of whom is a congenital idiot. We shall leave it to others to identify which of us is Benji. Our learned discussants would, no doubt, wish to complete the line in William Shakespeare's 'Macbeth', from which Faulkner drew his title: ... 'it is a tale told by an idiot, full of sound and fury, signifying nothing'.

3.1 Introduction

This chapter is about the comparative performance of the standard UK measure of broad money, M4, and its corresponding Divisia index. We do not spend time setting out the well-known theoretical case for choosing one or the other. What may be less familiar to some however, is the institutional and policy environment in the UK, so it is this that we outline first.

From the Second World War until 1972, the UK operated a fixed exchange rate. Text book theory tells us that under a fixed exchange rate (especially with mobile capital) the domestic monetary authorities have no independent

* The authors are grateful to Sophie Haincourt for her excellent research assistance, and Drake and Chrystal gratefully acknowledge financial support from the ESRC (Research Grant Ref. No: R000234614).

discretion. In practice, the UK authorities did have some limited discretion in this period, because they had a very rigid system of exchange controls. However, their main method of controlling the domestic money supply was by direct quantitative controls on the banking system. Banks were told year by year at what rate they could increase loans. There were cartel arrangements between the banks and between building societies (the UK equivalent of S&Ls) so there was no effective competition for loans and deposits and there was credit rationing. Quantitative ceilings (in their 1960s incarnation) were swept away in September 1971, in the reforms known as Competition and Credit Control. A surge in bank intermediation and associated rapid growth in the broad money supply (then called £M3) followed. Rapid inflation ensued a couple of years later. The observation of a growth rate of £M3 above 25 per cent in 1972–3, followed by inflation of the same order in 1974–5, persuaded the authorities that there was a link between monetary growth and inflation. Quantitative ceilings, of a sort (limits on the growth rate of banks' eligible liabilities, known as the Corset) were restored at the end of 1973. Monetary targeting, based on £M3 targets, was introduced in 1976, though for a while targeting was achieved by direct controls rather than by base control or an interest rate policy. The strong correlation between £M3 and nominal GDP (with a lag) established in the mid-1970s left little doubt about which monetary aggregate was the best indicator of monetary conditions. However, at the end of the 1970s there was another significant regime change which undermined the economic significance of £M3. In the late 1970s there was a dramatic appreciation of the sterling real and nominal exchange rates. Part of the reason for this was the emergence of the UK as an oil producer (combined with a doubling of the oil price in 1979). The Thatcher Government abolished all exchange controls in October 1979. This made it impossible to maintain quantitative ceilings on the banking system, because banks were now free to intermediate off-shore what they could not intermediate on-shore. Accordingly, the Corset was abolished in June of 1980, though it went effectively at the end of 1979. There followed a period of gradual but substantial financial innovation. In 1980–1, the corporate sector was in severe recession, and banks immediately targeted the personal mortgage market (the traditional domain of building societies) as a sector into which to expand, and building societies fought back. In 1983, the building society cartel started to break up, with the effect that both mortgage and savings deposit markets became more competitive. Building societies offered transactions services (ATMs and credit cards) and interest-bearing cheque accounts. The 1986 Building Society Act gave them the right to convert to bank status and also to increase the levels of both wholesale funding and unsecured lending. In response to this new competition, banks were forced to offer high interest cheque and deposit accounts. The significance of all this for monetary aggregates is twofold. First, the surge of bank intermediation that followed the removal of the Corset was associated with rapid growth of £M3. This occurred at a time when real activity was declining fast and inflation was falling. Broad money continued to grow at rates in the high teens for most of the 1980s, but up to 1988 inflation stayed low. This did much to discredit the case for monetary targeting, and targets for broad money were officially abandoned in 1986. Secondly, the changing role of banks and building societies made it less sensible to have a broad monetary aggregate which includes one but not the other. The distortions to £M3 (and to M1) caused by the conversion of the Abbey National Building Society into a bank in 1989 led the authorities to drop M3 (and M1) as an aggregate entirely, and the standard broad money measure became M4, which included both bank and building society deposits.

Monetary policy still needs some guiding principles. It is well known that inflation and unemployment are lagging indicators, so good policy needs, at the very least, some leading indicator of overheating. For a while, the UK authorities tried an exchange rate target. At first, this was implicit (Nigel Lawson, the then UK Chancellor of the Exchequer, held the pound sterling close to DM3 in 1987–8) but it later became explicit when John Major took Britain into the ERM in October 1990. Since the UK's departure from the ERM in September 1992, the authorities claim to monitor a range of monetary aggregates (explicitly M0 and M4), and the Bank of England has started to publish a Divisia series in its Quarterly Bulletin (with historical data dating back to 1977). However, their only explicit target is an inflation target. So far this inflation target has been easy to hit because the economy has been well below potential output since 1992 (at the cost of a cumulative output loss of £70 billion at 1990 prices). Problems undoubtedly lie ahead, the main problem being to identify indicators of monetary conditions that will inform policy-makers sufficiently early of impending inflation so that they can control it in advance, rather than resort to another boom-and-bust correction of the sort experienced three times since the 1970s. Our purpose is to increase the level of understanding of the informational content of M4 and Divisia M4. Our hypothesis is that Divisia M4 is a better indicator of monetary conditions than M4. The logical case for this is that Divisia aggregation endogenises at least some of the major innovations that clearly distorted simple sum M4 in the 1980s, especially the payment of competitive interest rates on cheque and savings deposits. We begin by discussing the data and proceed to investigate the comparative empirical performance of the simple-sum and Divisia aggregates in a battery of tests.

3.2 Monetary data

The monetary data used in this study were supplied by the Bank of England and consist of the official M4 (simple-sum) aggregate together with its constituent asset components. These components are:

1. Notes and coins.
2. Non-interest-bearing sight deposits.

3. Interest-bearing sight deposits.
4. Time deposits.
5. Building society deposits.

In order to construct a Divisia M4 aggregate, we clearly need data on individual asset returns, together with a benchmark rate of return. With respect to the former, personal sector and company sector holdings form the bulk of M4 assets, but the interest rates paid to each sector on the same category of asset are often very different, with corporate customers typically receiving a higher rate of return (see Drake and Chrystal, 1994a, 1994b). Rather than apply a proxy interest rate for each asset, therefore, we chose to utilise data provided by the Bank of England (which was in turn provided by the financial institutions in question) on the rates of interest paid to corporate and personal-sector customers on each asset. In order to approximate the appropriate rate of return on aggregate asset holdings we simply calculated the weighted average return, with the weights calculated as the share of each sectors holdings in the asset totals. As is common in most money-demand studies, the own return on notes and coins and non-interest-bearing sight deposits is taken to be zero.

Turning now to the appropriate choice of benchmark rate of return, previous work by Drake and Chrystal (1994a, 1994b) on sectoral money demand used the maximum government bond yield in each period as the benchmark for the corporate sector, and the maximum retail rate offered by the Halifax Building Society (the largest UK building society) as the appropriate personal-sector benchmark. The latter was also used as a benchmark rate of return by Patterson (1991) in his non-parametric analysis of personal-sector decisions on consumption, liquid assets and leisure. Drake and Chrystal found that the use of these benchmarks worked well in terms of cointegration analysis on sectoral money demand, and it therefore seems appropriate to take the higher of the two returns in each period as the appropriate benchmark for this aggregate study.

In order to calculate the user cost or rental price for each asset component we use the following formula, developed by Barnett (1978):

$$RP_{it} = (R_t - r_{it})/(1 + R_t) \tag{3.1}$$

where RP_i is the rental price of the ith asset; R, is the benchmark rate of return; and r_i is the rate of return on asset i. These rental prices are the one-period holding costs for each asset and are the appropriate prices to enter into the Divisia computation of monetary aggregate indices and rental price indices.

The sample period for this study runs from 1977 Q1 to 1993 Q2, and the full monetary data set can be obtained from the authors. Although the Bank of England does produce a Divisia M4 index, this is constructed by applying the Divisia methodology to the personal and corporate-sector components of each

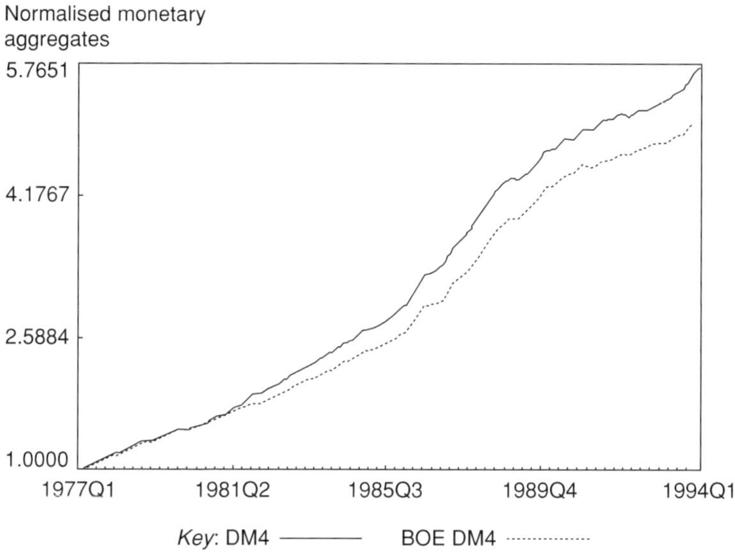

Figure 3.1 Divisia M4 and Bank of England Divisia M4

asset in order to construct an aggregate index (they also use a different benchmark rate). In order to facilitate a direct comparison with simple-sum M4, however, we felt it more appropriate to apply the Divisia methodology to the underlying aggregate asset components of official simple-sum M4. Both the evolution of the Bank of England series (BDM4) and our constructed Divisia series (DM4) are contrasted in Figure 3.1 over the sample period.

3.3 Graphical analysis

The purpose of this section is simply to contrast the behaviour of the Divisia M4 aggregate with its simple-sum counterpart over the sample period. Figure 3.2 plots the Divisia M4 index against an index of the simple-sum aggregate where both are normalised at unity in the base period. The most striking feature of this figure is that simple-sum M4 begins to increase much faster than the Divisia aggregate from the early 1980s, and the two aggregates diverge markedly after this time. This is largely because of the financial innovations that took place during the 1980s and involved rising interest yields on the 'broader – near-money' components of M4. The consequent increase in holdings of these near-money assets resulted in a sharp increase in the unweighted simple-sum aggregate but a much more moderate increase in Divisia M4 where these assets are recognised as providing fewer liquidity

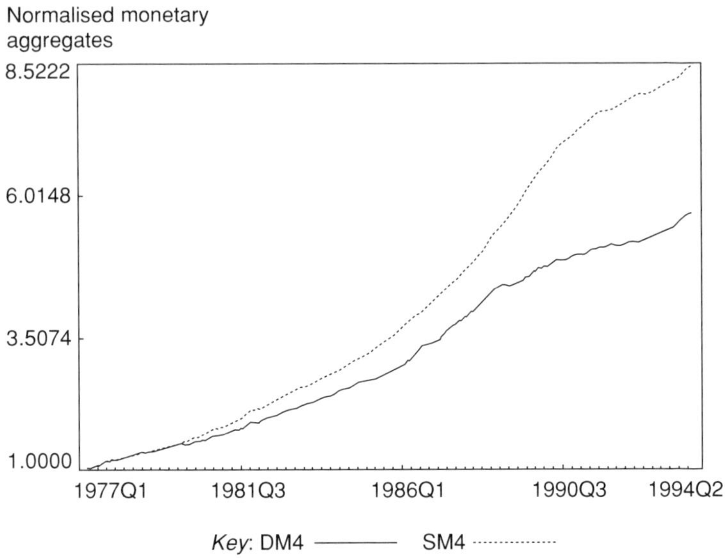

Figure 3.2 Divisia M4 and simple-sum M4 aggregates

services than the narrow money assets and are consequently given less weight in the construction of the aggregate.

Figure 3.3 shows the annual growth rates (based on quarterly data) of the two aggregates. It is quite clear that simple-sum M4 has at times shown very rapid growth when the Divisia counterpart exhibited much more moderate growth. A case in point is during 1988–9, when simple-sum M4 continued to grow very rapidly while the growth of Divisia M4 declined significantly, thus correctly anticipating the subsequent sharp decline in the rate of inflation from the middle of 1990. This type of episode is undoubtedly attributable to the failure of simple-sum aggregates to deal with the type of financial innovation outlined above and could lead to serious errors if the authorities are using the growth in the broad money aggregate as an indicator of subsequent movements in nominal income or prices.

Finally, Figure 3.4 plots indices of the velocity of circulation of both Divisia and simple-sum M4. It is clear that the simple-sum velocity has been exhibiting a relatively sharp trend decline since the early 1980s. Again, this probably reflects the failure of unweighted aggregates to take adequate account of the growth in 'broad money' assets as a consequence of financial innovation. In contrast, the Divisia velocity is much more stable over the sample period as a whole. Although the Divisia velocity index does show some modest decline in the early part of the 1980s, this is much less severe than is

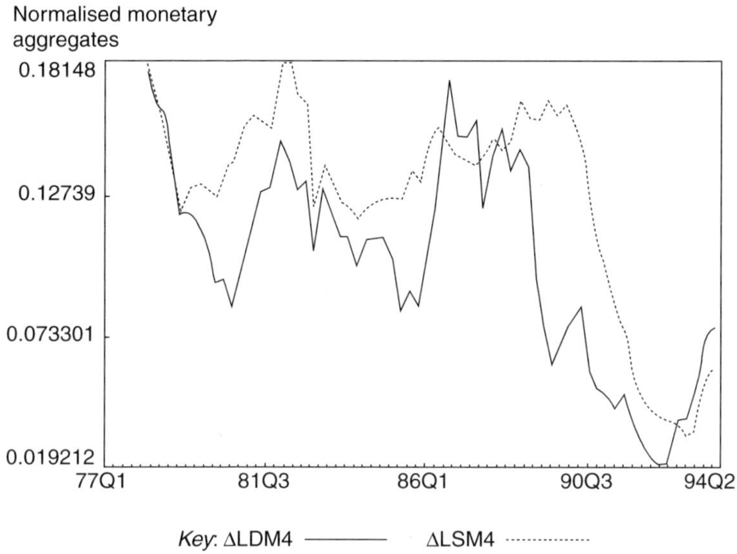

Figure 3.3 Annual growth rates of Divisia M4 and simple-sum M4 (quarterly data)

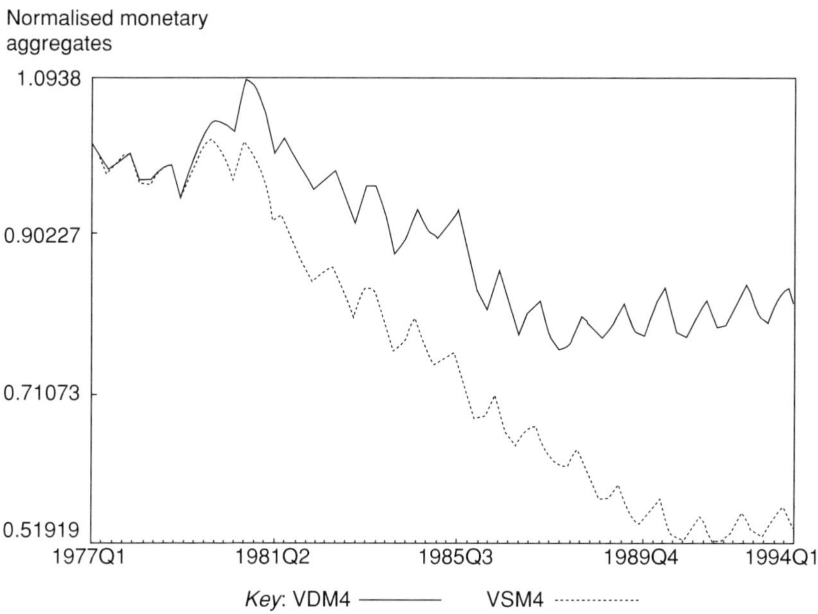

Figure 3.4 Velocity of circulation indices for Divisia and simple-sum M4

the case for simple-sum M4, and the Divisia velocity does appear to stabilise again after the mid-1980s.

3.4 Cointegration analysis

One important test of the suitability of a monetary aggregate is whether there exists a plausible long-run relationship between the aggregate and both real national income (or some alternative scale variable) and the price level. We test for the existence of such a relationship for both Divisia and simple-sum M4 using the Johansen maximum likelihood cointegration technique (Johansen, 1988; and Johansen and Juselius, 1990). Details of all the variables utilised in the cointegration analysis are:

DM4:	Divisia M4
SM4:	Simple-sum M4
YSM4:	Own yield on simple-sum M4
DPM4:	Rental price index for Divisia M4
R:	Benchmark rate of return
RGDP:	Real GDP
GDPDEF:	GDP deflator
RTFE:	Real total final expenditure
REXP:	Real consumer expenditure
TBR:	Treasury Bill rate

Note: The prefix (L) in the results indicates that the variable is in log terms.

Prior to embarking on the cointegration analysis, however, it is important to check the order of integration of all the variables. Table 3.1 reports order of integration tests based upon the standard DF/ADF test statistics (Dickey and Fuller, 1981) and the non-parametric tests $Z\alpha^*$ and $Z_t\alpha^*$ proposed by Phillips and Perron (1988). Although these test statistics do provide conflicting evidence for some variables, on the basis of the available evidence it seems reasonable to assume that all the variables in question are integrated of order 1, (I(1)), and hence are all valid candidates for inclusion in a cointegrating vector.

In the case of the Divisia monetary aggregate, it is clear that the relevant interest rate term is the rental price index corresponding to the monetary aggregate index. In the case of the simple-sum aggregate, however, the choice is not so clear-cut. In order to provide as much comparability as possible with the Divisia results, we chose to include both the own yield on simple-sum money and the benchmark rate of interest, with the latter acting as the opportunity cost variable. The own yield on money is proxied by the weighted average interest rate across all M4 assets. Clearly, our priors would suggest that the coefficient on the own yield should be positive, while the coefficient on the opportunity cost variable should be negative.

Table 3.1 Order of integration tests

	DF	*ADF (4)*	*Zα** (without trend)	*Ztα** (without trend)	*Zα** (with trend)	*Ztα** (with trend)
LDM4	−3.9218	−1.1642	−0.9242	−4.0679	0.2682	0.1570
LSM4	−4.3258	−1.2170	−0.7174	−4.2883	3.6974	2.2822
DPM4	−2.3783	−1.2310	−8.7684	−2.1539	−20.221	−3.4469
YSM4	−0.9187	−2.7965	−4.7318	−1.2938	−3.6982	−1.0158
R	−0.8875	−1.6571	−3.5446	−0.9969	−7.1549	−1.7904
TBR	−1.5190	−2.3821	−6.5847	−1.6062	−7.3643	−1.8042
LRGDP	−1.5550	−0.4359	−3.9962	−1.5069	−28.954	−4.1130
LRTFE	−1.1429	−0.5519	−1.9997	−1.1218	−16.933	−2.9779
LREXP	−1.7356	−0.5325	−3.9190	−1.6793	−32.989	−4.4333
LGDPDEF	−5.1048	−1.6633	−1.3924	−4.7357	−3.0799	−2.0799
ΔLDM4	−7.2916	−2.0690	−58.094	−7.2716	−74.030	−8.8057
ΔLSM4	−6.4836	−0.8726	−48.563	−6.3948	−68.475	−8.1393
ΔDPM4	−11.2288	−4.5433	−87.107	−11.254	−87.040	−11.158
ΔYSM4	−5.4623	−3.2997	−40.964	−5.4560	−42.995	−5.6859
ΔR	−7.5876	−3.0377	−63.177	−7.5899	−64.415	−7.6606
ΔTBR	−2.9119	−2.0837	−64.290	−7.9039	−65.542	−8.0727
ΔLRGDP	−8.8754	−2.0164	−72.155	−9.0015	−72.156	−8.9289
ΔLRTFE	−8.6136	−2.3365	−70.645	−8.6262	−70.656	−8.5602
ΔLREXP	−9.5207	−1.9793	−75.815	−9.6249	−75.900	−9.5759
ΔLGDPDEF	−4.9864	−1.8097	−35.536	−5.0224	−51.653	−6.5364
5% Critical values	−2.930	−2.930	−14.000	−2.880	−21.600	−3.430

It is now well established that the Johansen cointegration results can be sensitive to the lag specification in the VAR. Hall (1991), for example, has demonstrated that the coefficient estimates tend to be fairly robust across different lag specifications, but that the Johansen maximum likelihood tests for the number of cointegrating vectors present among the set of variables can be sensitive to the VAR lag specification. For this reason, we have chosen to report the Johansen cointegration results for VAR lags running from 4 to 8 for both Divisia and simple-sum M4. In addition to the relevant interest rate terms and the price index, we also report the cointegration results for a range of scale variables. These results are given in Tables 3.2 and 3.3. In the case where there is more than one cointegrating vector, we report only the vector which corresponds with our economic priors and indicate both the total number of cointegrating vectors and the number of the vector reported where these are numbered in descending eigenvalue order.

The first point to make about the results in Tables 3.2 and 3.3 is that for both simple-sum and Divisia M4 there is generally at least one sensible money demand specification. Furthermore, the coefficient estimates appear to be reasonably robust across the differing VAR lag specifications. An important

Table 3.2 Summary of Johansen cointegration results for Divisia M4 normalised coefficients

Lag length	*NB of coint. vectors*	*DPM4*	*LRGDP*	*LRTFE*	*LREXP*	*LGDPDEF*	*CON*
	1/2	0.10231	2.2362			0.97568′	–29.0978
4	1/2	0.07520		1.8719		0.93723′	–25.3674
	3/3	–0.22039			1.2265	0.96594′	–16.6568
	1	–0.00623	2.0116			0.94892*	–26.2477
5	1	0.00475		1.7723		0.95713*	–24.2213
	1	–0.02138			1.6944	0.80306′	–21.3061
	1	0.00472	2.0868			0.93454*	–27.0695
6	1	0.02388		1.8209		0.93513*	–24.7084
	1	–0.03484			1.7434	0.76758′	–21.6862
	1/3	–0.02895	1.8160			1.0567′	–24.4845
7	1	–0.03055		1.5721		1.0309*	–22.1301
	1	–0.10583			1.3633	0.98739*	–18.3931
	2/2	0.02660	2.0875			0.92161′	–27.0185
8	1	–0.09262		1.2752		1.1623′	–19.1397
	1	–0.10657			1.2371	1.0626*	–17.3124

Notes: The sample covers the period until 1993Q2.
* and ′ denote that the test of a unit coefficient on LGDPDEF was accepted/rejected.

difference between the simple-sum and Divisia results, however, is that it proved impossible to find a unique cointegrating vector for any simple-sum specification. This result echoes the work of Hall *et al.* (1989), who reported that no cointegrating relationships could be found for aggregate simple-sum M4 without the inclusion of proxy variables for financial innovation.

In contrast, it was the norm to find a unique vector for Divisia M4. This is clearly significant given the controversy surrounding the inferences that can be made about specific coefficient estimates in cases of multiple cointegrating vectors. It is also noteworthy that, although the coefficient estimates generally conform with *a priori* expectations, formal tests of price homogeneity are satisfied in only three out of fourteen specifications for simple-sum M4, in contrast to seven out of fifteen specifications for Divisia M4. Furthermore, in those cases where the formal test is rejected, the coefficients on the GDP deflator are generally close to unity.

Turning now to the specific coefficient estimates, it is clear from Table 3.3 that the coefficient on the simple-sum own yield is consistently small but

Table 3.3 Johansen cointegration results for simple-sum M4 (Normalised coefficients)

Lag length	*NB of coint. vectors*	*YSM4*	*R*	*LRGDP*	*LRTFE*	*LREXP*	*LGDPDEF*	*CON*
	3/3	0.03611	–0.03234	1.5441			1.3949*	–22.4410
4	2/2	0.01668	–0.06101		1.8147		0.99673*	–23.8708
	1/2	0.06674	–0.09975			1.6075	0.77632′	–19.3000
	2/2	0.03492	–0.05958	1.4747			1.3276′	–21.0625
5	2/4	0.01868	–0.04587		1.5819		1.1792′	–22.2009
	2/2	0.06244	–0.09406			1.2930	0.98540*	–16.7566
	2/4	0.03238	–0.04404	1.4417			1.3687′	–20.9974
6	2/4	0.03264	–0.04462		1.2929		1.3416′	–19.6538
	2/4	0.03877	–0.05396			1.5515	0.92621′	–19.5693
	4/5	0.02258	–0.02142	1.8896			1.0017′	–24.4459
7	1/4	0.03010	–0.0273		1.4022		1.3542′	–21.1822
	1/4	0.02496	–0.02472			1.7112	1.0731′	–22.3103
	no sensible results							
8	1/3	0.01189	–0.00957		1.8324		1.2099′	–25.6980
	1/5	0.01514	–0.01651			1.8173	1.0713′	–23.5036

Notes:
The sample covers the period until 1993Q2.
* and ′ denote that the test of a unit coefficient on LGDPDEF was accepted/rejected respectively.

positive, while the coefficient on the benchmark return (the opportunity cost variable) is consistently small but negative. In contrast, the rental price coefficient in the Divisia estimation (Table 3.2), which might have been expected to be small and negative, in fact varies between small and positive and small and negative. The likely explanation for this is that the rental price has two channels of influence on Divisia money. The first is the usual demand effect whereby an increase in the rental price of an asset will reduce the demand for that asset. The second is the compositional influence whereby an increase in the rental price of an asset will imply that its weight in the composition of the Divisia aggregate will increase. This is likely to be particularly significant during periods of declining interest rates, when the own yields on the interest bearing assets decline by more than the benchmark return. In these cases the rental price will increase and the compositional effect may outweigh the demand effect, producing a positive coefficient on the rental price.

With respect to the coefficients on the scale variables, it is interesting to note that in the Divisia estimations the coefficient on real GDP is consistently close to two. This is much higher than the coefficient obtained in traditional money demand studies which have tended to find income coefficients of unity or just above unity. If we contrast the results obtained in Tables 3.2 and 3.3, however, one possible explanation emerging is that the use of simple-sum aggregates in previous broad money demand studies has 'biased downwards' the income elasticity estimate. Our simple-sum income coefficients in Table 3.3 are typically in the range 1.4 to 1.5, in contrast to the estimates of around 2.0 from the Divisia estimates (Table 3.2). The range 1.4 to 1.5 is still somewhat higher than the typical values obtained in earlier studies, however, suggesting that this is not the full explanation. A further possible explanation is that, by using cointegration, we are abstracting from the short-run deviations in income and capturing a type of permanent income or wealth influence on money demand. As this is likely to capture both transactions and asset demands for money, we might expect to find a higher coefficient on this variable than on variables capturing only the transactions demand. This hypothesis is given some credence by the fact that the coefficient estimates obtained in Table 3.2, when real TFE and real consumer expenditure are used as scale variables, are typically much lower and closer to unity. For the VAR lags of 7 and 8, for example, the price homogeneity restriction is satisfied, the coefficient on the rental price is small and negative, and the coefficients on the log of real consumer expenditure are 1.36 and 1.23, respectively.

Although we tried to include the separate influence of wealth on money demand in specifications including either real TFE or real consumer expenditure, no sensible cointegration results emerged. This may well be attributable to problems associated with the wealth data. In particular, we only had reliable data on gross and net financial wealth and it may be that a broader definition, including physical assets and human capital, would be more

Table 3.4 Johansen cointegration results for Divisia M4 incorporating both real GDP and real TFE, normalised coefficients

Lag length	*NB of coint. vectors*	*DPM4*	*LRGDP*	*LRTFE*	*LGDPDEF*	*CON*
5	2/2	0.010618	0.67756	1.1890	0.96313*	–25.1252

Notes: The sample covers the period until 1993Q2.
* denotes that the test of a unit coefficient on LGDPDEF was accepted.

appropriate. We did, however, test a specification which included both real GDP and real TFE, on the grounds that the former may be acting as a wealth variable in the context of approximating permanent income in the long-run cointegrating relationship, while the latter is acting as a straight transactions demand variable. Although we could not find a unique cointegrating vector for this specification, Table 3.4 illustrates that we did find a cointegrating vector that satisfies the price homogeneity restriction, produces a reasonable rental price coefficient and produces sensible coefficients on the wealth and transactions variables. Specifically, the wealth coefficient of 0.67 seems sensible in that it is less than unity, while the transactions coefficient of around unity also seems to accord with *a priori* expectations and previous empirical work. It is also interesting to note that this result suggests that there are no economies of scale in the aggregate transactions demand for money, which is in direct contradiction of Baumol/Tobin-type inventory theoretic models of the transactions demand for money.

A final possibility concerning the relatively high coefficient observed on real GDP in the Divisia cointegration results is that some aggregation bias is emerging because of the inappropriate aggregation of corporate and personal-sector asset holdings. Drake and Chrystal (1994a, 1994b), for example, found that there are important differences in the money demand functions across these two sectors. It is also interesting to note that Drake and Chrystal found coefficient estimates on real GDP in broad money demand specifications around 2.5 for the corporate sector and around unity for the personal sector. While these results might seem to conform well with our finding of an income elasticity of around 2 for aggregate M4, the fact that personal-sector holdings typically accounted for over 70 per cent of total M4 asset holdings over the sample period might suggest some degree of upward aggregation bias on the income elasticity estimate.

Regardless of any potential aggregation bias, however, the important issues in respect of aggregate M4 are whether an admissible stable money demand function can be established, and whether this aggregate has any predictive power in respect of variables of interest to policy-makers such as inflation and nominal GDP. We have already established the existence of unique cointegrating vectors for Divisia M4 and further examine the robustness and stability of the derived money-demand functions (for both Divisia and simple-sum M4) by estimating and testing dynamic error-correction models using lagged residuals derived from long-run money demand functions. The predictive power of both simple-sum and Divisia M4 is examined later in the Chapter in the context of nominal spending equations (St Louis equations) and formal causality tests using error-correction VAR models.

3.5 Dynamic error-correction models

The general to specific methodology was utilised in order to derive dynamic error correction models for both Divisia and simple-sum M4. Initially, general higher-order lag specifications incorporating the first differences of the cointegrating variables together with the lagged residuals from the long-run vectors were estimated for both aggregates. These were then sequentially tested down to arrive at the parsimonious preferred error-correction models detailed below.

Error-correction model for Divisia M4

$$\begin{aligned}\Delta LDM4_t = \; & \underset{(0.105)}{0.297^*\Delta LDM4_{t-2}} \; \underset{(0.097)}{+0.258^*\Delta LDM4_{t-3}} \; \underset{(0.114)}{+0.440^*\Delta LDM4_{t-4}} \\ & \underset{(0.079)}{+0.275^*\Delta LRGDP} \; \underset{(0.070)}{-0.193^*\Delta LRGDP_{t-1}} \; \underset{(0.193)}{-0.431^*\Delta LGDPDEF_{t-1}} \\ & \underset{(0.066)}{-0.205^*RES_{t-1}}.\end{aligned}$$

RES = the residuals from the unique cointegrating vector for a VAR lag = 5; figures in parentheses are standard errors; R^2 = 0.462; DW = 1.995; and residual sum of squares = 0.0088.

Lagrange multiplier test statistics

Normality (Jarque–Bera) test:	CHI-SQ(2) = 0.792
Serial correlation tests:	CHI-SQ(1) = 0.00006 CHI-SQ(4) = 3.489
	CHI-SQ(8) = 5.589
Heteroskedasticity test:	CHI-SQ(1) = 0.451
Autoregressive conditional heteroskedasticity (ARCH) tests:	CHI-SQ(1) = 1.489
	CHI-SQ(4) = 2.065 CHI-SQ(8) = 6.970
Functional form (RESET) test:	CHI-SQ(1) = 0.427
Predictive failure (CHOW second) tests:	CHI-SQ(4) = 0.799 CHI-SQ(8) = 1.874,
Parameter stability (CHOW) test:	CHI-SQ(7) = 1.876.

Error-correction model for simple-sum M4

$$\Delta LSM4_t = \underset{(0.054)}{0.168^*\Delta LSM4_{t-1}} \; \underset{(0.087)}{+0.254^*\Delta LSM4_{t-2}} \; \underset{(0.104)}{+0.613^*\Delta LSM4_{t-4}}$$

$$\underset{(0.001)}{+0.004 * \Delta R_{t-1}} \; \underset{(0.031)}{-0.104^*\Delta LRGDP_{t-1}} \; \underset{(0.027)}{-0.075^*\Delta LRGDP_{t-2}}$$

$$\underset{(0.134)}{-0.195^*\Delta LGDPDEF_{t-2}} \; \underset{(0.109)}{-0.290^*\Delta LGDPDEF_{t-3}} \; \underset{(0.020)}{-0.062^*RES_{t-1}}.$$

RES = the residuals from the second cointegrating vector (of two) for a VAR lag = 5; standard errors are White heteroskedasticity consistent; $R^2 = 0.706$; DW = 2.1941; and residual sum of squares = 0.004.

Lagrange multiplier test statistics

Normality (Jarque–Bera) test:	CHI-SQ(2) = 21.631
Serial correlation tests:	CHI-SQ(1) = 0.711 CHI-SQ(4) = 6.284
	CHI-SQ(8) = 11.661
Heteroskedasticity test:	CHI-SQ(1) = 7.696
Autoregressive conditional heteroskedasticity (ARCH) tests:	CHI-SQ(1) = 0.316
	CHI-SQ(4) = 1.100 CHI-SQ(8) = 2.423
Functional form (RESET test):	CHI-SQ(1) = 0.732
Predictive failure (CHOW second) test:	CHI-SQ(4) = 0.585 CHI-SQ(8) = 1.236
Parameter stability (CHOW) test:	CHI-SQ(9) = 4.268.

It is clear that the error correction models pass most of the diagnostic tests. The simple-sum model, however, fails the Jarque–Bera test for the normality of the regression residuals. Furthermore, although both models pass the parameter constancy and post-sample forecasting test, Figures 3.5 and 3.6 illustrate that the Divisia model has much greater forecasting accuracy over a sixteen quarter forecast horizon. Figures 3.7 and 3.8 also show that the simple-sum model fails the CUSUMSQ test, while for the Divisia model the cumulative sum of squares of the recursive residuals remain firmly within the 5 per cent band throughout the sample period. This latter result suggests that the simple-sum model may well suffer from some mis-specification that causes a gradual deterioration in the model fit. This may well be attributable to the failure of simple-sum aggregates to deal adequately with some of the most important financial innovations of the 1980s. Specifically, those involving changing interest yields on the various components of money. This is just the type of financial innovation that can be handled appropriately by the Divisia methodology.

Finally, it is interesting to note that the coefficient of –0.205 on the error-correction term for Divisia M4 is much larger than the corresponding coefficient of –0.062 for simple-sum M4. This implies that, following

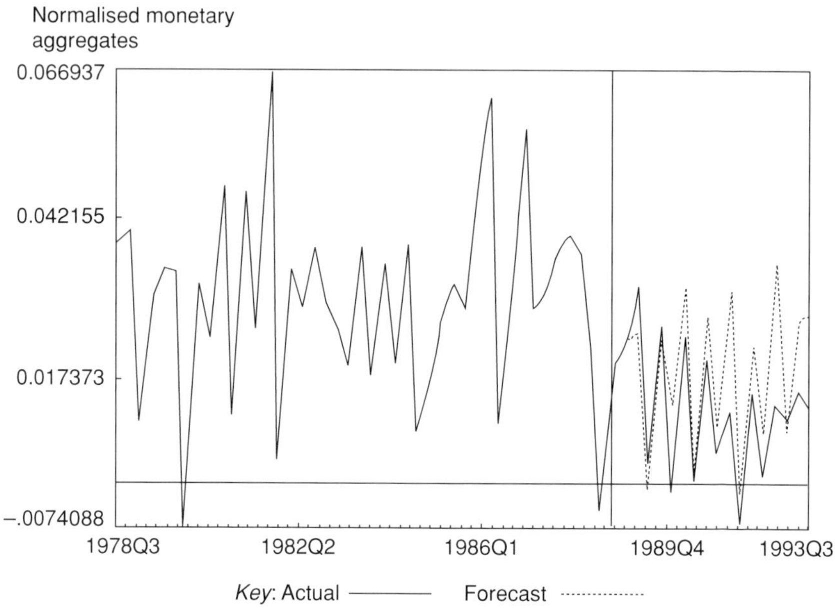

Figure 3.5 Sixteen-quarter ECM forecasts of Divisia M4 and actual Divisia M4

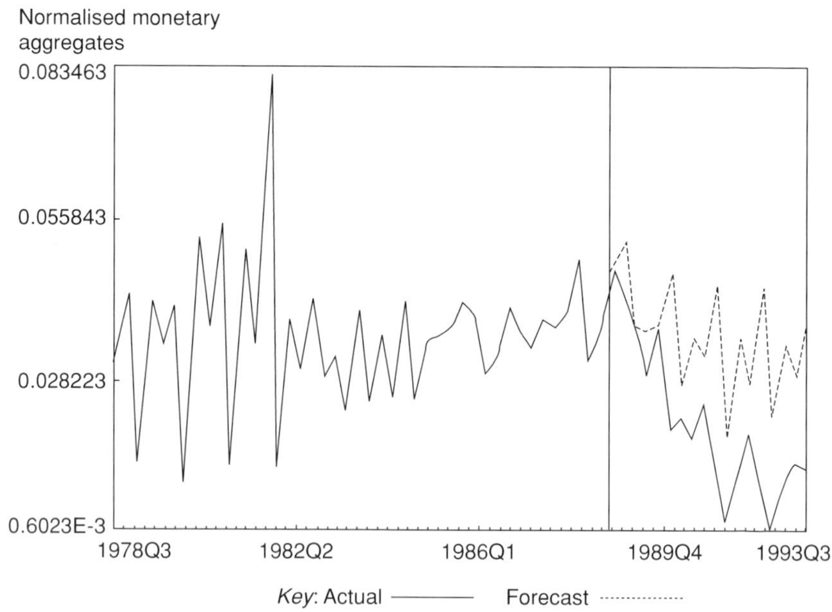

Figure 3.6 Sixteen-quarter ECM forecasts of simple-sum M4 and actual simple-sum M4

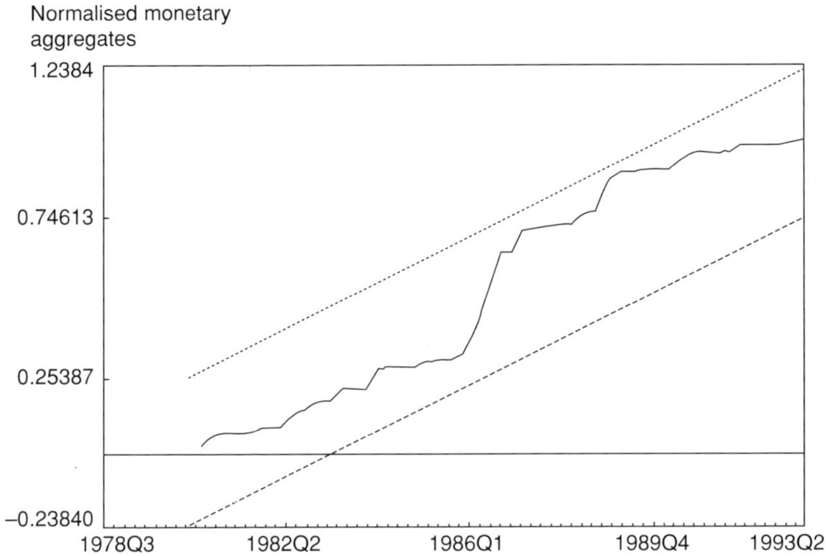

Note: The straight lines represent critical bounds at 5% significance level.

Figure 3.7 CUSUMSQ test statistic for Divisia M4 ECM

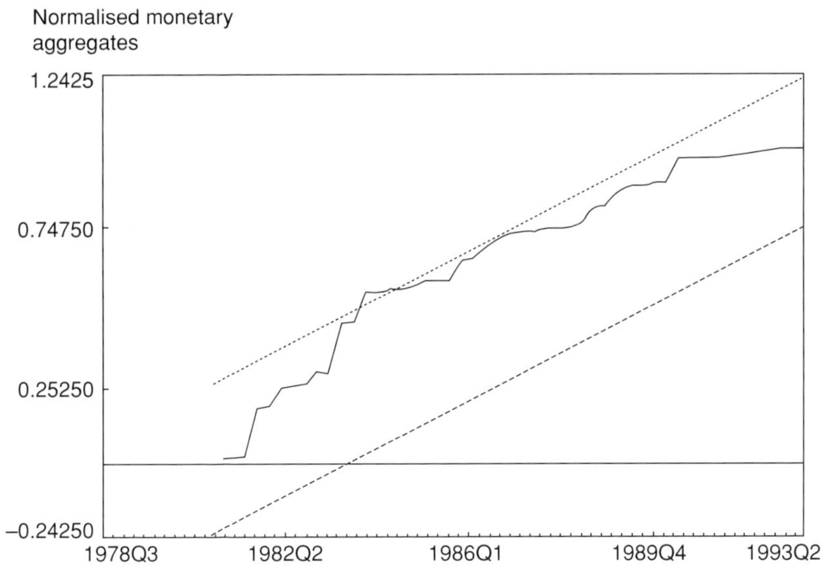

Note: The straight lines represent critical bounds at 5% significance level.

Figure 3.8 CUSUMSQ test statistic for simple-sum M4 ECM

disturbance in the equilibrium level of money holdings, equilibrium will be restored within five quarters for Divisia M4. In contrast, our estimates suggest that simple-sum M4 holdings will be in disequilibrium for approximately sixteen quarters following such a disturbance.

3.6 St Louis equations

As was alluded to earlier, if Divisia aggregates are to be useful as monetary indicators it should be demonstrable that they provide superior information to simple-sum aggregates on final policy objectives. A traditional linear test of a variable's usefulness as a monetary indicator is its performance in an aggregate spending equation. In this section, however, we compare the performance of Divisia M4 against simple-sum M4 in the environment of a modified St Louis nominal spending equation, and use non-nested tests to identify superior information content. Although there are acknowledged difficulties associated with the use of St Louis equations, they do offer simplicity and transparency, and provide a feel for the properties of the data in question.

The dependent variable in our estimated St Louis equation is the first difference of the log of nominal GDP while the independent control variable is the first difference of the log of nominal general government expenditure with lags of the order 0 to 4. In our initial specification we also included the lagged dependent variable (lags 1 to 4) as well as the first difference of either Divisia or simple-sum M4, with lags running from 0 to 4. Three test statistics are reported for comparisons between the two St Louis specifications, the Schwarz and Akaike information criteria, and the Davidson and MacKinnon J-test. It is clear from Table 3.5 that all three tests favour Divisia M4 over the simple-sum alternative. It is also interesting to note that although the R^2 statistics are reasonably high in both cases, the Divisia specification does explain a higher percentage of the variation in nominal GDP. We also undertook an F-test on this specification to test the null hypothesis that all the money coefficients are jointly zero; that is, to test whether 'money' could be excluded from the equation entirely. It is clear from Table 3.5 that the null hypothesis is rejected at the 5 per cent level for Divisia M4, but very decisively accepted in the case of simple-sum M4.

Finally, we utilised an alternative St Louis specification which omitted the lagged dependent variables. Again, Table 3.5 indicates that the three test statistics unambiguously favour Divisia M4; the F-test for the exclusion of 'money' is rejected for Divisia M4 but accepted for simple-sum M4; and the R^2 goodness of fit statistic is superior for the Divisia specification.

Notwithstanding the criticisms that can be made of the St Louis methodology, these results represent powerful evidence that Divisia M4 carries a superior information content relative to simple-sum M4 in the context of subsequent fluctuations in nominal GDP. Furthermore, the results strongly suggest that it was an error of policy in the UK to downgrade the use

Table 3.5 St Louis equation: non-nested tests

Dependent variable: DLNGDP (first difference of log nominal GDP).
Independent control variable: DLGGTE (first difference of log General Government nominal Total Expenditure) and lagged DLGGTE (1–4 lags).

Specification 1	**Including lagged dependent variables**	
Akaike's information criterion		favours DIVISIA M4 (6.2016)
Schwarz's Bayesian information criterion		favours DIVISIA M4 (6.2016)
J-test		favours DIVISIA M4 (0.8735; 4.3952)
	Divisia M4	**Simple-sum M4**
R^2	0.82394	0.78425
F-test for the exclusion of money from the St Louis equation		
Divisia M4	F (5, 46) = 2.6094 [0.037]	
Simple-sum M4	F (5, 46) = 0.43653 [0.821]	
Specification 2	**Excluding lagged dependent variables**	
Akaike information criterion		favours DIVISIA M4 (5.1275)
Schwarz's Bayesian information criterion		favours DIVISIA M4 (5.1275)
J-test		favours DIVISIA M4 (0.8758; 3.8629)
	Divisia M4	**Simple-sum M4**
R^2	0.60839	0.53669
F-test for the exclusion of money from the St Louis equation		
Divisia M4	F (5, 50) = 3.2510 [0.013]	
Simple-sum M4	F (5, 50) = 1.2005 [0.323]	

of broad money aggregates in the mid-1980s. While this was probably justifiable in the context of simple-sum aggregates, the evidence suggests that it was certainly not justifiable in the context of Divisia M4.

3.7 Causality tests of Divisia and simple-sum M4

In this section of the chapter we compare Divisia and simple-sum M4 in the context of formal Granger causality tests. Our causality tests are based on the specification of a VAR system that includes the following variables: real GDP; the GDP deflator; the Treasury Bill rate; and the relevant measure of the money supply. Defining our causality vector in this way facilitates the modelling of the separate impact that monetary impulses may have on the real and price components of GDP. The Treasury Bill rate is included in the specification because of the well-known spurious money – output causality results which can emerge if the interest rate effect is excluded from the analysis.

As the variables under consideration are all assumed to be I(1) it is important that the VAR is specified in first difference terms in order to ensure that all the variables entering the causality vector are stationary. In addition, however, it is now well established that if cointegrating relationships can be established between the variables, the VAR should also include the lagged cointegrating error term in addition to the first differenced variables. If this error correction term is not included, the Granger representation theorem (Granger, 1981) asserts that the resultant VAR will be mis-specified in the sense that it will exclude important long-run information contained in the levels of the variables.

The cointegration results for the vector of variables outlined above is given in Table 3.6. It is clear from this table that unique cointegrating vectors exist for VAR lag (in the Johansen specification) of 3 and 6 for simple-sum M4, and 6 and 7 for Divisia M4. For reasons of comparability, therefore, we have chosen to incorporate the lagged residuals from the cointegrating vectors obtained with a VAR lag of 6 in both cases. Before embarking on the formal causality tests, however, it was necessary to establish the appropriate lag order to incorporate in the causality VAR system. Utilising criteria such as the Schwarz Bayesian and Akaike Information criteria as well as the maximised log of the likelihood function did not prove illuminating, as they tended to produce significantly different results. We were also conscious of the monetarist dictum that money affects output and prices with long and variable lags which, in the case of prices, might be as long as two years or more. Hence, we were wary of setting an overly short lag over specification in our causality tests, particularly with respect to prices (inflation).

In order to cast some light on the appropriate lag order specification in the VAR, as well as acting as a sort of case study of the recent UK experience, we chose to focus on the relationship between the annual growth of the M4 aggregate (Divisia and simple-sum) and the annual rate of inflation. In both cases we use quarterly data to calculate annual growth rates for money and prices for the period 1985 Q1 to 1993 Q2. This is an interesting period in the context of the UK economy in the sense that it includes the period of the so-called 'Lawson Boom' of the mid-1980 (which incorporated a rapid increase in the rate of inflation) and the post-1989 recessionary period (which was a period of relatively rapid deflation). Figure 3.9 illustrates the annual growth rate of both Divisia and simple-sum money lagged 2 years or 8 quarters plotted against the contemporary rate of price inflation and it is clear that, particularly in the case of Divisia M4, the rapid growth of the monetary aggregate seems to correspond very closely with the rapid increase in price inflation from the mid-1980s. The growth in the Divisia M4 aggregate also seems to be a remarkably good predictor (two years hence) for the decline in price inflation in the early

Table 3.6 Cointegration results for the 'causality vector' based on the maximal eigenvalue of the stochastic matrix

	Simple-sum M4 *Null*	*Likelihood Ratio test statistic*		*Divisia M4* *Null*	*Likelihood Ratio test statistic*
VAR = 3	r = 0	48.2610	VAR = 6	r = 0	30.4013
	r ≤ 1	17.1351		r ≤ 1	12.0208
VAR = 6	r = 0	50.7483	VAR = 7	r = 0	47.3490
	r ≤ 1	19.2251		r ≤ 1	21.3804

Notes: 1. The variables included in the 'causality vector' are LDM4 (LSM4, alternatively), LRGDP, LGDPDEF, and the quarterly Treasury Bill rate.
2. The 95% critical values are 28.1380 for the null $r = 0$, and 22.0020 for the null $r \leq 1$.

1990s. The correspondence between prior changes in the growth of simple-sum M4 and subsequent changes in inflation, although evident in some periods, is much less clear-cut than is the case with the Divisia aggregate.

Although we should be wary of reading too much into a simple graphical analysis, it does seem that the monitoring of Divisia M4 in the mid-1980s could have provided an important early warning signal regarding the subsequent inflation of the 'Lawson Boom' period. Ironically, the mid-1980s marked the period in the UK when broad monetary aggregates had fallen into disrepute (because of the earlier disappointing performance of the official simple-sum aggregates) and the government began to place much greater emphasis on narrow money in the form of M0, and on the exchange rate. As Figure 3.10 illustrates, however, these indicators failed the government in the sense that base rates were clearly being adjusted in response to current changes in the inflation rate, whereas Divisia M4 growth was acting as a two-year leading indicator for inflation. To take a specific example, inflation began to increase sharply from 1988 Q1 and base rates were also increased gradually from this time. In contrast, Divisia M4 started to increase rapidly from 1985 Q1, some nine quarters prior to the acceleration in inflation.

With respect to the causality analysis, the evidence from Figure 3.9 is supportive of the monetarist dictum that monetary changes may take at least

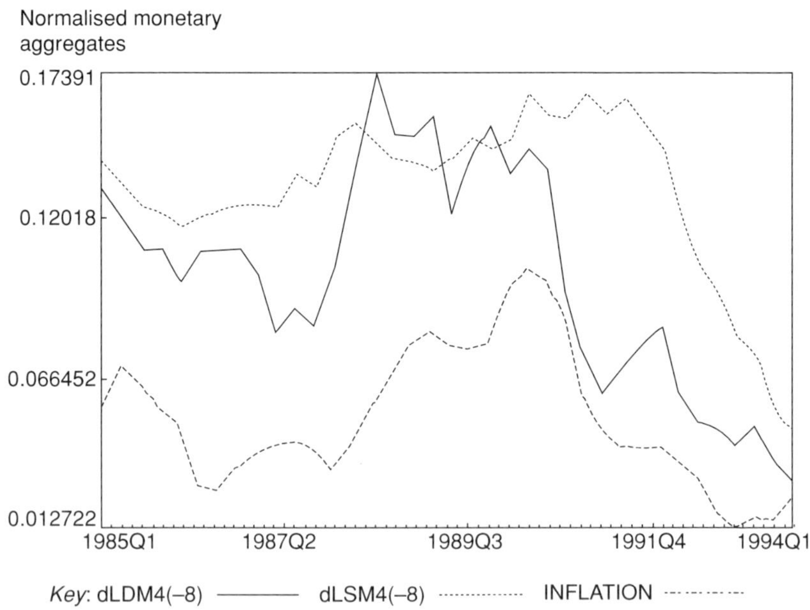

Figure 3.9 Annual growth rates of Divisia and simple-sum M4 (lagged 2 years) and the annual rate of price inflation

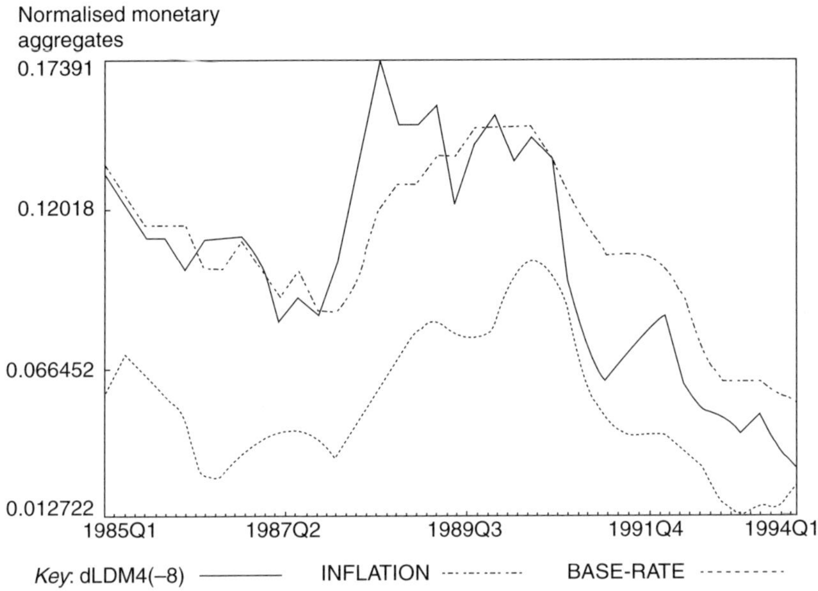

Figure 3.10 Divisia M4 growth (lagged 2 years), base rate and inflation

two years to have their full impact on prices and inflation. Bearing this in mind, we elected to utilise 10th order lags on the first differences of the variables in the VAR. The results of the causality tests are indicated in Table 3.7 and are Wald exclusion tests on the lagged changes in the relevant monetary

Table 3.7 Granger causality tests

Dependent variable	Divisia M4	Simple-sum M4
ΔLRGDP	CHI-SQUARE (10) = 6.555 (18.31)	CHI-SQUARE (10) = 26.320 (18.31)
ΔLGDPDEF	CHI-SQUARE (10) = 25.414 (18.31)	CHI-SQUARE (10) = 10.491 (18.31)
ΔTBR	CHI-SQUARE (10) = 20.147 (18.31)	CHI-SQUARE (10) = 17.002 (18.31)

Notes: 1. The vectors are unique vectors from cointegration, using Johansen procedure and a Var of 6.
2. The figures are Wald test statistics of the exclusion of the 10th order lags of first difference of money in the equations where first difference of log real GDP, first difference of log GDPDEF, and first difference of Treasury Bill rate are the dependent variables, respectively.
3. Figures in parentheses are 5% critical values of the chi-square distribution.

aggregate in the equations for the first difference of real GDP, the price index and the Treasury Bill rate respectively. Hence, the null hypothesis in each case is that prior changes in the monetary aggregate do not Granger-cause subsequent changes in these variables. Not surprisingly, given the previous graphical analysis, the results indicate that Divisia M4 Granger causes changes in the price level while simple-sum M4 does not. Interestingly, the results suggest that the greatest impact of changes in Divisia M4 on prices occurs after nine quarters, confirming that Divisia M4 is likely to be a useful leading indicator of inflation.

With respect to real GDP, we obtain the result that Divisia M4 does not Granger-cause real GDP, but that simple-sum M4 does Granger-cause real GDP. An inspection of the coefficients in the real GDP VAR equation, however, reveals that this observed causality arises over the short term, as would be expected. Hence, these results suggest that simple-sum M4 may act as a short-run leading indicator for nominal GDP, acting through real GDP, while Divisia M4 acts as a longer leading indicator for nominal GDP acting through its influence on inflation.

Finally, the results indicate that Divisia M4 Granger-causes changes in short-term interest rates, but that simple-sum M4 does not.

3.8 Vector autoregressive modelling and impulse response functions

In this final section we undertake further multivariate analysis in the form of vector autoregressive (VAR) model building with associated impulse response functions in order to investigate the macroeconomic policy implications of the two alternative monetary aggregates. We again utilise the error-correction VAR methodology outlined previously, but rather than estimating an unrestricted VAR system, as in the causality tests, we now employ a general to specific modelling strategy in order to arrive at a parsimonious system. This resulted in the specifications given in Tables 3.8 and 3.9 for the simple-sum M4 and Divisia M4 systems, respectively.

It is interesting to note that the error correction term (RES_{t-1}) does not appear in the interest-rate equation for the simple-sum model, implying that money, real GDP and prices are endogenous, while the interest rate is weakly exogenous (Engle *et al.*, 1983). The fact that only lagged own terms appear in the equation for ΔTBR_t also suggests that interest rates are strongly exogenous in the simple-sum system. In contrast, all four variables are endogenously determined in the Divisia M4 model.

The vector autoregressive models are precisely determined in both cases, and provide a reasonably detailed representation of the macro economy. As the standard errors are lower in three out of the four equations in the Divisia system relative to the simple-sum system, it should be possible to forecast output prices and interest rates with greater accuracy in the Divisia economy.

Table 3.8 Vector autoregressive models: Simple-sum M4

$$\Delta LSM4_t = \underset{(0.095)}{0.200^*\Delta LSM4_{t-2}} + \underset{(0.087)}{0.543^*\Delta LSM4_{t-4}} - \underset{(0.049)}{0.180^*\Delta LRGDP_{t-1}} - \underset{(0.047)}{0.169^*\Delta LRGDP_{t-2}} - \underset{(0.130)}{0.452^*\Delta LGDPDEF_{t-2}} + \underset{(0.001)}{0.002^*\Delta R_{t-1}} - \underset{(0.026)}{0.123^*\Delta RES_{t-1}}$$

$R^2 = 0.74$ $\quad DW = 2.096$ $\quad$ S.E of regression $= 0.008$

$$\Delta LRGDP_t = \underset{(0.055)}{0.855^*\Delta LRGDP_{t-4}} + \underset{(0.164)}{0.412^*\Delta LRGDPDEF_{t-4}} + \underset{(0.022)}{0.060^*RES_{t-1}}$$

$R^2 = 0.834$ $\quad DW = 2.328$ $\quad$ S.E of regression $= 0.015$

$$\Delta LGDPDEF_t = \underset{(0.051)}{-0.235^*\Delta LRGDP_{t-1}} - \underset{(0.034)}{0.110^*\Delta LRGDP_{t-2}} - \underset{(0.046)}{0.099^*\Delta LRGDP_{t-3}} + \underset{(0.001)}{0.002^*\Delta R_{t-3}} - \underset{(0.009)}{0.130^*RES_{t-1}}$$

$R^2 = 0.458$ $\quad DW = 1.888$ $\quad$ S.E of regression $= 0.009$

$$\Delta R_t = \underset{(0.114)}{-0.250^*\Delta R_{t-10}}$$

$R^2 = 0.065$ $\quad DW = 1.954$ $\quad$ S.E of regression $= 1.250$

$$\Omega = \begin{bmatrix} 5.90 & 0 & 0 & 0 \\ & 22.60 & 0 & 0 \\ & & 6.77 & 0 \\ & & & 153.6 \end{bmatrix} \times 10^{-5}$$

Note: 1. RES are the residuals from the cointegrating vector for a Var lag = 6.
2. Standard errors are shown in parentheses.

Table 3.9 Vector autoregressive models: Divisia M4

$$\Delta \mathrm{LDM4}_t = \underset{(0.095)}{0.275} * \Delta \mathrm{LDM4}_{t-1} + \underset{(0.091)}{0.662} * \Delta \mathrm{LDM4}_{t-4} - \underset{(0.058)}{0.120} * \Delta \mathrm{LRGDP}_{t-2} - \underset{(0.067)}{0.262} * \Delta \mathrm{LRGDP}_{t-9} - \underset{(0.197)}{0.513} * \Delta \mathrm{LGDPDEF}_{t-1} - \underset{(0.001)}{0.004} * \Delta \mathrm{R}_{t-3}$$

$$- \underset{(0.001)}{0.003} * \Delta \mathrm{R}_{t-7} - \underset{(0.039)}{0.146} * \mathrm{RES}_{t-1}$$

$R^2 = 0.510$ $DW = 2.22$ S.E of regression $= 0.012$

$$\Delta \mathrm{LRGDP}_t = \underset{(0.051)}{0.669} * \Delta \mathrm{LRGDP}_{t-4} + \underset{(0.048)}{0.283} * \Delta \mathrm{LRGDP}_{t-5} + \underset{(0.157)}{0.487} \Delta \mathrm{LRGDPDEF}_{t-2} + \underset{(0.148)}{0.35} * \Delta \mathrm{LGDPDEF}_{t-4} + \underset{(0.114)}{0.245} * \Delta \mathrm{LGDPDEF}_{t-7} + \underset{(0.033)}{0.254} * \Delta \mathrm{RES}_{t-1}$$

$R^2 = 0.916$ $DW = 1.92$ S.E of regression $= 0.011$

$$\Delta \mathrm{LGDPDEF}_t = \underset{(0.058)}{0.206} * \Delta \mathrm{LDM4}_{t-1} + \underset{(0.058)}{0.140} * \Delta \mathrm{LDM4}_{t-9} - \underset{(0.033)}{0.108} * \Delta \mathrm{LRGDP}_{t-1} + \underset{(0.089)}{0.247} * \Delta \mathrm{LGDPDEF}_{t-8} - \underset{(0.093)}{0.212} * \Delta \mathrm{LGDPDEF}_{t-9} + \underset{(0.017)}{0.090} * \mathrm{RES}_{t-1}$$

$R^2 = 0.550$ $DW = 1.56$ S.E of regression $= 0.008$

$$\Delta \mathrm{R}_t = \underset{(0.387)}{-0.853} + \underset{(10.168)}{26.270} * \Delta \mathrm{LDM4}_{t-9} + \underset{(5.922)}{16.918} * \Delta \mathrm{LRGDP}_{t-2} + \underset{(5.242)}{13.503} * \Delta \mathrm{LRGDP}_{t-9} + \underset{(19.540)}{53.751} * \Delta \mathrm{LGDPDEF}_{t-3} + \underset{(0.120)}{0.290} \Delta \mathrm{R}_{t-6} + \underset{(3.867)}{15.600} * \mathrm{RES}_{t-1}$$

$R^2 = 0.333$ $DW = 2.073$ S.E of regression $= 1.116$

$$\Omega = \begin{bmatrix} 13.40 & 0 & 0 & 0 \\ & 11.50 & 0 & 0 \\ & & 5.61 & 0 \\ & & & 109.6 \end{bmatrix} \times 10^{-5}$$

Note: 1. RES are the residuals from the cointegrating vector for a Var lag = 6.
2. Standard errors are shown in parentheses.

Furthermore, the Divisia systems correspond well with the earlier causality results in the sense that lagged monetary changes are significant in both the price and interest rate equations, but not the real GDP equation. The inclusion of the 9th order lag on the first difference of Divisia M4 in the price equation also serves to confirm the earlier results, which suggested that Divisia M4 can play an important role as a leading inflation indicator. In contrast, we note that lagged monetary changes do not enter into any of the three non-monetary equations in the simple-sum M4 system and, in the case of the real GDP equation, this result is in conflict with the earlier causality results which suggested that simple-sum M4 had a direct causal influence on real GDP.

The covariance matrices illustrated in Tables 3.8 and 3.9 are clearly diagonal and show that no significant contemporaneous correlation exists between the equation innovations; that is the elements of the error vector are orthogonal to each other. Hence the dynamics of the two alternative systems may be ascertained by computing the impulse responses associated with innovations to each of the variables. We recognise that these functions of the model parameters are dependent on the ordering of the equations employed to obtain them. Following Sims (1981), however, the impulse response functions were recalculated using a variety of orderings and found to be robust and invariant to the prior theorising, as would be expected given the absence of any contemporaneous correlations in the vector of residuals.

The impulse response functions for the ordering (LM4, LRGDP, LGDPDEF, TBR) are displayed in Figures 3.11 to 3.13. As we are interested mainly in the response of these variables to monetary innovations, these charts illustrate the responses of LRGDP, LGDPDEF and TBR, respectively, to separate one-unit shocks in the monetary innovations for both Divisia M4 and simple-sum M4. It is quite clear from the figures that innovations to simple-sum M4 have relatively little impact upon these three variables. This is most clearly illustrated in the case of the Treasury Bill rate, and illustrates the strong exogeneity of interest rates in the simple-sum economy. In contrast, innovations to Divisia M4 produce distinct cyclical fluctuations in each of the variables of interest. Specifically, a positive innovation to Divisia M4 monetary growth would be expected to produce inflationary pressure; an increase in real GDP growth; and rising nominal interest rates in the short-to-medium term. This would be followed by a recessionary phase in which inflation moderates, real GDP declines, and short-term interest rates are reduced.

Figures 3.11 to 3.13 clearly demonstrate, therefore, that Divisia M4 is likely to be a much better leading indicator of future economic activity than simple-sum M4. In the case of prices, the response of the GDP deflator to Divisia M4 monetary innovations is clearly a product of both the direct causal influence of money on prices and the full-model interactions and feedbacks between the variables. In the case of real GDP, it is the latter that is responsible for producing the cycle in real GDP. It is also worth noting that the strong

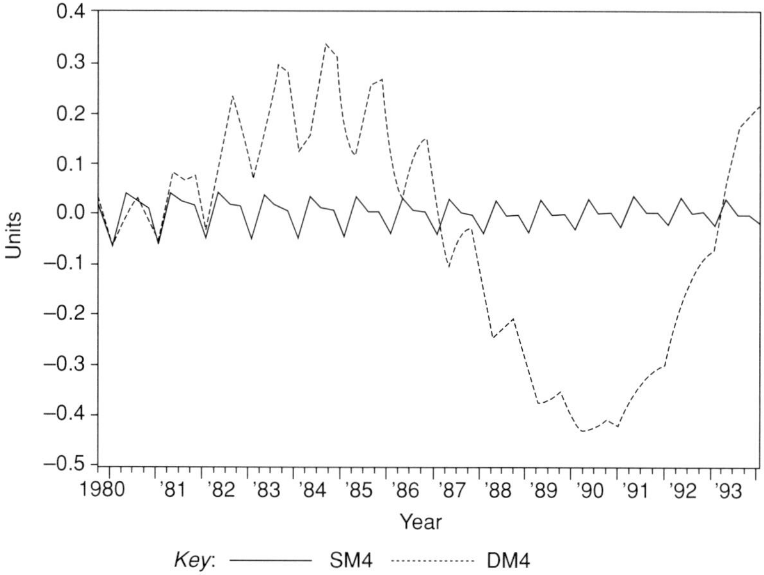

Figure 3.11 LRGDP responses to money shocks

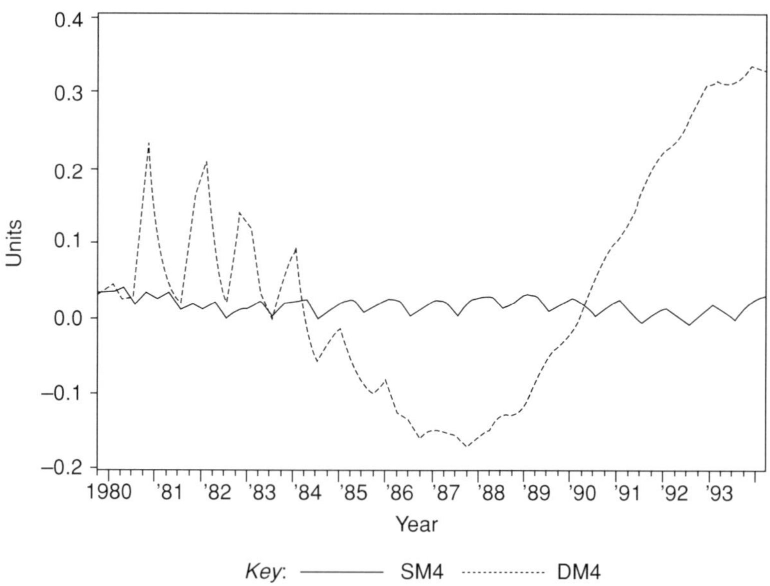

Figure 3.12 LGDPDEF responses to money shocks

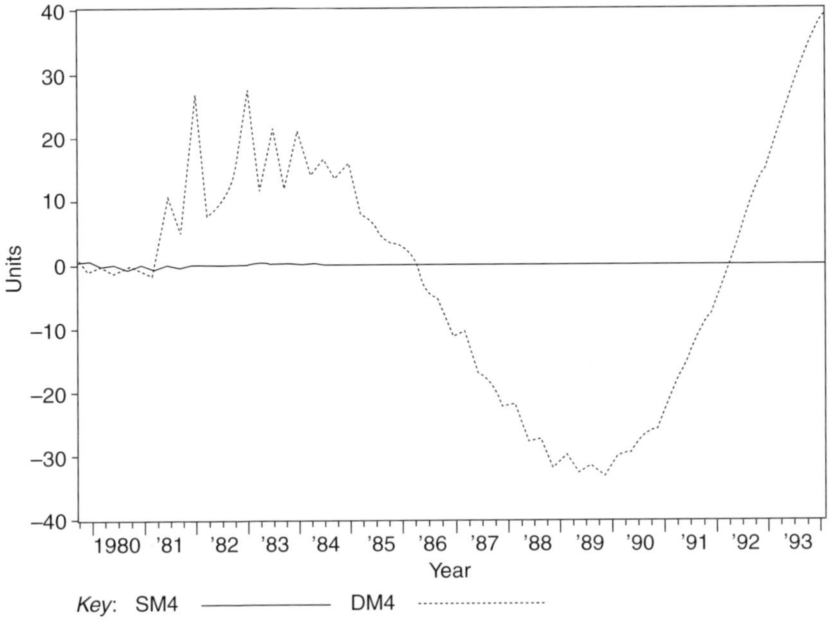

Figure 3.13 TBR responses to money shocks

interactions between money and other economic variables in the Divisia system, combined with the relatively long lag lengths, results in long-lived effects of Divisia monetary shocks on the economy. This suggests that, if the authorities were to adopt a policy of benign neglect with respect to broad money aggregates, the resultant erratic Divisia monetary growth could produce a good deal of instability in the economy. This potential instability is clearly underestimated when focusing purely on simple-sum measures of broad money.

Finally, it is probably worth entering a few caveats regarding the use of VAR systems and, in particular, impulse response functions. Firstly, it is important to note that the standard errors associated with the impulse response coefficients could be quite large and hence precise inference is somewhat hazardous (see Runkle, 1987). Second, the analysis is open to the usual Lucas critique. If, for example, a monetary shock were to be followed by a policy response, it is quite possible that the underlying model parameters would not be invariant to this policy change. Again, this makes precise inference difficult in the context of impulse response functions.

Having entered these caveats, however, our results make it quite clear that there are important and significant differences between the way in which

Divisia M4 and simple-sum M4 interact with the economy. In general, these differences echo our earlier St Louis equation and Granger-causality results, and confirm that Divisia M4 is an important leading indicator for the UK economy.

3.9 Summary and conclusions

We have submitted simple-sum M4 and Divisia M4 to a battery of alternative tests. As always with empirical work, the results are mixed. However, at least on the evidence of the 1980s, the Divisia aggregate has better leading indicator properties of inflation than does simple-sum M4. Of course, nobody knows what is going to happen in the future. Financial innovation is certainly not over, and the likely technological innovations ahead may be less favourable to Divisia than were the competitive innovations of the 1980s. Accordingly we do not suggest rigid policy rules based on Divisia monetary aggregates. Rather, we recommend that the behaviour of Divisia monetary aggregates be taken seriously by both policy-makers and academic economists who use 'money' in their research.

References

Barnett, William A. (1978) 'The User Cost of Money,' *Economic Letters,* vol. 1, pp. 145–9.

Barnett, William A. (1980) 'Economic Monetary Aggregates: An Application of Aggregation and Index Number Theory', *Journal of Econometrics,* vol. 14, no. 1. (September), pp. 11–48.

Barnett, William A. (1982) 'The Optimal Level of Monetary Aggregation', *Journal of Money, Credit and Banking,* vol. 14, no. 4, p. 2, (November), pp. 687–710.

Barnett, William A. (1990) 'Developments in Monetary Aggregation Theory', *Journal of Policy Modelling,* vol. 12, no. 2, pp. 205–57.

Barnett, William A. and Seugnmook Choi (1986) 'A Monte Carlo Study of Tests of Blockwise Separability', mimeo, University of Texas, Austin.

Barnett, William A., Edward Offenbacker and Paul Spindt (1984) 'The New Divisia Monetary Aggregates', *Journal of Political Economy,* vol. 92, no. 6 (December), pp. 1049–85.

Barnett, William A., Douglas Fisher and Apostolis Serletis (1992) 'Consumer Theory and the Demand for Money', *Journal of Economic Literature* (December), pp. 2086–119.

Batchelor, Roy (1987) 'Monetary Developments', *City University Business School Economic Review* (Autumn), pp. 17–22.

Belongia, Michael T. and James A. Chalfant (1989) 'The Changing Empirical Definition of Money: Some Estimates from a Model of the Demand for Money Substitutes', *Journal of Political Economy,* vol. 87, no. 2 (April), pp. 387–97.

Belongia, Michael T. and K. Alec Chrystal (1991) 'An Admissible Monetary Aggregate for the United Kingdom', *The Review of Economics and Statistics,* vol. 73, no. 3 (August), pp. 497–503.

Cagan, Phillip, (1982) 'The Choice among Monetary Aggregates as Targets and Guides for Monetary Policy', *Journal of Money, Credit and Banking,* vol. 14, no. 4 (November), pp. 661–686.

Chalfant, James A, and Julian M. Alston (1988) 'Accounting for Changes in Tastes', *Journal of Political Economy* (April), pp. 391–410.

Cockerline, J. P. and J. D. Murray (1981) 'A Comparison of Alternative Methods of Monetary Aggregation: Some Preliminary Evidence', Bank of Canada Technical Reports No. 28.

Dickey, D. A. and W. A. Fuller (1981) 'Likelihood Ratio Statistics for Autoregressive Time Series with a Unit Root', *Econometrica*, vol. 49, pp. 1057–72.

Diewert, W. Erwin. (1978) 'Superlative Index Numbers and Consistency in Aggregation', *Econometrica*, vol. 46 (July), pp. 883–900.

Diewert, W. Erwin (1986) 'Exact and Superlative Index Numbers', *Journal of Econometrics* vol. 4 (May), pp. 115–46.

Drake, Leigh (1992) 'The Substitutability of Financial Assets in the UK', *The Manchester School*, vol. LX, no. 3, (September), pp. 221–48.

Drake, Leigh and K. Alec Chrystal (1994a) 'Company Sector Money Demand: New Evidence of a Stable Long run Relationship for the UK', *Journal of Money, Credit and Banking*, vol. 26, no. 3 (August), pp. 480–94.

Drake, Leigh and K. Alec Chrystal (1994b) 'Personal Sector Money Demand in the UK', Loughborough University Discussion Paper 94/8.

Engle, R. F. and C. W. J. Granger (1987) 'Cointegration and Error Correction: Representation, Estimation and Testing', *Econometrica*, vol. 55, pp. 251–76.

Engle, R. F., D. F. Hendry, and J. F. Richard (1983) 'Exogeneity', *Econometrica*, vol. 51, pp. 277–304.

Fischer, P., S. Hudson and M. Pradhan (1993) 'Divisia Indices for Money: An Appraisal of Theory and Practice', Bank of England Working Paper Series No. 9 (April).

Fluri, Robert and Piyu Yue (1991) 'Divisia Monetary Services Indexes for Switzerland: Computation and Behaviour', *Federal Reserve Bank of St. Louis Review* (September/October).

Granger, C. W. J. (1981) 'Some Properties of Time Series Data and their Use in Econometric Specification', *Journal of Econometrics*, vol. 16, pp. 121–30.

Hall, S. G. (1991) 'The Effect of Varying Lag Length VAR Models on the Maximum Likelihood Estimates of Cointegrating Parameters', *Scottish Journal of Political Economy*, vol. 38, pp. 317–23.

Hall, S. G., S. G. B. Henry and J. B. Wilcox (1989) 'The Long run Determination of the UK Monetary Aggregates', Bank of England Discussion Paper No. 41 (August).

Hancock, Diana (1986) 'The Financial Firm: Production with Monetary and Non-Monetary Goods', *Journal of Political Economy* (October), pp. 859–80.

Ishida, Kazuhiko (1984) 'Divisia Monetary Aggregates and Demand for Money: A Japanese Case', *Bank of Japan Monetary and Economic Studies* (June), pp. 49–80.

Johansen, Soren (1988) 'Statistical Analysis of Cointegration Vectors', *Journal of Economic Dynamics and Control*, vol. 12, pp. 231–54.

Johansen, Soren and Katarina Juselius (1990) 'Maximum Likelihood Estimation and Inference on Cointegration – With Applications to the Demand for Money', *Oxford Bulletin of Economics Statistics*, vol. 52, no. 2, pp. 169–210.

Patterson, K. D. (1991) 'A Non-Parametric Analysis of Personal Sector Decisions on Consumption, Liquid Assets and Leisure', *Economic Journal*, vol. 101, no. 408 (September), pp. 1103–16.

Phillips, P. C. B. and P. Perron (1988) 'Testing for Unit Roots in Time Series Regressions', *Biometrika*, vol. 75, pp. 335–46.

Runkle, D. E. (1987) 'Vector Autoregressions and Reality', *Journal of Business and Economic Statistics*, vol. 5, pp. 437–42.

Sims, C. A. (1981) 'An Autoregressive Index Model for the US 1948–1975', in J. Kmenta and J. B. Ramsey (eds), *Large scale Macroeconomic Models* (Amsterdam: North Holland), pp. 283–327.

Spencer, P. (1994) 'Portfolio Disequilibrium: Implications for the Divisia Approach to Monetary Aggregation', *The Manchester School*, vol. LXII, no. 2, pp. 125–50.

Swofford, James L. and Gerald A. Whitney (1986) 'Flexible Functional Forms and the Utility Approach to the Demand for Money: a Nonparametric Analysis', *Journal of Money, Credit and Banking* (August), pp. 383–9.

Swofford, James L. and Gerald A. Whitney (1987) 'Nonparametric Tests of Utility Maximisation and Weak Separability for Consumption, Leisure and Money', *The Review of Economics and Statistics*, vol. 69 (August), pp. 458–64.

Swofford, James L. and Gerald A. Whitney (1988) 'A Comparison of Non-Parametric Tests of Weak Separability for Annual and Quarterly Data on Consumption, Leisure and Money', *Journal of Business Economics and Statistics*, vol. 6, no. 2 (April), pp. 241–6.

Taylor, Mark P. (1987) 'Financial Innovation, Inflation and the Stability of the Demand for Broad Money in the UK', *Bulletin of Economic Research*, vol. 39, no. 3, pp. 225–33.

Varian, Hal. R. (1982) 'The Nonparametric Approach to Demand Analysis', *Econometrica*, pp. 945–74.

Varian, Hal, R. (1983) 'Non-Parametric Tests of Consumer Behaviour', *Review of Economic Studies*, vol. 50, no. 1 (January), pp. 99–110.

4
Weighted Monetary Aggregates for Germany*

Heinz Herrmann, Hans-Eggert Reimers and Karl-Heinz Toedter

4.1 Introduction

Financial innovations and regulatory changes are often associated with the deterioration of previously stable monetary relationships in several countries. 'Missing money' and 'velocity puzzles' have led to frequent redefinition of monetary aggregates and, finally, particularly in the USA and the UK, to the abolishment of monetary targeting strategies. In these circumstances it is not surprising that research on alternative monetary aggregates, based on sound microfoundations and consistent with economic aggregation and index theory, has been intensified.[1]

This chapter provides empirical evidence on weighted monetary aggregates for Germany in comparison to traditional M3. Section 4.2 explains the shift of the Deutsche Bundesbank from central bank money stock to M3 in the 1980s, and reflects on the experience with monetary targeting in Germany. Section 4.3 discusses some problems with aggregation of assets providing monetary services. Section 4.4 derives Divisia-type weighted monetary aggregates within a unifying cost minimisation framework. Section 4.5 provides details on the all-German data and construction of monetary aggregates with constant, current and smoothed weights. In Section 4.6, cointegration properties and error-correction dynamics of money demand functions for weighted aggregates and simple-sum M3 are estimated. In Section 4.7 the link between the different monetary aggregates and prices is investigated empirically using the P-star approach. In Section 4.8 the relationship between monetary policy instruments and monetary aggregates on the one hand, and between money and prices on the other (that is, the control error and the projection error of

* This chapter is based on a paper with the same title presented at the conference 'Divisia Monetary Aggregates: Right in Theory – Useful in Practice?', held at the University of Mississippi, Oxford 17–18 October 1994. We thank M. Belongia, A. Mullineux and the participants of this conference for their extremely helpful comments. The views expressed here are solely of the authors and are not necessarily shared by the Deutsche Bundesbank or other members of its staff.

monetary policy) is investigated for the alternative monetary aggregates. Finally, Section 4.9 summarises and concludes the chapter.

4.2 Experience with monetary targeting in Germany

The Bundesbank has always regarded the money stock as its most important monetary policy indicator. There are two major reasons for this. First, by law, the Bundesbank has been assigned the function of regulating 'the amount of money in circulation and of credit supplied to the economy ... with the aim of safeguarding the currency'; this is generally interpreted as being a commitment to safeguarding price stability. Second, the money stock showed a far more stable correlation with major macroeconomic variables (and especially with prices) than was the case in many other countries. It was therefore a logical consequence that the Bundesbank was the first central bank to adopt a policy of pre-announced monetary targets after the end of the exchange-rate system of Bretton Woods in 1975, and that it has used the money stock continuously as an intermediate target variable ever since (see Issing, 1992).

From the middle of the 1970s until the second half of the 1980s the Bundesbank used the 'central bank money stock at constant reserve ratios' as its key reference variable. That variable constitutes the sum of currency in circulation and reserve-carrying bank deposits, each weighted with its reserve ratio of January 1974. The relative weighting between the bank deposits was seen as being roughly commensurate with their degree of liquidity; however, it was agreed at the same time that currency in circulation was overrepresented relative to the other components of the money stock. In view of a number of other advantages that the central bank money stock exhibited in the context of the Bundesbank's monetary strategy, this drawback was of little significance at first. Foremost among these favourable features was the fact that the central bank money stock displayed negative interest elasticity, thus enabling the Bundesbank to control the aggregate in principle. In addition, the interest elasticities of money demand and GNP were balanced in a favourable manner.

A different situation arose in the second half of the 1980s: in particular, currency in circulation, which is highly responsive to interest rate changes, rose strongly, since interest rates were exceptionally low. Moreover, the growth of currency in circulation was reinforced by a number of expansionary special factors: these included, for example, increased demand for DM notes abroad and the hoarding of currency in connection with a planned change in the taxation of interest income. Hence the overshooting of the monetary targets at that time owed a great deal to currency in circulation. Empirical studies suggested that the demand for central bank money was no longer stable. Against this background, the disproportionately great weight of currency in the intermediate target variable – which was ill-substantiated theoretically – was increasingly felt to be a problem. This is why, from 1988 onwards, the Bundesbank has used the money stock M3 as its intermediate target variable. That variable comprises virtually the same bank deposits as the central bank money stock, but its individual components are aggregated by simple summation. In other words, the 'experiment' of differentiating according to various degrees of liquidity was not followed up any further.

Experience in succeeding years went on to show that such an unweighted monetary aggregate has weaknesses as well as strengths relative to a weighted aggregate. The transition to M3 turned out to be favourable in the German case in view of a number of other disturbances in the demand for currency. They affected the unweighted money stock M3 far less than they would have influenced a more narrowly defined or weighted aggregate. That aggregate also turned out to be unproblematic in the face of shifts between the demand for savings deposits (at three months' notice) and the demand for time deposits for up to four years. Such shifts started on a massive scale in 1988. These shifts out of savings deposits, whose interest rates were traditionally well below markets rates, into time deposits with market-related interest rates, were fostered to some extent by the widening of interest rate differentials at that time. But a new, cost-conscious cash management stance on the part of households was apparently also of significance. This can be interpreted as a symmetric shift in the demand functions of different assets included in M3. However, there was little evidence that this shift within M3 was connected with efforts to modify liquidity-holding, with implications for non-bank spending behaviour. Since the money stock M3 failed to respond to these shifts, in this respect it presented, all in all, an accurate picture of actual conditions.

Yet the unweighted aggregation of money stock components turned out to be a disadvantage in two respects: during the early 1990s, in the wake of a prolonged period of low capital market rates and an inverse interest rate pattern, there were indications that domestic non-banks – in view of the comparatively high level of time deposit rates and the substantial uncertainties about future trends in capital market rates, which were already low – were increasingly holding their financial assets in liquid forms without having any intention of disbursing them. To the extent that this shift did indeed take place, mainly on speculative grounds, the money stock M3 distorted the monetary trends of the economy. A suitably weighted monetary aggregate would have been advantageous in this case.

Finally, the use of unweighted monetary aggregates also posed problems in connection with the spread of liquid financial assets outside M3. These include, in particular, Euro-deposits bearing interest at market-related rates, which have grown strongly since the early 1980s, and, since 1994, money-market funds. While the close substitutive relationship with domestic time deposits made the inclusion of such deposits in a money stock concept seem advisable (and the Bundesbank does indeed monitor such an extended money stock), an extended money stock turned out to be unsuitable for use as an intermediate target variable, since it no longer exhibited a significant negative interest elasticity. Such problems could perhaps have been avoided, or at least mitigated, if these funds had been taken into consideration as part of a weighted aggregate because, in any such monetary aggregate, these components would have been included with a relatively small weight.

4.3 Problems of monetary aggregation

The definition of a monetary aggregate comprises three aspects:

1. Which assets provide monetary services?
2. How should they be aggregated?
3. Which weights should be used?

The discussion about the most appropriate aggregate to serve as an indicator or intermediate target of monetary policy often centres around the first question only. Whereas orthodox monetarists prefer narrow aggregates such as M1 (currency plus sight deposits), which exclude interest-bearing components, central banks often adopt wider definitions, including savings deposits and time deposits (M2, M3). When stability problems with conventional money demand functions arise, often associated with financial innovations and regulatory changes (Judd and Scadding, 1982), the definition of the monetary aggregate is called into question. After observed breaks in previously stable trend velocities in the 1980s, Switzerland, the UK and the USA all shifted emphasis to broader definitions of money. But while this change in focus has given the appearance of stable velocities for broad simple-sum measures, Barnett and Zhou (1994) discuss why this may be a statistical illusion rather than an indication of a better definition of money.

Traditional simple-sum aggregates can be defined and analysed within the statistical framework of the consolidated balance sheet of the banking sector. As such, they provide a measure of that part of the stock of financial wealth of the private sector that is likely to provide monetary services. Clearly, this is closely related to the function of money as a store of wealth. The role of money as a medium of exchange, however, requires a measure of the flow of liquidity services from holding a certain stock and composition of monetary assets. Simple summation implies that the financial assets included in the monetary aggregate are perfect substitutes. This feature of simple-sum aggregates is regarded as being highly implausible from a theoretical point of view and has been rejected strongly by empirical evidence on elasticities of substitution for monetary assets.

Aggregation can either be performed by summation of the stock of liquid assets (additive aggregates) or by some non-linear aggregation procedure – that is, by summation of their rates of growth (multiplicative aggregates).[2] In contrast to additive (linear) aggregates, multiplicative (non-linear) aggregates do not imply perfect substitutability; no single monetary asset can be replaced completely by the others. Rather, to perform the transaction needs a – not necessarily fixed –

Table 4.1 Aggregation and weighting schemes of monetary assets

Aggregation	*Weighting scheme*	
	Constant	*Variable*
Additive	M1, M2, M3, CBM	Currency equivalent (CE)
Multiplicative	TM	Divisia (DM, SM)

blend of all assets. The weighting scheme of monetary assets can either be constant or time-varying. In either case, the weights may or may not depend on the opportunity costs of holding wealth in liquid form in terms of interest forgone.

M1, M2, M3 and CBM are all additive aggregates with constant weights. The currency equivalent aggregate (CE) developed by Rotemberg *et al.* (1995) is an additive aggregate, its weights depending on the interest rate differential relative to a benchmark rate. Divisia indices with current (DM) and smoothed (SM) weights are multiplicative aggregates with variable weights. *Multiplicative aggregates with constant weights* have apparently been neglected widely in the literature. This is somewhat surprising, because monetary aggregates with constant weights are easy to interpret. The weights of a monetary aggregate used as an intermediate target of monetary policy should not depend directly on changes in the interest rates. Hence, multiplicative aggregates with constant weights should be potentially useful for monetary policy purposes because they simultaneously overcome two objections raised against alternative monetary aggregates: the perfect substitutability assumption of additive aggregates and the volatility of the weighting scheme of Divisia and, in particular, CE-aggregates. In the following we include the multiplicative *transactions orientated monetary aggregate* (TM), explained in the next section, into our study (Toedter, 1994). Table 4.1 summarises the preceding discussion.

4.4 The transaction costs approach to monetary aggregation

In the following we assume that there is a benchmark asset with yield R_t which provides no monetary services and is held solely to transfer wealth intertemporally. Holding the liquid asset i with yield r_{it} costs $R_t - r_{it}$ per D-Mark in period t. Total transaction costs in period t (that is, expenditures for monetary services) can be expressed as:

$$K_t = \sum_{i=1}^{L}(R_t - r_{it})M_{it} \tag{4.1}$$

and, accordingly, the expenditure share of the ith asset is:[3]

$$S_{it} = \frac{(R_t - r_{it})M_{it}}{K_t} = \frac{(R_t - r_{it})M_{it}}{\sum(R_t - r_{it})M_{it}} \tag{4.2}$$

Table 4.2 Expenditure on monetary services, 1989 (DM bn)

	$R - r_i$	M_i	$(R - r_i)\ M_i$
Currency plus sight deposits	0.070	419	29.4
Savings deposits	0.046	482	22.2
Time deposits	0.015	293	4.5
Total		1 194	56.1

As shown in Table 4.2 transaction costs in Germany in 1989 (the year before unification) amounted to DM 56 bn or 2.56 per cent of GNP. To derive a constant weight index, assume that the transactions technology can be described by a Cobb-Douglas function:

$$TM_t = m_o \prod_{i=1}^{L} M_{it}^{\alpha} i \tag{4.3}$$

For linear homogeneity, the restriction $\Sigma\alpha_i = 1$ has to be imposed. The coefficient α_i is the elasticity of *TM* with respect to the ith monetary asset. The elasticity of substitution between any two assets included in the multiplicative aggregate *TM* is unity. Regardless of the weights used to calculate Equation (4.3), *TM* is a geometrically weighted average of nominal monetary components and, hence, itself a nominal monetary index. A real monetary index (TM_t/P_t) would be obtained by weighting the deflated quantities M_{it}/P_t.

Facing transactions technology of Equation (4.3), rational economic agents minimising expenditures (Equation (4.1)), demand the amount:

$$M_{it}^{*} = \alpha_i \frac{K_t}{R_t - r_{it}} \qquad \forall\, i = 1 \ldots L \tag{4.4}$$

of the ith asset. This demand will be higher as the overall budget for transaction purposes (K_t) rises, and the price (opportunity cost $R_t - r_{it}$) falls.[4] Alternatively, the result in Equation (4.4) can be expressed as follows: expenditures on monetary assets are minimised if the share s_{it} of the component i in expenditures is equal to its constant elasticity:

$$S_{it}^{*} = \alpha_i \quad \forall\, i = 1 \ldots L \tag{4.5}$$

The empirical content of the proposition in Equation (4.5) is high. The theory predicts that expenditure shares are constant. More generally, in a stochastic setting, the expenditure shares should be stationary. This implication can be tested empirically by checking the expenditure shares for unit roots. If the null hypothesis of a unit root (non-stationarity) is rejected, unbiased estimates of α_i can be obtained by OLS:

$$\hat{\alpha}_i = \bar{s}_i \tag{4.6}$$

Table 4.3 Weighted monetary aggregates

Aggregate	*Weighting scheme*
Transactions oriented monetary aggregate (TM)	Constant: $\bar{s}_i$
Divisia monetary aggregate (DM)	Current: $\tilde{s}_{it} = (1/2)(s_{i,t} + s_{i,t-1})$
Smoothed Divisia monetary aggregate (SM)	Smoothed: $\hat{s}_{it} = \hat{\lambda} s_{i,t-1} + (1 - \hat{\lambda})\bar{s}_i$

where s_i is the average expenditure share of the i^{it} asset in the estimation period. We refer to the monetary measure with constant weights defined in Equation (4.6) as a transactions orientated monetary aggregate (*TM*), where its log-rate of growth is:

$$\mathrm{d}\log TM_t = \sum \bar{s}_i \, \mathrm{d}\log M_{it} \tag{4.7}$$

This contrasts with the Divisia monetary aggregate (*DM*), which uses variable weights:

$$\mathrm{d}\log DM_t = \sum \tilde{s}_{it} \, \mathrm{d}\log M_{it}, \quad \tilde{s}_{it} = (s_{it} + s_{i,t-1})/2 \tag{4.8}$$

The theory presented so far does not account for adjustment lags resulting from adjustment costs and/or information lags. Minimising a quadratic function in the adjustment costs $(s_{it} - s_{i,t-1})$ and in the disequilibrium costs $(s_{it} - S^* >_{it})$ yields the partial adjustment scheme:

$$s_{it} = \lambda_i s_{i,t-1} + (1 - \lambda_i)\bar{s}_i \tag{4.9}$$

Equation (4.9) suggests fitting a regression of s_{it} on its lagged values and a constant term in order to estimate λ_i. The weights, that is the fitted values,

$$\hat{s}_{it} = \hat{\lambda}_i s_{i,t-1} + (1 - \lambda_i)\bar{s}_i \tag{4.10}$$

are a weighted mean of the lagged and the average expenditure shares. Hence, this procedure yields an empirically-based compromise between the variable weight (Divisia) and the constant weight (*TM*) index. Even if the expenditure shares are stationary, they may contain an autoregressive component that would be picked up by smoothing the weights as described by Equation (4.10). This approach is similar in spirit to Spencer (1994), who accounts for sluggish portfolio adjustment by smoothing the user costs before using them to construct a Divisia aggregate. Henceforth, we refer to the monetary aggregate with smoothed weights defined in Equation (4.10) as Smoothed Divisia (*SM*). Table 4.3 summarises the preceding discussion.

4.5 The data and construction of aggregates for Germany

Since M3 is used by the Bundesbank for monetary targeting, we confine our study to the components of this broad monetary aggregate.[5] M3 contains four

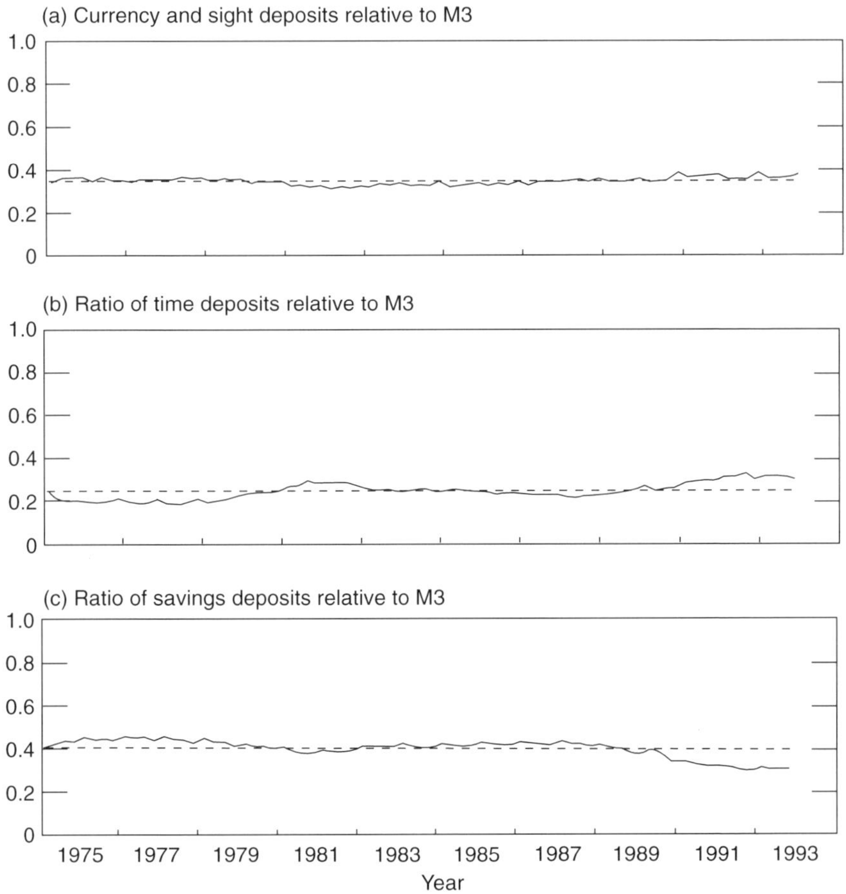

Figure 4.1 Shares of the components of M3

different components: currency, sight deposits, time deposits, and savings deposits at three months notice for domestic non-banks. More precisely, the Bundesbank defines currency as currency in circulation, excluding cash balances of banks. The major share of time deposits are borrowed for three months or less. Sight deposits bear no interest rate, except for some banks that offer their customers a low rate of 0.5 per cent per annum, which is more or less fixed. Therefore, currency and sight deposits are regarded as one composite non-interest-bearing component. In the following it is denoted as M_1 while the time deposits are M_2 and savings deposits M_3. Using this notation, simple sum M3 is defined as $\text{M3} = M_1 + M_2 + M_3$. The shares of the components M_1, M_2 and M_3 relative to M3 are shown in Figure 4.1, for the period ranging from 1975:1 to 1993:4. The share of M_1 in the aggregate M3 is nearly constant over the whole period. The shares of time deposits and savings exhibit somewhat more pronounced fluctuations around their mean values (indicated by the dashed line in Figure 4.1). Substitution between savings deposits and time deposits is clearly present.

For the construction of weighted monetary aggregates (TM3, DM3, SM3), we use the following corresponding interest rates: for time deposits, the average interest rate on deposits with agreed maturities from one to three months, accounting for the major share of time deposits (r_2); for savings deposits, the average interest rate on savings deposits at three months' notice (r_3). Finally, as a benchmark rate of return we use the yield on public bonds outstanding (R). All rates are stated on a one-year basis, and no adjustments have been made to account for different maturities (Thornton and Yue, 1992). The interest rates are shown in Figure 4.2.

To construct real opportunity costs, theory suggests the use of the price dual of the respective monetary index. For simple sum M3 this is $R - \max(r_i)$, and for the weighted aggregates (TM3, DM3, SM3) this is the geometrically weighted mean of the interest rate differences $R - r_i$, with weights defined in Equation (4.6), (4.8) and (4.10), respectively (see Note 4). However, when the time deposit rate is close to the bond yield, as in a few quarters of our sample period, the difference $R - r_2$ almost vanishes. An arithmetical mean of the interest rate differences does not have this problem and facilitates comparison because it can be applied to all four monetary aggregates. Hence, we use $R - r_e$ as real opportunity costs, where $r_e = 0.24r_2 + 0.42r_3$ denotes the own interest rate and 0.24 (0.42) is the mean share of time deposits (savings deposits) in M3 in the estimation period.

The expenditure shares s_{it} are calculated according to Equation (4.2). As can be seen in Figure 4.3, these shares fluctuate around their mean values (dashed lines), depending on the interest rate cycle. In line with the assumption made for the transaction-orientated monetary aggregate (TM) they appear to be mean-reverting in the long run. Unit root tests reported in Toedter (1994) reject the null hypothesis of non-stationarity. The empirical means of the expenditure shares are OLS estimates of the transactions elasticities:

$$\hat{\alpha}_i = \bar{s}_i = \frac{1}{T}\sum_{t=1}^{T} s_{it} \quad \forall\, i = 1, 2, 3 \tag{4.11}$$

The weights $\hat{\alpha}_i$ are estimated for the period from 1975:1 to 1993:4. The estimates (standard errors in parentheses) are:

$\bar{s}_1 = 0.54\ (0.06)$ for currency and sight deposits (M_1);
$\bar{s}_2 = 0.10\ (0.05)$ for time deposits (M_2); and
$\bar{s}_3 = 0.36\ (0.03)$ for savings deposits (M_3).

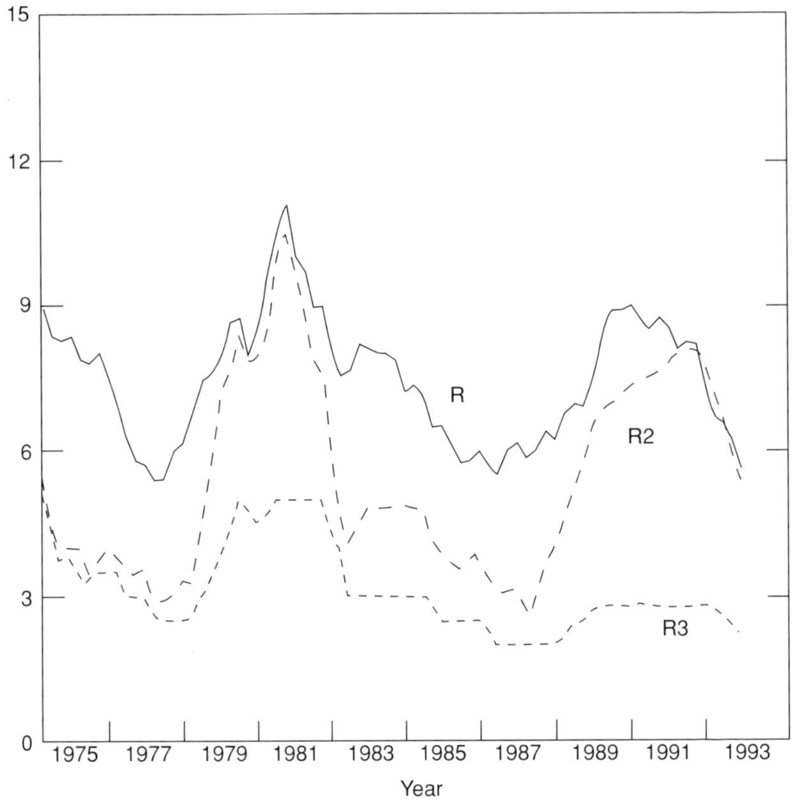

Key:
R = Yield on public bonds outstanding
R2 = Rate on time deposits
R3 = Savings rate

Figure 4.2 Interest rates

Using these estimated coefficients the transactions-orientated money aggregate (TM3) can be determined according to Equation (4.3).

For Divisia-M3 (DM3) the weights $\tilde{s}_{it}$ were calculated as the average of the current and the previous quarter expenditure shares. For the smoothed Divisia aggregate (SM) the weights were constructed according to the partial adjustment mechanism given in Equation (4.10). Estimation of the coefficients λ_i yielded values around 0.9 for all three components. Hence, for simplicity, we use $\hat{\lambda} = 0.9$ as a common value for constructing the smoothed Divisia aggregate (SM3). All weighted aggregates (TM3, DM3, SM3) are normalised on the value of M3 in 1975:1. Quarterly values for the levels and

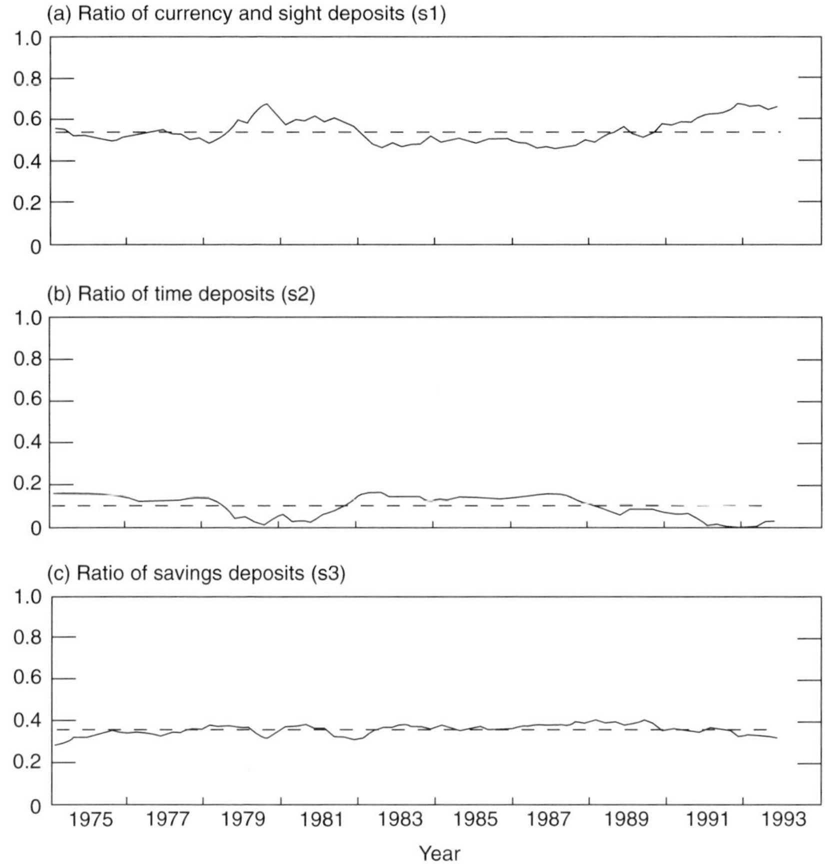

Figure 4.3 Share values around mean

the annual growth rates of the four series are shown in Figure 4.4. According to the ADF-tests, all four series are integrated of order 1 ($I(1)$. The jump of the monetary aggregates in 1990 is because of German monetary unification. Since end-of-quarter values are used, the jump appears in 1990:2. It is interesting to note that, in periods of high interest rates, the growth rates of the weighted aggregates TM3, SM3 and DM3 are below the growth rates of M3, and vice versa.

Completing the data description, the other series used in the money demand equations and the relationships between money and prices are discussed briefly. The price variable is represented by the deflator of domestic demand (P). This deflator is calculated as ratio between the nominal and real

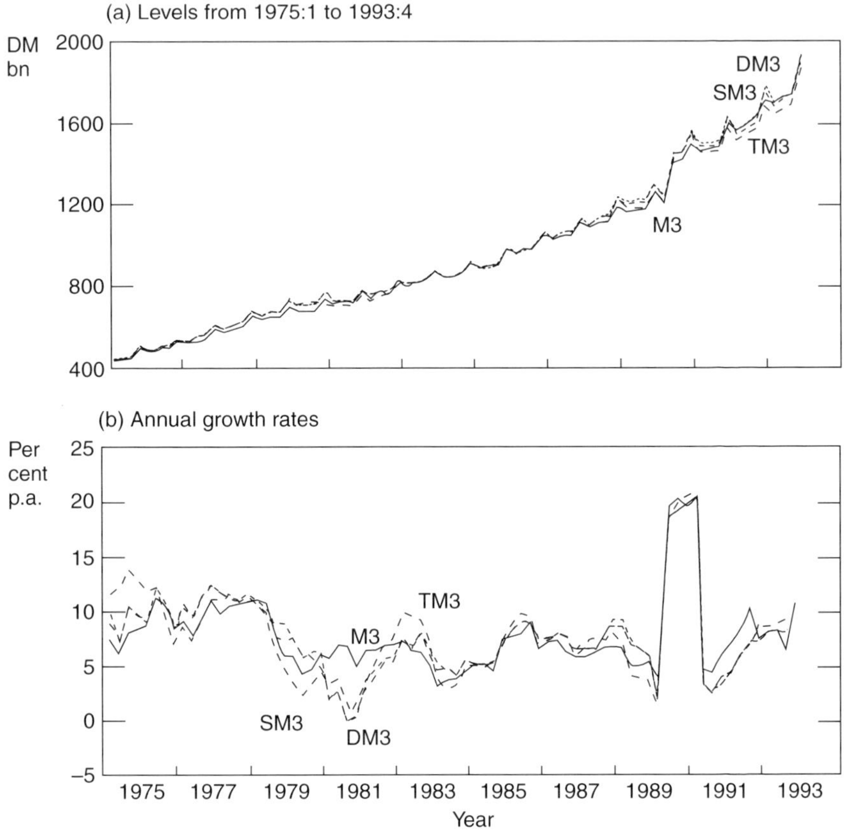

Figure 4.4 Monetary aggregates

domestic demand of West Germany and East Germany. The East Germany data are available from 1990:3 on. All-German real GDP (at 1991 prices) (Y) approximates the volume of transactions. All-German potential output ($Y(^*)$) is also composed of a West German and an East German part. Because of the ongoing structural changes, it is difficult to obtain reliable estimates of the East German component. In this study, we simply add the actual East German gross domestic product to the West German potential output.

Testing the data for stationarity is confronted with the problem of seasonal fluctuations and breaks in the series because of German unification. To account for seasonality in output and prices, seasonal dummies are used. Moreover, an impulse dummy (DWU) for the change from West German data to all-German data is used in the stationarity tests. The ADF tests are conducted for the period from 1975:1 to 1993:4, where an appropriate lag specification is selected to get white noise residuals. According to these tests (not reported here) money, output and prices are difference-stationary at the 1 per cent level. For the interest rate differential ($R - r_e$) the null hypothesis of non-stationarity is rejected at the 5 per cent level, but cannot be rejected at the 1 per cent level.

4.6 Money demand and its dynamics in the long run

A money demand function for a broad money aggregate may be written as follows:

$$M/P = f(Y, R - r_e) \tag{4.12}$$

where P denotes the price level, and Y is real GDP. The interest rate differential $R - r_e$ serves as a measure of the real opportunity costs of holding money for all four monetary aggregates, as was pointed out in Section 4.5. Since economic theory suggests that people care about the real quantities of goods and services (McCallum, 1989), money demand is specified in real (price-deflated) terms. Since the purpose of holding money is to facilitate transactions, real money balances respond positively to real transactions planned, approximated by real GDP. The cost of holding money is the interest that is sacrificed. Hence, money demand responds negatively to the opportunity costs of holding money: that is, the difference between the yield of a non-monetary benchmark asset and the own rate of return. Adopting a log-linear functional form, Equation (4.12) can be rewritten as:

$$m - p = \beta_0 + \beta_1(R - r_e) + \beta_2 \tag{4.13}$$

where small letters denote the logarithms of a variable, except for the interest rate r_e. In contrast to this long-run money demand function, actual money holdings respond dynamically to changes of the explanatory variables and to deviations from long-run equilibria inherited from the past. Both dynamic influences may be summarised in an error-correction equation of the form:

$$\begin{aligned}\Delta_4(m - p) = \gamma_0 + \gamma_1\Delta_4 y + \gamma_2\Delta_4\mathrm{DWU} + \gamma_3\Delta_4 p + \gamma_4\Delta_4(R - r_e) \\ + \gamma_5\Delta_4(m - p)_{-1} + \gamma_6\sum_{i=1}^{4} 0.25\mathrm{ECM}_{-i} + \varepsilon\end{aligned} \tag{4.14}$$

where ECM represents the estimated residuals of the long-run money demand Equation (4.13), and the operator Δ_4 denotes four-period differences of a series: that is, $\Delta_4 X_t = X_t - X_{t-4}$. Assuming that price homogeneity holds in the long run only, the dynamic equation includes the inflation rate. This framework is investigated for all four aggregates: M3, TM3, DM3 and SM3.

Reunification increased all-German potential GDP by about 9 per cent. To account for this we have adjusted the money and income data by subtracting 9 per cent from both series for the period 1990:2 to 1993:4. The estimated

Table 4.4 Long-run money demand equations $(m - p)$

Variable	*M3*	*TM3*	*DM3*	*SM3*
y	1.55	1.44	1.53	1.52
$R - r_e$	–1.89	–2.56	–2.47	–2.50
R^2	0.98	0.96	0.97	0.97
DW	0.73	0.53	0.81	0.77

Notes: Estimation period = 1975: 1 to 1993: 4. All monetary series and real GDP are break-adjusted according to $m - DV \log(1.09)$ and $y - DV_{-1} \log(1.09)$, where the dummy variable DV is one from 1990: 2 to 1993: 4, and zero otherwise.

income elasticity in the cointegrating regression of the Engle–Granger (1987) procedure is in all cases around 1.5, implying a pronounced downward trend in velocity (see Table 4.4). The interest rate semi-elasticity is –1.9 for M3 and around –2.5 for the weighted aggregates. Hence, the weighted aggregates react more strongly to changes of the interest rate differential than does M3.

As a result of the seasonal pattern of the series, the dynamic equation uses data that are four-period differences. The estimates of these equations and their t-ratios in parentheses are shown in Table 4.5. The residuals pass a battery

Table 4.5 Dynamic money demand equations $(\Delta_4(m - p))$

Variable	*M3*	*TM3*	*DM3*	*SM3*
C_0	0.03 (4.91)	0.02 (3.29)	0.02 (3.26)	0.02 (3.45)
$DWU - DWU(-4)$	0.05 (5.03)	0.07 (7.61)	0.08 (8.18)	0.07 (7.57)
$\Delta_4 y$	0.08 (1.44)	0.18 (2.97)	0.18 (2.96)	0.19 (3.00)
$\Delta_4 p$	–0.59 (5.62)	0.55 (4.51)	–0.43 (4.05)	–0.47 (4.15)
$\Delta_4(R - r_e)$	–0.14 (0.81)	–0.61 (3.29)	–0.63 (3.13)	–0.71 (3.45)
$\Delta_4(m - p)_{-1}$	0.70 (10.06)	0.79 (13.63)	0.76 (13.92)	0.73 (12.60)
$\sum_{i=1}^{4} 0.25ECM_{-i}$	0.34 (4.33**)	0.30 (4.72**)	–0.24 (2.82)	–0.22 (2.65)
R^2	0.82	0.89	0.88	0.87
SER in %	1.11	1.20	1.18	1.22
DW	1.87	1.52	1.97	2.10
LB(8)	12.53(*)	10.52	7.62	11.11
ARCH(4)	2.21	6.79	6.74	2.52
CHOW(4)	2.93(**)	0.25	0.32	0.21
CHOW(8)	2.33(**)	0.30	0.49	0.34
CHOW(12)	1.71(*)	0.27	0.54	0.49

Notes: Estimation period = 1976: 3 to 1993: 4; y and $m - p$ break-adjusted as in Table 4.4. DW: Durbin–Watson statistic. LB(8): Ljung-Box test for 8th order autocorrelation. ARCH(4): Auto-regressive conditional heterosskedasticity test for 4 lags. CHOW(4): Prediction test of Chow (1960) for the last 4, 8 and 12 observations, respectively. Critical values from MacKinnon (1991) for testing the ECM-coefficient: 3.54 for the 10% and 3.86 for the 5% test level. * ** denote significance at 10% (5%) levels respectively.

of tests without any indication of misspecification except for the possible presence of autocorrelation in the M3 equation. Chow (1960) prediction tests do not indicate instabilities associated with German unification in the equations with weighted aggregates. For M3 the Chow tests signal a structural break. This, however, is not associated with German unification but results from strong M3-growth in the second half of 1993.

The estimated coefficients have the expected signs and are significantly different from zero. One exception is the insignificant coefficient of the interest-rate variable in the M3 equation. Cointegration of the long-run relationship in Equation (4.13) is tested by the estimated *t*-value of the error correction coefficient. Kremers *et al.* (1992) point out that this test is more powerful than the commonly used residuals-based Dickey–Fuller (ADF) test. The reason for this result is that the latter imposes common-factor restrictions that are not likely to be valid. Using the critical values of MacKinnon (1991) for the coefficients of the error-correction terms the ECM-coefficients in the equations for M3 and TM3 are significant at the 5 per cent level, suggesting cointegration in Equation (4.13). The ECM terms of DM3 and SM3 are not significant even at the 10 per cent level, indicating the possibility that the variables in these equations may not form a cointegrated relationship.

Summarising the results, we find evidence for cointegration in the money demand equations for M3 and TM3. The evidence for cointegration is weak, however, for SM3 and DM3. It is worth noting that the Chow prediction test does not indicate instabilities associated with German reunification for any of the weighted monetary measures. The apparent instabilities in the case of M3 result from strong money growth in 1993 and not from instabilities associated with German reunification.

4.7 The link between money and prices

The familiar equation of exchange:

$$PY = MV \tag{4.15}$$

states that the product of the price level and real GDP equals the product of the stock of money and its average velocity of circulation (V). Leaning on this identity, Hallman *et al.* (1991) define the long-run equilibrium price level (P^*) as money per unit of real potential output (Y^*) at the equilibrium level of velocity (V^*):

$$P^* = \frac{M}{Y^*} V^* \tag{4.16}$$

The basic idea of this approach is that more money increases the price level if it is not absorbed by a larger supply of goods or lower velocity. Provided the actual price level (P) and P^* are cointegrated, P^* can be used as an indicator of the development of prices in the future. If the prevailing price level is below its equilibrium level ($P^* > P$) a future acceleration of inflation is indicated, whereas, in the opposite case ($P^* < P$), a reduction of the rate of inflation is to be expected.

To calculate P^*, empirical estimates of potential output and trend velocity are required (see Toedter and Reimers, 1994). If velocity fluctuates randomly around a constant we may treat equilibrium velocity as a constant. However, in Germany the velocity of M3 has exhibited a pronounced downward trend in the past. If money demand develops according the Equation (4.13) in the long run, a downward trend of velocity can occur, for two reasons: either income elasticity of money is high ($\beta > 1$), or the interest rate differential ($R - r_e$) is downward-trending. The latter explanation can be discarded empirically because the interest rate differential in Germany exhibits cyclical ups and downs, but not a permanent downward movement. On the other hand, given a growth rate of potential output between 2 per cent and 3 per cent, the estimated income elasticity ($\hat{\beta} = 1.5$ – see Table 4.4) is able to explain the velocity trend rate of -1 to -1.5 per cent observed in the past. Following this line of reasoning, we treat the interest rate differential as a constant and define long-run velocity as:

$$V^* = V_0 + (1 - \beta)y^* \tag{4.17}$$

Using the estimated long-run income elasticities ($\hat{\beta}_i$) of the four monetary aggregates estimated in the previous section, the following equations for p^*;

$$p_i^* = m - \hat{\beta}_i y^* + \hat{V}_{0i} \quad i = 1, \ldots 4 \text{ (for } M3, TM3, DM3, SM3) \tag{4.18}$$

were obtained from fitting regressions of p on $m - \hat{\beta}_i y$ and the contrast terms, v_{oi}, which include seasonal dummies. The fitted values of these regressions provide our measure of p^* for the four monetary aggregates considered. The regressions ensure that the series are normalised such that the price gap ($p_i^* - p$) is, on average, zero. The four different price gaps are alternatively used to explain the rate of inflation. Because of the seasonal pattern of the series we use the four-period differences in the dynamic price equations. Correspondingly, a lagged four-quarter average of the price gap is specified. To take into consideration import price fluctuations the dynamic equations, include the inflation rate of the import price deflator ($\Delta_4 pim$) as an additional regressor:

$$\Delta_4 p = \sum_{j=1}^{4} \delta_{1j} \Delta_4 p_{-j} + \delta_2 \Delta_4 pim + \delta_3 \Delta_4 p_i^* = \delta_4 \sum_{j=1}^{4} 0.25(p_i^* - p)_{-j} + \varepsilon \tag{4.19}$$

A lag length of two for the endogenous variable turned out to be sufficient to remove autocorrelation (see Table 4.6). Moreover, the data failed to reject the equality restriction $\delta_3 = \delta_4$ for the coefficients of $\Delta_4 p^*$and the price gap in all four equations. Interpreting the *t*-values of the ECM terms as tests for cointegration, they indicate (using the critical values of MacKinnon, 1991) that

Table 4.6 Dynamic price equations in four-period differences ($\Delta_4 p$)

Variable	$\Delta_4 p$ *(M3)*	$\Delta_4 p$ *(TM3)*	$\Delta_4 p$ *(DM3)*	$\Delta_4 p$ *(SM3)*
$\Delta_4 p_{-1}$	0.62 (5.64)	0.63 (5.61)	0.63 (5.49)	0.63 (5.53)
$\Delta_4 p_{-2}$	0.23 (2.23)	0.25 (2.34)	0.25 (2.35)	0.21 (2.29)
$\Delta_4 pim$	0.07 (4.29)	0.07 (4.13)	0.06 (3.62)	0.06 (3.70)
$\Delta_4 p(*)$	0.07	0.05	0.05	0.05
$\sum_{i=1}^{4}(p(*)_{-i} - p_{-i})$	0.07 (4.41**)	0.05 (3.93**)	0.05 (3.64**)	0.05 (3.57**)
R^2	0.97	0.97	0.97	0.97
DW	1.87	1.89	1.82	1.89
SER	0.628	0.643	0.652	0.654
LB(8)	10.03	11.27	10.80	11.01
ARCH(4)	2.39	4.20	3.69	3.70
CHOW(4)	1.00	1.15	1.17	1.16
CHOW(8)	1.08	1.14	1.20	1.18
CHOW(12)	1.87*	2.11**	2.21**	2.15**

Notes: Estimation period = 1976: 3 to 1993: 4. Critical values at the 10% (5%) level for the *t*-statistic of the ECM-term from MacKinnon (1991): 3.10 (3.42). * ** denote significance at 10% (5%) level respectively.

the actual price level and equilibrium price level based on M3, TM3, SM3 and DM3 are cointegrated at the 5 per cent level. Comparing the coefficients of the same variables across equations, the differences are very small. However, the Chow tests for the last twelve quarters indicate some problems with short-run stability. The reason is that the dynamic equations do not fully explain the increase of the all-German inflation rate from 2.8 per cent in the first quarter of 1991 to more than 5.5 per cent by the fourth quarter of that year, because of various administrative price and indirect tax rate adjustments.

To summarise the findings of this section, we obtained cointegrating relationships between the actual price and the equilibrium price level p^*, based on all four monetary aggregates. Probably associated with transition of the regulated prices to market prices in East Germany after unification, there is evidence of instability in all four dynamic price equations. Monte Carlo simulation results performed for M3 suggest, however, that the underlying long-run relationship between p and p^* remained stable after unification.

4.8 Control and projection error of monetary aggregates

The money demand and price equations estimated in the previous two sections empirically establish a link between the alternative monetary aggregates and prices. On this criterion alone, these measures can be considered as useful indicators of monetary policy. However, a monetary aggregate, serving as an intermediate target for monetary policy, must also be controllable by monetary policy instruments. According to Belongia and Batten (1992, p. 2).

> identifying a stable long-run relationship between a monetary aggregate and the price level, while necessary for a variable monetary policy process based on an intermediate target strategy, is not a sufficient condition for its success. Missing in virtually all discussions of which monetary aggregate might best suit a central bank's goals and procedures is evidence on whether the central bank can use its instruments to control the behavior of the aggregate.

In this section, following Belongia and Batten (1992) and Andersen and Karnosky (1977), we take into account the controllability of the monetary aggregates by the Bundesbank, using an interest rate instrument.

The framework developed so far may be summarised in stylised form by the following three equations, determining money (m), P-star (p^*) and prices (p):

$$m - p = f(y, R - r_e) + \varepsilon \tag{4.20}$$

$$p^* \equiv m - \hat{\beta}y^*; \text{ and} \tag{4.21}$$

$$\Delta p = g(p^* - p) + u \tag{4.22}$$

The Deutsche Bundesbank controls the target variable mainly by interest rate policy. As a representative central bank interest rate, the Bundesbank's rate for open market transactions in securities under repurchase agreements (r_c) is used in the following estimations. The demand for money does not depend directly on this instrument but is modelled as a function of the difference between the long-run benchmark rate and the own interest rate: $R - r_e$. Hence we estimate the link between these interest rates and the instrument by simple dynamic term structure equations of the form:

$$R = h(R_{e-1}, r_c) + \eta; \text{ and} \tag{4.23}$$

$$r_e = h_e(r_{e-1}, r_c) + \eta_e \tag{4.24}$$

The residual terms η, η_e and ε contribute to the control error, while the residual term u in the price equation is called the projection error of the process. Even if the Bundesbank could control its intermediate target perfectly, and even if it had accurate forecasts of the 'exogenous' variables of the process, it would not be able to control the rate of inflation perfectly because of the projection error. On the other hand, if – for example – M3 had the closest relationship to the rate of inflation but it was controllable only with large errors, one of the weighted aggregates might perform better because of a smaller control error. To investigate the whole process – that is, the total error – we calculate a series of stepwise forecasts using the estimated money demand and price equations for the four different monetary aggregates, together with the interest rate

Table 4.7 Forecast errors of the inflation rate (1987: 1 to 1993: 4)

Measure	*Horizon*	*M3*	*TM3*	*DM3*	*SM3*
RMSFE	1 step	0.689	0.700	0.703	0.703
MAFE	1 step	0.512	0.534	0.520	0.522
RMSFE	4 step	0.948	1.023	1.091	1.062
MAFE	4 step	0.729	0.699	0.796	0.773
RMSFE	8 step	1.362	1.227	1.042	0.959
MAFE	8 step	1.033	0.991	0.866	0.794

Notes: RMSFE = Root mean squared forecast error; MAFE = mean absolute forecast error.

equations. It should be noted, however, that the results of this exercise are conditional on the 'exogenous' variables output (y), potential output (y^*) and import prices (*pim*). Moreover, using the historical values of the interest rate instrument (r_c) disregards the problem that the Bundesbank would have set its rates differently if it had aimed at one of the weighted aggregates rather than M3. Hence, the procedure may be somewhat in favour of M3.

To calculate the one-step, four-step and eight-step forecasts of the inflation rate, we start by re-estimating Equations (4.20) to (4.24) for the shorter period ranging from 1976:3 to 1986:4. In the next round, the information base is extended by one quarter. The equations are re-estimated again and new forecasts are calculated. The procedure is repeated until 1991:4 to determine the last eight-step forecast, until 1992:4 to get the last four-step forecast, and until 1993:3 to get the last one-step forecast. In summary, there are twenty-one eight-step forecasts, twenty-five four-step forecasts, and twenty-eight one-step forecasts. The forecast performance is measured by the mean absolute forecast error (MAFE) and by the root mean squared forecast error (RMSFE). The results are presented in Table 4.7. It is apparent that the errors increase with the forecast horizon. The one-step forecast errors are slightly higher than the standard errors of estimation. In the short-run forecasts (one-step horizon), there are no marked differences between the four monetary aggregates. In the four-step forecasts (one-year horizon), the most important ones, because the Bundesbank announces annual targets for monetary growth, M3 slightly outperforms the weighted aggregates. The reverse is true for the eight-step forecasts (two years ahead). On the whole, judged by this forecast performance, which takes into account the control error as well as the projection error, there is no clear ranking among the four aggregates under consideration.[6]

4.9 Summary and conclusions

In this chapter, three weighted monetary aggregates were investigated and compared to traditional M3, the Bundesbank's monetary target. Emphasising the role of money as a medium of exchange, a measure of the flow of monetary services provided by a given stock and composition of monetary assets is needed. The weighted aggregates analysed in this study are composed of the same components as M3. The weighting scheme, however, is derived from a microeconomic expenditure minimisation problem consistent with economic aggregation and index theory. In contrast to simple-sum M3, the weighted aggregates do not imply perfect substitutability among included assets. For the three weighted aggregates examined, Divisia M3 (DM3) uses current expenditure shares as weights, whereas the transactions orientated aggregate (TM3) has constant (average) expenditure shares, and the smoothed Divisia index (SM3) applies a weighted average of current and constant expenditure shares. For all four aggregates, the chapter analyses long-run as well as dynamic money demand functions, and the relationship between money and prices using the *P*-star approach. Finally, the complete link between monetary policy instruments and inflation is investigated by a series of forecast exercises, comprising the control as well as the projection error of the whole process.

As can already be inferred from inspecting Figure 4.4, the development of the levels of the four time series show no marked differences. The rates of growth, however, indicate a stronger responsiveness of the weighted aggregates to changes in interest rates. These features of the data are reflected in the estimated long-run functions for real money demand. The long-run income elasticities of all four aggregates is around 1.5, reflecting the pronounced downward trend of velocity observed in the past. The estimated semi-elasticity of the difference between the long-term (benchmark) yield and the own interest rate is −1.9 for M3 and around −2.5 for the weighted indices. While real M3 and TM3 pass tests for cointegration based on the *t*-statistics of the estimated error correction term in the dynamic money demand function, the evidence for cointegration among real DM3 and SM3 and their determinants is somewhat weaker.

In the next part of our analysis we use the monetary aggregates to construct measures of the long-run equilibrium price level (*P*-star). The price gap – that is, the difference between *P*-star and the actual price level – serves as an indicator for future developments of the inflation rate, provided *P* and *P*-star are cointegrated. Tests based on the error correction term in the estimated dynamic equation for the inflation rate confirm the cointegration hypothesis for all four aggregates. The evidence does not show any differences between simple-sum M3 and the weighted aggregates. Prediction tests, however, do indicate some problems with the stability of simple-sum M3 after unification.

In the final part of our analysis we take into account the short-term interest rate as the instrument of monetary control used by the Bundesbank (the open market rate) and estimate its link with the benchmark yield and the own rate of monetary assets. The purpose of this exercise is to investigate the link between the open market rate, the main monetary policy instrument of the Bundesbank, the monetary aggregates, *P*-star, and the final goal of monetary stabilisation policy, the rate of inflation. Both the failure to control monetary aggregates by the interest rate instrument, and failure of the intermediate target to track prices contribute to prediction errors in the rate of inflation. *Ex-post* forecasts show that all four monetary aggregates perform almost equally well.

The empirical evidence presented in this chapter is not unequivocal. Hence, it is not easy to strike a final balance. Perhaps the most remarkable result of out study is that traditional M3, despite its theoretical weaknesses, stands up to comparison with the weighted monetary indices considered.

Notes

1. See, for example, Barnett (1980, 1982) and Barnett, Offenbacher and Spindt (1984). Barnett, Fisher and Serletis (1992) provide a comprehensive overview of these efforts. Chrystal and McDonald (1994) discuss empirical evidence for seven countries. Economists in several central banks have explored the properties of Divisia and related monetary aggregates: that is, Thorton and Yue (1992) for the USA; Fisher *et al.* (1993) for Great Britain; Fluri (1990) and Yue and Fluri (1991) for Switzerland; Ayuso and Vega (1993) for Spain; Gaiotti (1994) for Italy; and Issing *et al.* (1993) for Germany.
2. *Additive aggregates* correspond to the *arithmetic mean*, and *multiplicative* aggregates to the *geometric mean* of their components. More general schemes such as the 'weighted mean of order rho' are also possible.
3. Note, that our user cost measure $R_t - r_{it}$ in Equation (4.1) differs slightly from Barnett's (1978) *real* user costs derived from intertemporal utility maximisation, i.e. $(R_t - r_{it})/(1 + R_t)$. However, this difference is inconsequential for the expenditure shares in Equation (4.2) and all subsequent derivations. Moreover, applying *nominal* user costs $P_t\ (R_t - r_{it})/(1 + R_t)$ (where P is a cost of living index) to real money holdings M_t/P_t has no effect on the results.
4. Re-inserting the demand functions of Equation (4.4) into Equation (4.3) results in $TM_t = K_t/TS_t$, with $TS_t = z_o\Pi\ (R_t - r_{it}^{\alpha}$ and $z_o^1 = m_o\Pi\alpha_1^{\alpha_1})$. TS is a geometrically weighted mean of the prices $(R - r_i)$ and can be interpreted as the real price dual to the quantity index TM. Formally, we have $(TM \times TS) = (TM/P) \times (P \times TS) = K$, i.e. total expenditures K are equal to nominal money TM times the real price dual TS, or to real money TM/P times the nominal price dual $P \times TS = z_o\Pi[P\ (R_t - r_{it})]^{\alpha_1}$.
5. Weak separability tests for Germany presented in Belongia (this volume) suggest that time deposits should not be part of a monetary aggregate. We have investigated an alternative asset composition, excluding time deposits. The result was a stronger responsiveness of the aggregate to interest rate changes. The link between money and prices was somewhat weaker, however.
6. Dorsey (this volume) used German data in a neural network design to evaluate inflation forecasts and found that Divisia measures dominate simple-sum aggregates.

References

Andersen, L. C. and D. S. Karnosky (1977) 'Some Considerations in the Use of Monetary Aggregates for the Implementation of Monetary Policy', *Federal Reserve Bank of St Louis Review*, September, pp. 2–7.

Ayuso, J. and J. L. Vega (1993) 'Weighted Monetary Aggregates: the Spanish Case', Banco de Espana, Servicio de Estudios, Documento de Trabajo No. 9303.

Barnett, W. A. (1978) 'The User Cost of Money', *Economics Letters*, vol. 1, pp. 145–9.
Barnett, W. A. (1980) 'Economic Monetary Aggregates – an Application of Index Number and Aggregation Theory', *Journal of Econometrics*, vol. 14, pp. 11–48.
Barnett, W. A., and G. Zhou (1994) 'Commentary', *Federal Reserve Bank of St Louis Review* (November–December), pp. 53–61.
Barnett, W. A., E. K. Offebacher and P. A. Spindt (1984) 'The New Divisia Monetary Aggregates', *Journal of Political Economy*, vol. 92, pp. 1049–85.
Barnett, W. A., D. Fisher and A. Serletis (1992) 'Consumer Theory and the Demand for Money', *Journal of Economic Literature*, vol. XXX, pp. 2086–119.
Belongia, M. T. (2000) 'Consequences of Money Stock Mismeasurement: Evidence From Three Countries', Chapter 13, this volume.
Belongia, M. T. and D. S. Batten (1992) 'Selecting an intermediate Target for variable Monetary Policy: Monetary Control and Policy Objectives', Discussion paper of the Federal Reserve Bank of St. Louis working paper, 92–008, November.
Chow, G. C. (1960) 'Tests for Equality between Sets of Coefficients in Two Linear Regressions', *Econometrica*, vol. 28, pp. 591–605.
Chrystal, K. and R. McDonald (1994) 'Empirical Evidence on the Recent Behavior and Usefulness of Simple sum and Weighted Measures of the Money Stock', *Federal Reserve Bank of St. Louis Review*, (March/April) pp. 73–109.
Dorsey, R. E. (2000) 'Neural Networks with Divisia Money: Better Forecasts of Future Inflation?', Chapter 2 in this volume.
Engle R. F. and C. W. J. Granger (1987) 'Co-integration and Error Correction: Representation, Estimation and Testing', *Econometrica*, vol. 55, pp. 251–76.
Fisher, P., S. Hudson and M. Pradhan (1993) 'Divisia Measures of Money', *Bank of England Quarterly Bulletin* (May), pp. 240–55.
Fluri, R. (1990) 'Monetäre Divisia-Aggregate – eine Alternative zu den traditionellen Geldmengenindikatoren?', *Geld, Währung und Konjunktur*, Swiss National Bank (December), pp. 343–54.
Gaiotti, E. (1994) 'Measuring Money with a Divisia-Index: An Application to Italy', Banca d'Italia, Temi di discussione, No. 223 (April).
Hallman, J. J., R. D. Porter and D. H. Small (1991) 'Is the Price Level Tied to the M2 Monetary Aggregate in the Long Run?', *American Economic Review*, vol. 81, pp. 841–58.
Issing, O. (1992) 'Theoretical and Empirical Foundations of the Deutsche Bundesbank's Monetary Targeting', *Intereconomics*, vol. 27, no. 6, pp. 289–300.
Issing, O., K.-H. Toedter, H. Herrmann and H.-E. Reimers (1993) 'Zinsgewichtete Geldmengenaggregate und M3 – ein Vergleich', *Kredit und Kapital*, vol. 26, no. 1, pp. 1–21.
Judd, J. P. and J. L. Scadding (1982) 'The Search for a Stable Money Demand Function: A Survey of the Post-1973 Literature', *Journal of Economic Literature*, vol. XX, pp. 993–1023.
Kremers, J. J. M., N. R. Ericsson and J. J. Dolado (1992) 'The Power of Cointegration Tests', *Oxford Bulletin of Economics and Statistics*, vol. 54, pp. 325–48.
McCallum, B. T. (1989) *Monetary Economics – Theory and Policy* (New York: Macmillan).
MacKinnon, J. (1991) 'Critical Values for Cointegration Tests', in R. F. Engle and C. W. J. Granger (eds); *Long-Run Economic Relationships – Readings in Cointegration* (Oxford University Press).
Rotemberg, J. J., J. C. Driscoll and J. M. Poterba (1995) 'Money, Output and Prices: Evidence from a New Monetary Aggregate', *Journal of Business and Economic Statistics*, vol. 13, no. 1, pp. 67–83.

Spencer, P. (1994) 'Portfolio Disequlibrium – Implications for the Divisia Approach to Monetary Aggregation', *The Manchester School*, vol. LXII, no. 2, pp. 125–150.

Thornton, D. L. and P. Yue (1992) 'An Extended Series of Divisia Monetary Aggregates' *Review of the Federal Reserve Bank of St Louis Review* (November/December), pp. 35–52.

Toedter, K.-H. (1994) 'Eine transaktionsorientierte Geldmenge', *Kredit und Kapital*, vol. 27, pp. 319–47.

Toedter, K.-H. and H.-E. Reimers (1994) 'P-Star as a Link Between Money and Prices in Germany', *Weltwirtschaftliches Archiv*, vol. 130, pp. 273–89.

Yue, P. and. R. Fluri (1991) 'Divisia Monetary Services Indexes for Switzerland: Are They Useful For Monetary Targeting?, *Federal Reserve Bank of St Louis Review* (September/October), pp. 19–33.

5
Simple-sum versus Divisia Money in Switzerland: Some Empirical Results*

Robert Fluri and Erich Spoerndli

5.1 Introduction

This paper is divided into four parts. Section 5.2 describes the Swiss National Bank's (SNB) internally used monetary indicator and reporting system, of which the Divisia aggregates are part. Through financial innovations and the increasing importance of non-cash payments, the SNB is currently revising the definitions of its simple-sum as well as of its Divisia monetary aggregates. We sketch the main aspects of the revision in Section 5.3. In Section 5.4, we present different empirical tests, evaluating the relative performance of the present and newly defined aggregates. To determine the short-run predictive information content of money, traditional Granger-causality tests within low dimension vector auto-regressive (VAR) systems in terms of first differenced variables are carried out. Vector error correction models (VECMs) are also used, to shed light on the relative importance of different monetary aggregates, when possible long-run relationships between money, prices, interest rates and output are explicitly taken into account. Tests of additional predictive information of lagged money in a structural Keynesian price equation supplement the VAR–Granger tests. As a final exercise, a series of Engle–Granger (1987) cointegration regressions of income velocity on the yield of government bonds are carried out. Section 5.5 concludes. The main findings of the investigations are as follows: for most of the measures studied, money does – as expected – help to predict prices and output in the short run as well as in the long run. The predictive information content of money regarding shorter-run price movements is in general not impressively high when other available information is incorporated. However, the various aggregates perform differently. The more narrowly-defined Divisia measures tend to perform best in these comparisons. Evidence from tests using long-run information content

* We thank Jeanne Gobat and Michel Peytrignet for their helpful comments and suggestions.

of money is, however, somewhat mixed for Divisia measures. Simple-sum aggregates M2 and M3 in general perform poorly.

5.2 Divisia aggregates used by the Swiss National Bank

The Swiss National Bank uses the seasonally adjusted monetary base as its official target monetary aggregate. It is the Bank's policy to increase the monetary base with an average growth rate of 1 per cent per annum in the medium term. Apart from the monetary base, the SNB uses broader aggregates as helpful indicators to assess the effects of its monetary policy on prices and income. These aggregates are defined in accordance with common practice among central banks. The SNB also sums up different assets providing monetary services. Consequently, M1 consists of highly liquid assets such as currency in circulation and demand deposits, whereas the aggregates M2 and M3 contain close substitutes to the M1 components (see below).

Definitions of the official monetary aggregates/components

M1: Currency in circulation
Demand deposits with banks
Demand deposits with the postal giro system
M2: Time deposits
M3: Savings deposits

Since 1990 the SNB has also computed Divisia aggregates (see Yue and Fluri, 1991). The computation of the Divisia aggregates is based on the above-mentioned components. However, in contrast to the simple-sum aggregates M2 and M3, we also include the maturity of time deposits (for more detail see Appendix 1). The reason is that the interest rates offered for time deposits are maturity-dependent. As far as M1 is concerned, we do not compute the respective Divisia aggregate, because the shares of each monetary component for simple-sum and Divisia M1 move almost uniformly. Thus the differences between M1 simple-sum and M1 Divisia are negligible.

The Divisia aggregates are not published in the official publications of the SNB. They are, however, part of the internally used monetary indicator and reporting system, along with the simple-sum aggregates. Experience shows that the Divisia aggregates – especially Divisia M2 – are valuable additional monetary indicators.

The weighting procedure eliminates the not very helpful features of the simple-sum M2. In periods when monetary policy is restrictive, or in phases when the SNB eases off its policy, M2 tends to move in the opposite direction from the other simple-sum and the Divisia aggregates. In periods of restrictive policy, as was the case between 1989 and 1992 (see Figure 5.1), these movements were a result of the change in the term structure from normal to inverse. Investors shifted funds from savings into time deposit accounts.

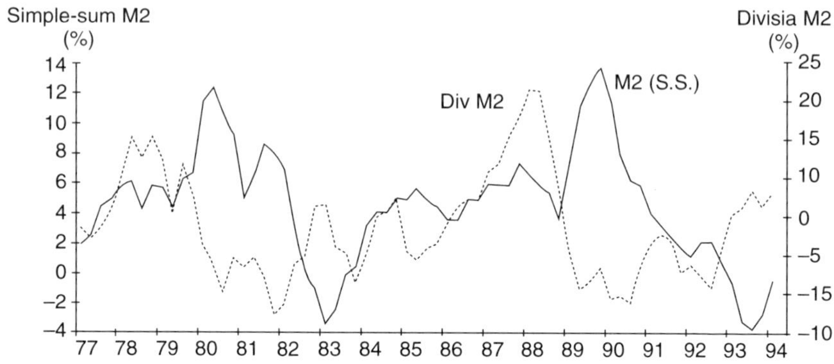

Figure 5.1 Divisia M2 versus simple-sum M2

Furthermore, asset-holders shifted funds from lower yielding securities and other financial assets not included in the monetary aggregates into time deposits. These shifts caused the volume of time deposits – and consequently M2 – to increase dramatically. However, the changes in interest rates produced quite different movements in the Divisia M2. Because of the inverse term structure, the interest rate on short-term time deposits became the reference interest rate. Since the opportunity or user cost of time deposits declined, the monetary service flows for a given quantity of time deposits also fell, and approached a value close to zero. This slowed down the growth of the Divisia aggregate.

Granger-causality tests have shown that Divisia M2 performs better in helping to predict inflation than the other aggregates, especially M1 (Fluri, 1990). This indicates that it makes sense to include time-deposits in a Divisia aggregate. However, the predictive power gain of Divisia M2 over simple-sum M1 is limited (see Figure 5.2).

5.3 The revision of monetary statistics

In Switzerland, non-cash payments have gained increasing importance since the late 1980s. The number of transactions carried out by credit or debit cards increased from 15 million in 1988 to 50 million transactions in 1992. The commercial banks also facilitated the use of banknotes by enlarging the network of automatic teller machines (ATM). In Switzerland, 2700 ATM units were installed in 1994, compared to 400 in 1982. Such instruments of cash and non-cash payment systems (credit cards, cheques, ATM, home banking and so on) are usually linked with accounts specially created for transaction purposes (in the following called 'transaction accounts'). Statistically they are part of savings deposits and, until now, have not been collected separately in banking statistics. Consequently, they are part of M3. However, the transaction

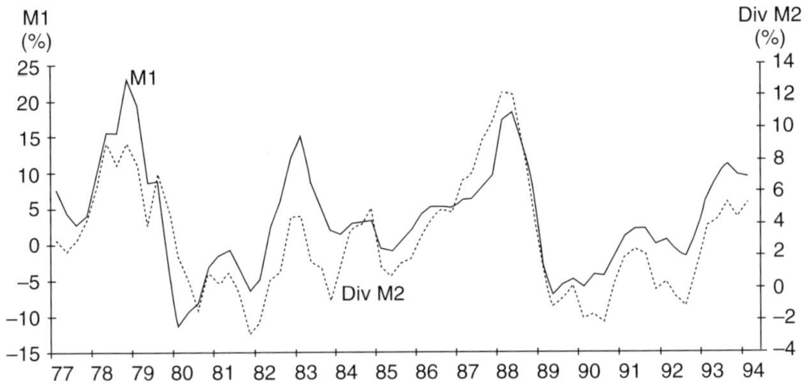

Figure 5.2 Simple-sum M1 versus Divisia M2 (old)

accounts, in principle, are more liquid than savings deposits, as the holders of these accounts have immediate access to their deposits. Furthermore, since around 1993 the interest rates paid for deposits on transaction accounts decreased while the difference between the savings rate and the transaction account rate increased. This means that transaction accounts are now hardly used for store-of-value purposes and should be part of M1 than of M3.

In spite of the well-known shortcomings of simple-sum aggregates, the SNB intends to continue observing and publishing broader simple-sum aggregates. The SNB therefore recently started collecting the transactions accounts deposits separately, to adjust M1. Simultaneously, M2 has also been redefined. It has – as mentioned above – not very helpful indicator features. Since savings deposits in Switzerland are more liquid than time-deposits, whose maturities can exceed the one-year limit substantially, while savings deposits can be withdrawn within a period of notice of six months at most, time-deposits in M2 were replaced by savings deposits. M3 remained unchanged. Since the final definitions are not yet official, provisional approximations of the new aggregates are used. The redefined aggregates are labelled M1a and M1b (see below), and the corresponding Divisia aggregates Divm1a and Divm1b (see Appendix 1).

Definitions of the revised monetary aggregates/components

M1a: Currency in circulation
Demand deposits with banks (mainly held by business)
Demand deposits with the postal giro system
Deposits on transaction accounts (mainly held by customers)

M1b: Savings deposits

M3: Time deposits

5.4 Empirical comparisons of simple-sum and Divisia aggregates

Test set-up and methods employed

In order to evaluate the relative performances of the various monetary aggregates, several empirical tests are implemented below. Three main questions are to be – provisionally – answered by these tests:

1. Does money help to predict prices and output in the Swiss economy? In the short run and/or in the long run?
2. If the answers to the first set of questions are affirmative, are there then some monetary aggregates that perform consistently better than others?
3. And, in particular, do all the Divisia aggregates or just one of them, tend generally to perform better than simple-sum measures of money?

A number of different testing environments are used to get evidence regarding these questions.

To determine the short-run predictive information content of money, traditional Granger-causality tests within low dimension vector auto regressive (VAR) systems in terms of first differenced variables are carried out.[1]

As has meanwhile become common knowledge, Granger-causality testing in first-differenced VAR equations may be hampered by misspecification problems [see, for example, Chrystal and MacDonald (1994), pp. 83 ff.]. The reason is that important long-run relationships among cointegrated I(1) variables may exist – and they are neglected in simple first-differenced VARs. The Johansen-procedure (Johansen, 1988; Johansen and Juselius, 1990) for maximum likelihood estimation of VECMs corrects for this potential problem of normal VAR systems. Therefore, VECMs are also used below to shed light on the relative importance of different monetary aggregates, when possible long-run relationships between money, prices, interest rates and output are taken into account explicitly.

The long-run relationships – if they exist – are of interest by themselves. If the estimated long-run elasticities of money measures with respect to the other variables are in line with theoretically expected values, the cointegrating relationships may with some confidence be interpreted as long-run money-demand functions. Moreover, Granger-causality in the long run may be evaluated by testing the significance of a (single) cointegrating relationship as an error-correction term in the different equations of the VECM.[2]

The normal Granger tests for short-term information content of money regarding inflation are supplemented by a different procedure. There, a structural price equation much in Keynesian spirit is first estimated (see a similar equation in a 'Keynesian model' used in a different context by Judd and Motley, 1992). After that, a test on additional predictive information of lagged money is carried out by including lagged differences of the various monetary aggregates.

The final exercise conducted in these comparisons is a series of two-step Engle–Granger (1987) cointegration regressions of income velocity on the yield of government bonds. Previous studies (Fischer and Peytrignet, 1990) suggest that there may be a long-term relationship between government bond yield and velocity for at least some of the aggregates considered here.[3]

Data used in the tests are the various measures of simple-sum and Divisia money, together with p, y, r_b, and – in the special case of M1a – r_{ta}; p stands for the log of the Swiss consumer price index, y for the log of real gross domestic product, r_b is the yield of federal government bonds, and r_{ta} finally represents the own-rate of interest on transaction accounts. The variables r_b and r_{ta} are scaled in the following way: if R represents the interest rate (yield) in per cent, r is set to log $(1 + R/100)$. Coefficients of r_b or r_{ta} in the long-run relation–ships are thus semi-elasticities. All data except the interest (yield) series are seasonally adjusted by the X-11 procedure.[4]

A general warning is appropriate here before results are presented: sample lengths are extremely limited. The tests conducted are thus marred by possible problems of overparameterisation. As will be seen below, parsimonious modelling[5] is necessary because of the short series available.

Estimations are carried out by means of the *E-Views*® econometric package (QMS, 1994).

Granger causality tests in first-differenced VARs

Bivariate VAR tests of Δm helping to predict Δp

Over the sample period 1980:1 to 1994:1; Granger causality tests with quarterly data yield the following results.

If, in the VAR equation:

$$\Delta p_t = c + \sum_{i=1}^{k} \alpha_i \cdot \Delta\, p_{t-i} + \sum_{i=1}^{l} \beta_i \cdot \Delta\, m_{t-i} + \varepsilon_t \tag{5.1}$$

the information of monetary variables is at first omitted, estimates of:

$$\Delta p_t = c + \sum_{i=1}^{k} \alpha_i \cdot \Delta\, p_{t-i} + \varepsilon_t \tag{5.2}$$

indicate that only Δp_{t-1} needs to be included in the equation according to the Akaike information criterion. Therefore, k is set equal to one, and various lags of Δm_t are then included in Equation (5.2), to yield:

$$\Delta p_t = c + \alpha \cdot \Delta p_{t-i} + \sum_{i=1}^{l} \beta_i \cdot \Delta m_{t-i} + \varepsilon_t \tag{5.3}$$

OLS-estimates of Equation (5.3) lead to the following results for most of the monetary aggregates considered here:

Table 5.1 Test results of equation $\Delta p_t = c + \alpha \cdot \Delta p_{t-1} + \beta_{11} \cdot \Delta m_{t-11} + \varepsilon_t$

	t-statistic	*Prob. (10^{-2})*	*S.E.E. (10^{-2})*	*Rank*
M1	3.21	0.218	.4509	6
M2[1]	0.95	34.5	.4855	11
M3	2.74	0.813	.4603	9
M1a	3.43	0.111	.4460	5
M1b	2.03	4.66	.4727	10
Divm1a	3.45	0.105	.4456	4
Divm1b	3.62	0.06	.4419	3
Divm2	4.07	0.014	.4315	1
Divm2alt	3.87	0.028	.4362	2
Divm3	3.11	0.293	.4530	7
Divm3alt	3.06	0.33	.4539	8

Notes: 1. Special case: significant at lag 6: (*t*-value: 2.18, Prob: $.337 \cdot 10^{-2}$, S.E.E. $.4597 \cdot 10^{-2}$).

- If only short lags l for lagged money growth are included, no significant short-run 'influence' of money on prices can be detected. In addition, and in contrast to results obtained for other countries, the b_is are negative for a number of quarters.
- Lags need to be extended to as far as eleven quarters in order to get significant evidence on predictive information of money growth on inflation. Moreover, if all eleven lags of Δm are included in the equation, the F-test of the hypothesis that all their coefficients are zero leads to a marginal significance level below the 5 per cent mark only for the M1a aggregate.
- But, for all aggregates except M2, the hypothesis that all coefficients of Δm_{t-1} are zero at lags $i = 1, 2, \ldots 10$ can, by far, not be rejected. Therefore, only the eleventh lag is retained in the equation. In the following, significant *t*-statistics for Δm_{t-11} emerge for all monetary aggregates except M2 (see Table 5.1).
- M2 is a special case. Evidence of significant information about future inflation is visible only when the *sixth* lag of the growth in M2 is included in Equation (5.3). Causality in this case is, however, not as one would normally expect. Large M2 growth is not a sign of a currently very expansive monetary policy, but rather a consequence of monetary tightening, as explained above in Section 5.2.

The results in Table 5.1 rank the narrower Divisia measures Divm2 to Divm1a ahead of the simple-sum aggregates. But the additional explanatory power of money growth in the equation is not substantially different among the various aggregates, as the relatively small differences in standard errors of the various equations show.

The results of the estimates between money growth on the eleventh lag and inflation, as well as the rankings of Divm2old, M1, Divm3old, M3 and M2 correspond to the findings reported in Fluri (1990), where a sample period from 1978:4 to 1990:3 was used.[6]

Four-variable VAR tests of money growth helping to predict real output growth

Granger causality tests of money changes containing information on future output growth are conducted using the following equation of a four-variable VAR system:[7]

$$\Delta y_t = c + \sum_{i=1}^{h} \alpha_i \cdot \Delta y_{t-i} + \sum_{i=1}^{j} b_i \cdot \Delta p_{t-i} + \sum_{i=1}^{k} \gamma_i \cdot \Delta r_{b,t-i} + \sum_{i=1}^{l} \delta_i \cdot \Delta m_{t-i} + \varepsilon_t \tag{5.4}$$

Based on the knowledge from earlier results, we again allow for long lag lengths *h, j, k, l* of up to eleven quarters. Because of lack of enough degrees of freedom, a parsimonious VAR equation is estimated for every monetary aggregate. Applying general to specific search, in several steps lags with lowest *t*-statistics are eliminated. The elimination process is stopped when only lagged changes of variables with *t*-statistics exceeding 1.0 in absolute value are left.[8]

Testing the joint hypothesis that all retained lagged money growth rates are zero in this output growth equation leads to the following results (see Table 5.2):

- Short-term changes in all monetary aggregates clearly contain significant information about future real GDP growth.

Table 5.2 Test results of equation

$$\Delta y_t = c + \sum_{i=1}^{h} \alpha_i \cdot \Delta y_{t-i} + \sum_{i=1}^{j} \beta_i \cdot \Delta p_{t-i} + \sum_{i=1}^{k} \gamma_i \cdot \Delta r_{b,t-i} + \sum_{i=1}^{l} \delta_i \cdot \Delta m_{t-i} + \varepsilon_t$$

	F-statistic[1]	*S.L.*[2] *(10^{-4})*	*S.E.E.* *(10^{-2})*	*Rank based on S.E.E.*
M1	6.47	0.52	.379	1
M2[3]	6.58	0.52	.381	2
M3	4.81	5.11	.422	6
M1a	5.83	1.85	.417	5
M1b	4.61	15.20	.453	8
Divm1a	5.44	1.94	.409	4
Divm1b	6.50	0.50	.401	3
Divm2	2.89	123.17	.501	11
Divm2alt	5.30	8.99	.480	10
Divm3	4.14	10.87	.466	9
Divm3alt	5.53	1.80	.447	7

Notes: 1. Test of joint significance of Δm_{t-i} – terms.
2. Marginal significance level.
3. Sum of $\Delta M2_{t-i}$ – coefficients negative.

- M2 again turns out as a special case: the sum of coefficients of its lagged differences is negative, whereas it is positive for all other aggregates.
- Divisia measures do not perform as well as in the case of predictive information on inflation. M1 is 'best' in terms of the standard error of the equation, and Divisia aggregates only do well in their very narrow definitions Divm1b and Divm1a.

Information content of money about the long run? Tests in four-variable VECMs

The four-variable setting Δm, Δp, Δr_b, Δp is again used in the following tests within VECMs. The latter are estimated by the Johansen M. L. procedure implemented in *E-Views*. Because of the limited number of degrees of freedom, again parsimonious modelling is needed. Thus, based on prior knowledge regarding the importance of the eleventh lag of money growth, the four variable VECMs are specified throughout, with the first four plus the eleventh lagged differences of all variables. To assess the existence of possible long-run relationships, Johansen cointegration tests are first performed within the VECM. Johansen's Eigenvalue L. R. test allows us to reject the null hypothesis of no cointegration for all money measures at the 1 per cent significance level in favour of the alternative hypothesis of at least one cointegrating vector. In all cases, a constant term but no deterministic trend is assumed in the cointegrating equations, and a linear deterministic trend in the data is allowed for. M1a, the new transactions money aggregate is an exception in this four-variable cointegration analysis. The hypothesis of non-cointegration can only be rejected (again at a marginal significance level below 1 per cent) when a fifth variable is included in the VECM – namely, the own-rate of interest on transaction accounts, r_{ta}.

The further hypothesis, that there is at most one cointegrating relationship in the VECM, can – in most cases by far – generally *not* be rejected by the L.R. test. Exceptions here are the simple-sum aggregates M2 and M3. For M3, rejection is possible at 1 per cent, for M2 at 5 per cent significance levels. These aggregates thus do not seem related to the other variables of the system by a single long-run (cointegrating) equation. They are therefore not considered in the further investigations of this section.[9]

Table 5.3 displays first the *t*-values of the eleventh lag of money growth, as measured by the various aggregates' corresponding price change equations of the four variable VECMs.[10] These *t*-tests supplement the ones given for the bivariate VAR framework above. They are more appropriate than the latter since the error correction (EC) term – that is, the single cointegrating relationship – clearly plays a significant role in the inflation equation of each VECM. The values of the *t*-statistic of the EC term all exceed 3.0 except in the case of Divm2[11] according to its new definition.

The ranking of the aggregates according to the *t*-statistic of the eleventh lag of their growth rates, and, more importantly, according to the standard errors

Table 5.3 VECM with lags 1 to 4 plus lag 11 for Δs of m, p, y, r_b plus r_{ta} for M1a and error correction term (cointegrating equation), including a constant term but no deterministic trend*

	t-statistic[1]	*S.E.E.*[2] *(10^{-2})*	*Rank S.E.E.*	*Long-run elasticities* ε_p	ε_y
M1	1.06	.3662	8	0.96	0.75
M2		More than one cointegrating vector			
M3		More than one cointegrating vector			
M1a[3]	2.77	.3534	1	0.83	1.71
M1b	1.07	.3677	9	1.21	0.90
Divm1a	1.45	.3579	3	1.08	0.82
Divm1b	1.00	.3610	4	1.01	0.62
Divm2	2.48	.3613	5	0.64	1.28
Divm2alt	2.06	.3564	2	0.51	1.23
Divm3	1.78	.3616	6	0.60	1.20
Divm3alt	1.71	.3647	7	0.60	1.14

Notes: *A trend is allowed for in the data.
1. for Δm_{t-11} in the Δp equation.
2. for Δp – equation.
3. incl. r_{ta}.

of the price-change equations of the VECM, show a slightly different picture than the results discussed in Section 5.3 (see Table 5.1).

The first choice in the present case is simple-sum narrow money in its new definition, M1a, including transactions accounts previously contained in savings deposits. It thus appears that, for this aggregate's information value to be correctly assessed, a simple equation from a bivariate VAR containing only inflation and money growth is particularly inappropriate. Another result worth mentioning concerns Divm2 in its new, more finely subdivided, definition. This aggregate loses its leading position in the bivariate case and falls back to fifth place in the more general model here.

Table 5.3 furthermore displays the estimates of the long-term price and real income elasticities of money as implied by the cointegrating relationship of each VECM. As the long-run relationship not necessarily reflects only the long-run *demand* function for money, no definitive conclusions can be drawn from these elasticities. Nevertheless, it seems worth pointing out that for narrow aggregates such as M1 and Divm1a or Divm1b, the estimated price elasticities lie very close to one. The latter is the value theoretically expected in a money-demand function. As to elasticities, with respect to real GDP (y), they are all positive and thus again compatible with money-demand theory. Yet the high values for broadly-defined Divisia measures, and especially for M1a, raise some doubts. These aggregates perhaps reflect not only the transactions services of money balances but also their services as a store of value. If so, high income elasticities might just capture the effect of rising wealth on money balances held for store of value purposes. Finally, elasticities with respect to the interest rate level, r_b, are not shown in Table 5.3. They are all negative, however, and are thus again compatible with the interpretation that the cointegrating equation reflects mainly a long-term money-demand relationship.

The cointegrating relationship appears, for our data and sample period, with significant *t*-statistics in several of the VECM equations. In the case of M1, for example, it *needs* to be included in the equations for Δm, Δp, and Δy. Even in the Δr_b equation of the VECM for M1, the EC term displays a *t*-statistic of –1.7.

These results – if they correctly reflect reality[12] – have some important implications. First, the presence of the EC-term in the inflation (Δp) equation of the VECM means that money helps to predict prices in the long run.[13] In other words, there is long-term information on future price developments contained in the movement of monetary aggregates. Since the EC term also appears to influence the Δm equation of the VECMs, there is no long-term unidirectional Granger-causality running from money to prices and other variables of the system. Instead, the long-run Granger 'causality' appears to be running both ways: that is, a 'feedback' relationship between money, prices, bond yield and output.[14]

Tests based on a 'structural' price-change equation

In this section, a structural inflation equation is modelled first. It follows 'Keynesian'-type 'sticky price' reasoning with a specification[15] of price change being 'explained' basically by the lagged influence of the output gap between actual and potential GDP. Apart from this, the current quarter change of the (trade-weighted) exchange rate and of foreign (German) consumer prices are supposed to exert short-term influences on Swiss inflation. As in the VAR equations above, one lag of Δp is included. The starting equation appears as follows:

$$\Delta p_t = c + \alpha \cdot \Delta p_{t-1} + \beta \cdot (y_{t-1} - y^*_{t-3}) + \gamma \cdot \Delta \hat{e}_t + \delta \cdot \Delta p^f_t + \epsilon_t \qquad (5.5)$$

where y stands for actual output and y^* for 'potential output',[16] p^f is the log of the foreign CPI, and $\Delta \hat{e}$ is an estimate of the log change of the exchange rate.[17]

After these preliminaries, it is asked, in this Keynesian environment, whether money has – apart from influencing the variables already included in the relationship – additional predictive value for inflation. Including the eleventh quarter lag of money (based on exclusion tests for lags 1 to 10 and on results in VAR equations above) leads to the results documented in Table 5.4.

Lagged money growth clearly has some additional explanatory power when introduced into Equation (5.5). Results are – as in the VAR equations above – again favourable to Divisia indexes such as Divm2. Yet, as in the previous tests, broadly-defined Divisia measures (Divm3) do not perform very well. Again, as in

Table 5.4 Keynesian model

	t-statistic[1]	*S.E.E.* *(10^{-2})*	*Rank*
M1	2.75	.3626	6
M2	0.10	.3868	11
M3	2.07	.3726	9
M1a	3.35	.3526	3
M1b	2.04	.3730	10
Divm1a	3.25	.3543	4
Divm1b	3.49	.3501	1
Divm2	3.46	.3506	2
Divm2alt	2.84	.3613	5
Divm3	2.61	.3649	7/8
Divm3alt	2.61	.3649	7/8

Note: 1. With respect to Δm_{t-11}.

the previous exercise, additional predictive power of the best compared to the worst aggregates appears to be relatively small; standard errors of the various equations clearly differ but, among the more useful aggregates, by not very much.

Engle–Granger unit root tests of a long-term relationship between income velocity and bond yield

A final comparison of our aggregates is done by unit root tests of the residuals from Engle–Granger-type OLS cointegrating regressions of income velocity on the federal bond yield r_b. Logs of velocity (nominal GDP divided by a monetary aggregate) are used in these regressions, both with and without allowing for a linear deterministic trend. Table 5.5 shows the results of the unit root tests of the residuals. Unit root tests are conducted as augmented Dickey–Fuller regressions. The sample period for the unit root regressions runs from 1977:2 to 1994:1. Four lagged changes in residuals of the cointegrating regressions were included in the test equations. Critical values were calculated according to MacKinnon (1991), p. 275.

As Table 5.5 demonstrates, only M1a (at the 5 per cent level) and M3 (at 10 per cent) appear cointegrated with the bond yield if no deterministic trend is allowed for.[18] But if a trend is included in the cointegrating regression, narrowly-defined Divisia aggregates and M1b also pass the cointegration test at the 5 per cent and 10 per cent confidence levels, respectively.

5.5 Conclusions

In order to evaluate the relative performance of various measures of simple-sum and Divisia money, several empirical comparisons were carried out. The main findings of these investigations are summarised as follows:

Table 5.5 ADF-cointegration tests for velocity and bond yield (1977:2 – 1994:1)

	t-statistic[1] *(without trend)*	*t-statistic*[2] *(including trend)*
M1	–0.998	–3.54
M2	–2.75	–2.02
M3	–3.32*	–3.06
M1a	–3.46**	–3.43
M1b	–3.10	–4.20**
Divm1a	–1.39	–3.91*
Divm1b	–0.947	–3.80*
Divm2	–1.16	–3.87*
Divm2alt	–1.06	–3.19
Divm3	–1.24	–3.55
Divm3alt	–1.28	–3.46

Notes: ** 5% S.L.; * 10% S.L.C.V.s are –3.44 (5%) or –3.11(10%) for tests without a trend, and –3.94 (5%) or –3.61 (10%) for tests allowing for a linear deterministic trend in the cointegration equation.

- First of all, for most of the measures studied, money does – as expected – help to predict prices and output in the short run as well as in the long run. The evidence regarding the short run stems from the Granger–causality tests in first differenced VAR equations, as well as in a Keynesian-type 'structural' price-change equation. As to the long run, the existence of a single cointegrating relationship between the levels of money, prices, output and interest rates (bond yields) emerges from tests implemented in VECMs estimated by the Johansen procedure.
- The predictive information content of money regarding shorter-run price movements is in general not impressively high when other available information (such as the lagged inflation rate, the output gap and so on) is taken into account. Nevertheless, there are clearly visible differences between the performance of different aggregates. The more narrowly defined Divisia measures (Divm2, Divm1a, Divm1b) tend to perform best in these comparisons, while Divm3 and Divm3old do not appear as particularly useful measures. The revised, more finely subdivided Divisia index, based on components of M2 (Divm2), outperforms Divm2old, and thus illustrates that good measurement matters.
- Predictive information content with respect to short-term output movements is highest for narrowly defined aggregates – simple-sum and narrow Divisia. This comparison is not as important as others, since interest in money measures mainly stems from their potential use as indicators for future inflation.
- Evidence from tests concerning long-run information content of money is somewhat mixed for Divisia measures. Velocity appears – in contrast to

simple-sum measures M1 and M2 – to be cointegrated with the yield on government bonds for Divm2 and the narrower Divisia aggregates, according to single equation cointegrating regressions. On the other hand, long-run price and GDP elasticities implied by the cointegrating relationships estimated within VECMs appear somewhat implausible for broadly-defined Divisia measures (Divm2, Divm3).

- The revised simple sum aggregate for narrow (transactions) money, M1a, clearly leads to improvements over the present measure, M1. Inclusion of transaction accounts formerly contained in savings deposits appears worthwhile.
- Simple-sum aggregates M2 and M3 in general perform very poorly; and simple-sum M1b does not fare much better. Test results for narrow money M1 are somewhat more promising on the whole; but they appear worse than the ones for simple-sum M1a and better among the Divisia aggregates.

Overall, then, Belongia's (1996) conclusion that 'measurement matters' in applied money research is certainly supported by our results.[19] Simple-sum aggregates, especially the broadly-defined ones such as M2 and M3, may be expected to distort results of empirical work involving money. But, while Divm2 appears to be a good measure of Swiss money on most counts, it cannot be recommended that even its use can be relied on exclusively. A good way of proceeding in practice may be to check on results obtained using simple sum M1a or M1 by repeating estimates and tests with Divm2.

For policy purposes, the use of a Divisia aggregate as the main policy indicator would, in the Swiss case, probably not prove to be very helpful. The SNB at present uses a medium-term target path for the monetary base as a rough guideline for its monetary policy (see SNB, 1993, 1994). The base has the important advantage of being observable daily, whereas broader money is only available for month ends, with a lag, and for a sample of Swiss banks only. Since strict adherence to a medium-term target path is not considered advisable in Switzerland,[20] choice of the aggregate used as the main policy indicator does not appear to be an important policy problem. However, Divm2 is, together with narrow money measures, routinely watched by the SNB to complement the signals it gets from monetary base developments. In this sense, Divisia money has already been useful as a policy indicator in the past – and it will remain so in the future.

Appendix 1

To calculate the Divisia monetary services index we used (except for the transaction accounts) the components according to the definition established in 1975 (for more details, see SNB, 1985 and Fluri, 1994). As far as Divisia M2 and M3 are concerned, we used two versions: in the first, transaction accounts were not taken into account as a separate component. These aggregates correspond to those that have been in use since

1990, called Divisia M2old and Divisia M3old. In the second, we incorporated the transaction accounts as a separate component (called Divisia M2 and Divisia M3).

The different Divisia monetary aggregates consist of the following assets held by individuals and non-bank institutions:

Divm1a	Currency in circulation	(C)
	Demand deposits with banks	(DB)
	Demand deposits with the postal system	(DP)
	Deposits on transaction accounts with banks	(TA)
Divm2	Time deposits: 1976:1–1978:11	
	<3-month residual maturity (r.m.)	(TD3)
	>3-month r.m.	(TD3*p*)
	Time deposits: 1984:12–1994:3	
	<1-month r.m.	(TD1)
	>1-month <3-month r.m.	(TD3)
	>3-month <12-month r.m.	(TD12)
	>12-month r.m.	(TD12*p*)
Divm3	Savings deposits	(SD)
Divm2old	*Without* transaction accounts	
Divm3old	Transaction accounts not separately weighted (same weight as savings accounts)	
Divm1b	Components of Divm1a plus savings deposits	

Own interest rates:

C	Zero
DB	0.25
DP	0.50
TA	Weighted average of the interest rates paid by the Cantonal Banks and the three largest Swiss banks.
TD1	1-month rate } on time deposits at the Euromarket
TD3	2-month rate } on time deposits at the Euromarket
TD12	6-month rate } on time deposits at the Euromarket
TD12*p*/TD3*p*	12-month rate } on time deposits at the Euromarket
SD	Saving rate based on the so-called year-end statistics of the Swiss National Bank; monthly value interpolated by using the average savings rate of the Cantonal Banks.

Benchmark rate

This is the highest rate in each period from the following interest rates: the secondary market yield of federal government bonds, interest rates on cash certificates with the Cantonal and the three largest Swiss banks, the savings rate and the short-term interest rates on deposits at the Euromarket.

Notes

1. No unit root tests are shown; but there are numerous studies relating to the variables concerned which suggest that all the variables used in the tests are I(0) when differenced once.
2. Fischer and Peytrignet (1994) and the sources referred to there [Granger (1986) and Toda and Phillips (1994)].

3. They find cointegration for velocity based on M1b.
4. We are aware of the fact that modern econometricians usually avoid working with seasonally adjusted data. We use the old-fashioned way.
5. See, for example, Davis (1993), p. 13, who restricts a VAR system by application of general-to-specific simplification search to get a PVAR (parsimonious VAR). He estimates a full PVAR system using OLS and a GLS method (SUR), and finds little differences in estimated coefficients. See also Clements and Mizon (1991).
6. The eleven-quarter lag also turns out to be significant when the rationality of Swiss consumers' expectations is tested (Fluri and Spörndli, 1988). The monetary aggregate used in the respective orthogonality tests is the base; the sample includes quarterly data from 1973:4 to 1986:3.
7. For similar tests, see for example, Belongia (1996) or Friedman/Kuttner (1993), where, however, a deterministic trend term was included in the equations as an additional regressor.
8. In the case of M1, the following lag structure is obtained by the described procedure: lags of Δy: 1 to 8, and 10; lags of Δy: 2 to 5, 9, 10, 11; lags of Δr_b 1, 4, 6, 8, 9, 10; lags of Δm: 1 to 5, 7, 8, 10, 11.
9. The existence of more than one cointegrating vector makes economic interpretation of the long-run relationships difficult.
10. Five variables in the case of M1a.
11. The *t*-statistic is 2.92 in this case.
12. Fischer and Peytrignet (1994) (F/P) get different results for a similar VECM in their study of the M1b aggregate. They find, for example, only in the money change equation a significant influence of the EC term, the single cointegrating vector. F/P work with a longer sample period (beginning in 1973) than is used here, and their data are not seasonally adjusted. Furthermore, they only include lags up to four quarters in the VECM. Further research will be necessary to explain the differing results regarding M1b between F/P and the present study.
13. Fischer and Peytrignet (1994) and Granger (1986).
14. As Fischer and Peytrignet (1994) indicate, estimation of single-equation money-demand functions might produce misleading results in such a situation.
15. Judd and Motley (1992) use a similar equation in their 'Keynesian model' to simulate monetary policy rules. The equation used here – Switzerland being a small, open economy – includes changes in the exchange rate and in foreign prices as additional variables.
16. y^* is proxied by a linear deterministic trend of y estimated from 76:1 to 94:1.
17. e is measured as an index of the foreign currency price of the Swiss franc. $\Delta\hat{e}$ is the fitted value from a first stage regression using Δp_t^f, Δr_t^f (change in the 3-month Euro–DM rate) and lagged values of Δp, Δe, e, and Δr_s (change in the 3-month Euro–SWF rate) as instruments. Estimation of this first stage equation spans from 77:1 to 94:1.
18. C.V.s are –3.44 (5%) or –3.11 (10%) for tests without a trend, and –3.94 (5%) or –3.61 (10%) for tests allowing for a linear deterministic trend in the cointegration equation.
19. Our results and conclusions are also broadly in line with the international comparisons presented by Chrystal and MacDonald (1994). Their tests for Swiss money measures are, however, not comprehensive enough. Comparison only of simple-sum M1 and M2 measures with their Divisia counterparts is in the Swiss case a very weak test of the superiority of Divisia indices.
20. Even for the best-measured aggregates, a scientifically precise setting of the medium-term target path is not feasible, because of uncertainty about the correct long-run demand function for money.

References

Belongia, M. T. (1996) 'Measurement Matters: Recent Results from Monetary Economics Re-examined', *Journal of Political Economy*, October, pp. 1065–83.

Chrystal, K. A. and R. MacDonald (1994) 'Empirical Evidence on the Recent Behavior and Usefulness of Simple-sum and Weighted Measures of the Money Stock', in *Money Stock Measurement, Federal Reserve Bank of St Louis Review*, vol. 76, March/April, pp. 73–109.

Clements, M. P. and G. E. Mizon (1991) 'Empirical Analysis of Macroeconomic Time Series – VAR and Structural Models', *European Economic Review*, vol. 35, pp. 887–932.

Davis, E. P. (1993) 'VAR Modelling of the German Economy with Financial Spreads as Key Indicator Variables', Discussion Paper No. 159, LSE Financial Markets Group, London (May).

Engle, R. F. and C. W. J. Granger (1987) 'Cointegration and Error Correction: Representation, Estimation, and Testing', *Econometrica*, vol. 55, pp. 251–76.

Fischer, A. and M. Peytrignet (1991) 'The Lucas Critique in Light of Swiss Monetary Policy', *Oxford Bulletin of Economics and Statistics*, vol. 53, pp. 481–93.

Fischer, A. and M. Peytrignet (1994) 'Geldmengenaggregate: Was bringt die Ausklammerung der Termingelder?', *Geld, Währung und Konjunktur*, Schweizerische Nationalbank, 12/3.

Fluri, R. (1990) 'Monetäre Divisia-Aggregate – eine Alternative zu den traditionellen Geldmengenindikatoren?', *Geld, Währung und Konjunktur*, Schweizerische Nationalbank, 8/4.

Fluri, R. (1994) 'Die Erweiterung der Geldmenge M1 der Schweizerischen Nationalbank um liquide Einlagen auf den Depositen- und Sparkonti', mimeo, Swiss National Bank.

Fluri, R. and E. Spörndli (1988) 'Rationality of Consumers' Price Expectations – Empirical Tests Using Swiss Qualitative Survey Data', in K. H. Oppenländer and G. Poser (eds), *Contributions of Business Cycle Surveys to Empirical Economics* (Aldershot: Gower).

Friedman, B. and K. N. Kuttner (1993) 'Another Look at the Evidence on Monetary-Income Causality', *Journal of Econometrics*, pp. 189–203.

Granger, C. W. J. (1986) 'Developments in the Study of Cointegrated Economic Variables', *Oxford Bulletin of Economics and Statistics*, vol. 51, pp. 451–64.

Johansen, S. (1988) 'Statistical Analysis of Cointegration Vectors', *Journal of Economic Dynamics and Control*, vol. 12, pp. 231–54.

Johansen, S. and K. Juselius (1990) 'The Role of the Constant Term in Cointegration – with Applications to the Demand for Money', *Oxford Bulletin of Economics and Statistics*, vol. 52, pp. 169–210.

Judd, J. P. and B. Motley (1992) 'Controlling Inflation with an Interest Rate Instrument', *Economic Review*, Federal Reserve Bank of San Francisco, No. 3, pp. 3–22.

MacKinnon, James G. (1991) 'Critical Values for Cointegration Tests', in R. F. Engle and C. W. J. Granger (eds), *Long-Run Economic Relationships* (Oxford University Press).

QMS (1994) 'EViews, MicroTSP for Windows, Version 1.0', © Quantitative Micro Software, Irvine Calif.

SNB (Schweizerische Nationalbank) (1993) 'Monetary policy in 1994', *Geld, Währung und Konjunktur*, 11/4.

SNB (Schweizerische Nationalbank) (1994) *Annual Report 1993*.

Toda, H. Y. and P. C. B. Phillips (1994) 'Vector Autoregression and Causality: A Theoretical Overview and Simulation Study', *Econometrics Review*, vol. 13, no. 2, pp. 259–85.

Yue, P. and R. Fluri (1991) 'Divisia Monetary Services Indexes for Switzerland: Are They Useful for Monetary Targeting?', *Federal Reserve Bank of St Louis Review*, vol. 73, September/October, pp. 19–33.

6

Weighted Dutch and German Monetary Aggregates: How Do They Perform as Monetary Indicators for The Netherlands*

Norbert G. J. Janssen and Clemens J. M. Kool

6.1 Introduction

In the 1970s, the heyday of monetarism, 'money matters' gradually became incorporated into mainstream macroeconomics. It was generally recognised that shocks to the money supply formed an important source of business-cycle fluctuations, and that excessive money growth caused inflation in the intermediate run. As a consequence, many central banks switched to a policy of targeting growth rates of monetary aggregates to control inflation. Prime examples are the USA, Switzerland and Germany. Over the years since then, however, most central banks in the industrialised world have again abandoned monetary targeting, although inflation control – or even price stability – remains their dominant policy objective.

An important reason for the current lack of interest in the development of monetary aggregates appears to be the breakdown of money-demand functions in many countries. Structural breaks in the trend path of velocity are considered to be serious impediments to the effective use of monetary targeting.[1] The observed money demand instabilities are often attributed to the occurrence of innovations in financial markets and to the existence of severe measurement error. Simple-sum aggregates are just not appropriate to measure the flow of monetary services when the component assets of these aggregates are imperfect substitutes. Closely related to the observed substitution processes between financial assets are the problems encountered by monetary authorities in defining monetary aggregates properly. Such measurement errors and definition problems are particularly obvious during

* Comments by Coen Oort and Martin Fase on an earlier version of this chapter are gratefully acknowledged. Any remaining errors are, of course, our own.

periods of financial innovation, when the relative degree of liquidity of various financial assets within and outside monetary aggregates is due to change. Weighted aggregates based on index number theory may be more robust in this respect (see Chrystal and MacDonald, 1994 for an extensive cross-country overview).

In this chapter, we add to the existing literature by presenting new empirical evidence on the relative performance of simple-sum and weighted (Divisia) monetary aggregates in the Netherlands over the period 1979–93, with quarterly data. At the M2 and harmonised M3 aggregation level, the indicator[2] properties of simple-sum and Divisia money measures are compared, and simple-sum M1's behaviour is also analysed. Divisia M1 is not investigated, because its indicator properties are similar to sum M1's properties. To date, hardly any work has been done in this direction with Dutch data.[3]

First, the usefulness of simple-sum and Divisia aggregates as monetary policy indicators is evaluated with cointegration and multivariate regression techniques to test for causality between money growth, real growth, inflation and interest rates. Next, the stability of the estimated relations between, on the one hand, the growth of monetary aggregates, and, on the other, inflation and real growth in the Netherlands, is investigated, using out-of-sample forecasts of Dutch inflation and real growth.

Over most of the period investigated in this chapter, the Netherlands has had a fixed exchange rate with Germany. According to the monetary theory of the balance of payments for small, open economies, this makes the Dutch money supply endogenous.[4] Because of the openness of the Dutch economy and the almost fixed exchange rate between the Dutch guilder and the German Mark, real economic growth and inflation in the Netherlands are also heavily affected by foreign developments. Under fixed exchange rates, a country's long-run equilibrium price level should be determined mainly by the anchor country's price level (Kool and Tatom, 1994). Since the anchor country in the EMS is Germany, whose price level is mainly determined by the Bundesbank's anti-inflationary monetary policy, it might additionally be argued that German monetary aggregates affect the Dutch economy. We therefore also analyse the indicator properties of German simple-sum and Divisia aggregates for Dutch inflation and real growth, using the same testing techniques as for Dutch aggregates. By also including Dutch exports of goods and services in the causality analysis, we can examine whether German money growth provides incremental explanatory power for Dutch inflation and real income growth.

The chapter is organised as follows. In Section 6.2 we give a short overview of Dutch monetary policy in past decades. Section 6.3 briefly discusses the data. In Sections 6.4 and 6.5 short- and long-run dynamics are taken into account in the causality test, using Dutch and German (simple-sum and Divisia) monetary aggregates, respectively. Section 6.6 presents out-of-sample forecasts of Dutch inflation and real growth obtained with Dutch and German aggregates. Section 6.7 contains a summary and conclusions.

6.2 Dutch monetary policy: an overview

From an institutional point of view, the Dutch central bank (DNB) is not absolutely independent, because the so-called 'Bank law' points out that the Minister of Finance has the right to give directions to the DNB with respect to policy. However, exercising this right would entail a very arduous procedure in which the government has to justify in parliament its decision to give directions to the DNB. To date, the Dutch Minister of finance has never exercised this right. *De facto*, therefore, the Dutch central bank may be regarded as one of the most independent central banks in the world. Its policy, though taking into account real developments, is primarily orientated towards inflation control, and Dutch inflation has been among the lowest in the world for many years.

In a small, open economy like that of the Netherlands, the nominal and real effects of domestic monetary policy, of course, depend significantly on the prevailing exchange-rate system. Under the Bretton Woods system of fixed but adjustable exchange rates, domestic output stabilisation was the main internal policy goal for monetary authorities in most countries, including the Netherlands. Stabilisation of the exchange rate of the guilder was achieved by foreign-exchange market interventions. The Dutch central bank usually imposed (relatively successfully) direct credit restrictions on the banking system in order to control domestic money creation. Monetary aggregates were used as indicators of real economic growth.

After the breakdown of the Bretton Woods system the guilder entered a period characterised by unstable exchange rates, although the fluctuations with respect to European currencies were relatively small because of the 'snake' arrangement. Domestic monetary policy in this period was formulated in terms of the planned rate of growth of a broad monetary aggregate (M2). Indirect credit restrictions were used to obtain the target, while the liquidity ratio (defined as the broad money supply (M2) divided by nominal GNP) served as the main policy indicator both for inflation and for real growth. Interest rates were not used as policy instruments, but resulted from the policy aimed at stabilising the liquidity ratio (Fase, 1985). However, the Dutch central bank was not very successful in achieving its objectives during the 1970s. High inflation and low economic growth resulted.

Since the beginning of the European Monetary System (EMS) in 1979, the Dutch central bank's primary intermediate policy objective has been to keep the exchange rate of the guilder fixed to the German Mark by using interest rates. The reason behind this specific policy is that price stability (which by now has become the single domestic monetary policy objective) in a small country such as the Netherlands can best be achieved by keeping the exchange rate credibly fixed to the currency of a country where the inflation rate is low (Svensson, 1994).

During the early 1980s, the DNB continued to use the liquidity ratio as a monetary policy indicator. Recognising the essential endogeneity of the money supply under fixed exchange rates and (almost) perfect capital mobility, the DNB initially aimed at restraining the domestic component of M2 through credit controls to support the credibility of the exchange-rate policy. Both the increased magnitude of international capital flows and the observed trend breaks in the liquidity ratio in the 1980s[5] have led the DNB to give ever more priority to the objective of exchange-rate stability *per se* (Kool, 1995). In October 1992, the harmonised M3 monetary aggregate was adopted as the monetary indicator in the context of the co-ordination of monetary policy in Europe. This indicator is currently monitored to contribute to the maintenance of the exchange rate of the guilder.

Even though the Dutch money supply is largely endogenous because of the fixed exchange rate, however, it is still possible that Dutch monetary aggregates serve as an indicator of inflation or future economic activity. This may be true, especially because of the Dutch policy of adapting the discount rate almost immediately in response to changes in the German discount rate. In the empirical part, we test for the appropriateness of Dutch simple-sum and Divisia money measures as indicators for real growth and/or inflation in the Netherlands. Interest rates are also included in the analysis because of their important role in Dutch exchange-rate policy. The Dutch central bank can control short-term interest rates to some extent with the discount rate. If short interest rates are also closely related to the state of the economy, they may serve as an alternative indicator of future inflation or real growth in the Netherlands.

6.3 Description of the data

The monetary aggregates[6] in this chapter (M1, M2 and harmonised M3) are calculated using quarterly data on monetary asset quantities and their respective user costs in the Netherlands over the period 1979:4–1993:4, according to the definitions adopted by the DNB since 1992. Currency and demand deposits together constitute the narrow aggregate M1. M2 consists of M1 plus short-term time-deposits with a maturity of less than two years (since their introduction in 1986 also including Certificates of Deposit) and foreign currency deposits held in banks located in the Netherlands. The broadest aggregate (harmonised M3) is obtained by adding short-term savings deposits to M2.

Generally, the assets included in the monetary aggregates are risk-free, so that different returns should reflect differences in liquidity. Quarterly data on quantities and interest rates of the financial assets are mainly taken from the quarterly bulletins published by the DNB.[7] All series were seasonally adjusted before we used them in the empirical part of this chapter.

The Divisia aggregates (Q_t) are constructed using Barnett's method (1980) with 1962:1 as the base quarter for Divisia M2, and 1970:4 as the base for Divisia M3. In logarithmic form this gives:

$$\log Q_t = \log Q_{t-1} + \sum_{i=1}^{N} s^*_{i,t}(\log m_{i,t} - \log m_{i,t-1}) \tag{6.1}$$

where m_i is the stock of monetary asset i, and t is a time subscript. $S^*_{i,t}$ (the average expenditure share of asset i) is defined in Equation (6.2):

$$s^*_{i,t} = 0.5(s_{i,t} + s_{i,t-1}) \tag{6.2}$$

where

$$s_{i,t} = \frac{p_{i,t}m_{i,t}}{\sum_{i=1}^{N} p_{i,t}m_{i,t}} \tag{6.3}$$

in Equation (6.3) p_i represents the opportunity cost of holding asset i during one quarter. This opportunity cost is defined analogously to Barnett (1978):

$$p_{i,t} = 0.25\pi^*_t \frac{(R_t - r_{i,t})}{(1 + R_t)^{0.25}} \tag{6.4}$$

where π is the level of the CPI, R denotes the benchmark interest rate (the highest rate achievable regardless of risk and maturity), and r_i is the own interest rate on monetary asset i. The benchmark asset is a non-monetary asset with a high interest return, which is known with certainty for a given time period; the benchmark asset is mainly held to transfer wealth intertemporally. The benchmark interest rate used here is the highest holding-period yield among the following: the yield on long-term government bonds; on call money; local government liabilities; euroguilder deposits; and three-month AIBOR plus 0.25 per cent (used as a proxy for short-term notes issued by the private sector).

In periods in which new financial assets are introduced, Fisher's Ideal index (Q^F_t) is used instead of the Divisia index. This index is computed with the following equation:

$$Q^F_t = Q_{t-1}\left[\frac{\sum_{i=1}^{M} p_{i,t}m_{i,t} \sum_{i=1}^{N} p_{i,t-1}m_{i,t}}{\sum_{i=1}^{N} p_{i,t}m_{i,t-1} \sum_{i=1}^{N} p_{i,t-1}m_{i,t-1}}\right]^{0.5} \tag{6.5}$$

where N is the number of assets before the introduction of new assets and M is the number of assets after this introduction. The Divisia index cannot be used to take into account new assets, because it adds the weighted growth rates of individual financial assets. In the period following the introduction of new assets, we again use the Divisia index (Equation (6.1)). Then, Q_{t-1} is replaced by the Fisher index from the previous period (Q^F_{t-1}). With this procedure, new

Table 6.1 Summary statistics for quarterly growth rates of monetary aggregates (1979:4–1993:4)

	Mean	*Standard deviation*
Sum M1	0.0152	0.0206
Sum M2	0.0192	0.0210
Divisia M2	0.0176	0.0197
Sum M3	0.0164	0.0112
Divisia M3	0.0158	0.0113

assets can easily be incorporated into the Divisia aggregate time series without causing serious breaks.[8] As Barnett (1980, 1981) shows, the difference between the Fisher Ideal and the Divisia index is only in the third decimal. Both indices belong to the class of superlative indices (Diewert, 1974).

Table 6.1 presents summary statistics for the growth rates of M1, M2, M3, and Divisia M2 and Divisia M3. It appears that the mean quarterly growth rates of the Divisia aggregates are lower than the corresponding values for their sum equivalents. The standard deviation of Divisia M2's growth rate is smaller than the one for sum M2. Overall, sum M1 has the lowest mean growth rate, but the M3 aggregates' growth rates show lower standard deviations. Apparently, the non-M1 components (which possess some degree of liquidity) have been responsible for most of the growth in the broad simple-sum aggregates in the Netherlands. This may also explain why the Divisia M2 and Divisia M3 aggregates have grown at a higher rate than simple-sum M1. It also indicates that a monetary aggregate consisting solely of the M1 components currency and demand deposits does not measure the total flow of monetary services appropriately.

6.4 Causality tests and long-run dynamics

The quantity theory of money hypothesises a proportional relationship between money growth and inflation in the long run, assuming velocity growth of monetary aggregates and real income growth (or better, potential output growth) are stationary series. In the short run, however, real national income varies considerably, which may be partly caused by money growth. Testing the relation between money growth on the one hand, and real income growth and inflation on the other, may provide useful insights into the role of money in the determination of nominal income. In this section, we investigate the causality between money (defined either as simple-sum or Divisia aggregates), prices, income and interest rates over the sample period 1979–93.

To investigate the (short-run) causal relations between the monetary and the real sectors of the economy, we have to take into account the time-series properties of the individual variables and any long-run relationships between them. First, the variables in the causality vectors should be stationary. Furthermore, a test on cointegration between the variables should determine whether any error correction terms have to be added to the causality vectors in order to incorporate some longer-run information that is present in the variables.

The stationarity of the variables included in the causality tests is examined by testing for unit roots in each variable separately, using the ADF-statistic (see Dickey and Fuller, 1979). The results from these tests are also used to decide on the correct order of differencing of the variables in the cointegration tests.[9] Only the short-term interest rate is stationary over the levels. At the 10 per cent significance level, all other variables contain a unit root. We assume these series to be I(1) from now on.

Next, we focus on the existence of cointegrating vectors among real national income, the price deflator, a monetary aggregate (all in logarithms), and the level of the short-term interest rate. In total, we have to analyse the cointegrating properties for five cases (since we distinguish five money measures). The variables appearing in the respective vectors should be I(1) or I(0) processes (see Johansen, 1988, 1991; and Johansen and Juselius, 1990).[10] The test statistics used to evaluate the number of cointegrating vectors are the trace statistics which test the null hypothesis that there are at most r cointegrating relationships against the alternative of n (=4) vectors, and the maximum Eigenvalue test statistic (λ_{max}), which tests the null hypothesis of r cointegrating vectors against the alternative of $r + 1$ vectors.

Table 6.2 gives the results of the Johansen–Juselius (1990) test on cointegration for the sample 1979:4–1993:4, using four lags of the levels of

Table 6.2 Trace and λ_{max} statistics (1979:4–1993:4)

Null hypothesis	*5% critical value*	*Sum M1*	*Trace* *Sum M2*	*Div. M2*	*Sum M3*	*Div. M3*
$r \leq 3$	9.24	0.21	0.23	0.01	0.41	1.05
$r \leq 2$	19.96	13.56	11.48	12.05	11.41	12.21
$r \leq 1$	34.91	41.68*	29.66	30.44	37.26*	36.71*
$r = 0$	53.12	82.49*	60.79*	58.82*	67.10*	69.22*
Null hypothesis	*5% critical value*	*Sum M1*	*Sum M2*	*Div. M2*	*Sum M3*	*Div. M3*
$r = 3$ or $r = 4$	9.24	0.21	0.23	0.01	0.41	1.05
$r = 2$ or $r = 3$	15.67	13.35	11.25	12.04	11.01	11.16
$r = 1$ or $r = 2$	22.00	28.12*	18.18	18.39	25.84*	24.50*
$r = 0$ or $r = 1$	28.14	40.81*	31.12*	28.38*	29.84*	32.51*

*Note:** Significant at 5 per cent level.

the respective variables in the cointegration analysis. Critical values are taken from Osterwald-Lenum (1992). We conclude that, in the five cases analysed, either one or two cointegrating vectors exist that have to be incorporated in the causality tests.

The Granger-causality tests are carried out with a vector consisting of stationary variables: consequently, real national income growth, inflation, the growth rate of a monetary aggregate, and the short-term interest rate level are included in the causality vector. In this set-up, the monetary effects on real income growth and inflation can be examined separately.

Causality is then analysed by testing the null hypothesis that all lags of a variable can be omitted from the regression. The number of lags for the variables is determined by the lag selection criterion and the variance–covariance matrix of the estimated coefficients is adjusted for heteroskedasticity. Linear Wald statistics, which have a central chi-squared distribution, are presented in Table 6.3, with p-values in parentheses.[11] Additionally, variables can have a long-run effect through the error-correction (ECM) terms. Our interest is mainly in the relative performance of simple-sum and Divisia monetary aggregates as indicators of monetary policy, and in the interest rate's performance. A full discussion of these results is available from the authors.

For each monetary aggregate, the four dependent variables are estimated with a VAR system in which a possible correlation between the residuals of the different equations is taken into account. In order to arrive at a parsimonious VAR system, we use the results of univariate causality regressions to ensure that only lags of the different variables with a t-statistic larger than one are included in the VAR regressions. Of course, this leads to a bias of rejecting the null hypothesis that all lags of a certain variable can be excluded from the regression. Most results of the exclusion tests appear to be significantly different from zero.

Table 6.3 shows that the error-correction terms are significant in all regressions, except in the inflation equation with sum M2 as the money measure. Furthermore, all monetary aggregates, except sum M3, turn out to be good indicators of real income growth via the short-run (all error-correction terms for real growth are also significant). Inflation is significantly influenced by all aggregates, except sum M2. Overall, the indicator properties of the respective monetary aggregates are very similar in this VAR system; only sum M2 appears unfit as an indicator of inflation.

The causality test results obtained with multivariate regression techniques may give rise to the following monetary policy implications. Short-term interest rates may be used as the main indicator of inflation because of the Fisher effect. On the other hand, the Dutch central bank can control short-term interest rates relatively easily with the discount rate. Since interest rates are affected both by inflationary expectations and by the discount rate, the exact relationship between short interest rates and inflation may be ambiguous. If the Fisher effect dominates, interest rates and inflation will

Table 6.3 Exclusion tests in VAR causality regressions (1979:4–1993:4)[†]

	Y_r	*SM1*	*P*	*R*
SM1	14.22 (0.0066)	19.80 (0.0002)	20.73 (0.0139)	10.01 (0.0185)
Y_r	83.54 (0.0000)	9.49 (0.0087)	81.47 (0.0000)	3.49 (0.3221)
P	35.53 (0.0000)	22.95 (0.0000)	140.98 (0.0000)	0.45 (0.8004)
R	–	66.59 (0.0000)	9.74 (0.0018)	244.67 (0.0000)
ECM	13.32 (0.0013)	21.38 (0.0000)	27.88 (0.0000)	5.56 (0.0619)
	Y_r	*SM2*	*P*	*R*
SM2	9.31 (0.0095)	37.31 (0.0000)	1.51 (0.2198)	9.94 (0.0069)
Y_r	61.81 (0.0000)	10.64 (0.0049)	164.31 (0.0000)	0.18 (0.9123)
P	53.09 (0.0000)	18.71 (0.0003)	120.57 (0.0000)	1.48 (0.6857)
R	5.21 (0.0225)	18.43 (0.0004)	3.70 (0.0546)	434.93 (0.0000)
ECM	4.22 (0.0400)	10.49 (0.0012)	0.64 (0.4232)	19.44 (0.0000)
	Y_r	*DM2*	*P*	*R*
DM2	21.98 (0.0012)	16.22 (0.0010)	10.91 (0.0276)	2.38 (0.1230)
Y_r	98.54 (0.0000)	26.60 (0.0002)	151.89 (0.0000)	5.99 (0.1121)
P	54.1 (0.0000)	34.97 (0.0000)	230.37 (0.0000)	11.61 (0.0205)
R	5.74 (0.0166)	52.85 (0.0000)	–	226.88 (0.0000)
ECM	23.61 (0.0000)	18.84 (0.0000)	27.72 (0.0000)	8.08 (0.0045)
	Y_r	*SM3*	*P*	*R*
SM3	2.45 (0.1174)	47.90 (0.0000)	16.79 (0.0021)	7.05 (0.3162)
Y_r	80.40 (0.0000)	–	108.26 (0.0000)	0.04 (0.9798)
P	52.32 (0.0000)	19.48 (0.0001)	162.71 (0.0000)	1.65 (0.6473)
R	4.74 (0.0294)	8.29 (0.0403)	8.98 (0.0027)	236.22 (0.0000)
ECM	18.24 (0.0001)	32.10 (0.0000)	25.33 (0.0000)	11.87 (0.0026)
	Y_r	*DM3*	*P*	*R*
DM3	5.54 (0.0626)	23.55 (0.0006)	18.50 (0.0003)	2.91 (0.9834)
Y_r	77.50 (0.0000)	0.64 (0.4231)	98.13 (0.0000)	2.65 (0.6181)
P	51.84 (0.0000)	20.02 (0.0002)	134.69 (0.0000)	0.32 (0.5696)
R	3.52 (0.0606)	6.48 (0.0109)	14.89 (0.0001)	271.48 (0.0000)
ECM	11.98 (0.0025)	21.10 (0.0000)	18.94 (0.0001)	8.47 (0.0145)

Notes: [†]Column headings indicate the dependent variable. Entries are Wald statistics with probability values in parentheses. – indicates that lags of this variable are not included in the regression because of insignificance.

move in the same direction. But if the DNB's control over short-term interest rates dominates, an increase in the discount rate will cause short interest rates to rise as well. In turn, this may lead to less inflation in the future. In addition, the ambiguous relationship between short interest rates and inflation may be a consequence of the feedback from inflation to the discount rate. Because of the Bundesbank's tight anti-inflationary policy, higher inflationary pressures in Germany may cause the Bundesbank to raise the discount rate. The close relation between the German and the Dutch inflation rate (see Berk and Winder, 1994) will usually imply that, in such circumstances, Dutch inflation is also higher.[12] In order to stabilise the guilder/DMark exchange rate (and to reduce inflation) the Dutch discount rate will be raised as well, and short-term interest rates will rise. In the future, these higher interest rates may reduce inflation (assuming that the anti-inflationary policy is effective). Short-term interest rates, then, are also useful indicators of future inflation. Of course, the credibility of the DNB's policy in keeping the exchange-rate fixed (and, consequently, in fighting inflation) is a crucial factor in the final relationship between the discount rate and inflation. If short interest rates are relatively easily controllable via the discount rate, and if these interest rates are, on the other hand, closely related to inflation, using these interest rates as indicators of future inflation contributes to the effectiveness of the DNB's anti-inflationary monetary policy.

The results in Table 6.3 also show that, in particular, the Divisia monetary aggregates could be adopted as additional indicators of inflation. Of these, Divisia M3 might be preferred because it has very good indicator properties for inflation and also appears to be a reasonable indicator for real income growth. We do not like to choose Divisia M2 as the inflationary indicator, since weak separability tests have thrown some doubt on the appropriateness of using M2 as a monetary aggregate (see Janssen, 1995).[13] M1 could also be used as real and/or nominal indicator of monetary policy, but M1 does not measure the flow of monetary services appropriately (see Section 6.3). For simplicity, it should also be preferred to use as few monetary indicators as possible. Summarising, short-term interest rates could be used as the primary nominal indicator, and Divisia M3 as an additional nominal and primary real indicator.

6.5 The impact of German monetary aggregates on the Dutch economy

In this section we test the indicator properties of German monetary aggregates for Dutch inflation and real income growth. In a fixed exchange rate system such as the EMS, the equilibrium domestic price level in a small country is determined by the ratio between, on the one hand, the product of the nominal exchange rate (in domestic currency units per unit of foreign currency) plus the foreign price level, and, on the other, the equilibrium real exchange rate (see Kool and Tatom, 1994). Since the nominal exchange rate is fixed, the main determinant of the long-run domestic price level is then the foreign price level. As a consequence of the pegging of the exchange rate, the domestic money stock in a small country becomes endogenous (demand-determined).

Theoretically, equilibrium price levels and inflation in the smaller EMS member countries will, among other factors, be determined primarily by price developments in Germany. The German Bundesbank has been using monetary targeting for many years in order to achieve domestic price stability. This policy has contributed to the relatively close link between money and prices (and inflation) in Germany. Since the Bundesbank determines monetary policy in the EMS, it is likely that economic developments – and particularly inflation – in other countries participating in the EMS will also be closely related to the German money supply. Kool and Tatom (1994) use the P^* approach to show that German monetary conditions have a more important impact on inflationary pressures in the surrounding small countries than do monetary conditions within these countries. This holds in particular for Austria and the Netherlands. The Dutch inflation rate has been very closely related to the German inflation rate over the EMS era (Berk and Winder, 1994).

The Netherlands has followed the German lead almost perfectly in the 1980s, except in 1983, when a 2 per cent devaluation of the guilder took place. Because of the exchange rate agreement, the Dutch central bank uses interest rates to stabilise the exchange rate, causing the money supply to be largely endogenous. Since the economies of Germany and the Netherlands are so closely integrated and the Bundesbank adheres to an anti-inflationary policy of monetary targeting, German monetary aggregates may be good indicators of Dutch inflation and real growth. A crucial factor for this relationship to be present is the credibility of the fixed exchange rate policy of the Dutch central bank.[14] Data for German simple-sum and Divisia aggregates are available for the period 1975–93.[15] We investigate causality relations between the growth rates of German monetary aggregates and Dutch real income growth, inflation, short-term interest rates, and the growth rate of Dutch exports of goods and services. The latter are included in the analysis because of their important role for the Dutch economy.

Table 6.4 shows the results of cointegration tests between German monetary aggregates (sum and Divisia M2 and M3) and the Dutch real income, price level, short-term interest rate and exports. Generally we find evidence of one cointegration relationship over the sample 1979:4–1993:4. Table 6.5 displays the results of multivariate causality tests when the role of various German aggregates and Dutch exports for the Dutch economy is taken into account. Lag selection tests lead us to include long lag lengths for German monetary aggregates and for exports in the equations for Dutch real income growth, inflation and the short interest rate, indicating that the Dutch economy reacts more slowly to foreign factors than to corresponding domestic developments.

Overall, significant results dominate in the VAR system. All error-correction terms are (highly) significant, except in the equations for real income growth and inflation when Divisia M3 is included. Thus generally there is evidence of the cointegrating vector affecting the short-run dynamics between German money and the Dutch economy. All four German aggregates have a highly

Table 6.4 Trace and λ_{max} statistics with German monetary aggregates (1979:4–1993:4)[†]

		Trace	
Sum M2	*Divisia M2*	*Sum M3*	*Divisia M3*
0.17	0.06	3.73	0.15
12.92	12.08	8.03	7.04
26.74	24.82	25.98	25.56
52.07	46.90	53.16	50.73
90.01*	84.11*	92.31*	89.29*
		λ_{max}	
Sum M2	*Divisia M2*	*Sum M3*	*Divisia M3*
0.17	0.06	3.73	0.15
12.75	12.02	4.30	6.88
13.82	12.74	17.95	18.52
25.33	22.08	27.18	25.18
37.94*	37.22*	39.15*	38.56*

Note: [†]For an explanation of symbols, test statistics and critical values see Table 6.2.

significant impact on Dutch real income. Dutch interest rates appear to be explained well by German sum M2 and the two M3 aggregates (directly and indirectly), whereas Divisia M2 only affects Dutch interest rates significantly via the error-correction term. Since monetary targets in Germany are expressed in terms of the growth rates of M3, and the Dutch central bank uses short-term interest rates to stabilise the exchange rate of the guilder, it should not be surprising that we find evidence of a close relationship between both German M3 aggregates and the Dutch interest rate.

All German monetary aggregates, except Divisia M3, appear as significant determinants of Dutch inflation (Divisia M2 is only marginally significant). With regard to the error-correction terms, there is hardly any difference in explanatory power of these three German aggregates for Dutch inflation. This confirms the theoretical view that the Dutch inflation rate is determined by German monetary policy through long-run equilibrium-restoring tendencies. With respect to the (short-run) indicator properties of German aggregates for Dutch inflation, the two simple-sum aggregates dominate their Divisia counterparts. This outcome is consistent with the results obtained for sum M3 in Germany in Herrmann *et al.* (1995). Dutch exports of goods and services appear significant in explaining Dutch inflation and real growth. Overall, the VAR system results for German monetary aggregates indicate that these foreign money measures, in addition to Dutch exports, contain important information about the behaviour of Dutch inflation and real income growth.

Table 6.5 Exclusion tests in VAR causality regressions between German monetary aggregates and the Dutch real economy (1979:4–1993:4)[†]

	Y_r	P	R
SGM2**	35.02 (0.0000)	37.07 (0.0000)	186.02 (0.0000)
Y_r	113.77 (0.0000)	45.13 (0.0000)	41.47 (0.0000)
P	85.09 (0.0000)	191.47 (0.0000)	85.07 (0.0000)
R	–	23.76 (0.0000)	12.70 (0.0017)
X	28.27 (0.0001)	60.25 (0.0000)	–
ECM	18.73 (0.0000)	31.37 (0.0000)	52.86 (0.0000)
DGM2**	23.15 (0.0000)	2.21 (0.1373)	0.65 (0.4197)
Y_r	67.41 (0.0000)	243.71 (0.0000)	1.74 (0.6278)
P	54.26 (0.0000)	149.96 (0.0000)	0.82 (0.8441)
R	–	10.19 (0.0014)	223.79 (0.0000)
X	35.84 (0.0000)	54.37 (0.0000)	0.12 (0.7290)
ECM	12.95 (0.0003)	7.68 (0.0056)	25.79 (0.0000)
SGM3	42.85 (0.0000)	12.45 (0.0060)	51.89 (0.0000)
Y_r	157.91 (0.0000)	173.85 (0.0000)	0.91 (0.6356)
P	82.68 (0.0000)	167.98 (0.0000)	8.53 (0.0363)
R	18.59 (0.0000)	–	295.74 (0.0000)
X	57.89 (0.0000)	13.61 (0.0035)	9.47 (0.0504)
ECM	4.20 (0.0403)	4.09 (0.0431)	16.70 (0.0000)
DGM3	7.66 (0.0217)	1.46 (0.2263)	10.89 (0.0043)
Y_r	95.15 (0.0000)	182.02 (0.0000)	6.68 (0.0829)
P	42.18 (0.0000)	111.49 (0.0000)	3.59 (0.3087)
R	4.05 (0.0443)	6.71 (0.0096)	225.93 (0.0000)
X	21.23 (0.0034)	48.98 (0.0000)	–
ECM	2.28 (0.1309)	1.45 (0.2290)	17.89 (0.0000)

Notes: [†] See Table 6.3 for an explanation of the layout and symbols used in this table.
** SGM2 and DGM2 refer to German sum and Divisia M2, respectively.

We also find evidence that interest rates significantly influence inflation, except when German sum M3 is the explanatory money stock variable. This confirms the results from the causality tests with Dutch aggregates (Table 6.3) where the short-term interest rate also turns out to be a good indicator of inflation. In combination, the significant influence of German simple-sum monetary aggregates and of the Dutch short-term interest rate on Dutch inflation may be a result of the credible Dutch policy of stabilising the guilder/DMark exchange rate with short-term interest rates. It may also be an indication that the relative weight of price stability in the objective function of the Dutch central bank has increased over the sample.

6.6 Out-of-sample forecasts of Dutch inflation and real income growth

As an additional test on the relative performance of simple-sum and Divisia monetary aggregates we analyse the stability of the estimated relationships between, on the one hand, the growth of the respective (Dutch and German) monetary aggregates, and on the other, inflation and real growth in the Netherlands. This section presents one-period and eight-period ahead out-of-sample forecasts for Dutch inflation and real income growth, applying univariate regressions of inflation and real income growth. Using rolling regressions, the inflation and real income equations are first re-estimated over the sample 1979:4–1985:4. Then we forecast one period (1986:1) and eight periods (1987:4) ahead. In the eight-period-ahead forecasts of inflation and real growth we use forecast values for the first seven lags of the respective dependent variable. After these first forecasts, the initial sample is extended with one observation and the same procedure is repeated until the last forecasts are obtained. With this method, we get thirty-two one-period-ahead forecasts, and twenty-five eight-period-ahead forecasts for inflation and real income growth in the Netherlands for each monetary aggregate. The relative performance of the aggregates is evaluated in Table 6.6 by the root mean square forecast error (RMSE) and the mean absolute forecast error (MAE).

In general, it is clear that the forecast errors increase with the forecast horizon, although Dutch M1 and Divisia M3 forecast inflation better over a longer horizon than just one quarter ahead. According to the RMSE, the same applies to real growth forecasts obtained with Dutch Divisia M2. The differences in forecasting performance of the monetary aggregates are

Table 6.6 Forecast errors of Dutch real income growth and inflation in percentages (initial estimation sample: 1979:4–1985:4)

	Real income growth				*Inflation*			
	One period ahead		*Eight periods ahead*		*One period ahead*		*Eight periods ahead*	
	RMSE	*MAE*	*RMSE*	*MAE*	*RMSE*	*MAE*	*RMSE*	*MAE*
Dutch M1	0.7500	0.5985	0.9360	0.7919	0.7367	0.4636	0.6122	0.4565
Dutch M2	0.8613	0.6738	0.9026	0.7479	0.4715	0.3863	0.4628	0.3954
Dutch Divisia M2	0.6195	0.4831	0.6039	0.4905	0.4904	0.4051	0.5826	0.5209
Dutch M3	0.8323	0.6349	0.9806	0.7658	0.5239	0.4273	0.7723	0.6086
Dutch Divisia M3	0.7923	0.6454	0.9170	0.6764	0.4565	0.3260	0.3853	0.3151
German M2	0.8867	0.7011	0.7909	0.6496	0.5104	0.3952	0.7958	0.5215
German Divisia M2	1.0624	0.7697	1.1901	0.9933	0.3896	0.3454	0.4746	0.4041
German M3	0.8850	0.6739	0.8077	0.6268	0.6786	0.4670	0.9287	0.5758
German Divisia M3	0.8177	0.6509	0.9242	0.7722	0.4061	0.3319	0.4872	0.3995

relatively small. The magnitude of the forecast errors obtained with German monetary aggregates is similar to the errors with Dutch aggregates. Concerning real income growth, our results from previous estimations are confirmed, in that the Dutch Divisia aggregates show smaller forecast errors than their simple-sum equivalents. Overall, Dutch Divisia M2 shows the smallest forecast errors for real income growth at both intervals. These findings are consistent with the results in Section 6.4, where Divisia M2 is the best real indicator, and where Divisia aggregates perform marginally better than their sum equivalents. In the main, sum M1 forecasts real growth and inflation with larger errors than do the two Divisia aggregates (only the short-run forecast errors of real growth are smaller with M1 than with Divisia M3). This may be another indication that M1 does not measure the flow of monetary services appropriately. At the one-period horizon, German Divisia M3 forecasts Dutch real income growth best of all four German aggregates. The German sum aggregates forecast real growth better at the longer horizon than just one period ahead. As a result, German sum aggregates outperform their Divisia counterparts as real income growth indicators at this longer forecast horizon.

With respect to inflation, Dutch Divisia M3 outperforms its sum equivalent. This aggregate also has the overall best forecasting performance at longer horizons. This confirms our view that Divisia M3 should be used as an indicator of inflation. Sum M3 has the worst inflation-forecasting ability at longer horizons. Dutch sum M2 predicts inflation slightly better than Divisia M2, an outcome that contradicts the results obtained before. These ambiguous results at the M2 aggregation level may be caused by the inappropriateness of M2 as a weakly separable aggregate. The German Divisia aggregates always forecast Dutch inflation with smaller errors than their simple-sum equivalents. This observation is in contrast with the results provided by the causality tests (see Table 6.5), where German sum aggregates appear to be better indicators of Dutch inflation. The relation between the German Divisia aggregates and Dutch inflation seems more stable than the corresponding relationship of German sum aggregates. According to the RMSE, German Divisia M2 performs even better than the Dutch aggregates as an indicator of inflation at the one-period horizon.

6.7 Conclusion

In this chapter we focused on the relative performance of simple-sum and Divisia monetary aggregates as indicators of future real growth and inflation in the Netherlands. Because the Dutch central bank has been targeting the exchange rate with Germany during the 1970s and 1980s to ensure price stability, this chapter also analyses whether German money measures are potential indicators of Dutch inflation and real growth. The importance of the short-term interest rate for the stabilisation of the exchange rate of the guilder to the German Mark leads us to include the short-term interest rate as a potential monetary indicator as well.

Taking into account short- and long-run considerations, it appears that all Dutch monetary aggregates, except sum M2, show a significant impact on inflation between 1979 and 1993. Divisia aggregates' growth rates outperform their simple-sum equivalents as indicators of real growth and inflation. In addition, the interest rate explains inflation well. Divisia M3 appears as the preferred indicator for real growth. All German aggregates, except Divisia M3, appear as significant determinants of Dutch inflation in the short-run, whereas all four German aggregates explain real income growth in the Netherlands equally well. Dutch short-term interest rates are well explained by the two German M3 aggregates and by sum M2. Divisia aggregates generally show smaller forecast errors of real growth than do their sum counterparts. Especially at longer horizons, the Dutch Divisia M3 aggregate provides the best out-of-sample forecasts of Dutch inflation. Generally, the differences in indicator performance of the German aggregates for the Dutch economy are only marginal.

Overall, the evidence is in favour of using Divisia aggregates as indicators of inflation and real growth, although not as strongly as might theoretically be expected. One explanation for this observation is the low and gradual degree of financial innovation in the Netherlands. Generally, the information content of Dutch and German aggregates for the Dutch economy is similar, probably because of the exchange-rate policy of the Dutch central bank, which in effect makes the Dutch money supply into an endogenous variable, closely responding to developments in German monetary conditions.

Notes

1. See Judd and Scadding (1982), and Boughton (1991, 1992) for an overview of the literature on money-demand instability. Nelson (1994), on the other hand, correctly argues that the ability to exploit the money–income relationship for monetary policy is not necessarily destroyed by the nonstationarity of velocity.
2. A good monetary policy indicator should be closely and predictably related to the ultimate target variables of monetary policy, inflation and real growth. Additionally, it may be advantageous if the indicator's value is controllable by the monetary authorities to some extent. Here, we focus on the link between indicator and ultimate target.
3. Fase (1985, 1987) is an exception.
4. See Kool (1995) for an overview and analysis.
5. These two points may be related. In the 1980s the structure of international financial markets changed markedly. Currency substitution, portfolio adjustments and the liberalisation of international capital flows may be determinants of money-demand instabilities in the Netherlands. Within the Netherlands, markets for commercial paper (CP) and certificates of deposit (CD) were introduced in 1986.
6. All three aggregates have passed tests for weak separability from other monetary assets, using Varian's (1982, 1983) non-parametric test. For details on the outcomes, see Janssen (1995).
7. Details on the data used are available from the authors.

8. We also calculated a reservation price for financial innovations in the period prior to their introduction, using Diewert's (1980) approach. This hardly has an effect on the Fisher Ideal index.
9. Details on the outcomes of the unit root tests are available from the authors.
10. The exact procedure to determine the presence of any cointegration vectors and the interpretation of these vectors are available from the authors.
11. The interest rate is indicated by R, Y_r means real national income, P is the consumer price deflator, ECM is the error-correction term, sum aggregates are abbreviated as SM2, for example, and Divisia aggregates as DM2. The Wald statistics for the ECMs are the result of a test of the joint significance of either one or two cointegrating vectors, depending on the number of cointegrating vectors for the respective monetary aggregates.
12. The higher (expected) inflation rate in the Netherlands may be observed in higher short interest rates.
13. Particularly if financial asset stocks are adjusted for budget increases over time, the NONPAR test reveals significant violations of weak separability of M2 from the other financial assets.
14. See Svensson (1994) for a discussion of the importance of credibility in maintaining a fixed exchange-rate system.
15. We are indebted to Chrystal and MacDonald (1994) and Herrmann *et al.* (1995) for making these series available to us. German monetary unification is incorporated as in Herrmann *et al.* (1995). In the subsequent analysis, German monetary aggregates have been converted into Dutch guilders using the actual guilder/DMark exchange rate.

References

Barnett, W. A. (1978) 'The User Cost of Money', *Economics Letters*, vol. 1, pp. 145–9.

Barnett, W. A. (1980) 'Economic Monetary Aggregates, An Application of Index Number and Aggregation Theory', *Journal of Econometrics*, vol. 14, pp. 11–48.

Barnett, W. A. (1981) *Consumer Demand and Labour Supply: Goods, Monetary Assets, and Time* (Amsterdam: North-Holland).

Berk, J. M. and C. C. A. Winder (1994) 'Price Movements in the Netherlands and Germany and the Guilder-Dmark Peg', *De Economist*, vol. 142, no. 1, pp. 63–74.

Boughton, J. M. (1991) 'Long-run Money Demand in Large Industrial Countries', *IMF Staff Papers*, vol. 38, pp. 1–32.

Boughton, J. M. (1992) 'International Comparisons of Money Demand: A Review Essay', *IMF Working Papers*.

Chrystal, K. A. and R. MacDonald (1994) 'Empirical Evidence on the Recent Behaviour and Usefulness of Simple-Sum and Weighted Measures of the Money Stock', *Federal Reserve Bank of St. Louis Review*, vol. 76, March/April, pp. 73–109.

De Nederlandsche Bank, *Quarterly Bulletin*, various issues (Amsterdam).

Dickey, D. A. and W. A. Fuller (1979) 'Distribution of the Estimators for Autoregressive Time Series with a Unit Root', *Journal of the American Statistical Association*, vol. 74, pp. 427–31.

Diewert, W. E. (1974) 'Applications of Duality Theory', in M. D. Intriligator and D. A. Kendrick (eds), *Frontiers of Quantitative Economics*, vol. II (Amsterdam: North-Holland), pp. 106–76.

Diewert, W. E. (1980) 'Aggregation Problems in the Measurement of Capital', in D. Usher, *The Measurement of Capital, Studies in Income and Wealth*, vol. 45 (University of Chicago Press), pp. 433–538.

Fase, M. M. G. (1985) 'Monetary Control: The Dutch Experience', in C. van Ewijk and J. J. Klant (eds), *Monetary Conditions for Economic Recovery*, Financial and Monetary Policy Studies 11 (Dordrecht: Martinus Nijhoff), pp. 95–125.

Fase, M. M. G. (1987) 'Geld en Inkomen: En Macro-economisch Debat van 25 Jaar', in H. W. J. Bosman and J. C. Brezet, *Sparen en Investeren, Geld en Banken* (Leiden/Antwerp: Stenfert Kroese), pp. 187–214.

Fuller, W. A. (1976) *Introduction to Statistical Time Series* (New York: John Wiley).

Herrmann, H., H.-E. Reimers and K.-H. Toedter (1995) *Weighted Monetary Aggregates for Germany*, Ch. 4 in this volume.

Janssen, N. G. J. (1995) *The Definition and Policy Relevance of Monetary Aggregates in the Netherlands*, Ph.D thesis, University of Limburg, Maastricht.

Johansen, S. (1988) 'Statistical Analysis of Cointegration Vectors', *Journal of Economic Dynamics and Control*, vol. 12, pp. 231–54.

Johansen, S. (1991) 'Estimation and Hypothesis Testing of Cointegration Vectors in Gaussian Vector Autoregressive Models', *Econometrica*, vol. 59, no. 6, pp. 1551–80.

Johansen, S. and K. Juselius (1990) 'Maximum Likelihood Estimation and Inference on Cointegration – with Applications to the Demand for Money', *Oxford Bulletin of Economics and Statistics*, vol. 52, no. 2, pp. 169–210.

Judd, J. P. and J. L. Scadding (1982) 'The Search for a Stable Money Demand Function', *Journal of Economic Literature*, vol. 20, pp. 993–1023.

Kool, C. J. M. (1995) 'Monetary Policy under Fixed Exchange Rates: Lessons from the Netherlands, Belgium, and Austria: 1973–1992', *De Economist*, vol. 143, no. 3, pp. 329–51.

Kool, C. J. M. and J. A. Tatom (1994) 'The P-Star Model in Five Small Economies', *Federal Reserve Bank of St Louis Review*, vol. 76, May/June, pp. 11–29.

Nelson, C. R. (1994) 'Commentary', *Federal Reserve Bank of St Louis Review*, vol. 76, March/April, pp. 110–16.

Osterwald-Lenum, M. (1992) 'A Note with Quantiles of the Asymptotic Distribution of the Maximum Likelihood Cointegration Rank Test Statistics', *Oxford Bulletin of Economics and Statistics*, vol. 54, no. 3, pp. 461–72.

Svensson, L. E. O. (1994) 'Fixed Exchange Rates as a Means to Price Stability: What Have We Learned?', *European Economic Review*, vol. 38, pp. 447–68.

Varian, H. R. (1982) 'The Nonparametric Approach to Demand Analysis', *Econometrica*, vol. 50, pp. 945–73.

Varian, H. R. (1983) 'Nonparametric Tests of Consumer Behaviour', *Review of Economic Studies*, vol. 50, pp. 99–110.

7

Divisia Aggregates and the Demand for Money in Core EMU

Martin M. G. Fase

Knowledge of money-holding behaviour in the private sector – that is, households and businesses – is of great importance for assessing the impact of monetary and other shocks on the economy, and the effectiveness of monetary policy. This, together with the fact that the theory of the demand for money is fairly well developed and with the required data readily available, explains why the demand for money has been so well explored econometrically. The underlying thought in all this work has been the belief that money demand should be stable (see Fase 1993, 1994). This chapter follows this research tradition but with a slight shift of emphasis away from econometric techniques and towards the substantial issues of considering various money concepts and geographical areas. Our main concern is the stability of money demand across geographical areas within EMU for various simple-sum versus index number, theory-based aggregates. Of these, the Divisia measure is a prominent example. As to geographical areas, we accept the view that Germany is the anchor country for EMU and should therefore have a relatively stable money demand *vis-á-vis* other member countries such as the Netherlands.

This chapter examines the narrow problem of money demand stability across a particular set of EMU countries.

7.1 Aggregation and the Divisia index

Aggregation method

A difficult problem in constructing monetary and income aggregates across countries is the conversion of national units into a common unit. A similar problem arises in constructing common price and interest-rate variables. Because no unique conversion method exists, arbitrary decisions need to be made. This perhaps affects the monetary picture and the resulting policy diagnosis, the sensitivity of which is shown, in part, by comparisons of results from some of the conversion techniques most prevalent in other research. Before addressing this important issue we first discuss the aggregation issue in general.

For the construction of (sub) EMU-wide data, several options are open. In order to place the monetary aggregates and nominal national products of the various countries on the same footing, current and 1985 exchange rates and purchasing power parities were successively used as the conversion factor, resulting in a total of four options. Moreover, we experimented with the current US dollar for conversion to illustrate the importance of the conversion method for the results.

In the study by Fase and Winder (1994) on Divisia aggregates for EMU, four options were tested, the monetary aggregates and nominal national products of the individual EMU countries being expressed in Deutsche Marks, with 1985 as the base period. The data for the member states' national products in 1985 prices were converted into 1985 Deutsche Mark prices using the 1985 exchange rates and purchasing power parities against the Deutsche Mark. The resulting series of (sub) EMU-wide monetary aggregates and (sub) EMU's supra-national product in current and constant prices were obtained by summing the corresponding standardised variables for the individual member states. The price index at the (sub) EMU level was determined as the quotient of (sub) EMU product in current and constant prices.

The (sub) EMU short- and long-term interest rates were calculated as weighted averages of the corresponding interest rates in the individual countries, using both a constant and a time-varying weighting scheme. In the constant weighting scheme, the weights chosen were the current shares of the EMU currencies in the ECU. The time-varying weighting scheme consists of the shares of the national products of the individual countries in aggregated EMU product. Since four different conversion factors were used in calculating aggregated EMU product, this leads to four weighting schemes on the basis of the income shares of the individual member states, so that a total of five weighting schemes result for short- and long-term interest rates.

Divisia aggregates

For monetary aggregation we use the Divisia index as it focuses on money for transactions purposes, adjusted for money holding for portfolio or speculative purposes. The notion of a monetary index was first brought to the fore in a series of articles by François Divisia, published in the French *Revue d'Economie Politique* in the 1920s (see Divisia, 1925, 1926), and rediscovered by Barnett (1978, 1980) almost half a century later. As is known, Divisia aggregates take explicit account of, and seek to adjust for, the differences in degrees of moneyness of the various liquid assets.

Divisia indices for (sub) EMU-wide money stock were determined in two ways: directly and indirectly. In the *direct* manner of calculation, data were first constructed for the monetary aggregates and short- and long-term interest rates at the EMU level, after which the corresponding Divisia indices were calculated. This resulted in four different definitions of monetary aggregates (depending on the conversion factor chosen), while five different interest rates (depending on the weighting scheme chosen) were used. In the calculation of the Divisia indices, two definitions of the EMU interest rate were considered for each of the four monetary aggregates: that based on euro weights; and that based on an income-weighting scheme, that particular scheme being selected which follows from the calculation of EMU product using the same conversion factor as for the monetary aggregate. Consequently, if the monetary aggregate was determined on the basis of current exchange rates, the income-weighting scheme based on current exchange rates was similarly used. In the *indirect* manner of calculation, Divisia indices were first calculated for the individual countries, the Divisia indices at the (sub) EMU level subsequently being determined as the weighted averages of the individual Divisia indices. The same five weighting schemes – euro and the four different income shares – were used in the construction of the EMU interest rates. The various possible combinations produce the thirteen different series for both Divisia M2 and M3 shown in Table 7.1. This paper focuses in particular on the subset resulting from the direct manner of calculation and (sub) EMU interest rates based on ecu shares. Divisia indices for M2 and M3 were calculated in conformity with the definition discussed above by weighting the growth rates of the components M1 and M2–M1 and M3–M1, respectively, with the two-period moving averages of the expenditure shares. The user cost required to this end is dependent on the benchmark interest rate carried by the illiquid asset and the return rates on the various monetary assets.

Following, for example, Belongia and Chrystal (1991), the benchmark interest rate was taken to be the long-term rate, raised by a constant equal to the maximum differential between short- and long-term rates during the sample period 1970: 1–1992: 4. This procedure warrants positive user cost. As Barnett *et al.* (1992, p. 2) points out, however, another, and perhaps preferred method, consistent with the consumer's optimisation problem, is to choose the maximum available holding period yield in each period as the benchmark rate. As regards the return on the liquid assets themselves, it has been assumed that for M1 it is equal to zero and for M2–M1 and M3–M1 to the short-term interest rate. The Divisia indices thus constructed are based on a relatively rough breakdown of the broadly defined monetary aggregate. However, further refinement to distinguish between more categories of liquid assets with their rates of return would give rise to serious data problems in an analysis at the (sub) EMU level.

Preliminary analysis of Divisia aggregates for core EMU

To gain some feeling for the meaning of Divisia aggregates as monetary measure, Table 7.2 sets out summary statistics for possible core EMU countries Germany *plus* the Benelux. The table shows a close correspondence between

Table 7.1 Various methods of constructing Divisia monetary measures for (sub) EMU monetary aggregates:

Method of calculation	*Aggregation method: monetary aggregates*	*Weighting scheme interest rates*				
		euro shares	*Income shares*			
			Exchange rates		*PPP*	
			Current	*Base period*	*Current*	*Base period*
Direct	Exchange rates					
	Current	x	x	•	•	•
	Base period	x	•	x	•	•
	PPP					
	Current	x	•	•	x	•
	Base period	x	•	•	•	x
Indirect		x	x	x	x	x

Note: x means considered in this chapter; • means not considered.

Table 7.2 Summary statistics for core EMU countries Germany *plus* Benelux; all variables in growth rates

Conversion technique	*Variable*	*Mean*	*Standard deviation*	*Correlation with*	
				M1	*y*
Current DM exchange rates	M1	7.45	4.48	1.00	0.38
	M2	8.54	4.04	0.26	0.62
	M3	8.05	2.79	0.70	0.54
	DiM2	7.43	3.69	0.85	0.60
	DiM3	7.46	3.46	0.94	0.50
	Real income	2.73	2.63	0.38	1.00
	Price	3.95	1.85	0.20	–0.20
1985 DM exchange rates	M1	7.82	4.24	1.00	0.39
	M2	8.89	4.07	0.20	0.61
	M3	8.38	2.71	0.66	0.54
	DiM2	7.80	3.48	0.82	0.64
	DiM3	7.80	3.23	0.93	0.52
	Real income	2.73	2.63	0.39	1.00
	Price	4.20	1.78	0.11	–0.21
Current DM–PPP	M1	7.48	4.17	1.00	0.42
	M2	8.59	4.13	0.22	0.61
	M3	8.12	2.63	0.65	0.59
	DiM2	7.47	3.53	0.82	0.65
	DiM3	7.50	3.20	0.93	0.56
	Real income	2.73	2.63	0.42	1.00
	Price	3.99	1.63	0.04	–0.20
1985 DM–PPP	M1	7.81	4.22	1.00	0.39
	M2	8.89	4.05	0.20	0.61
	M3	8.39	2.70	0.66	0.54
	DiM2	7.79	3.46	0.82	0.63
	DiM3	7.80	3.22	0.93	0.52
	Real income	2.73	2.63	0.39	1.00
	Price	4.21	1.78	0.12	–0.21

the M1 growth rate and the two Divisia aggregates M2 and M3, while the correlation of the latter with M1 of 0.80 to almost 0.95 is quite impressive. This seems to support the view that the relevant monetary expansion – that is, the growth rate of transaction money – is close to the growth of M1, which is in line with the growth of real income y. This picture changes very little with the conversion technique used: the same holds for the core countries Germany, the Benelux plus France (see Appendix 2). At the same time, the simple-sum variants of M2 and M3 demonstrate a much lower correlation with M1 than the equivalent Divisia indices.

7.2 Money demand and simple-sum aggregates

General theoretical framework

A traditional demand for money relationship typically expresses that the desired demand for money is determined by real income, the rate of inflation, and short- and long-term interest rates. Assuming a price elasticity possibly unequal to one, the following macroeconomic demand for money equation is postulated:

$$M = AP^{\alpha_1} y^{\alpha_2} \exp(\alpha_3 r_s + \alpha_4 r_\ell + \alpha_5 \dot{p}) \tag{7.1}$$

with M being the desired money stock in a steady state situation; P the price index – so that M/P is the real money stock; y real income; $\dot{p}$ the rate of inflation; r_s the short-term interest rate; and r_p the long-term interest rate. The price and income elasticities are equal to α_1 and α_2, respectively; α_3, α_4 and α_5 measure the relative change in the demand for money due to a one percentage point change in short- and long-term interest rates and inflation respectively. These coefficients are therefore semi-elasticities. Following for example, den Butter and Fase (1981) and a recent study of Boughton (1991), the usual assumption of a price elasticity of one – that is, price homogeneity of order 1 – is not made *a priori*, but considered as a testable hypothesis.

Equation (7.1) describes the relationship between the optimum nominal amount of liquid assets held, on the one hand, and the expected equilibrium value of the explanatory variables, on the other. As such, Equation (7.1) is a description of the long-run equilibrium relationship based on an aggregated macroeconomic approach. An advantage of this approach is its fundamental distinction between the steady state and the short run, which makes such an expression especially suitable for practical purposes such as forecasting. In this case, where it is desirable to model deviations from the equilibrium relationship, a dynamic formulation of Equation (7.1) is required for the estimation process and the long-run properties of the demand for money are determined jointly with the short-run adjustment processes. An error-correction specification was chosen for this purpose, together with the introduction of lags. In accordance with our earlier studies (see Fase and Kuné, 1974a and 1974b; Fase, 1979; den Butter and Fase, 1981; and Fase and Winder, 1990, 1993), a cyclical indicator, conj – defined as some measure of unused capacity – was used to describe the short-run dynamics of the demand for money. This variable represents the tendency of money-hoarding in times of recession and of dishoarding during an economic boom. An alternative, and perhaps deeper, economic interpretation is to regard this variable as a proxy for the costs of real assets, for which liquid financial assets provide a substitute. In this view, hoarding and dishoarding reflect substitution processes.

With respect to the long-run relationship in Equation (7.1), income represents the influence of the transaction volume or wealth, while the rate of inflation and the two interest rates determine the composition of the monetary aggregate, for which the holding of, for example, less liquid financial assets such as bonds offers an alternative. Including both short- and long-term interest rates is also intended to take into account the influence of the yield curve on the demand for money.

The above leads to the following general dynamic specification of the demand for money:

$$\alpha(L)\ln M = \beta_1(L)\ln P + \beta_2(L)\ln y + \beta_3(L)r_s + \beta_4(L)r_\ell + \beta_5(L)\dot{p} + \beta_6(L)\,\text{conj} \quad (7.2)$$

with

$$\alpha(L) = 1 - \alpha_1 L - \ldots - \alpha_p L^p \text{ and } \beta_i(L) = \beta_{io} + \beta_{il}L + \ldots + \beta_{ip_i}L^{pi}$$

where $i = 1, \ldots, 6$. Of course, the indices p and pi rather than i indicate the number of lags. The parameters of $\beta_1(L)$ and $\beta_5(L)$ are not all identified as a result of perfect multicollinearity between the ln P and $\dot{p}$. This identification problem can be solved by imposing *a priori* restrictions on the polynomials concerned.

One possible method is to consider real money balances as the dependent variable. This means – in terms of Equation (7.2) – that the restriction $\beta_{10} = 1$ and $\beta_{li} = -\alpha_i$, for $i = 1, \ldots 1, p$ are imposed. These $p + 1$ restrictions imply that the long-run price elasticity is equal to 1. As only p restrictions are needed, the imposed restrictions are sufficient, but not necessary, to obviate the identification problem. In the present study we deliberately impose the restrictions $\beta_{1i} = -\alpha_i$ for $i = 1, \ldots, p$. Because these restrictions serve to avoid the identification problem, they cannot be tested.

In view of this, Equation (7.2) can be rewritten as:

$$\begin{aligned}\alpha(L)\ln(M/P) = (\beta_{10} - 1)\ln P + \beta_2(L)\ln y + \beta_3(L)r_s + \beta_4(L)r_\ell \\ + \beta_5(L)\dot{p} + \beta_6(L)\,\text{conj}\end{aligned} \quad (7.3)$$

so that it is no longer assumed a priori that the price elasticity equals 1.

For further analysis we consider the following reformulation of Equation (7.3):

$$\begin{aligned}\overline{\alpha}(L)\Delta\ln(M/P) = (\beta_{10} - 1)\ln P - \alpha\ln(M/P)_{-1} - \ln y_{-1} \\ + (\beta_2 - \alpha)\ln y_{-1} + \beta_3 r_s + \beta_4 r_\ell + \beta_5\dot{p} + \overline{\beta}_2(L)\Delta\ln y \\ + \overline{\beta}_3(L)\,\Delta r_s + \overline{\beta}_4(L)\Delta r_\ell + \overline{\beta}_5(L)\,\Delta\dot{p} \\ + \beta_6(L)\,\text{conj}\end{aligned} \quad (7.4)$$

with $\alpha = 1 - \alpha_1 - \ldots - \alpha_p$, $\beta_i = \beta_{io} + \ldots + \beta_{ipi}$, i $= 2, \ldots, 6$, while $\overline{\alpha}$(L) and $\overline{\beta}_i(L)$, $i = 2, \ldots, 5$, are lag polynomials of order p–1 and p_i–1. The parameters of $\overline{\alpha}(L)$

and $\overline{\beta}_i(L)$ are linear combinations of those of $a(L)$ and $\beta_i(L)$. For example, $\overline{\alpha}_i = -\sum_{j-i+1}^{p} \alpha_j, i = 1, \ldots, p-1$, with $\overline{\alpha}_i$ the parameters of polynomial $\overline{\alpha}(L)$.

Equation (7.4) serves as the general formulation for the estimation and specification analysis. Estimating Equation (7.4) instead of Equation (7.3) has several advantages. The most important is that it provides the possibility of obtaining the long-run (semi-) elasticities in a relatively simple way, as they equal the quotient of two estimates. The long-run semi elasticities are β_3/α for the short-term interest rate, β_4/α for the long-term rate, β_5/α for the rate of inflation, and the elasticity is β_2/α for real income. Obviously, the hypothesis that the income elasticity equals one corresponds with the restriction that the coefficient of ln y_{-1} equals zero. The price elasticity is equal to $(\beta_{10} - 1 + \alpha)/\alpha$. Thus the hypothesis of the price elasticity equal to one can be tested by assessing the significance of the estimate of the coefficient of ln P. This, together with the identifying restrictions $\beta_{li} = -\alpha_i$ for $i = 1, \ldots, p$, implies that the polynomial $\beta_1(L) - \alpha(L)$ has a unit root. Therefore this is an alternative interpretation of the hypothesis that $\alpha_{10} - 1 = 0$. The economic interpretation is that the price elasticity equals one. The second advantage of Equation (7.4) over Equation (7.3) is that Equation (7.4) circumvents the multicollinearity problem by expressing the explanatory variables in first differences.

It is also worth noting that the formulation in Equation (7.4), which belongs to the class of error-correction models, is also in line with the early studies into the demand for money. This linkage is made by noting that the error-correction term represents the inverse velocity of circulation, the dependent variable in Latané's (1954) study of the demand for money. Christ (1993) offers a thorough review of this relationship between early and modern studies.[1]

Estimation results for simple-sum aggregates

To begin with, Equation (7.4) was estimated for the simple-sum monetary aggregates M1, M2 and M3 for Germany, Belgium, the Netherlands and France as well as for the potential core countries Germany and the Benelux – let us call them GB and GB plus France. A full report of the estimation results is given in Appendix 1. By way of illustration we report here the estimation result for M3 for the core group Germany *plus* the Benelux. Using the current DM exchange rates as conversion methods, s_i as seasonal dummies, $\text{dum}_{90:\text{III}}$ a binary variable to account for the German unification in October 1990, and the sample period of 1971:2–1992:4, the estimated equation is:

$$\begin{aligned}\Delta \ln (M3/P) = \; & -\underset{(4.39)}{0.1056} \, (\ln (M3/P)_{-1} - \ln y) + \underset{(2.51)}{0.0381} \ln y_{-1} \\ & + \underset{(1.31)}{0.0010} \, r_s - \underset{(2.18)}{0.0024} \, \Delta r_{s_{-1}} - \underset{(3.42)}{0.0046} \, r_{\ell_{-0.5}} - \underset{(7.14)}{0.0018} \, \dot{p}\end{aligned}$$

$$
\begin{aligned}
&- \underset{(2.18)}{0.0003}\, \Delta\dot{p}_{-2} - \underset{(2.03)}{0.0019}\, \text{conj}_{-4} - \underset{(1.39)}{0.1149} + \underset{(0.11)}{0.0005}\, s_1 \\
&+ \underset{(1.06)}{0.037}\, s_2 - \underset{(5.07)}{0.0197}\, s_3 + \underset{(36.80)}{0.0928}\, \text{dum}_{90:\text{III}}
\end{aligned}
$$

$\overline{R}^2 = 0.88 \quad \text{SE} = 0.006.$

Without firm guidance from theory, the choice of the conversion method is an important decision for the examination of monetary behaviour across countries. This is the more so as several alternatives are reasonable. To illustrate the potential effects of these choices, Equation (7.4) was re-estimated using data converted by current DM purchasing power parity. The resulting estimated equation for Germany plus the Benelux is:

$$
\begin{aligned}
\Delta \ln (\text{M3}/P) = &- \underset{(4.39)}{0.1001}\, (\ln (\text{M3}/P) - \ln y) + \underset{(2.35)}{0.0350} \ln y_{-1} \\
&+ \underset{(2.52)}{0.00102} r_s - \underset{(5.56)}{0.0045}\, r_{\ell_{-3.5}} - \underset{(5.15)}{0.0144}\, \Delta\, r_{\ell_{-1.5}} - \underset{(13.03)}{0.0024}\, \dot{p} \\
&- \underset{(3.37)}{0.0026}\, \text{conj}_{-3} - \underset{(1.19)}{0.0956} - \underset{(3.28)}{0.0093}\, r_1 + \underset{(3.17)}{0.0088}\, s_2 \\
&- \underset{(6.89)}{0.0165}\, s_3 + \underset{(33.29)}{0.0924}\, \text{dum}_{90:\text{III}}
\end{aligned}
$$

$\overline{R}^2 = 0.90 \qquad \text{SE} = 0.006.$

The above two examples show remarkable differences in empirical specification and estimation results, but not in the error-correction term and goodness of fit. In any case, the two equations illustrate that the method of conversion might affect the results. To investigate this matter further we also estimated the equation for data converted by using the US dollar exchange rate rather than the DM exchange rate. This yields:

$$
\begin{aligned}
\Delta \ln (\text{M3}/P) = &- \underset{(2.14)}{0.0842}\, (\ln (\text{M3}/P)_{-1} - \ln y) + \underset{(1.19)}{0.0316} \ln y_{-1} \\
&+ \underset{(1.56)}{0.0019}\, r_s - \underset{(2.22)}{0.0035} \Delta r_{s-1} - \underset{(3.65)}{0.0072}\, r_{\ell_{-1.5}} - \underset{(1.12)}{0.0001}\, \dot{p} \\
&- \underset{(2.36)}{0.0001}\, \Delta\dot{p}_{-2} - \underset{(2.44)}{0.0031}\, \text{conj}_{-4} - \underset{(0.51)}{0.0581} + \underset{(7.75)}{0.0232}\, s_1 \\
&+ \underset{(3.46)}{0.0137}\, s_2 - \underset{(3.33)}{0.0108}\, s_3 + \underset{(24.81)}{0.1002}\, \text{dum}_{90:\text{III}}
\end{aligned}
$$

$\overline{R}^2 = 0.76 \qquad \text{SE} = 0.009.$

Table 7.3 Equilibrium elasticities for M3

	Short-term interest rate	*Long-term interest rate*	*Inflation*
Current DM exchange rates			
Germany and Benelux	0.07	–0.35	–0.07
Idem, *plus* France	0.04	–0.24	–0.02
Current DM PPP			
Germany and Benelux	0.09	–0.37	–0.10
Idem, *plus* France	0.13	–0.33	–0.06
Current US$ exchange rates			
Germany and Benelux	0.16	–0.70	–0.01

Obviously, these results differ from those obtained with the other equations. Consequently the long-run or equilibrium elasticities also differ, as Table 7.3 illustrates, doubling the size of the long-run interest rate elasticity, which seems implausible.

One explanation of this difference is that movements in the price variable are influenced by the specific exchange rate used. When expressing the national aggregates in another currency, the change in the transformed price is the result of changes in both domestic prices and exchange rates. To illustrate this, Figure 7.1 presents the inflation rates in Belgium, Germany and the Netherlands with the DM conversion method and the US dollar conversion method. When using the dollar as the conversion factor, the first half of the 1980s shows strong deflation, whereas in 1985–6 excessive inflation is in evidence. Naturally, this reflects the change in the value of the US dollar.

7.3 Money demand with Divisia measures in core EMU

This section discusses estimated money demand equations using Divisia monetary measures for the hard core of EMU, focusing in particular on stability issues of Divisia measures *vis-à-vis* simple-sum aggregates discussed in Section 7.1. In addition, the statistical properties of the estimated equation are examined briefly.

Estimation results for Divisia measures

As before, the estimated equations are based on the general theoretical framework set out in Section 7.1, and particularly in Equation (7.4). As before for simple-sum aggregates, this equation was estimated for Divisia M2 and M3 for Germany, the Netherlands, Belgium and France, as well as for the potential core countries Germany and the Benelux (GB), and for GB plus France. A full

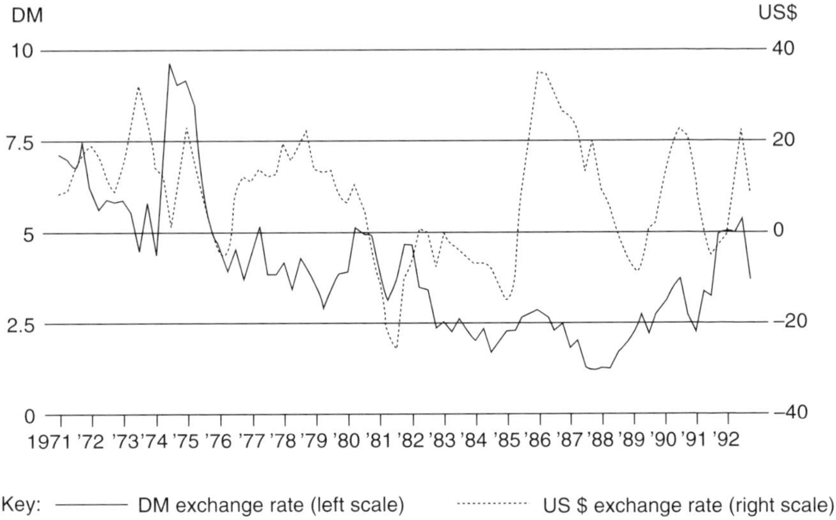

Figure 7.1 Inflation in Germany *plus* Benelux, using DM and US$ exchange rates

report of the estimation results is given in Appendix 1. By way of illustration we report below the estimated equation for Divisia M3 in the core group Germany–Benelux. Using the 1985 DM exchange rate as the conversion technique, oc2 the user costs of M3, s_i as seasonal dummies; $\text{dum}_{90:\text{III}}$ is a binary variable to account for the German unification in October 1990 and sample period 1971:2–1992:4; the estimated equation is:

$$
\begin{aligned}
\Delta \ln(\text{DiM3}/P) = {} & -\underset{(2.01)}{0.0736}\,(\ln(\text{DiM3}/P)_{-3} - \ln y) + \underset{(3.78)}{0.3659}\,\Delta \ln(\text{DiM3}/P)_{-4} \\
& + \underset{(2.32)}{0.0022}\,\text{oc2}_{-2.5} - \underset{(1.69)}{0.0055}\,\Delta R - \underset{(2.32)}{0.0022}\,\dot{p} - \underset{(3.00)}{0.0042}\,\text{conj}_{-1} \\
& - \underset{(0.98)}{0.0184} + \underset{(0.97)}{0.0044}\,s_1 + \underset{(2.95)}{0.0113}\,s_2 - \underset{(3.18)}{0.0148}\,s_3 \\
& + \underset{(29.86)}{0.0900}\,\text{dum}_{90:\text{III}}
\end{aligned}
$$

$\bar{R}^2 = 0.70$, SE $= 0.011$, and *t*-values in parenthesis.

The estimation results for Divisia measures of money also depend on the conversion technique chosen. We therefore also present the corresponding estimates, using 1985 DM purchasing power parity as conversion method. The estimated equation is:

$$\begin{aligned}\Delta \ln (\text{DiM3}/P) = & -\underset{(2.02)}{0.0738}\ (\ln (\text{DiM3}/P)_{-3} - \ln y) + \underset{(3.80)}{0.3694}\ \Delta \ln (\text{DiM3}/P)_{-4} \\ & -\underset{(2.32)}{0.0021}\ \text{oc2}_{-2.5} - \underset{(1.68)}{0.0054}\ \Delta R - \underset{(2.32)}{0.0021}\ \dot{p} - \underset{(3.02)}{0.0043}\ \text{conj}_{-1} \\ & +\underset{(1.01)}{0.0192} + \underset{(0.98)}{0.0044}\ s_1 + \underset{(2.96)}{0.0113}\ s_2 - \underset{(3.18)}{0.0149}\ s_3 \\ & +\underset{(29.42)}{0.0900}\ \text{dum}_{90:\text{III}}\end{aligned}$$

$\bar{R}^2 = 0.71, \quad \text{SE} = 0.011$

Comparing the two equations shows that in this case the technique of conversion affects the specification and estimates only slightly. The results differ substantially, however, if the US dollar or current value of DM are used (see Appendix 1). The size of the standard error of residuals, which is a measure of stability – which is our main focus – is only slightly affected by the conversion method but larger than for simple-sum money demand. Therefore we may conclude that money demand stability for the Divisia measure and simple-sum aggregate differ considerably.

Finally Table 7.4 sets out the (semi) elasticities over countries/area and monetary aggregates, showing that very often the results are rather plausible. They are also in agreement with the implications of the simple-sum estimates.

A closer look at the results

Relative stability is our main concern in this chapter. The statistic for stability used here is the residual standard error for the monetary aggregate over two core EMU countries set out in Table 7.5. This table also includes the standard errors for the equations for Belgium, France, Germany and the Netherlands.

The results shown in Table 7.5 indicate first that, regardless of the monetary measure used, stability measured by standard errors of residuals is greater for Germany and France than for the other countries. Second, stability does not increase by using Divisia measures, although the pattern according to the size of the countries still holds. Third, Table 7.5 suggests a slight increase in stability for the core EMU. However, stability is much greater for EMU as a whole.

Table 7.5 shows the remarkable result that aggregation across countries reduces the standard error of residuals in the demand for money. As far as this standard error is the measure for stability, it increases stability for the particular countries considered. This result suggests that aggregation across countries should be examined further. Table 7.5 also shows that M3 is more stable than the narrowly-defined aggregates, a result that constitutes a justification for considering M3 as the central monetary policy variable.

Table 7.4 Long-run properties of money demand

	Monetary aggregate	*Elasticities*		*Semi-elasticities*		
		Price	*Income*	*Short-term interest rate*	*Long-term interest rate*	*Inflation*
Germany	DiM2	1	1	0.012	–0.029	–0.029
	DiM3	1	1	0.021	–0.032	–0.032
The Netherlands	DiM2	1	1	0.011	–0.029	–0.029
	DiM3	1	1	0.022	–0.034	–0.039
Belgium	DiM2	0.746	1	0.025	–0.058	–0.011
	DiM3	0.745	1	0.039	–0.059	–0.026
France	DiM2	0.830	1	0.004	–0.010	–0.010
	DiM3	0.849	1	0.004	–0.007	–0.007
Germany plus Benelux 1985 DM exchange rates	M1	1	1.391	–0.010	–0.010	–0.010
	M2	1	1.229	0.041	–0.041	–0.041
	M3	1	1	0.021	–0.043	–0.043
	DiM2	1	1	0.014	–0.035	–0.035
	DiM3	1	1	0.019	–0.029	–0.029
Current DM exchange rates	M3	1	1.361	0.010	–0.043	–0.017
Germany plus Benelux 1985 DM–PPP	M1	1	1.384	–0.010	–0.010	–0.010
	M2	1	1.225	0.041	–0.041	–0.041
	M3	1	1	0.021	–0.043	–0.043
	DiM2	1	1	0.014	–0.035	–0.035
	DiM3	1	1	0.019	–0.029	–0.029
Current DM–PPP	M3	1	1.349	0.012	–0.045	–0.024

Table 7.4 (*continued*)

	Monetary aggregate	*Elasticities*		*Semi-elasticities*		
		Price	*Income*	*Short-term interest rate*	*Long-term interest rate*	*Inflation*
Germany, France plus Benelux 1985 DM exchange rates	M1	1	1	–0.007	–0.007	–0.008
	M2	1	1	0.054	–0.054	–0.054
	M3	1	1	0.035	–0.035	–0.035
	DiM2	1	1	0.015	–0.035	–0.015
	DiM3	1	1	0.015	–0.024	–0.024
Current DM exchange rates	M3	1.254	1	0.004	–0.027	–0.004
Germany, France plus Benelux 1985 DM–PPP	M1	1	1	–0.007	–0.007	–0.007
	M2	1	1	0.054	–0.054	–0.054
	M3	1	1	0.035	–0.035	–0.035
	DiM2	1	1	0.015	–0.036	–0.015
	DiM3	1	1	0.015	–0.024	–0.024
Current DM–PPP	M3	1	1.289	0.015	–0.037	–0.015

Table 7.5 Standard error of residuals ($\times 10^3$)

	M1	*M2*	*M3*	*DiM2*	*DiM3*
Germany *plus* Benelux	14	12	8	12	11
Germany, France *plus* Benelux	8	11	8	9	9
EMU[a]	6	6	5	7	7
Germany[b]	11	13	9	14	12
France[b]	10	12	8	11	9
Belgium[b]	12	14	9	15	15
Nederland[b]	20	25	16	19	19

Notes: The results for (sub) EMU follow by using 1985 DM exchange rates as the conversion factor.
[a] The results for M1, M2 and M3 are calculated as a weighted average of the country results in Fase and Winder (1993). The results for DiM2 and DiM3 are found in Fase and Winder (1994).
[b] The results for M1, M2 and M3 are obtained from Fase and Winder (1993).

Statistical properties

The demand for money equations discussed in this chapter have been subjected to an econometric specification analysis. The results are summarized in Appendix 3, upon which the following discussion draws. First, the constraints imposed upon the parameters are tested. Subsequently, the residuals of the estimated equations have been tested for autocorrelation. Finally, a cointegration analysis of the long-run relationships is set out.

The estimated demand-for-money Equation (7.4) includes a number of constraints imposed on the parameters and long-run elasticities. These constraints constitute testable hypotheses, whose validity has been examined with *t* and *F* tests. The test for these constraints, set out in Table 7.C.1, indicate that these constraints need not be rejected.

Subsequently, we have tested whether the residuals of the demand-for-money equations show autocorrelation. To this end, the Ljung–Box test statistic, based on the first p autocorrelations of the residuals – $p = 2$, 4, 8 and 12 – has been calculated. Under the null hypothesis of white noise disturbances, the test statistics are distributed $\chi^2(p)$. The results are shown in Table 7.C.2, and indicate that no significant autocorrelation is present.

The long-run relationships implied by the estimated dynamic demand-for-money have been examined further by means of cointegration tests to verify whether the deviations from the equilibrium path follow a stationary process. As the data used are seasonally adjusted, the procedure of Hylleberg *et al.* (1990) has been used. The estimated equation is:

$$\Delta_3 x_t = \pi_1 y_{1t-1} + \pi_2 y_{2t-1} + \pi_3 y_{3t-2} + \pi_4 y_{3t-1} + \varepsilon_t \qquad (7.5)$$

where x_t represents the deviations from the equilibrium path, $y_{1t} = (1 + L + L^2 + L^3)x_t$, $y_{2t} >= -(1 - L)(1 + L^2)x_t$, $y_{3t} = -(1 - L)(1 + L)x_t$ and ε_t^{15} a disturbance term. Lags of $\Delta_4 x_t$ have been added to eliminate any autocorrelation in the residuals. The constraint $\pi_1 = 0$ corresponds to a unit root, $L = 1$. The constraint $\pi_2 = 0$ implies that a unit root equal to $L = -1$ is present. If π_3 and π_4 are both equal to zero, the complex roots $L = \pm i$ are present. These various constraints can be tested with the t-ratios of π_i, $i = 1, \ldots 4$ and the F test for the constraint $\pi_3 = \pi_4 = 0$. However, the test statistics do not have the standard distributions. Hylleberg *et al.* (1990) present the critical values for the test statistics obtained with simulation experiments.

The cointegration test was carried out by estimating Equation (7.5) with seasonal dummies, a constant term and the first four lags of $\Delta_4 x_t$ being included as additional explanatory variables. Subsequently, in several rounds, the most insignificant of the lags of $\Delta_4 x_t$ was eliminated successively from the equation. The results of the above t and F tests for the ultimate equation are listed in Table 7.C.3, showing that cointegration can be accepted for the core EMU, including France. On the other hand, cointegration has to be rejected for the monetary aggregates for Germany plus Benelux, with the exception of M2. According to the results in Table 7.C.3, seasonal unit roots are absent.

7.4 Conclusion

The main objective of this chapter was to examine the properties of the demand for money measured as a simple-sum and Divisia aggregate for various groups of EMU countries. The groups studied are the core EMU countries, in particular the country set Germany, Belgium and the Netherlands, and this country set extended with France.

Our analysis results in five clear-cut conclusions. First, we found statistical evidence for the hypothesis of price homogeneity. Second, the method of converting individual country data to a common basis does affect the estimation results in some instances. Third, the estimation results differ slightly according to the monetary aggregate used, but are consistent between potential core EMU countries and the EMU as a whole. Fourth, money demand in the core countries has a similar stability as in Germany, a finding that holds for both simple-sum and Divisia aggregates. The empirical results also indicate that for the EMU as a whole, demand for Divisia monetary aggregates displays greater stability than for core EMU. Finally, the monetary picture resulting for Divisia aggregates differs substantially from that given by the traditional monetary aggregates but converges to simple-sum M1 monetary growth.

Appendix 1: estimation results

Germany

$$\Delta \ln (\text{DiM2}/P) = \underset{(1.80)}{-\,0.0629} \,(\ln (\text{DiM2}/P)_{-3} - \ln y) + \underset{(2.59)}{0.2565}\, \Delta \ln (\text{DiM2}/P)_{-4}$$

$$\underset{(2.14)}{-\,0.0018}\, \text{oc1}_{-2} \underset{(2.47)}{-\,0.0085}\, \Delta R_{-1.5} \underset{(2.14)}{-\,0.0018}\, \dot{p}$$

$$\begin{array}{llll} -\ \underset{(0.50)}{0.0008}\ \text{conj} & +\ \underset{(0.66)}{0.0131} & -\ \underset{(2.55)}{0.0174}\ s_1 & -\ \underset{(0.48)}{0.0024}\ s_2 \end{array}$$

$$-\ \underset{(2.82)}{0.0157}\ s_3 +\ \underset{(29.69)}{0.1324}\ \text{dum}_{90:\text{III}}$$

Sample period: 1971:2–1992:4 $\quad \overline{R}^2 = 0.64 \quad \text{SE} = 0.014$

$$\Delta \ln (\text{DiM3}/P) = -\ \underset{(2.16)}{0.0681}\ (\ln (\text{DiM3}/P)_{-3} - \ln y) + \underset{(2.20)}{0.2424}\ \Delta \ln (\text{DiM3})_{-4}$$

$$-\ \underset{(2.24)}{0.0022}\ \text{oc2}_{-3} - \underset{(2.72)}{0.0081}\ \Delta R_{-1} - \underset{(2.24)}{0.0022}\ \dot{p}$$

$$-\ \underset{(1.50)}{0.0022}\ \text{conj}_{-1.5} + \underset{(0.57)}{0.0066} + \underset{(0.44)}{0.0021}\ s_1 + \underset{(0.20)}{0.0007}\ s_2$$

$$-\ \underset{(2.47)}{0.0103}\ s_3 +\ \underset{(35.91)}{0.1235}\ \text{dum}_{90:\text{III}}$$

Sample period: 1971:2–1992:4 $\quad \overline{R}^2 = 0.58 \quad \text{SE} = 0.012$

The Netherlands

$$\Delta \ln (\text{DiM2}/P) = -\ \underset{(1.71)}{0.0464}\ (\ln (\text{DiM2}/P)_{-1} - \ln y_{-1}) + \underset{(4.02)}{0.3833}\ \Delta \ln y$$

$$+\ \underset{(3.67)}{0.3334}\Delta \ln y_{-2} + \underset{(7.74)}{0.6607}\Delta \ln (\text{DiM2}/P)_{-4} - \underset{(2.44)}{0.0013}\ \text{oc1}_{-1}$$

$$-\ \underset{(2.89)}{0.0132}\ \Delta R - \underset{(2.44)}{0.0013}\ \dot{p} - \underset{(3.57)}{0.0090}\ \Delta \dot{p}_{-0.5} + \underset{(4.95)}{0.0117}\ \Delta \dot{p}_{-1.5}$$

$$-\ \underset{(1.28)}{0.0022}\ \text{conj}_{-1} + \underset{(0.89)}{0.0348} + \underset{(4.38)}{0.0429}\ s_1 + \underset{(2.66)}{0.0285}\ s_2$$

$$+\ \underset{(3.22)}{0.0560}\ s_3$$

Sample period: 1971:4–1992:4 $\quad \overline{R}^2 = 0.89 \quad \text{SE} = 0.019$

$$\Delta \ln (\text{DiM3}/P) = -\ \underset{(1.80)}{0.0512}\ (\ln (\text{DiM3}/P)_{-1} - \ln y_{-1}) + \underset{(4.44)}{0.3615}\ \Delta \ln y$$

$$+\ \underset{(2.68)}{0.2450}\ \Delta \ln y_{-2} + \underset{(7.95)}{0.6070}\ \Delta \ln (\text{DiM2}/P)_{-4}$$

$$-\ \underset{(2.99)}{0.0017}\ \text{oc2}_{-2} - \underset{(3.46)}{0.090}\ \Delta\ \text{oc2} - \underset{(2.99)}{0.0017}\ \dot{p} - \underset{(1.84)}{0.0031}\ \text{conj}_{-2}$$

$$+ \underset{(1.40)}{0.0605} - \underset{(3.05)}{0.0514}\, s_1 + \underset{(1.73)}{0.0143}\, s_2 + \underset{(2.42)}{0.0394}\, s_3$$

Sample period: 1971:2–1992:4 $\bar{R}^2 = 0.86$ SE = 0.019

Belgium

$$\Delta \ln (\text{DiM2}/P) = -\underset{(2.59)}{0.1211} (\ln (\text{DiM2}/P)_{-1} - \ln y_{-1}) + \underset{(3.37)}{0.2838}\, \Delta \ln (\text{DiM2}/P)_{-4}$$
$$- \underset{(1.08)}{0.1328}\, \Delta \ln y_{-1.5} + \underset{(2.29)}{0.0308}\, \ln P - \underset{(3.89)}{0.0070}\, \text{ocl}_{-4} + \underset{(1.66)}{0.0013}\, \dot{p}$$
$$- \underset{(3.15)}{0.0073}\, \Delta \dot{p} - \underset{(1.19)}{0.0022}\, \text{conj}_{-3} - \underset{(1.74)}{0.0769} - \underset{(0.26)}{0.0029}\, s_1$$
$$+ \underset{(2.24)}{0.0375}\, s_2 - \underset{(3.82)}{0.0329}\, s_3$$

Sample period: 1971:2–1992:4 $\bar{R}^2 = 0.83$ SE = 0.015

$$\Delta \ln (\text{DiM3}/P) = -\underset{(0.69)}{0.0440} (\ln (\text{DiM3}/P)_{-1} - \ln y_{-1}) + \underset{(3.20)}{0.3615}\, \Delta \ln (\text{DiM3}/P)_{-4}$$
$$- \underset{(1.09)}{0.0112}\, \ln P - \underset{(1.87)}{0.0026}\, \text{oc2}_{-4} - \underset{(1.13)}{0.0011}\, \dot{p} + \underset{(2.97)}{0.0078}\, \Delta \dot{p}$$
$$- \underset{(1.40)}{0.0032}\, \text{conj}_{-3} - \underset{(0.30)}{0.0203} - \underset{(1.31)}{0.0062}\, s_1 + \underset{(4.20)}{0.0206}\, s_2$$
$$- \underset{(1.85)}{0.0238}\, s_3$$

Sample period: 1971:2–1992:4 $\bar{R}^2 = 0.79$ SE = 0.015

France

$$\Delta \ln (\text{DiM2}/P) = -\underset{(2.71)}{0.1823} (\ln (\text{DiM2}/P)_{-1} - \ln y) - \underset{(3.02)}{0.0310}\, \ln P$$
$$- \underset{(3.32)}{0.0018}\, \text{oc1}_{-1} - \underset{(3.32)}{0.0018}\, \dot{p}_{-1} - \underset{(3.22)}{0.0042}\, \text{conj}_{-3}$$
$$- \underset{(2.11)}{0.1091} - \underset{(9.41)}{0.0365}\, s_1 - \underset{(1.53)}{0.0066}\, s_2 + \underset{(1.44)}{0.0193}\, s_3$$

Sample period: 1971:4–1992:4 $\bar{R}^2 = 0.67$ SE = 0.011

$$\Delta \ln (\text{DiM3}/P) = -\underset{(1.66)}{0.0930} (\ln (\text{DiM3}/P)_{-1} - \ln y) - \underset{(2.97)}{0.0140}\, \ln P$$

$$+ \underset{(3.85)}{0.3417}\ \Delta \ln (\mathrm{DiM3}/P)_{-4} - \underset{(2.30)}{0.0007}\ \mathrm{oc2} - \underset{(2.30)}{0.0007}\ \dot{p}$$

$$- \underset{(7.30)}{0.0079}\ \Delta \dot{p} - \underset{(4.13)}{0.0039}\ \mathrm{conj}_{-3} - \underset{(1.26)}{0.0506} - \underset{(4.55)}{0.0187}\ s_1$$

$$- \underset{(1.67)}{0.0057}\ s_2 + \underset{(0.66)}{0.0072}\ s_3$$

Sample period: 1971:2–1992:4 $\bar{R}^2 = 0.71$ SE = 0.009

Germany plus Benelux

(1985 DM exchange rates)

$$\Delta \ln (\mathrm{M1}/P) = - \underset{(2.09)}{0.1134}\ (\ln (\mathrm{M1}/P)_{-2} - \ln y) - \underset{(4.44)}{0.3682}\ \Delta \ln y_{-4}$$

$$+ \underset{(2.21)}{0.0443}\ \ln y_{-1} - \underset{(2.74)}{0.0011}\ r_{s_{-2}} - \underset{(2.74)}{0.0011}\ r_{l_{-2}} - \underset{(2.74)}{0.0011}\ \dot{p}$$

$$- \underset{(5.74)}{0.0094}\ \mathrm{conj}_{-2} - \underset{(2.13)}{0.2991} - \underset{(0.63)}{0.0075}\ s_1 - \underset{(6.91)}{0.0323}\ s_2$$

$$- \underset{(4.25)}{0.0244}\ s_3 + \underset{(18.91)}{0.0874}\ \mathrm{dum}_{90:\mathrm{III}}$$

Sample period: 1971:2–1992:4 $\bar{R}^2 = 0.82$ SE = 0.014

$$\Delta \ln (\mathrm{M2}/P) = - \underset{(3.02)}{0.0837}\ (\ln (\mathrm{M2}/P)_{-3} - \ln y_{-1} + \underset{(3.99)}{0.3527}\ \Delta \ln (\mathrm{M2}/P)_{-4}$$

$$+ \underset{(2.70)}{0.2936}\ \Delta \ln y + \underset{(3.02)}{0.0192}\ \ln y_{-1} - \underset{(3.78)}{0.0034}\ r_s - \underset{(3.78)}{0.0034}\ r_\ell$$

$$+ \underset{(2.07)}{0.0069}\ \Delta r_{\ell_{-2}} - \underset{(3.78)}{0.0034}\ \dot{p} + \underset{(2.01)}{0.0047}\ \Delta \dot{p}_{-2} + \underset{(2.85)}{0.0048}\ \mathrm{conj}_{-3.5}$$

$$- \underset{(2.91)}{0.0978} + \underset{(2.52)}{0.0315}\ s_1 + \underset{(2.50)}{0.0114}\ s_2 + \underset{(0.33)}{0.0023}\ s_3$$

$$+ \underset{(10.98)}{0.0985}\ \mathrm{dum}_{90:\mathrm{III}}$$

Sample period: 1971:2–1992:4 $\bar{R}^2 = 0.68$ SE = 0.012

$$\Delta \ln (\mathrm{M3}/P) = - \underset{(2.96)}{0.0600}\ (\ln (\mathrm{M3}/P)_{-3} - \ln y) + \underset{(2.60)}{0.3168}\ \Delta \ln (\mathrm{M3}/P)_{-4}$$

$$+ \underset{(1.90)}{0.0013}\ r_s - \underset{(2.20)}{0.0028}\ \Delta r_{s_{-1}} - \underset{(2.97)}{0.0026}\ r_{\ell_2} - \underset{(2.12)}{0.0064}\ \Delta r_{\ell_{-2.5}}$$

$$- \underset{(2.97)}{0.0026}\,\Delta \dot{p}_{-1} - \underset{(2.48)}{0.0073}\,\Delta \dot{p}_{-0.5} + \underset{(3.14)}{0.0090}\,\Delta \dot{p}_{-1.5}$$

$$- \underset{(2.50)}{0.0029}\,\text{conj}_{-3.5} + \underset{(3.19)}{0.0668} - \underset{(4.52)}{0.0184}\,s_1 + \underset{(2.12)}{0.0052}\,s_2$$

$$+ \underset{(2.94)}{0.0095}\,s_3 + \underset{(30.49)}{0.1015}\,\text{dum}_{90:\text{III}}$$

Sample period: 1971:4–1992:4 $\bar{R}^2 = 0.82$ SE = 0.008

$$\Delta \ln(\text{DiM2}/P) = - \underset{(1.34)}{0.0529}\,(\ln(\text{DiM2}/P)_{-3} - \ln y) + \underset{(3.78)}{0.3352}\,\Delta \ln(\text{DiM2}/P)_{-4}$$

$$- \underset{(2.89)}{0.0018}\,\text{oc1}_{-2} - \underset{(2.28)}{0.0081}\,\Delta R_{-0.5} - \underset{(2.89)}{0.0018}\,\dot{p}$$

$$- \underset{(2.06)}{0.0030}\,\text{conj}_{-2} - \underset{(0.09)}{0.0026} - \underset{(1.34)}{0.0080}\,s_1 + \underset{(2.73)}{0.0121}\,s_2$$

$$- \underset{(3.48)}{0.0202}\,s_3 + \underset{(29.51)}{0.0931}\,\text{dum}_{90:\text{III}}$$

Sample period: 1971:2–1992:4 $\bar{R}^2 = 0.75$ SE = 0.012

$$\Delta \ln(\text{DiM3}/P) = - \underset{(2.01)}{0.0736}\,(\ln(\text{DiM3}/P)_{-3} - \ln y) + \underset{(3.78)}{0.3659}\,\Delta \ln(\text{DiM3}/P)_{-4}$$

$$- \underset{(2.32)}{0.0022}\,\text{oc2}_{-2.5} - \underset{(1.69)}{0.0055}\,\Delta R_{-1} - \underset{(2.32)}{0.0022}\,\dot{p}$$

$$- \underset{(3.00)}{0.0042}\,\text{conj}_{-1} - \underset{(0.98)}{0.0184} + \underset{(0.97)}{0.0044}\,s_1 + \underset{(2.95)}{0.0113}\,s_2$$

$$- \underset{(3.18)}{0.0148}\,s_3 + \underset{(29.86)}{0.0990}\,\text{dum}_{90:\text{III}}$$

Sample period: 1971:2–1992:4 $\bar{R}^2 = 0.70$ SE = 0.011

Germany plus Benelux

(1985 DM-purchasing power parities)

$$\Delta \ln(\text{M1}/P) = - \underset{(2.04)}{0.1111}\,(\ln(\text{M1}/P)_{-2} - \ln y) - \underset{(4.42)}{0.3644}\,\Delta \ln y_{-4}$$

$$+ \underset{(2.16)}{0.0426}\,\ln y_{-1} - \underset{(2.72)}{0.0011}\,r_{s_{-2}} - \underset{(2.72)}{0.0011}\,r_{\ell_{-2}}$$

$$- \underset{(2.72)}{0.0011}\,\dot{p} - \underset{(5.73)}{0.0093}\,\text{conj}_{-2} - \underset{(2.08)}{0.2877} - \underset{(0.60)}{0.0072}\,s_1$$

$$- \underset{(7.02)}{0.0328}\, s_2 - \underset{(4.21)}{0.0245}\, s_3 + \underset{(18.93)}{0.0867}\, \mathrm{dum}_{90:\mathrm{III}}$$

Sample period: 1971:2–1992:4 $\quad \bar{R}^2 = 0.82 \quad \mathrm{SE} = 0.014$

$$\begin{aligned}
\Delta \ln (\mathrm{M2}/P) = {} & - \underset{(3.00)}{0.0826} (\ln (\mathrm{M2}/P)_{-3} - \ln y_{-1} + \underset{(4.03)}{0.3579}\, \Delta \ln (\mathrm{M2}/P)_{-4} \\
& + \underset{(2.68)}{0.2917}\, \Delta \ln y + \underset{(3.00)}{0.0186} \ln y_{-1} - \underset{(3.80)}{0.0034}\, r_s - \underset{(3.80)}{0.0034}\, r_\ell \\
& + \underset{(2.08)}{0.0069}\, \Delta r_{\ell_{-2}} - \underset{(3.80)}{0.0034}\, \dot{p} + \underset{(1.99)}{0.0047}\, \Delta \dot{p}_{-2} + \underset{(2.87)}{0.0048}\, \mathrm{conj}_{-3.5} \\
& - \underset{(2.90)}{0.0943} + \underset{(2.52)}{0.0317}\, s_1 + \underset{(2.53)}{0.0117}\, s_2 + \underset{(0.38)}{0.0027}\, s_3 \\
& + \underset{(10.91)}{0.0973}\, \mathrm{dum}_{90:\mathrm{III}}
\end{aligned}$$

Sample period: 1971:4–1992:4 $\quad \bar{R}^2 = 0.68 \quad \mathrm{SE} = 0.012$

$$\begin{aligned}
\Delta \ln (\mathrm{M3}/P) = {} & - \underset{(2.96)}{0.0597} (\ln (\mathrm{M3}/P)_{-3} - \ln y) + \underset{(2.63)}{0.3224}\, \Delta \ln (\mathrm{M3}/P)_{-4} \\
& + \underset{(1.91)}{0.0013}\, r_s - \underset{(2.18)}{0.0028}\, \Delta r_{s_{-1}} - \underset{(2.98)}{0.0026}\, r_{\ell_{-1}} - \underset{(2.14)}{0.0065}\, \Delta r_{\ell_{-2.5}} \\
& - \underset{(2.98)}{0.0026}\, \Delta \dot{p}_{-1} - \underset{(2.51)}{0.0073}\, \Delta \dot{p}_{-0.5} + \underset{(3.16)}{0.0091}\, \Delta \dot{p}_{-1.5} \\
& - \underset{(2.54)}{0.0029}\, \mathrm{conj}_{-3.5} + \underset{(3.19)}{0.0668} + \underset{(4.49)}{0.0182}\, s_1 + \underset{(2.11)}{0.0052}\, s_2 \\
& - \underset{(2.93)}{0.0095}\, s_3 + \underset{(29.99)}{0.1003}\, \mathrm{dum}_{90:\mathrm{III}}
\end{aligned}$$

Sample period: 1971:4–1992:4 $\quad \bar{R}^2 = 0.82 \quad \mathrm{SE} = 0.008$

$$\begin{aligned}
\Delta \ln (\mathrm{DiM2}/P) = {} & - \underset{(1.33)}{0.0526} (\ln (\mathrm{DiM2}/P)_{-3} - \ln y) + \underset{(3.80)}{0.3384}\, \Delta \ln (\mathrm{DiM2}/P)_{-4} \\
& - \underset{(2.89)}{0.0018}\, \mathrm{oc1}_{-2} - \underset{(2.27)}{0.0081}\, \Delta R_{-0.5} - \underset{(2.89)}{0.0018}\, \dot{p} \\
& - \underset{(2.08)}{0.0030}\, \mathrm{conj}_{-2} - \underset{(0.11)}{0.0032} - \underset{(1.29)}{0.0078}\, s_1 + \underset{(2.78)}{0.0122}\, s_2 \\
& - \underset{(3.47)}{0.0202}\, s_3 + \underset{(29.51)}{0.0921}\, \mathrm{dum}_{90:\mathrm{III}}
\end{aligned}$$

Sample period: 1971:2–1992:4 $\quad \bar{R}^2 = 0.76 \quad SE = 0.012$

$$\begin{aligned}\Delta \ln (\text{DiM3}/P) = {} & -\underset{(2.02)}{0.0738} (\ln (\text{DiM3}/P)_{-3} - \ln y) + \underset{(3.80)}{0.3694}\, \Delta \ln (\text{DiM3}/P)_{-4} \\ & - \underset{(2.32)}{0.0021}\, \text{oc2}_{-2.5} - \underset{(1.68)}{0.0054}\, \Delta R - \underset{(2.32)}{0.0021}\, \dot{p} \\ & - \underset{(3.02)}{0.0043}\, \text{conj}_{-1} - \underset{(1.01)}{0.0192} - \underset{(0.98)}{0.0044}\, s_1 + \underset{(2.96)}{0.0113}\, s_2 \\ & - \underset{(3.18)}{0.0149}\, s_3 + \underset{(29.42)}{0.0890}\, \text{dum}_{90:\text{III}}\end{aligned}$$

Sample period: 1971:2–1992:4 $\quad \bar{R}^2 = 0.71 \quad SE = 0.011$

Germany plus Benelux

(current DM exchange rates)

$$\begin{aligned}\Delta \ln (\text{M3}/P) = {} & -\underset{(4.39)}{0.1056} (\ln (\text{M3}/P)_{-1} - \ln y) + \underset{(2.51)}{0.0381} - \ln y_{-1}) \\ & + \underset{(1.31)}{0.0010}\, r_s - \underset{(2.18)}{0.0024}\, \Delta r_{s_{-1}} - \underset{(3.42)}{0.0046}\, r_{\ell_{-0.5}} - \underset{(7.14)}{0.0018}\, \dot{p} \\ & - \underset{(2.18)}{0.0003}\, \Delta \dot{p}_{-2} - \underset{(2.03)}{0.0019}\, \text{conj}_{-4} - \underset{(1.39)}{0.1149} + \underset{(0.11)}{0.0005}\, s_1 \\ & - \underset{(1.06)}{0.0037}\, s_2 - \underset{(5.07)}{0.0197}\, s_3 + \underset{(36.80)}{0.0928}\, \text{dum}_{90:\text{III}}\end{aligned}$$

Sample period: 1971:2–1992:4 $\quad \bar{R}^2 = 0.88 \quad SE = 0.006$

(current DM purchasing power parities)

$$\begin{aligned}\Delta \ln (\text{M3}/P) = {} & -\underset{(4.39)}{0.1001} (\ln (\text{M3}/P)_{-1} - \ln y) + \underset{(2.35)}{0.0350} \ln y_{-1} \\ & + \underset{(2.52)}{0.0012}\, r_s - \underset{(5.56)}{0.0045}\, r_{\ell_{-3.5}} - \underset{(5.15)}{0.0144}\, r_{l_{-1.5}} - \underset{(13.03)}{0.0024}\, \dot{p} \\ & - \underset{(3.37)}{0.0026}\, \text{conj}_{-43} - \underset{(1.19)}{0.0956} + \underset{(3.28)}{0.0093}\, s_1 - \underset{(3.17)}{0.0088}\, s_2 \\ & - \underset{(6.89)}{0.0165}\, s_3 + \underset{(33.29)}{0.0924}\, \text{dum}_{90:\text{III}}\end{aligned}$$

Sample period: 1971:1–1992:4 $\quad \bar{R}^2 = 0.90 \quad SE = 0.006$

Germany, Benelux plus France

(1985 DM exchange rates)

$$
\begin{aligned}
\Delta \ln (\mathrm{M1}/P) = & - \underset{(4.33)}{0.2544} (\ln (\mathrm{M1}/P)_{-1} - \ln y) + \underset{(4.81)}{0.3282}\, \Delta \ln (\mathrm{M1}/P)_{-4} \\
& - \underset{(4.93)}{0.0017}\, r_s - \underset{(2.65)}{0.0038}\, \Delta r_{s_{-1}} - \underset{(4.93)}{0.0017}\, r_\ell + \underset{(2.24)}{0.0061}\, \Delta r_{\ell_{-2}} \\
& - \underset{(2.47)}{0.0020}\, \dot{p} - \underset{(3.03)}{0.0098}\, \Delta \dot{p}_{0.5} - \underset{(2.28)}{0.0059}\, \Delta \dot{p}_{1.5} - \underset{(2.41)}{0.0035}\, \mathrm{conj}_{1.5} \\
& - \underset{(0.65)}{0.0071} - \underset{(1.99)}{0.0100}\, s_1 + \underset{(2.18)}{0.0078}\, s_2 - \underset{(0.00)}{0.0000}\, s_3 \\
& + \underset{(6.81)}{0.0358}\, \mathrm{dum}_{90:\mathrm{III}}
\end{aligned}
$$

Sample period: 1971:4–1992:4 $\quad \bar{R}^2 = 0.89 \quad \mathrm{SE} = 0.008$

$$
\begin{aligned}
\Delta \ln (\mathrm{M2}/P) = & - \underset{(1.97)}{0.0453} (\ln (\mathrm{M2}/P)_{-1} - \ln y) + \underset{(4.78)}{0.5318}\, \Delta \ln (\mathrm{M2}/P)_{-4} \\
& + \underset{(2.27)}{0.3809}\, \Delta \ln y_{-1.5} + \underset{(2.24)}{0.0024}\, r_s - \underset{(2.24)}{0.0024}\, r_\ell - \underset{(2.24)}{0.0024}\, \dot{p} \\
& - \underset{(3.50)}{0.0084}\, \Delta \dot{p} - \underset{(1.57)}{0.0023}\, \mathrm{conj}_{-2} + \underset{(3.50)}{0.0497} - \underset{(2.96)}{0.0274}\, s_1 \\
& - \underset{(2.40)}{0.0243}\, s_2 - \underset{(2.94)}{0.0190}\, s_3 + \underset{(11.07)}{0.0564}\, \mathrm{dum}_{90:\mathrm{III}}
\end{aligned}
$$

Sample period: 1971:2–1992:4 $\quad \bar{R}^2 = 0.74 \quad \mathrm{SE} = 0.011$

$$
\begin{aligned}
\Delta \ln (\mathrm{M3}/P) = & - \underset{(2.26)}{0.0481} (\ln (\mathrm{M3}/P)_{-1} - \ln y) + \underset{(4.19)}{0.5719}\, \Delta \ln (\mathrm{M3}/P)_{-4} \\
& + \underset{(2.28)}{0.0017}\, r_s - \underset{(1.86)}{0.0027}\, \Delta r_{s-2.5} - \underset{(2.28)}{0.0017}\, r_{\ell-1} - \underset{(2.12)}{0.0045}\, \Delta r_{\ell-1} \\
& - \underset{(2.28)}{0.0017}\, \dot{p} - \underset{(3.15)}{0.0093}\, \Delta \dot{p}_{1.5} + \underset{(2.18)}{0.0053}\, \Delta \dot{p}_{-1.5} - \underset{(2.27)}{0.0028}\, \mathrm{conj}_{-3} \\
& + \underset{(2.59)}{0.0549} + \underset{(1.09)}{0.0026}\, s_1 - \underset{(1.08)}{0.0027}\, s_2 - \underset{(1.55)}{0.0096}\, s_3 \\
& + \underset{(11.85)}{0.0606}\, \mathrm{dum}_{90:\mathrm{III}}
\end{aligned}
$$

Sample period: 1971:4–1992:4 $\quad \bar{R}^2 = 0.82 \quad \mathrm{SE} = 0.008$

$$\Delta\ 1\text{n}\ (\text{DiM2}) = -\ \underset{(4.83)}{0.2017}\ (1\text{n}\ (\text{DiM2})_{-1} - 1\text{n}\ y) + \underset{(6.04)}{0.4480}\ \Delta 1\text{n}\ (\text{DiM2}/P)_{-4}$$

$$-\ \underset{(3.32)}{0.0071}\ \text{oc1} + \underset{(2.50)}{0.0075}\ \Delta\ \text{oc1}_{-1} + \underset{(2.74)}{0.0128}\ \Delta\ \text{oc1}_{-2.5} - \underset{(2.75)}{0.0030}\ \dot{p}$$

$$-\ \underset{(3.19)}{0.0107}\ \Delta\ \dot{p}_{-0.5} + \underset{(2.66)}{0.0069}\ \Delta\ \dot{p}_{-1.5} - \underset{(2.20)}{0.0037}\ \text{conj}_{-2} - \underset{(3.60)}{0.1076}$$

$$-\ \underset{(0.92)}{0.0042}\ s_1 + \underset{(1.94)}{0.0067}\ s_2 + \underset{(0.15)}{0.0011}\ s_3 + \underset{(8.81)}{0.0430}\ \text{dum}_{90:\text{IIIi}}$$

Sample period: 1971:4–1992:4 $\quad \bar{R}^2 = 0.84 \quad \text{SE} = 0.009$

$$\Delta\ 1\text{n}\ (\text{DiM3}) = -\ \underset{(2.86)}{0.1218}\ (1\text{n}\ (\text{DiM3}/P)_{-1} - 1\text{n}\ y) + \underset{(4.74)}{0.5449}\ \Delta\ 1\text{n}\ (\text{DiM3}/P)_{-4}$$

$$-\ \underset{(3.19)}{0.0029}\ \text{oc2}_{-0.5} + \underset{(2.93)}{0.0085}\ \Delta\ \text{oc2}_{-1} + \underset{(3.32)}{0.0109}\ \Delta\ \text{oc2}_{-2.5}$$

$$-\ \underset{(3.19)}{0.0029}\ \dot{p} - \underset{(3.56)}{0.0097}\ \Delta\ \dot{p}_{-0.5} + \underset{(2.57)}{0.0066}\ \Delta\ \dot{p}_{-1.5} - \underset{(1.97)}{0.0024}\ \text{conj}_{-3}$$

$$-\ \underset{(2.29)}{0.0688} - \underset{(0.06)}{0.0002}\ s_1 + \underset{(0.86)}{0.0028}\ s_2 - \underset{(0.55)}{0.0039}\ s_3$$

$$+\ \underset{(7.98)}{0.0420}\ \text{dum}_{90:\text{III}}$$

Sample period: 1971:4–1992:4 $\quad \bar{R}^2 = 0.81 \quad \text{SE} = 0.009$

Germany, Benelux plus France

(1985 DM purchasing power parities)

$$\Delta\ 1\text{n}\ (\text{M1}/P) = -\ \underset{(4.31)}{0.2546}\ (1\text{n}\ (\text{M1}/P)_1 - 1\text{n}\ y) + \underset{(4.82)}{0.3267}\ \Delta\ 1\text{n}\ (\text{M1}/P)_{-4}$$

$$-\ \underset{(4.99)}{0.0017}\ r_s - \underset{(2.65)}{0.0038}\ \Delta\ r_{s_{-1}} - \underset{(4.99)}{0.0017}\ r_\ell + \underset{(2.26)}{0.0061}\ \Delta\ r_{\ell_{-2}}$$

$$-\ \underset{(2.42)}{0.0019}\ \dot{p} - \underset{(3.06)}{0.0099}\ \Delta\ \dot{p}_{-0.5} + \underset{(2.29)}{0.0059}\ \Delta\ \dot{p}_{-1.5} - \underset{(2.41)}{0.0035}\ \text{conj}_{-1.5}$$

$$-\ \underset{(0.64)}{0.0070} - \underset{(1.99)}{0.0100}\ s_1 + \underset{(2.24)}{0.0081}\ s_2 - \underset{(0.02)}{0.0002}\ s_3$$

$$+\ \underset{(6.81)}{0.0357}\ \text{dum}_{90:\text{III}}$$

Sample period: 1971:4–1992:4 $\quad \bar{R}^2 = 0.89 \quad \text{SE} = 0.008$

$$\Delta \ln (M2/P) = -\underset{(1.97)}{0.0451} (\ln (M2/P)_{-1} - \ln y) + \underset{(4.82)}{0.5340} \Delta \ln (M2/P)_{-4}$$

$$+ \underset{(2.28)}{0.3822} \Delta \ln y_{-1.5} + \underset{(2.25)}{0.0024} r_s - \underset{(2.25)}{0.0024} r_\ell - \underset{(2.25)}{0.0024} \dot{p}$$

$$- \underset{(3.52)}{0.0084} \Delta \dot{p} - \underset{(1.56)}{0.0023} \text{conj}_{-2} + \underset{(3.51)}{0.0495} - \underset{(2.94)}{0.0272} s_1$$

$$- \underset{(2.40)}{0.0242} s_2 - \underset{(2.93)}{0.0189} s_3 + \underset{(11.01)}{0.0560} \text{dum}_{90:III}$$

Sample period: 1971:2–1992:4 $\quad \bar{R}^2 = 0.74 \quad SE = 0.011$

$$\Delta \ln (M3/P) = -\underset{(2.28)}{0.0483} (\ln (M3/P)_{-1} - \ln y) + \underset{(4.21)}{0.5739} \Delta \ln (M3/P)_{-4}$$

$$+ \underset{(2.31)}{0.0017} r_s - \underset{(1.87)}{0.0027} \Delta r_{s_{-2.5}} - \underset{(2.31)}{0.0017} r_{\ell_{-1}} - \underset{(2.15)}{0.0045} \Delta r_{\ell_{-1}}$$

$$- \underset{(2.31)}{0.0017} \dot{p} - \underset{(3.17)}{0.0093} \Delta \dot{p}_{-0.5} + \underset{(2.19)}{0.0053} \Delta \dot{p}_{-1.5} - \underset{(2.30)}{0.0028} \text{conj}_{-3}$$

$$+ \underset{(2.61)}{0.0551} + \underset{(1.13)}{0.0027} s_1 - \underset{(1.04)}{0.0026} s_2 - \underset{(1.54)}{0.0095} s_3 + \underset{(11.80)}{0.0602} \text{dum}_{90:III}$$

Sample period: 1971:4–1992:4 $\quad \bar{R}^2 = 0.82 \quad SE = 0.008$

$$\Delta \ln (DiM2) = -\underset{(4.77)}{0.2003} (\ln (DiM2)_{-1} - \ln y) + \underset{(6.04)}{0.4502} \Delta \ln (DiM2/P)_{-4}$$

$$- \underset{(3.33)}{0.0071} \text{oc1} + \underset{(2.51)}{0.0075} \Delta \text{ocl}_{-1} + \underset{(2.72)}{0.0127} \Delta \text{oc1}_{-2.5} - \underset{(2.69)}{0.0029} \dot{p}$$

$$- \underset{(3.21)}{0.0108} \Delta \dot{p}_{-1/2} + \underset{(2.65)}{0.0068} \Delta \dot{p}_{-1.5} - \underset{(2.19)}{0.0037} \text{conj}_{-2} - \underset{(3.57)}{0.1077}$$

$$- \underset{(0.90)}{0.0041} s_1 + \underset{(1.97)}{0.0068} s_2 + \underset{(0.14)}{0.0010} s_3 + \underset{(8.79)}{0.0428} \text{dum}_{90:III}$$

Sample period: 1971:4–1992:4 $\quad \bar{R}^2 = 0.84 \quad SE = 0.009$

$$\Delta \ln (DiM3) = -\underset{(2.87)}{0.1228} (\ln (DiM3/P)_{-1} - \ln y) + \underset{(4.76)}{0.5454} \Delta \ln (DiM3/P)_{-4}$$

$$- \underset{(3.19)}{0.0030} \text{oc2}_{-1.5} + \underset{(2.94)}{0.0085} \Delta \text{oc2}_{-1} + \underset{(3.30)}{0.0109} \Delta \text{oc2}_{-2.5}$$

$$- \underset{(3.19)}{0.0030} \dot{p} - \underset{(3.58)}{0.0097} \Delta \dot{p}_{-0.5} + \underset{(2.59)}{0.0066} \Delta \dot{p}_{-1.5} - \underset{(1.99)}{0.0024} \text{conj}_{-3}$$

$$- \underset{(2.30)}{0.0702} - \underset{(0.04)}{0.0001} s_1 + \underset{(0.90)}{0.0029} s_2 - \underset{(0.54)}{0.0038} s_3 + \underset{(7.97)}{0.0417} \text{dum}_{90:III}$$

Sample period: 1971:4–1992:4 $\quad \bar{R}^2 = 0.82 \quad SE = 0.009$

Germany, Benelux plus France

(current DM exchange rates)

$$\Delta \ln (M3/P) = -\underset{(2.79)}{0.1490} (\ln (M3P)_{-1} - \ln y) + \underset{(1.94)}{0.1376} \Delta \ln (M3/P)_{-4}$$
$$+ \underset{(2.18)}{0.0378} \ln P + \underset{(2.24)}{0.0007} r_{s_{-3.5}} - \underset{(4.22)}{0.0040} r_{\ell_{-2.5}} - \underset{(2.24)}{0.0007} \dot{p}_{-3.5}$$
$$- \underset{(2.10)}{0.0010} \Delta \dot{p} - \underset{(3.06)}{0.0033} \text{conj}_{-3.5} + \underset{(3.46)}{0.1669} + \underset{(1.95)}{0.0079} s_1 + \underset{(0.94)}{0.0038} s_2$$
$$- \underset{(0.05)}{0.0003} s_3 + \underset{(22.95)}{0.0552} \text{dum}_{90:\text{III}}$$

Sample period: 1972:1–1992:4 $\bar{R}^2 = 0.68$ SE = 0.007

(current DM purchasing power parities)

$$\Delta \ln (M3/P) = -\underset{(3.57)}{0.1843} (\ln (M3/P)_{-1} - \ln y) + \underset{(2.32)}{0.0530} \ln y_{-1} + \underset{(3.83)}{0.0028} r_s$$
$$- \underset{(4.88)}{0.0045} \Delta r_{s_{-1}} - \underset{(6.31)}{0.0068} r_{\ell_{-0.5}} - \underset{(3.83)}{0.0028} \dot{p} - \underset{(4.33)}{0.0034} \text{conj}_{-4}$$
$$- \underset{(1.32)}{0.1545} + \underset{(1.93)}{0.0041} s_1 + \underset{(0.48)}{0.0011} s_2 - \underset{(0.21)}{0.0010} s_3 + \underset{(20.25)}{0.0548} \text{dum}_{90:\text{III}}$$

Sample period: 1971:2–1992:4 $\bar{R}^2 = 0.72$ SE = 0.006

Appendix 2

Table 7.B.1 Summary statistics for core EMU: Germany, France plus Benelux

Conversion technique	*Variance*	*Mean*	*Standard deviation*	*Correlation with*	
				M1	*y*
Current DM exchange rates	M1	6.17	4.45	1.00	0.11
	M2	7.95	3.89	0.73	0.34
	M3	7.81	3.50	0.90	0.26
	DiM2	6.71	4.00	0.96	0.23
	DiM3	6.89	3.99	0.98	0.20
	Real income	2.70	1.96	0.11	1.00
	Price	3.83	2.80	0.69	–0.24
1985 DM exchange rates	M1	7.98	3.10	1.00	0.17
	M2	9.75	2.46	0.21	0.64
	M3	9.38	2.43	0.77	0.41
	DiM2	8.51	2.32	0.88	0.44
	DiM3	8.57	2.66	0.95	0.31
	Real income	2.70	1.96	0.17	1.00
	Price	5.13	1.90	0.37	–0.29
Current DM–PPP	M1	6.30	3.04	1.00	0.41
	M2	8.12	3.22	0.52	0.63
	M3	7.98	2.65	0.81	0.60
	DiM2	6.87	2.83	0.90	0.59
	DiM3	7.05	2.82	0.96	0.54
	Real income	2.69	1.96	0.41	1.00
	Price	3.96	1.59	0.26	–0.06
1985 DM–PPP	M1	7.97	3.10	1.00	0.16
	M2	9.74	2.46	0.21	0.64
	M3	9.38	2.43	0.77	0.41
	DiM2	8.50	2.32	0.88	0.44
	DiM3	8.57	2.66	0.95	0.31
	Real income	2.69	1.96	0.16	1.00
	Price	5.13	1.90	0.37	–0.29

Appendix 3

Table 7.C.1 Results of specification analysis, long-run relationship

	Monetary aggregate	*P elas = 1* ($\alpha_1 = 1$)	*Inc. elas = 1* ($\alpha_2 = 1$)	*Semi-elasticities* Restriction	Test statistic
Germany	DiM2	0.28	1.68	$\alpha_3 = \alpha_4$	0.68
	DiM3	0.74	1.21	$\alpha_3 = \alpha_4$	0.80
Netherlands	DiM2	1.10	0.75	$\alpha_3 = \alpha_4$	1.58
	DiM3	0.16	0.11	$\alpha_3 = \alpha_4$	0.15
Belgium	DiM2	2.29*	0.99	–	–
	DiM3	1.09	0.36	–	–
France	DiM2	3.02*	1.64	$\alpha_3 = \alpha_4$	0.77
	DiM3	2.97*	0.97	$\alpha_3 = \alpha_4$	1.76
Germany plus	M1	0.90	2.21*	$\alpha_3 = \alpha_4 = \alpha_5$	$F(2, 75) = 0.85$
Benelux	M2	0.62	1.74[a]	$\alpha_3 = -\alpha_4 = \alpha_5$	$F(2, 71) = 1.78$
1985 DM exchange	M3	0.85	1.06	$\alpha_3 = \alpha_5$	1.54
rates	DiM2	1.25	0.13	$\alpha_3 = \alpha_4$	1.91
	DiM3	0.21	0.98	$\alpha_3 = \alpha_4$	1.18
Current DM exchange rates	M3	0.64	2.51	–	–
Germany plus	M1	0.93	2.16*	$\alpha_3 = \alpha_4 = \alpha_5$	$F(2, 75) = 0.87$
Benelux	M2	0.63	1.76[a]	$\alpha_3 = -\alpha_4 = \alpha_5$	$F(2, 71) = 1.78$
1985 DM–PPP	M3	0.85	1.07	$\alpha_3 = \alpha_5$	1.56
	DiM2	1.27	0.10	$\alpha_3 = \alpha_4$	1.93
	DiM3	0.21	0.97	$\alpha_3 = \alpha_4$	1.20
Current DM–PPP	M3	1.22	2.35*	–	–
Germany, France	M1	0.97	1.13	$\alpha_3 = \alpha_4$	0.06
plus Benelux	M2	0.43	0.62	$\alpha_3 = -\alpha_4 = \alpha_5$	$F(2, 74) = 1.54$
1985 DM exchange rates	M3	1.23	0.03	$\alpha_3 = -\alpha_4 = \alpha_5$	$F(2, 70) = 1.23$
	DiM2	0.18	0.14	–	–
	DiM3	0.96	0.44	$\alpha_3 = \alpha_4$	0.72

Table 7.C.1 (continued)

	Monetary aggregate	*P elas = 1* *($\alpha_1 = 1$)*	*Inc. elas = 1* *($\alpha_2 = 1$)*	*Semi-elasticities*	
				Restriction	*Test statistic*
Current DM					
exchange rates	M3	2.18*	0.51	$\alpha_4 = -\alpha_5$	0.35
Germany, France	M1	0.90	1.09	$\alpha_3 = \alpha_4$	0.03
plus Benelux	M2	0.42	0.60	$\alpha_3 = -\alpha_4 = \alpha_5$	F (2, 74) = 1.53
1985 DM–PPP	M3	1.21	0.03	$\alpha_3 = -\alpha_4 = \alpha_5$	F (2, 70) = 1.24
	DiM2	0.23	0.09	–	–
	DiM3	0.92	0.43	$\alpha_3 = \alpha_4$	0.71
Current DM–PPP	M3	0.31	2.32*	$\alpha_4 = -\alpha_5$	1.03

Notes: Long-run relationship for M1, M2, M3:
$M = P^{a_1} y^{a_2} \exp(a_3 r_\ell + a_4 r_s + a_5 \dot{p})$; for DiM2, DiM3; $M = p^{a_1} y^{a_2} \exp(a_3 oc + a_4 \dot{p})$; unless stated otherwise, the values of the t-test statistic are given.
* Significant at significance level of 0.05.
[a] t-test for restriction implying that the price elasticities of M2 – M1 and M3 – M1 are equal to 1.

Table 7.C.2 LB tests on residual autocorrelation

	Monetary aggregate	Order p			
		1	4	8	12
Germany	DiM2	0.96	1.51	10.28	13.79
	DiM3	0.06	1.85	5.11	6.55
Netherlands	DiM2	1.67	7.56	12.58	15.11
	DiM3	0.75	5.56	10.93	13.17
Belgium	DiM2	1.66	2.04	4.92	13.89
	DiM3	0.90	1.84	3.70	11.84
France	DiM2	0.45	3.33	5.65	11.69
	DiM3	0.45	2.21	7.38	10.48
Germany plus	M1	0.44	1.11	2.70	5.55
Benelux	M2	0.11	0.80	2.40	5.68
1985 DM exchange	M3	1.66	2.20	6.08	10.94
rates	DiM2	1.30	3.76	14.17	16.45
	DiM3	0.62	7.77	10.91	11.94
Current DM exchange rates	M3	2.43	4.75	12.90	15.37
Germany plus	M1	0.46	1.13	2.76	5.64
Benelux	M2	0.13	0.87	2.44	5.82
1985 DM–PPP	M3	1.61	2.16	6.09	10.92
	DiM2	1.30	3.85	14.03	16.27
	DiM3	0.65	7.98	11.04	12.03
Current DM–PPP	M3	0.75	3.88	8.48	11.56
Germany, France	M1	0.07	3.79	4.73	7.78
plus Benelux	M2	1.18	3.34	4.25	6.43
1985 DM exchange	M3	0.14	0.63	2.90	5.87
rates	DiM2	0.02	4.37	5.04	12.73
	DiM3	0.05	4.49	6.31	10.83
Current DM exchange rates	M3	1.32	3.91	9.13	16.16
Germany, France	M1	0.08	3.84	4.74	7.73
plus Benelux	M2	1.14	3.35	4.34	6.48
1985 DM–PPP	M3	0.13	0.63	2.86	5.77
	DiM2	0.02	4.40	5.07	12.73
	DiM3	0.05	4.53	6.38	10.86
Current DM–PPP	M3	2.01	2.99	4.92	6.68

Table 7.C.3 Results of cointegration analysis

	Monetary	$t(\pi_1)$	$t(\pi_2)$	$t(\pi_3)$	$t(\pi_4)$	$F(\pi_3, \pi_4)$
Germany	DiM2	−1.20*	−4.51	−6.12	−4.53	44.66
	DiM3	−2.81	−4.56	−6.25	−4.64	47.87
Netherlands	DiM2	−1.86*	−6.04	−4.24	−3.90	20.93
	DiM3	−2.51*	−6.03	−4.78	−3.89	24.77
Belgium	DiM2	−2.83	−4.14	−5.28	−5.01	40.75
	DiM3	−4.08	−4.50	−4.84	−5.72	43.89
France	DiM2	−3.94	−2.05*	−2.64*	−1.83*	5.03*
	DiM3	−1.73*	−2.29*	−2.35*	−2.41	5.13*
Germany plus	M1	−1.57*	−4.14	−5.75	−2.29	21.33
Benelux	M2	−2.86	−4.85	−5.70	−6.01	60.71
1985 DM exchange	M3	−2.31*	−4.39	−6.47	−4.86	54.06
rates	DiM2	−1.78*	−4.06	−5.80	−5.39	51.50
	DiM3	−2.50*	−4.15	−5.60	−5.63	52.41
Current DM exchange rates	M3	−2.45*	−2.56*	−4.59	−1.29*	12.02
Germany plus	M1	−1.55*	−4.15	−5.79	−2.29	21.60
Benelux	M2	−2.86	−4.84	−5.70	−6.03	60.92
1985 DM–PPP	M3	−2.31(*)	−4.40	−6.49	−4.86	54.34
	DiM2	−1.79(*)	−4.06	−5.81	−5.38	51.58
	DiM3	−2.50(*)	−4.15	−5.61	−5.63	52.39
Current DM–PPP	M3	−3.02	−2.75	−3.15	−2.20	8.64
Germany, France	M1	−2.91	−3.98	−3.40	−2.50	9.36
plus Benelux	M2	−3.89	−5.27	−4.63	−6.23	47.36
1985 DM exchange	M3	−2.19*	−5.73	−1.54*	−4.25	10.51
rates	DiM2	−3.56	−4.85	−5.95	−5.45	54.39
	DiM3	−3.53	−4.35*	−5.69*	−5.67	54.25
Current DM exchange rates	M3	−3.37	−5.53	−6.85	−4.41	54.02
Germany, France	M1	−2.90	−3.99	−3.40	−2.47	9.27
plus Benelux	M2	−3.88	−5.27	−4.62	−6.24	47.42
1985 DM–PPP	M3	−2.21*	−5.72	−1.55*	−4.25	10.55
	DiM2	−3.57	−4.87	−5.95	−5.44	54.30
	DiM3	−3.55	−4.35	−5.71*	−5.66	54.35
Current DM-PPP	M3	−3.22	−4.82	−7.00	−4.26	53.59

Notes: * not significant at significance level of 0.10.
* in $t(\pi_1)$ column indicates absence of cointegration.

Note

1. Our formulation in Equation (7.4) differs from that used in the more technically-orientated cointegration literature put forward by Engle and Granger (1987). In this cointegration approach, the error-correction term is defined as the deviation from the equilibrium relationship in Equation (7.1), and hence is given a somewhat different interpretation. Collecting the level terms in Equation (7.4) yields the formulation commonly used in the cointegration literature, and shows that real income – the price level as well as interest rates and inflation – are important, in the long run.

References

Barnett, W. A. (1978) 'The User Cost of Money', *Economics Letters*, vol. 1, pp. 145–9.

Barnett, W. A. (1980) 'Economic Monetary Aggregates: An Application of Index Number and Aggregation Theory', *Journal of Econometrics*, vol. 14, pp. 11–48.

Barnett, W. A., D. Fisher and A. Serletis (1992) 'Consumer Theory and the Demand for Money', *Journal of Economic Literature*, vol. 30, pp. 2086–119.

Belongia, M. T. and K. A. Chrystal (1991) 'An Admissible Monetary Aggregate for the United Kingdom', *The Review of Economics and Statistics*, vol. 73, pp. 497–503.

Boughton, J. M. (1991) 'Long-run Money Demand in Large Industrial Countries', *IMF Staff Papers*, vol. 38, no. 1, pp. 1–32.

Butter, F. A. G. den and M. M. G. Fase (1981) 'The Demand for Money in EEC Countries' *Journal of Monetary Economics*, vol. 8, pp. 201–230.

Christ, C. F. (1993) 'Assessing Applied Econometric Results', in M. T. Belongia (ed.), *Dimensions of Monetary Policy, Essays in Honor of Anatol B. Balbach, Federal Reserve Bank of St Louis Review*, vol. 75, March/April, pp. 71–94.

Divisia, F. (1925, 1926) 'L'indice monétaire et la théorie de la monnaie', *Revue d'Economie Politique*, vol. 39, pp. 842–861; 980–1008; 1121–1151; and vol. 40, pp. 49–87.

Engle, R. F. and C. W. J. Granger (1987) 'Cointegration and Error Correction: Representation, Estimation and Testing', *Econometrica*, vol. 55, pp. 251–276.

Fase, M. M. G. (1979) 'The Demand for Financial Assets: Time Series Evidence for the Netherlands: 1963:II–1975:IV', *European Economic Review*, vol. 12, pp. 381–94.

Fase, M. M. G. (1993) 'The Stability of the Demand for Money in the G7 and EC Countries: A Survey', *De Nederlandsche Bank WO&E Research Paper*, no. 9321 (May) and *CEPS Working Document*, no. 81 (November).

Fase, M. M. G. (1994) 'In Search for Stability: An Empirical Appraisal of the Demand for Money in the G7 and EC Countries', *The Economist*, vol. 142, pp. 421–54.

Fase, M. M. G. and J. B. Kuné (1974a) 'Price and Income Expectations in the Demand for Money', Paper presented at ESEM, Grenoble.

Fase, M. M. G. and J. B. Kuné (1974b) 'De vraag naar liquiditeiten in Nederland, 1952–1971', *De Economist*, vol. 122, pp. 326–56.

Fase, M. M. G. and C. C. A. Winder (1990) 'The Demand for Money in the Netherlands Revisited', *The Economist*, vol. 138, pp. 276–301.

Fase, M. M. G. and C. C. A. Winder (1993) 'The Demand for Money in the Netherlands and the Other EC Countries', *The Economist*, vol. 141, pp. 471–96.

Fase, M. M. G. and C. C. A. Winder (1994) 'Money Demand Within EMU: An Analysis with the Divisia Measure', *De Nederlandsche Bank NV Quarterly Bulletin*, 1994/2 (September) pp. 25–55.

Hylleberg, S., R. F. Engle, C. W. J. Granger and B. S. Yoo (1990) 'Seasonal Integration and Cointegration', *Journal of Econometrics*, vol. 44, pp. 215–38.

Latané, H. A. (1954) 'Cash Balances and Interest Rates: A Pragmatic Approach', *Review of Economics and Statistics*, vol. 36, pp. 456–60.

Part III

Evidence from the Pacific Basin

8
Broad and Narrow Divisia Monetary Aggregates for Japan*

*Kazuhiko Ishida and Koji Nakamura**

8.1 Introduction

An application of the Divisia aggregation theory to Japanese monetary data was first made by Ishida (1984). This paper argued for the use of Divisia monetary aggregates in the case of broadly-defined money (M2 + CDs, M3 + CDs), whereas for narrowly defined money (M1) it was found that the aggregation method made no significant difference in the chosen empirical applications.

In that paper, Divisia M2 + CDs were considered to be more useful than simple-sum M2 + CDs as an indicator for monetary policy, mainly for these two reasons:

(i) The downward trend in velocity, which had been observed consistently for simple-sum M2 + CDs in Japan, was far less significant in the case of Divisia M2 + CDs. This suggested that Divisia M2 + CDs had a more stable long-run relationship with GDP.
(ii) The demand function for Divisia M2 + CDs was found to be more stable than that for simple-sum M2 + CDs.

It was also found, however, that Divisia and simple-sum M2 + CDs showed similar cyclical behaviour (developments in the growth rate or in the velocity around its trend).

There has been little research on Divisia monetary aggregates in Japan since then. The purpose of this chapter is to construct updated Divisia monetary aggregates for various definitions of money in Japan, and to investigate their usefulness. Special attention will be paid to the following developments of the past ten years, which are expected to affect the relative usefulness of Divisia monetary aggregates;

*The views expressed are those of the authors and do not necessarily reflect those of the Bank of Japan.

(i) The deregulation of interest rates on time deposits, the main components of 'quasi money', started in 1985 and was completed in 1993. This deregulation of time-deposit interest rates, along with other liberalisation measures, is thought to have changed substantially the meaning of money, especially for the components of broad monetary aggregates.
(ii) Large fluctuations in asset prices during the late 1980s and early 1990s affected the demand for money significantly through an increase in the weight of asset transactions as well as through their wealth effects.

Simultaneously affected by these two factors, simple-sum M2 + CDs, the main monetary indicator in Japan, has been very volatile since the late 1980s and has become more and more difficult to interpret. It might therefore be interesting to examine the behaviour of Divisia monetary aggregates during this period to see if more useful information could have been obtained from them.

8.2 Constructing Divisia monetary aggregates for Japan

In this chapter, Divisia aggregates for Japan have been calculated for both narrow and broad official definitions of money, namely M1, M2 + CDs and L (broadly defined liquidity). The Divisia aggregation theory, however, requires that the set of money components to be aggregated should satisfy certain separability conditions. In many studies, the sets of components included in the officially defined monetary aggregates have failed to satisfy those conditions.

In Japan's case, Kobayakawa (1993), applying Varian's GARP (generalized axiom of revealed preference) test method to various sets of money components, found that the set that consists of M2 + CDs failed to pass the GARP test (for a summary of Kobayakawa's results, see Appendix on page 196). It is therefore possible that the Divisia M2 + CDs calculated here, in fact, does not have a proper theoretical basis for aggregation. Kobayakawa also found that certain sets of components, which are not used as official monetary aggregates, passed the GARP test. For example, a set which includes M1 components and time-deposits with regulated interest rates (hereafter, referred to as A1) or a set which includes A1 components, postal savings and trust accounts (hereafter, referred to as A2) passed the GARP test. In contrast, Belongia (this volume) generally found for Japan, Germany and the USA that asset collections including time-deposits failed the GARP test.[1] Based on Kobayakawa's results, we have constructed Divisia aggregates for A1 and A2 as well as for the three official aggregates mentioned earlier. The major important points of the construction are as follows:

(i) Mainly taking account of data availability, L is divided into nineteen components, of which six are included in M1, and eleven in M2 + CDs.

For the components for which official money supply statistics are not available, estimates have been made using various public data sources.

(ii) Distinctions have been made for each component on the basis of whether it is held by individuals or corporations. This is necessary because regulatory restrictions for the holders of certain assets (for example, postal savings are not available to corporations) mean that different benchmark rates are applied for individuals and corporations.

(iii) For components to which different interest rates could be attached, the most representative rate has been adopted. All the interest rates are adjusted to a common one-year maturity, using the yield curve of bank debenture rates.

8.3 Developments in Divisia monetary aggregates

For each category of aggregates (M1, M2 + CDs, L, A1, A2), Divisia indices have been calculated and compared with simple-sum counterparts, which are indexed using the same base year. Growth rates (year-to-year) and velocity developments have also been compared. In the following, the main findings will be described by each category of aggregation.

M1

In the case of M1, the discrepancy between the Divisia index and the indexed simple-sum aggregates is very small (see Figure 8.1), which suggests that substitutability among M1 components, (that is, cash and demand deposits) is still rather high. This result seems quite natural, because there had been no significant institutional changes nor deregulation of interest rates concerning M1 components until October 1994, hence they still bear zero or very low interest rates.

The difference in the developments of the growth rate between Divisia and simple-sum M1 seems much smaller (see Figure 8.2). In fact, as is shown in Table 8.1, the basic descriptive statistics (the average and the standard deviation) concerning the growth rates of Divisia and simple-sum M1 do not differ much from each other, and the correlation coefficient between them is close to unity. In addition, although a very small discrepancy can be seen between the trends in the velocity of Divisia and simple-sum M1, their cyclical developments around the trend line seem to be almost the same (see Figure 8.3). These observations imply that cyclical policy signals obtained from Divisia and simple-sum M1 might not be much different from each other.

Given these results, it could be concluded that, as far as M1 is concerned, there is little need to adopt the Divisia aggregation method. One important reservation, however, must be made here. Deregulation of interest rates on demand deposits (excluding checkable current deposits) took place in October 1994, which is likely to expand the discrepancy between Divisia and simple-sum M1 in the future.

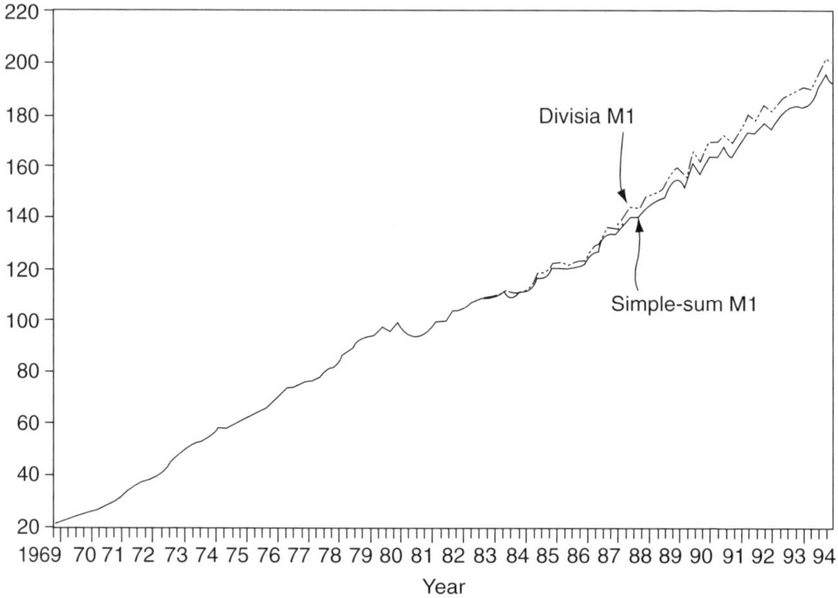

Figure 8.1 Simple-sum and Divisia M1 indices (1980/IQ = 100)

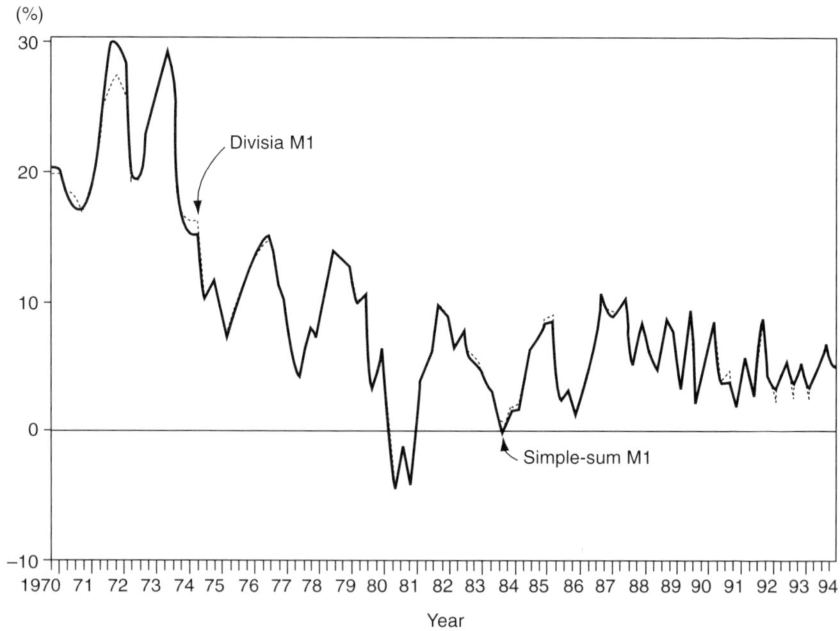

Figure 8.2 Growth rates of simple-sum and Divisia M1 (year-to-year)

Table 8.1 Basic statistics

(a) M1

		1Q/70–4Q/79	1Q/80–1Q/94	1Q/70–1Q/94
Average	SS	15.7	5.0	9.4
	DV	15.6	5.3	9.6
Standard	SS	7.3	3.3	7.5
Deviation	DV	6.7	3.3	7.1
Correlation coefficient		0.995	0.993	0.997

(b) M2 + CDs

		1Q/70–4Q/79	1Q/80–1Q/94	1Q/70–1Q/94
Average	SS	16.1	7.5	11.1
	DV	15.8	5.6	9.8
Standard	SS	4.9	3.5	5.9
Deviation	DV	5.3	2.4	6.3
Correlation coefficient		0.988	0.204	0.873

(c) L

		1Q/81–4Q/93
Average	SS	8.4
	DV	6.3
Standard	SS	2.7
Deviation	DV	2.1
Correlation coefficient		0.441

(d) A1

		1Q/81–4Q/93
Average	SS	2.1
	DV	3.1
Standard	SS	11.5
Deviation	DV	7.9
Correlation coefficient		0.984

(e) A2

		1Q/81–4Q/93
Average	SS	5.1
	DV	4.2
Standard	SS	7.7
Deviation	DV	6.7
Correlation coefficient		0.987

Notes: 1 Quarterly year-to-year change.
2 SS represents simple-sum index. DV represents Divisia index.

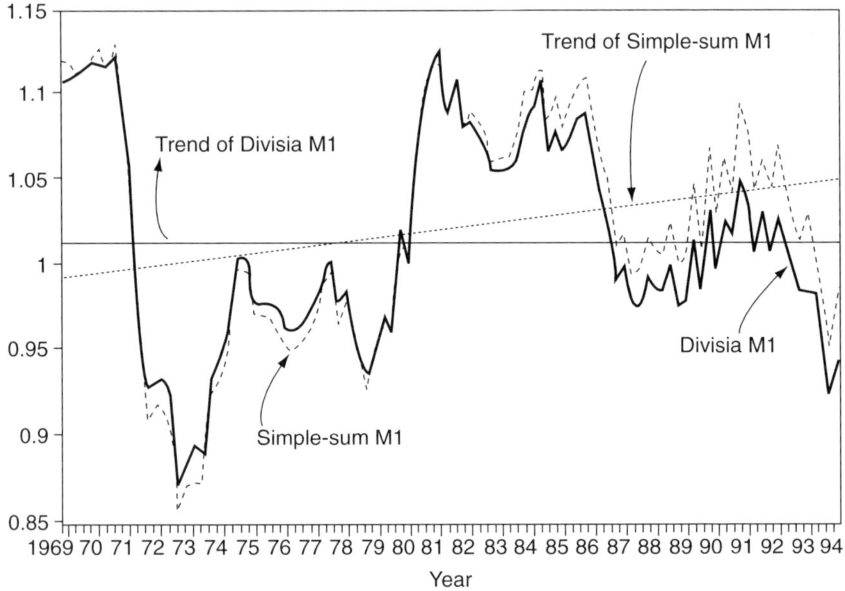

Figure 8.3 Velocity of simple-sum and Divisia M1 (trend: IQ/69–IQ/94) (1980/IQ = 1)

M2 + CDs

A large discrepancy, however, can be observed between Divisia and simple-sum M2 + CDs (see Figure 8.4). The discrepancy seems to have expanded since 1985, because simple-sum M2 + CDs grew far more rapidly during the late 1980s. The difference in the growth rates of the two aggregates is also substantial (see Figure 8.5). For example:

(i) The growth rate of simple-sum M2 + CDs generally accelerated between 1987 and 1989, whereas that of Divisia M2 + CDs decelerated gradually.
(ii) From 1990 to 1992, the growth rate of simple-sum M2 + CDs decelerated rapidly, while, on the other hand, that of Divisia M2 + CDs accelerated.

The discrepancy in the growth rates of Divisia and simple-sum M2 + CDs is also evidenced by the basic descriptive statistics (see Table 8.1). The differences in these statistics become much greater in the period after 1980 (IQ/80–IQ/94), compared to those during the 1970s (IQ/70–IVQ/79). The correlation coefficient, which was close to unity (0.988) in the 1970s, fell sharply to 0.204 after 1980. It should also be noted that the average growth rate of Divisia M2 + CDs is much smaller than simple-sum M2 + CDs in the period after 1980.

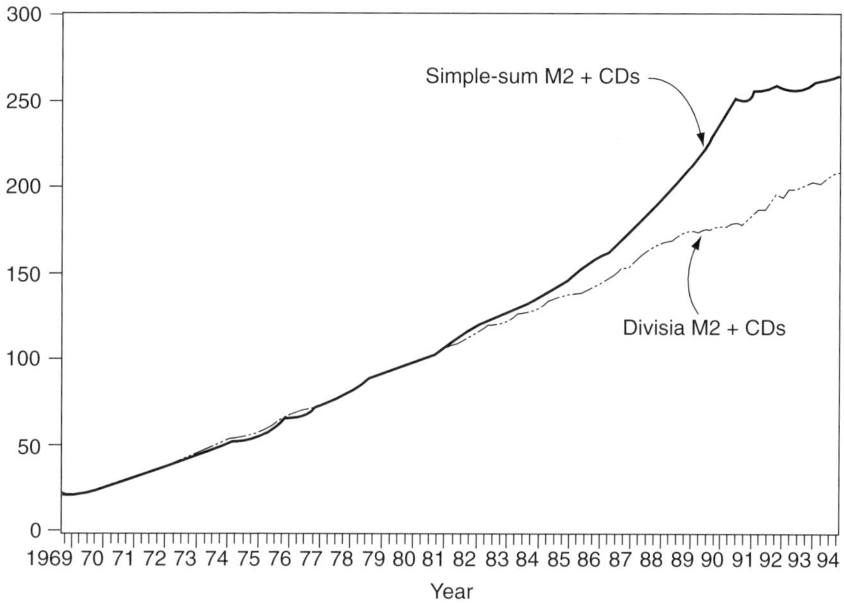

Figure 8.4 Simple-sum and Divisia M2 + CDs indices (1980/IQ)

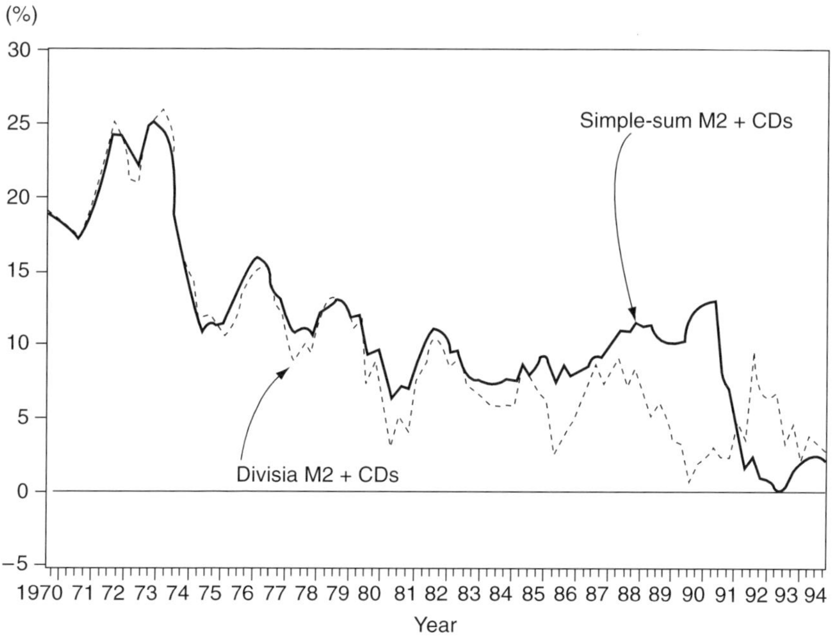

Figure 8.5 Growth rate of simple-sum and Divisia M2 + CDs (year-to-year)

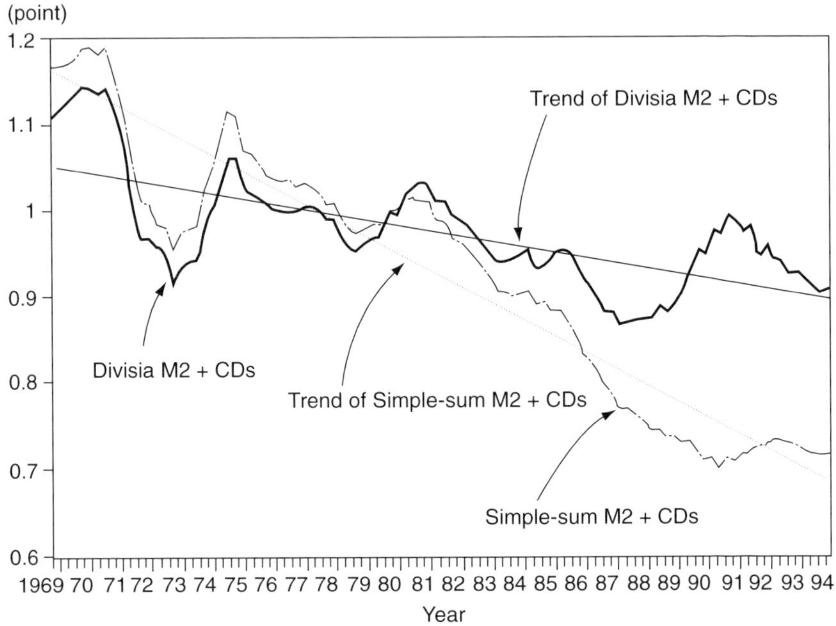

Figure 8.6 Velocity of simple-sum and Divisia M2 + CDs (trend: IQ/69–IQ/94) (1980/IQ = 1)

This implies that, contrary to the case of M1, cyclical signals obtained from Divisia and simple-sum M2 + CDs might be quite different. It seems that, in general, the cyclical movements in the growth rate of Divisia M2 + CDs is more consistent with monetary policy conditions that are represented by short-term interest rates. On the other hand, developments in the growth rate of simple-sum M2 + CDs are more difficult to explain by monetary conditions.[2]

As regards developments in their velocities, a persistent downward trend can be seen in the velocity of simple-sum M2 + CDs (see Figure 8.6). This downward trend has long been observed and is usually explained by an increase in money demand associated with accumulation of wealth, which has been much faster than income growth. In contrast, the velocity of Divisia M2 + CDs shows a far flatter trend, which suggests that Divisia M2 + CDs has a more stable long-run relationship with nominal GDP than does simple-sum M2 + CDs.

This seems quite natural, because Divisia monetary aggregates are thought to be measures of the total quantity of 'monetary services' (services provided by money as a medium of exchange (MOE)) consumed by economic agents, which, in principle, excludes the portfolio demand for money (money as a

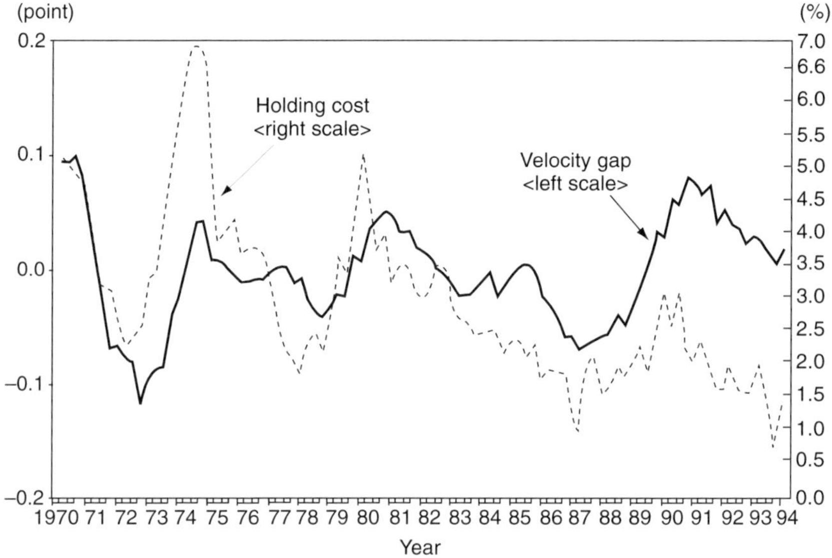

Notes: 1. Velocity gap: time trend of velocity minus actual velocity.
2. Holding cost: yields on bank debentures (5Y) minus rate of return for holding M2 + CDs

Figure 8.7 Velocity gap and holding cost of Divisia M2 + CDs

store of value (SOV)). As mentioned above, the persistent downward trend in the velocity of simple-sum M2 + CDs has been thought to reflect the rise in the portfolio demand for money (money as SOV), and the Divisia index does not count this rise as an increase in money (as MOE).

Furthermore, there is a substantial difference between the cyclical developments in the velocity of Divisia and simple-sum M2 + CDs around their trend lines. The divergence seems to have become particularly significant since 1987, and in many cases they have tended to move in the opposite direction. In general, as in the case of the growth rate, it seems that cyclical developments in the velocity of Divisia M2 + CDs are more consistent with monetary policy conditions or the movements in interest rates, compared with those of simple-sum M2 + CDs. In fact, Figure 8.7 shows almost parallel movement in the velocity of Divisia M2 + CDs (measured by the divergence from the trend line) and the holding cost of M2 + CDs.

This observation is the main difference with the result obtained in Ishida (1984), who found that the cyclical behaviour of the velocity of Divisia and simple-sum M2 + CDs had been similar despite the divergence in their trends. The difference is supposed to have been caused by major developments that have taken place after 1984, namely, (i) progress in interest rate deregulations;

and (ii) fluctuations in asset prices. The deregulation of interest rates on time deposits, for example, caused a large shift of funds to M2 + CDs. Most of this shift, however, has been associated with an increase in the portfolio demand for time-deposits (money as SOV). Fluctuations in asset prices also caused large movements in the portfolio demand for M2 + CDs through the rise and fall in total wealth.[3]

Since the simple-sum measure of M2 + CDs has been affected greatly by these developments, which are not always in line with movements in interest rates or income, it is quite natural that the cyclical behaviour of the velocity of simple-sum M2 + CDs has often been distorted by these developments and failed to exhibit a consistent cyclical signal for monetary policy. In contrast, Divisia M2 + CDs, which is, in principle, a measure of money as MOE, is not much affected by fluctuations in the portfolio demand for money, and hence has exhibited consistent behaviour with regard to income and interest rates.

L

As in the case of M2 + CDs, there is an apparent divergence in the developments in Divisia and simple-sum L (see Figure 8.8). The developments in the growth rate are also quite different (see Figure 8.9). The divergence, however, is much smaller than in the case of M2 + CDs because simple-sum L internalises most of the shift of funds to M2 + CDs from assets outside M2 + CDs, which has been one of the major reasons for the divergence between

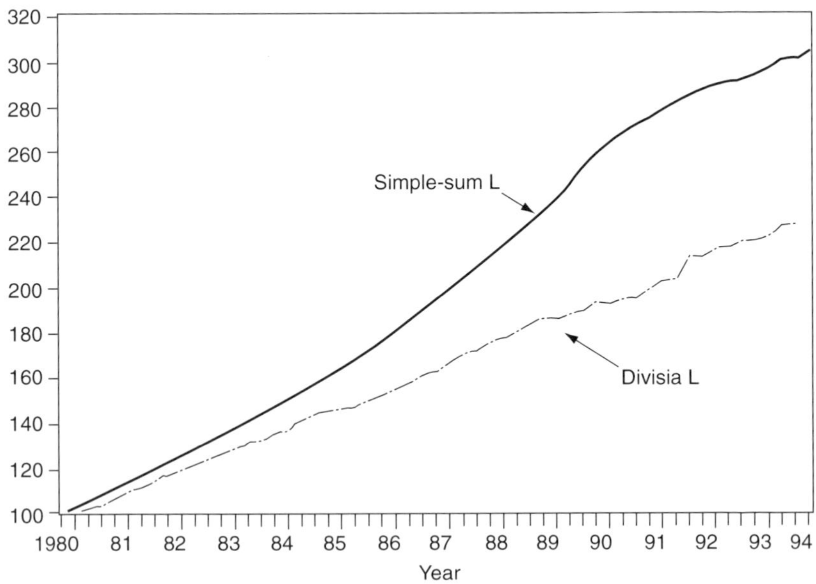

Figure 8.8 Simple-sum and Divisia L indices (1980/IQ = 100)

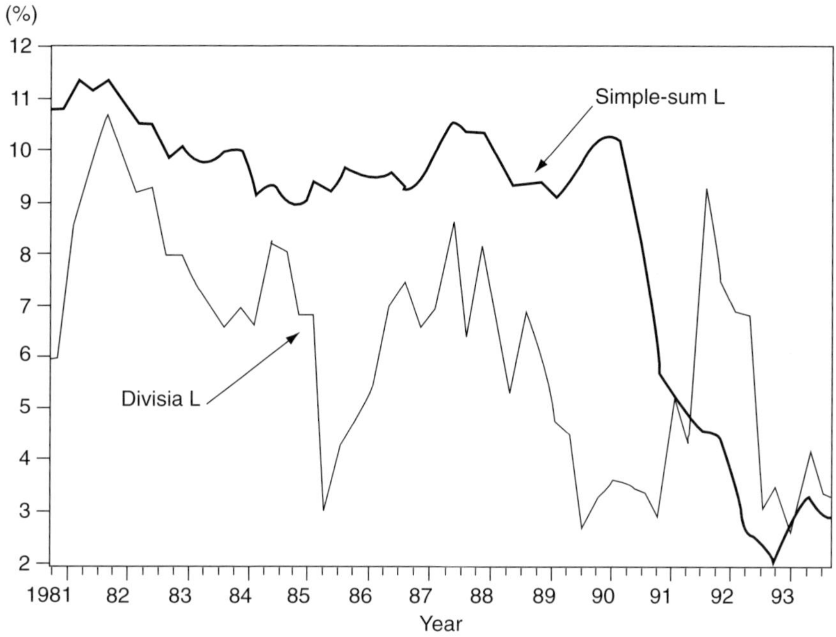

Figure 8.9 Growth rate of simple-sum and Divisia L (year-to-year)

Divisia and simple-sum M2 + CDs. Observations concerning the velocity of Divisia and simple-sum L are more or less the same as in the case of M2 + CDs; that is, the downward trend is much smaller and the cyclical behaviour seems more consistent with movements in interest rates in the case of Divisia L (Figure 8.10).

From these findings one might conclude that Divisia L could better serve as a policy indicator than simple-sum L. A more important observation concerning Divisia L, however, is that the difference between Divisia L and Divisia M2 + CDs is quite small, both in terms of their trends and in their cyclical behaviour, reflecting the lower marginal weights attached to the components (assets) included in L but not in M2 + CDs. This means that, if Divisia monetary aggregates are to be used for monetary policy, there would be little need to put much stress on Divisia L. It might be sufficient to use mainly Divisia M2 + CDs. This is particularly true if one takes account of the advantage of M2 + CDs in terms of availability and reliability of data.

A1

A1 is a set of money components that has been found to pass the GARP test by Kobayakawa (1993). It consists of M1 components and time deposits with

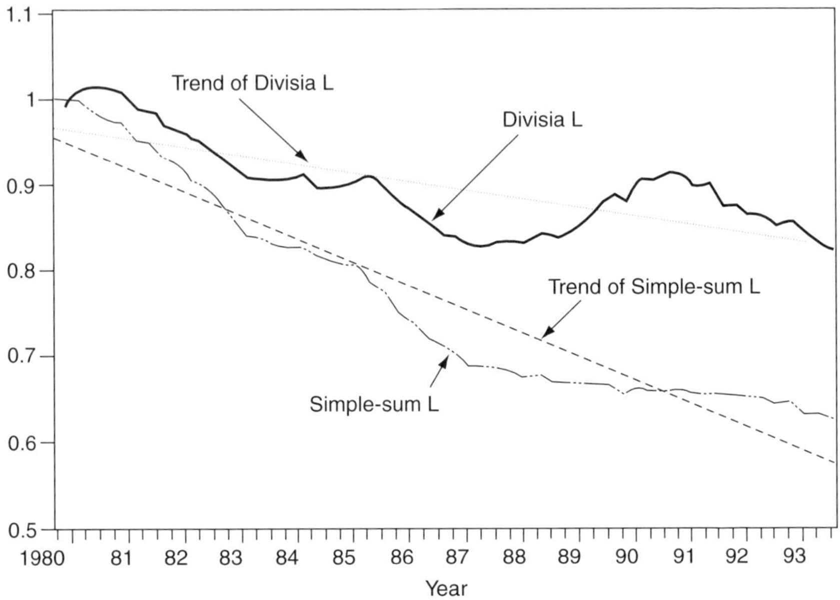

Figure 8.10 Velocity of simple-sum and Divisia L (trend: IQ/80–IVQ/93) (1980/IQ = 1)

regulated interest rates. Hence, A1 is broader than M1, but narrower than M2 + CDs, and it would also converge to M1 sufficiently after the completion of deregulation of time-deposit interest rates.

The developments in Divisia and simple-sum A1 and their velocities are shown in Figures 8.11 and 8.12, respectively. The difference in the trends and the cyclical behaviour between Divisia and simple-sum A1 is much smaller than in the case of M2 + CDs, which suggests higher substitutability among the assets included in A1.

Both Divisia and simple-sum A1, however, showed an extremely large fluctuation (a fall in the indices and a rise in the velocity) from 1989 to 1991, caused by a large shift of funds from A1 to time-deposits with deregulated interest rates. This extremely large fluctuation makes it difficult to find any meaningful relationship between A1 aggregates and key economic variables such as GDP or the inflation rate, at least for the moment. Thus, A1 aggregates, Divisia or simple-sum, currently seem to be of little use, despite their advantage of theoretical consistency. In addition, since A1 is expected to converge with M1 in the long run, it is unlikely that A1 aggregates would exhibit a particular role as a monetary indicator even in the future.

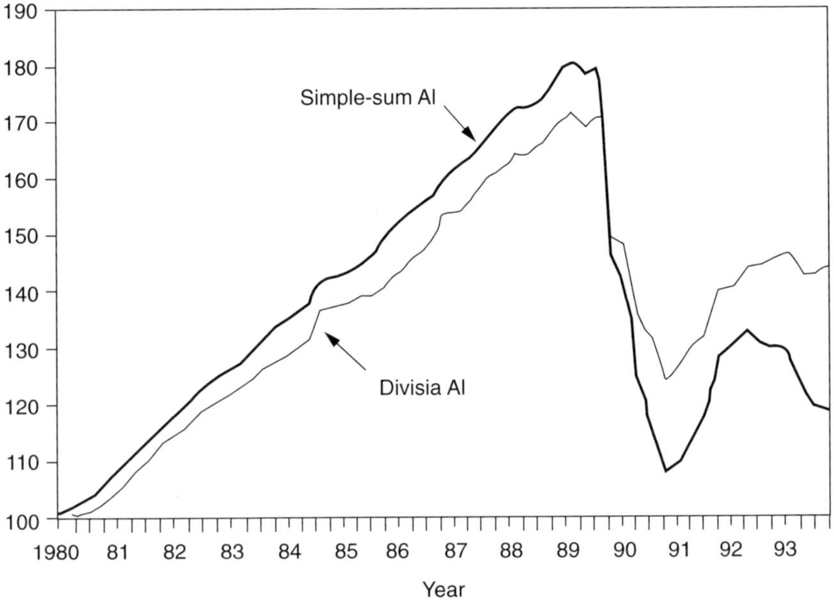

Figure 8.11 Simple-sum and Divisia A1 indices (1980/IQ = 100)

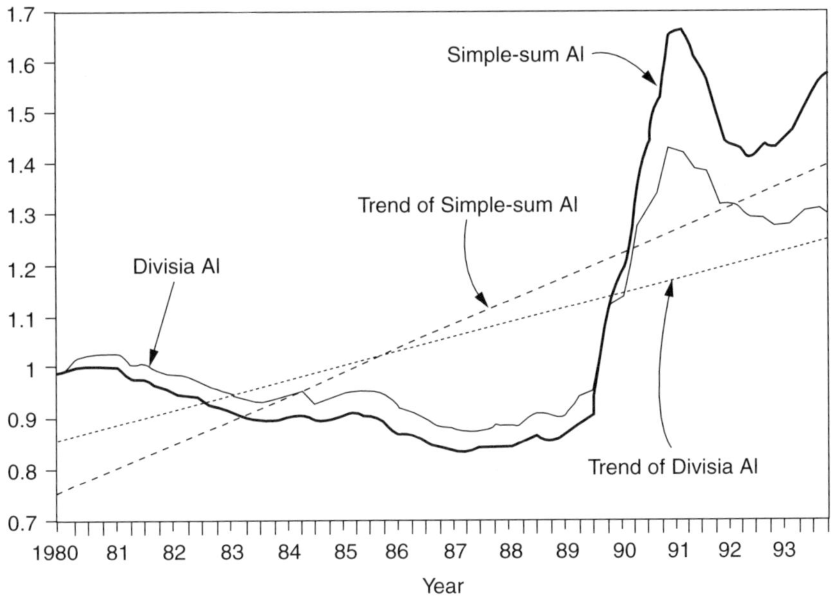

Figure 8.12 Velocity of simple-sum and Divisia A1 (trend: IQ/80 ~ IVQ/93) (1980/IQ = 1)

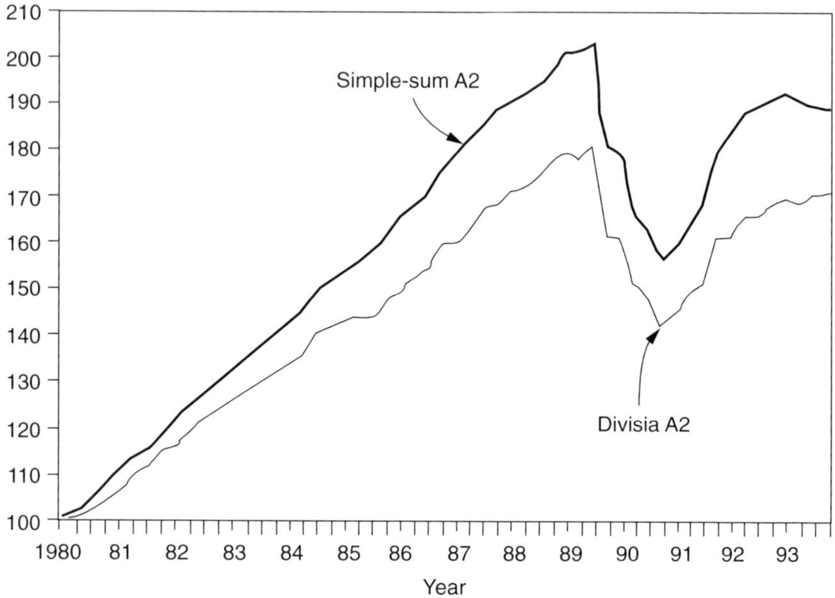

Figure 8.13 Simple-sum and Divisia A2 indices (1980/IQ = 100)

A2

A2 is also a set of money components that has passed the GARP test. A2 consists of A1, postal savings and outstanding balances in trust accounts (money trusts and loan trusts). It should be noted that postal savings and trust accounts are assets that are not included in M2 + CDs, since in the official definition of money they are considered to be less liquid than the components of M2 + CDs.

The developments in Divisia and simple-sum A2, and their velocities are shown in Figures 8.13 and 8.14, respectively. As in the case of A1, the divergence in the trends of Divisia and simple-sum A2 seems much smaller compared to the case of M2 + CDs, and their cyclical movements around the trend look quite similar. These observations suggest that, contrary to the assumption adopted in the official definition, the substitutability of A2 components is rather high, probably higher than that of M2 + CDs components.

However, A2 aggregates also showed a very large fluctuation from 1989 to 1991, again reflecting the shift of funds to time-deposits with deregulated interest rates, and hence are very difficult to interpret at the present time. In this chapter, therefore, it would be of little use to go into a more detailed analysis of A2 aggregates. Nonetheless, contrary to the case of A1, A2

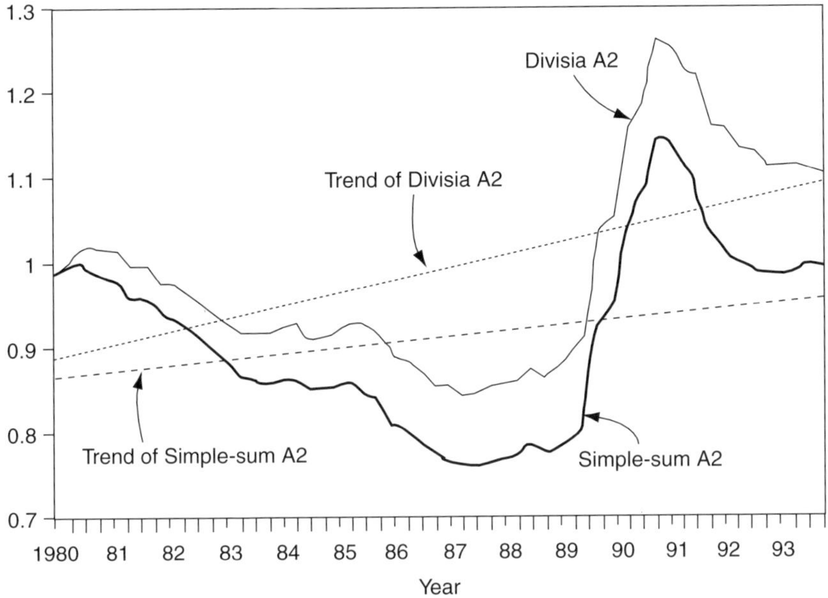

Figure 8.14 Velocity of simple-sum and Divisia A2 (trend: IQ/80 ~ IVQ/93) (1980/IQ = 1)

aggregates would be well worth re-investigating in the future, when the data for the period after the completion of deregulation have been sufficiently accumulated, because (i) A2 would continue to remain a set of assets that have a unique meaning, clearly different from official aggregates; and more importantly, (ii) it includes postal savings, which occupy a substantial share in Japan's financial system.

8.4 Analysis of money-demand functions

The existence of stable demand for a monetary aggregate is essential if the aggregate is to be used as an indicator or target for monetary policy. In this context, money demand functions for various Divisia and simple-sum monetary aggregates have been estimated. In the following, the results for the cases of M1 and M2 + CDs are reported.

In each case a traditional partial adjustment model for the demand for money function has been adopted:

$$(m-p)_t = a_0 + a_1(m-p)_{t-1} + a_2(y-p)_t + a_3 r_t + u_t \tag{8.1}$$

where:

m_t = log of money stock;
y_t = log of nominal total demand;
p_t = log of total demand deflator; and
r_t = holding cost of money[4]

In some cases, a variable which represents the wealth effect has been added to Equation (8.1).

Results for M1

The estimation results for M1 are shown in Table 8.2(a), from which the following points can be made:

(i) The results do not differ significantly between Divisia and simple-sum M1, which seems consistent with the observations depicted in Section 8.3.
(ii) In both cases, the income factor is not significant, whereas the holding cost variable is significant with the right sign.
(iii) Durbin's *h* statistic suggests the existence of serial correlation in the error term.
(iv) Including the wealth variable does not significantly improve the results in either case.

In addition, in order to check the stability of the estimated functions, the stepwise Chow test has been performed. The result, shown in Figures 8.15 and 8.16, suggests that the estimated functions are far from stable during the estimation period in both cases.

All these observations seem to imply that, as far as the simple partial adjustment models are concerned, it is difficult to find a sufficiently stable and meaningful M1 demand function which can be used for policy purposes, irrespective of whether the Divisia or simple-sum aggregation method is used.

Further investigation concerning demand functions of M1 is, of course, possible as well as desirable. For example, it could be asked whether a function with better performance could be found if more complicated models are adopted, or whether a stable function could be found if the estimation period were properly divided and so on. For the purposes of this chapter, however, it is sufficient to conclude that the use of Divisia or simple-sum M1 is unlikely to result in a significant difference in the results.

Results for M2 + CDs

The results for M2 + CDs are shown in Table 8.2(b), for which the following differences should be pointed out.

(i) The estimated demand function for Divisia M2 + CDs seems to exhibit a fairly reasonable performance. The coefficients for both income and

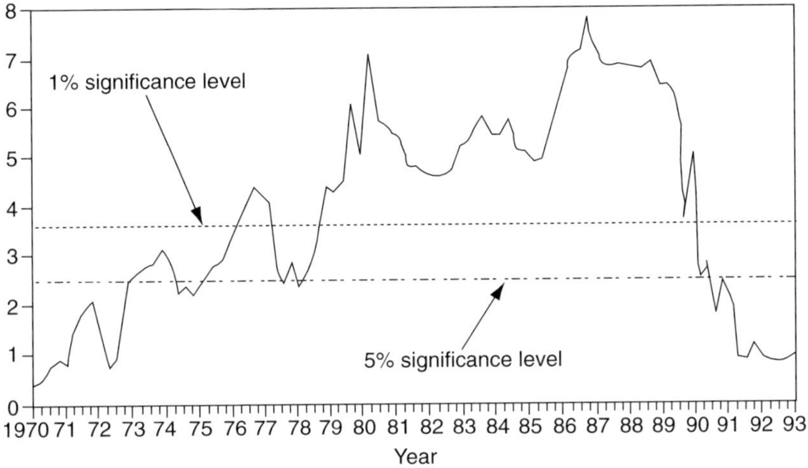

Figure 8.15 Results of stepwise Chow test (F-value) simple-sum M1

interest rate (holding cost) factor variables show the right sign and they are significant as well; and the absence of serial correlations in the error term is not rejected by Durbin's *h*.

(ii) On the contrary, in the demand function for simple-sum M2 + CDs, the coefficient for the income variable shows the wrong sign. Durbin's *h* also suggests the existence of serial correlation.

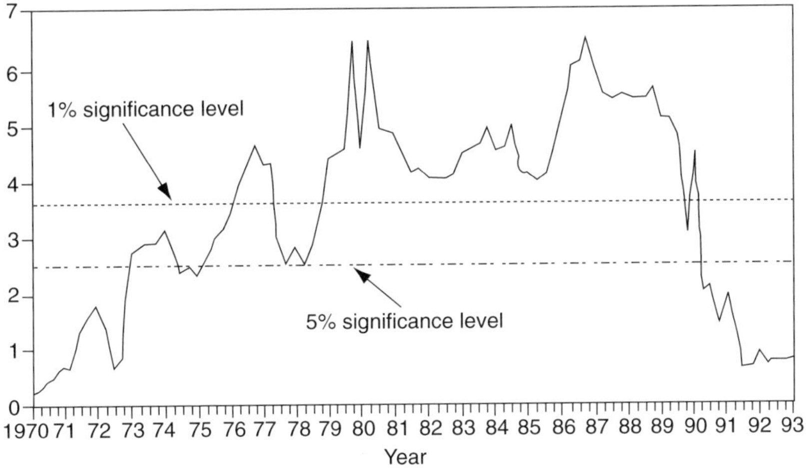

Figure 8.16 Results of stepwise Chow test (F-value) Divisia M1

Table 8.2 Estimation results of money demand functions

(a) Results of M1

Dependent variable	*constant*	$(m-p)_{t-1}$	*Explanatory variables* $(y-p)_t$	r_t	$(s-p)_t$	R^2, Durbin's h
SS M1	0.332** (6.29)	0.887** (27.18)	0.571×10^{-1} (1.78) <0.505>	-0.810×10^{-2}** (–5.80) <–0.072>	–	0.994, –1.63
Div M1	0.288** (5.92)	0.890** (26.48)	0.637×10^{-1} (1.85) <0.579>	-0.793×10^{-2}** (–6.06) <–0.072>	–	0.995, –1.91
SS M1	0.291** (5.07)	0.884** (27.28)	0.304×10^{-1} (0.86) <0.262>	-0.729×10^{-2}** (–4.98) <–0.063>	0.126×10^{-1} (1.67) <0.109>	0.994, –1.87
Div M1	0.246** (4.62)	0.883** (26.44)	0.399×10^{-1} (1.10) <0.34>	-0.712×10^{-2}** (–5.21) <–0.061>	0.130×10^{-1} (1.85) <0.11>	0.995, –2.20

(b) Results of M2 + CDs

Dependent variable	*constant*	$(m-p)_{t-1}$	*Explanatory variables* $(y-p)_t$	r_6	$(s-p)_t$	R^2, Durbin's h
SS M2 + CDs	0.246** (3.55)	0.982** (35.57)	-0.227×10^{-1} (–0.54) <–1.261>	$-0.119 \times^{-1}$** (–8.21) <–0.661>	–	0.999, 3.87
DV M2 + CDs	0.245** (6.67)	0.884** (29.97)	0.756×10^{-1}** (2.24) <0.652>	-0.135×10^{-1}** (–9.02) <–0.116>	–	0.999, –0.06

Table 8.2 (continued)

Dependent variable	*Explanatory variables* *constant*	$(m-p)_{t-1}$	$(y-p)_t$	r_6	$(s-p)_t$	R^2, Durbin's h
SS M2 + CDs	–0.206*	0.822**	0.141**	-0.117×10^{-1}**	0.318×10^{-1}**	0.999, 2.95
	(–2.08)	(22.43)	(3.06)	(–9.27)	(5.74)	
			<0.792>	<–0.066>	<0.179>	
Div M2 + CDs	0.219**	0.871**	0.752×10^{-1}**	-0.131×10^{-1}**	0.628×10^{-2}	0.999, –0.07
	(5.34)	(28.34)	(2.24)	(–8.70)	(1.40)	
			<0.583>	<–0.102>	<0.049>	

Notes: m = log of money stock.
y = log of nominal total demand.
p = log of total demand deflator.
r = holding cost of money (yields on bank debentures minus own rate of money: own rate is assumed to be zero for M1.
s = log of total amount of stocks evaluated at current prices in Tokyo Stock Exchange market
Sample period: 1Q/1969–1Q/1994.
t-value in upper parentheses.
Long-run elasticity in lower parentheses.
** represents significance at 1% level.
* represents significance at 5% level.

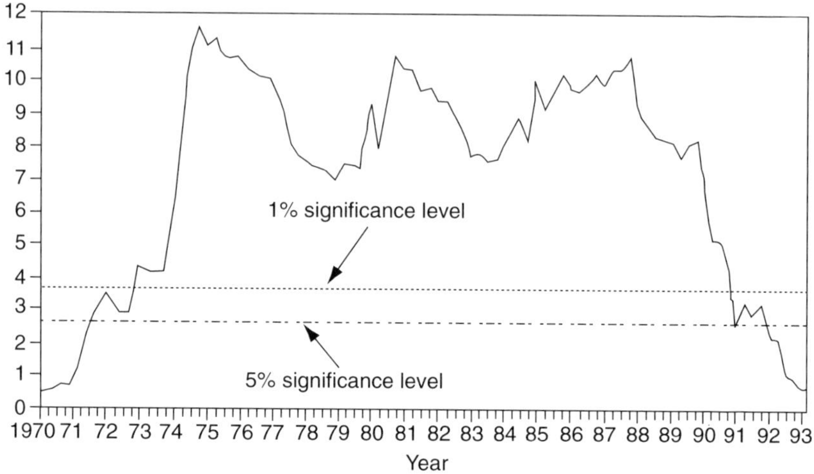

Figure 8.17 Results of stepwise Chow test (F-value) simple-sum M2 + CDs

As regards the stability of these functions, the results of the stepwise Chow test suggest that the demand function for Divisia M2 + CDs seems fairly stable, while stability is doubtful in the case of simple-sum M2 + CDs (see Figures 8.17 and 8.18). In fact, in the case of Divisia M2 + CDs, the F-values exceed the 5 per cent significance level only during the period from 1974 to 1976 (that is,

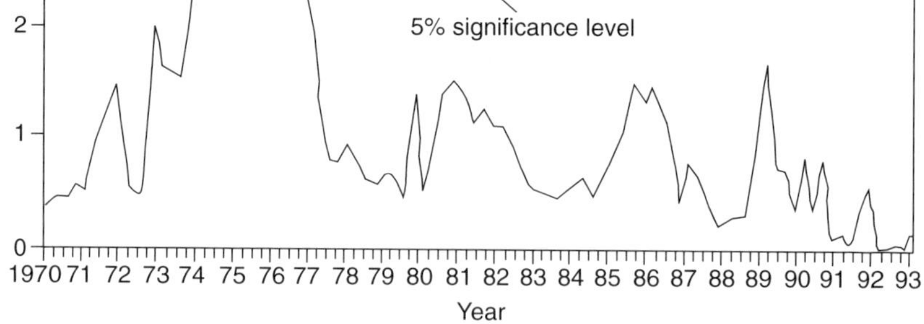

Figure 8.18 Results of stepwise Chow test (F-value) Divisia M2 + CDs

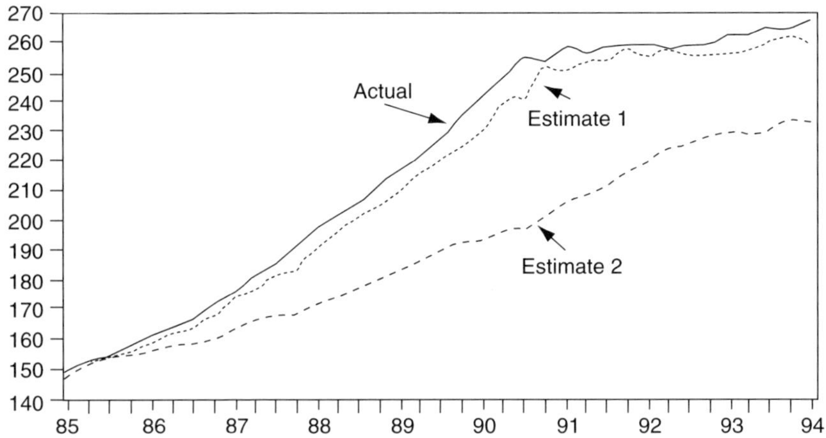

Notes: Estimate 1: Out-of-sample static simulation (IV Q/1985–I Q/1994)
Estimate 2: Out-of-sample dynamic simulation (IV Q/1985–I Q/1994)

Figure 8.19 Extrapolation test for money demand function of simple-sum M2 + CDs (1980/IQ = 100)

the period just after the first oil crisis), and never exceed the 1 per cent significance level. Compared with the case for simple-sum M2 + CDs, or M1 demand functions, this result can be interpreted as indicating a conspicuous stability of the Divisia M2 + CDs demand function.

As a further check on stability, extrapolation tests have been made. In these tests, demand functions estimated for the period until IIIQ/1985 have been used to produce forecast values after IVQ/1985, which were then compared with the actual values.[5] The results are shown in Figures 8.19 and 8.20. They show that the forecast values are considered to follow broadly the actual values in the case of Divisia M2 + CDs, while a persistent underestimation can be seen for simple-sum M2 + CDs. Thus, extrapolation tests also support the relative stability of the Divisia M2 + CDs demand function.

All the aforementioned results for simple-sum M2 + CDs, and in particular, the serial correlation and the persistent under-estimation in the extrapolation test, seem to suggest the existence of a missing variable in the demand function. As the observations described in Section 8.3 explain, a wealth variable is the most obvious possibility. Hence, demand functions for simple-sum M2 + CDs, as well as for Divisia M2 + CDs, have been estimated with the wealth factor added to the explanatory variables. The results are as follows:

(i) For simple-sum M2 + CDs, the estimation result substantially improves: the coefficients for the income and interest rate variables are now significant with the right sign, and for the wealth variables as well.

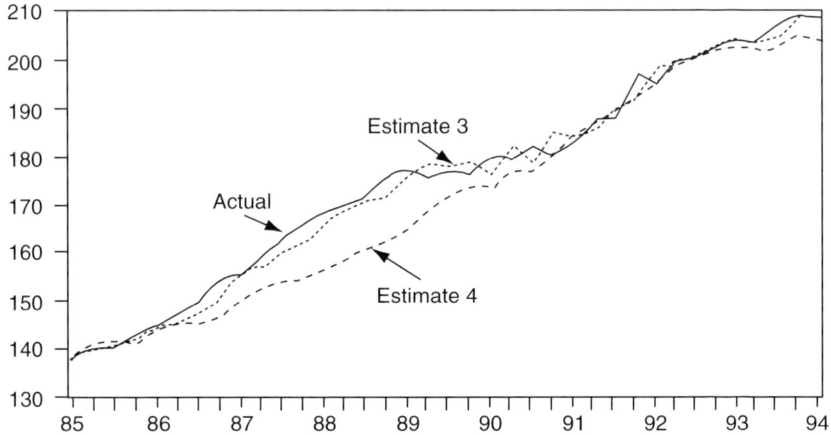

Notes: Estimate 3: Out-of-sample static simulation (IV Q/1985–I Q/1994)
Estimate 4: Out-of-sample dynamic simulation (IV Q/1985–I Q/1994)

Figure 8.20 Extrapolation test for money demand function of Divisia M2 + CDs (1980/IQ = 100)

(ii) The wealth variable exhibits no significant explanatory power in the Divisia M2 + CDs demand function. The coefficients for other variables are affected very little by adding the wealth variable.

These results seem to support the interpretation of the observed difference between Divisia and simple-sum M2 + CDs described in Section 8.3. That is, simple-sum M2 + CDs is substantially affected by the portfolio demand for money, while Divisia M2 + CDs, as a measure of money as MOE, is not. It has been found, however, that even the simple-sum M2 + CDs demand function estimated with the wealth variable does not seem stable. The F-values in the stepwise Chow test still far exceed the 1 per cent significance level for most points, and the extrapolation test still exhibits a persistent under-estimation (see Figure 8.21).

From these findings, it can be concluded that the demand function for Divisia M2 + CDs performs reasonably well and seems fairly stable, while for simple-sum M2 + CDs no stable and well-performing demand function has been found. This, in addition to the observations in Section 8.3, would give further support to the use of the Divisia aggregation in the case of M2 + CDs. This again illustrates the importance of weighting for a non-separable group, as described in Note 3 (see page 198). In this case, the missing assets (or the improper extra assets) act as shift variables would behave in a regression. Weighting minimises this effect, and hence leads to a more stable money demand function, as is shown by the result here.

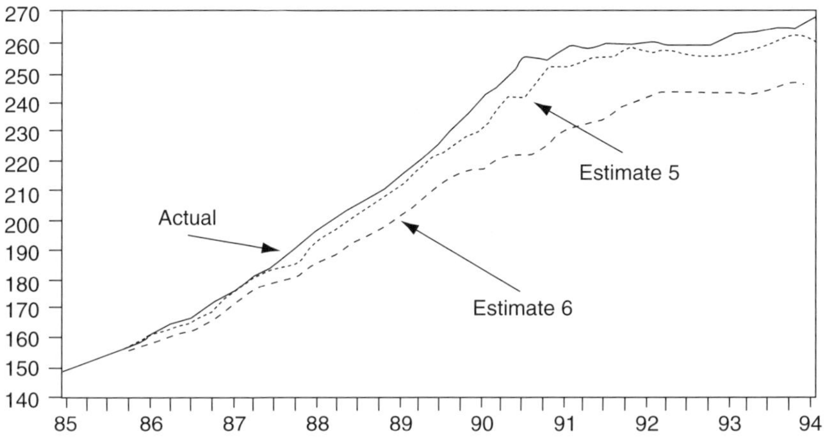

Notes: Estimate 5: Out-of-sample static simulation (IV Q/1985–I Q/1994)
Estimate 6: Out-of-sample dynamic simulation (IV Q/1985–I Q/1994)

Figure 8.21 Extrapolation test for money demand function of simple-sum M2 + CDs with wealth variable (1980/IQ = 100)

8.5 Conclusion

In this chapter, an updated series of broad and narrow Divisia monetary aggregates for Japan has been constructed and compared with their simple-sum counterparts in various analyses. The main findings, which generally seem to support the use of Divisia aggregates for broadly defined money, can be summarised as follows:

(i) Methods of aggregation cause no significant difference for narrowly-defined money, M1. The fluctuations in both Divisia and simple-sum M1 seem to have been large compared with, for example, fluctuations in GDP, and no stable demand functions have been found for both. This implies that the method of aggregation should not be the main focus of further research on the possible usefulness of M1.

(ii) For M2 + CDs, which has been the main monetary indicator in Japan, the Divisia aggregate seems to be superior to the simple-sum one in many respects: (a) the trend in its velocity is far flatter; (b) cyclical movements in the growth rates and velocities seem more consistent with developments in interest rates; and (c) the estimated demand function is more reasonable and stable.

The cyclical behaviour of simple-sum M2 + CDs has been particularly distorted since 1985 by the progress of interest rate deregulation and fluctuations in asset prices. On the contrary, Divisia M2 + CDs, as a measure of money as MOE, has been far less affected by these developments. Hence, at least as a cyclical indicator for monetary policy, it is likely that Divisia M2 + CDs could have served better than the simple-sum M2 + CDs that has in fact been used, particularly in recent periods.

(iii) The difference between Divisia and simple-sum L seems more or less similar to the case of M2 + CDs in many aspects. The more important finding, however, is that the difference between Divisia L and Divisia M2 + CDs is quite small in terms of both the trend and cyclical behaviour. This would reduce substantially the need to stick to L when the Divisia aggregation method is utilised, especially given the advantage of M2 + CDs in data availability and accuracy.

(iv) Theoretically consistent aggregates, A1 and A2, which have passed the GARP test, have been found to be less useful for the moment, as they have been too strongly affected by the large shift of funds caused by the deregulation of time-deposit interest rates.

However, before broad Divisia monetary aggregates, such as Divisia M2 + CDs, are used for the implementation of monetary policy, further considerations are needed. The following are examples:

(i) The finding that Divisia M2 + CDs is little affected by the portfolio demand for money (money as SOV) implies that it contains little information on the relationship between asset prices and money. If this relationship is believed to be important for monetary policy purposes, it would not be sufficient to look only at the Divisia aggregate.

(ii) If Divisia monetary aggregates were to be used as an intermediate target for monetary policy rather than simply as an indicator, a reasonable level of controllability is required. Since Divisia aggregates are constructed as a function of the holding costs of each component, controlling them seems to require the capability to affect many, though not necessarily all, own interest rates for each component individually as well as the benchmark rate. The relative difficulty in controlling Divisia monetary aggregates, however, should be tested empirically, and then compared with their simple-sum counterparts.

Appendix: GARP test for Japanese monetary data

Kobayakawa (1993) applied Varian's GARP test method to Japanese monetary data to check the separability of various sets of money components. To be consistent with the theory, he chose to restrict the analysis only to the components of monetary aggregates held by individuals. However, his findings are very informative and it seems worthwhile to introduce them here. Kobayakawa's main findings are as follows (see Table 8.3):

(i) M1, as well as certain combinations of assets in M1, passes the GARP test, though not always strictly.[6]

Table 8.3 Results of GARP Tests

(a) M1 components

	(1)	*(2)*	*(3)*	*(4)*	*(5)*	*(6)*	*(7)*	*(8)*	*(9)*
CC	*	*	*	*	*	*	*	*	*
CD	*	*	*	*	*	*	*		
OD		*	*	*				*	
DN			*	*	*		*		*
SP				*	*	*			*
Violations	0	10	12	10	2	0	2	10	2
Percentage of violations	0	1.5	1.8	1.5	0.3	0	0.3	1.5	0.3

(b) M2 + CDs components

	(10)	*(11)*	*(12)*	*(13)*	*(14)*	*(15)*	*(16)*
M1	*	*	*	*	*	*	*
QMR	*	*	*	*	*	*	*
IS		*	*	*	*	*	*
MD			*	*	*	*	*
MMC				*	*	*	
QMU					*	*	
CDS						*	*
Violations	72	49	30	485	397	397	30
Percentage of violations	10.0	7.0	4.4	42.9	39.3	39.3	4.4

(c) L components

	(17)	*(18)*	*(19)*	*(20)*	*(21)*	*(22)*	*(23)*
M1	*	*	*	*	*	*	*
QMR	*	*	*	*	*	*	*
IS	*	*	*	*	*	*	*
MD	*	*	*	*	*	*	*
MMC	*	*	*	*	*		
QMU	*	*	*	*	*		
OS	*	*	*	*	*	*	*
SC		*	*	*	*	*	*
MT			*	*	*		*
LT				*	*		*
CDS					*		
Violations	496	240	163	160	160	27	20
Percentage of Violations	45.3	27.4	20.7	20.7	19.8	4.0	3.0

Notes: CC = Cash currency in circulation; CD = Current deposits; DD = Ordinary deposits; DN = Deposits at notice; SP = Special deposits; QMR = Time deposits with regulated rates; IS = Instalment savings; MD = Maturity designated time deposits with regulated rates; MMC = Small money market certificates; QMU = Time deposits with unregulated rates; CDS = Certificates of deposits; OS = Postal ordinary savings; SC = Postal savings certificates; MT = Money in trust; LT = Loan trusts; * indicates that the asset is included in each data set; Percentage violation represents the number of inconsistent observations in GARP; Percentage violation represents the ratio of violations in GARP; Percentage M1 includes CC, CD, OD, DN and SP.

(ii) M2 + CDs failed to pass the GARP test, implying that the components of M2 + CDs do not form a separate subutility function, and hence M2 + CDs is not theoretically qualified for aggregation.
(iii) If time-deposits with deregulated interest rates (here, CDs, MMCs and large-denomination time-deposits) are excluded from M2 + CDs, the remaining set can be thought to pass the GARP test.
(iv) For broader sets of assets, it can be generally said that, as long as a set includes time-deposits with deregulated interest rates, it fails to pass the GARP test. If, on the contrary, they are excluded, a set tends to pass the test.

Notes

1. A possible reason for this difference in the result might be that Belongia (this volume) did not necessarily make a proper distinction between time-deposits with regulated interest rates and those with deregulated interest rates, probably because of data availability limitations.
2. It should, however, be noted that developments in the growth rate of Divisia M2 + CDs have not necessarily been completely consistent with monetary conditions. For example, the growth rate of Divisia M2 + CDs decelerated rapidly during 1987 and 1988 despite the fact that short-term interest rates were kept very low. This rapid deceleration was at least in part a result of the shift of funds from time-deposits with regulated interest rates to those with deregulated higher rates (hence, with smaller weights in the Divisia aggregation), which took place gradually during this period. Although this shift was an entirely *internal* substitution with M2 + CDs, the Divisia index was affected because the shift in fact reflected the introduction of new products to the aggregation set.
3. For example, a rise in stock prices would increase an investor's total wealth as well as the share of stocks in it, which would make the portfolio riskier than before. It is therefore likely that investors would shift part of their funds from stocks (or other risky assets) to safer assets, which might increase the demand for bank deposits. In cases such as this, however, one additional advantage of Divisia aggregation is revealed. If the group of assets being aggregated is not a separable group (as M2 + CDs appears to be), the measurement errors at least will be minimised by the smaller weights that will be given to the inappropriate assets included.
4. The holding costs of money are defined as follows:
   M1: yields on bank debentures (5Y)
   M2 + CDs: yields on bank debentures (5Y) minus rate of return for holding M2 + CDs (weighted average of the interest rates on major components of M2 + CDs).
5. The dividing point, IIIQ/1985, was chosen for the following reasons:
   (i) 1985 is the year when interest deregulation on time deposits started;
   (ii) the rise in asset prices generally accelerated from around 1985; and
   (iii) the Chow test result for Divisia M2 + CDs exhibits one of the local peaks (although insignificant) at IIIQ/1985.
6. Strictly speaking, the test does not allow a single violation of the GARP condition. However, Kobayakawa argued that, taking account of the possibility of measurement errors, and adjusting costs and periods, it is unrealistic to assume that no violation occurs even when the consumer exhibits optimising behaviour based on a well-defined utility function. He, instead, calculated the relative frequency of violations, and considered that a set of assets passed the test if the frequency of violations is sufficiently small (generally, below 5 per cent).

References

Belongia, B. (2000) – 'Consequences of money stock measurement', Chapter 13, this volume.

Ishida, K. (1984) 'Divisia Monetary Aggregates and Demand for Money: A Japanese Case', *Bank of Japan Monetary and Economic Studies* (June), pp. 49–80.

Kobayakawa, S. (1993) 'Shouhisha Riron To Tsuka Juyou Ni Tsuite' (Consumer Theory and Money Demand), *Kin'yu Kenkyu* (Japanese edition of *Bank of Japan Monetary and Economic Studies*) (December).

Varian, H. (1982) 'The Nonparametric Approach to Demand Analysis', *Econometrica* vol. 50 (July), pp. 945–73.

Varian, H. (1983) 'Nonparametric Test of Consumer Behavior', *Review of Economic Studies* vol. 50 (January), pp. 99–110.

9

The Signals from Divisia Money in a Rapidly Growing Economy*

Jeong Ho Hahm and Jun Tae Kim

9.1 Introduction

Since the mid-1970s, the Korean financial markets have experienced vast innovations and various regulatory policy changes, even though the speed of change has been more moderate than in many advanced industrial nations. Since the end of the 1980s, these financial innovations and regulatory changes have resulted in the rapid growth of non-bank financial institutions and the widespread introduction of various new financial assets in Korean financial markets. These developments have led to large fluctuations in the M2 measure of the money supply, which has been used as the official monetary target variable since 1979. Through portfolio shifts from components of M2 to other highly liquid assets with higher interest rates, which are offered mainly by non-bank financial institutions, higher volatility in M2 growth has raised questions about the appropriateness of M2 as an intermediate target or indicator of monetary policy. In order to overcome this situation, several researchers and practitioners have suggested the use of broader monetary aggregates such as M2B and M3 as replacements for M2.[1]

The question of whether the official monetary aggregate, M2, is useful as an intermediate target or information variable essentially centres on the fact that M2 is constructed as a simple-sum of financial assets offered by banking institutions alone. Two critical issues are associated with the definition of money. First, M2 includes even long-term time- and savings deposits with terms of maturity of two years or more, which are basically very distant substitutes for money. Second, M2 excludes all the components of non-bank financial assets as well as the highly liquid assets that the public may consider to be very strong substitutes for money. That is, M2 includes only the assets of

* The authors are grateful to Michael Belongia for his many helpful comments on earlier drafts of this chapter. Special thanks to William Barnett and James Swofford. The views expressed in this chapter are the authors and do not necessarily reflect those of the Bank of Korea.

banking institutions, but not those of other financial institutions, on the basis of the 'all or nothing' principle.

As is generally recognised, this approach to construction of the M2 aggregate suffers from at least two deficiencies on the grounds of aggregation and index number theory. First, in order for an aggregate to be admissible, the component assets within the aggregate must be weakly separable from other financial assets outside the aggregate. M2, being constructed over a set of financial assets of banking institutions alone, will not be an admissible aggregate unless the components are a weakly separable group.[2] Second, even if the M2 asset collection represents an admissible group, the simple-sum aggregate gives equal weight to each of its component assets, even though they are not perfect substitutes.[3] Because the M2 aggregate includes various assets, ranging from currency in circulation and non-interest-bearing demand deposits to long-term time and savings deposits yielding high interest rates, this index number problem only begs the question of how large the measurement error is.

In this chapter, our primary objective is to apply aggregation and index number theory to search for admissible Divisia monetary aggregates for Korea. After identifying and constructing these indexes, we evaluate their empirical performance against that of their traditional simple-sum equivalents. Specifically, we first conduct tests for weak separability of monetary component assets to identify admissible groups. We then apply one of Diewert's superlative index numbers to the admissible groups, to construct Divisia monetary aggregates.[4] Finally, the empirical performance of these Divisia money measures is evaluated against their traditional simple-sum counterparts in terms of various policy criteria, such as cointegration with the price level and error correction forecasts of inflation. Our main finding is that admissible Divisia money measures show better performance, especially at higher levels of aggregation.

The organisation of this chapter is as follows. Section 9.2 describes the data employed in the study and provides a general discussion of the computation of Divisia monetary aggregates. In Section 9.3, we conduct tests for weak separability of monetary asset groups to identify admissible monetary aggregates. Section 9.4 evaluates the empirical performance of admissible monetary aggregates identified in the previous section against their traditional simple-sum equivalents. Section 9.5 presents concluding remarks.

9.2 Computation of Divisia monetary aggregates

The data used in our study consist of quarterly Korean observations for the period 1980–1993 on various types of monetary (sub-) aggregates. Details about the data used to generate these aggregates are presented in Table 9.1. As can be seen from the table, there exists a total of 40 assets that the Bank of

Table 9.1 A taxonomy of monetary assets and interest rates series

Institution	*Monetary Assets*			*Own rate*	
Banking Institutions (BI)					
M1: (Narrow money)	1	CC	Currency	r_1	Zero by definition
	2	DDH*	Demand deposits for households	r_2	Zero by definition
			* *Total demand deposits × Share of DDH***		
			** *Share of DDH = ratio for all individual demand deposits to total demand deposits*		
	3	DDB*	Demand deposits for business	r_3	$r^*(1 - \text{MMRR})$
			* *Total demand deposits × (1 – Share of DDH)*	r^* = Interest rate on time deposits (3-month or more)	
				MMMR = Maximum reserve requirement on demand deposits	
	* *Memo: M1 identity M1 ≡ sum of assets 1 to 3*				
SS: (Short-term time and savings deposits)	4	SD	Savings deposits	r_4	Interest rate on SD
	5	ND	Notice deposits	r_5	Interest rate on ND
	6	LSD	Liberal savings deposits	r_6	Interest rate on LSD (3-month or more)
	7	CSD	Company savings deposits	r_7	Interest rate on CSD (3-month or less)
	8	STD	Short-term time deposits (less than 2-year)	r_8	Interest rate o TD (less than 2-year)
	9	OTSDBI	Other time and savings deposits at BI	r_9	Interest rate on TD (1-year)
	10	FCD	Deposits in foreign currencies	r_{10}	Interest rate on TD (3-month or more)
	**Memo: M2A identity M2A ≡ M1 + sum of assets 4 to 10*				
LS: (Long-term time and savings deposits)	11	LTD	Long-term time deposits (2-year or more)	r_{11}	Interest rate on TD (2-year or more)
	12	ISD	Instalment savings deposits	r_{12}	Interest rate on ISD (2-year)
	13	HPISD	Household preferential instalment savings deposit	r_{13}	Interest rate on HPISD (3-year)
	14	BID	Mutual instalment deposits	r_{14}	Interest rate on BID (3-year)
	15	HID	Housing instalment deposits	r_{15}	Interest rate on HID (3-year)

Table 9.1 (*continued*)

	No.	Symbol	Asset	Rate	Rate description
	16	WPFD	Workmen's property formation savings deposits	r_{16}	Interest rate on WPFD (3-year)
	17	WLSD	Workmen's long-term savings deposits	r_{17}	Interest rate on WLSD (3-year)
	**Memo: M2 identity M2 ≡ M2A + sum of assets 11 to 17*				
	18	CD	Certificates of deposit	r_{18}	Interest rate on CD (91-day or more)
Non-bank Financial Institutions (NFI) HL: (Short-term highly liquid assets)	**Development institutions**				
	19	DDDI	Demand deposits at DI	r_{19}	Interest rate on time deposits (less than 1-year)
	20	STDDI	Savings & time deposits at DI	r_{20}	Interest rate on time deposits (1-year or more)
	Investment institutions				
	21	BIL	Bills issued	r_{21}	Interest rate on bills issued (60-day or more)
	22	CMA	Cash management accounts	r_{22}	Interest rate on CMA (180-day)
	23	BC	Beneficial certificates	r_{23}	Yield on government and public bonds
	24	SIS	Securities investment savings	r_{24}	Yield on government and public bonds
	25	SFCD	Securities finance corporation deposits	r_{15}	Interest rate on securities finance liability certificates (60-day or more)
	Savings institutions				
	26	MT	Money in trust at bank trust accounts	r_{26}	Interest rate on development trusts (3-year)
	27	MSFCD	Mutual savings and finance companies' deposits	r_{27}	Interest rate on mutual instalment deposits (20-month)

Table 9.1 *(continued)*

	No.	Code	Asset	Rate	Description of rate
	28	MSFCB	Mutual savings and finance companies' borrowings from public	r_{28}	Interest rate on borrowings (1-year or more)
	29	MCCD	Mutual credit companies' deposits	r_{29}	Interest rate on mutual credit time deposits (1-year)
	30	CUD	Credit unions' deposit	r_{30}	Interest rate on credit union time deposits (1-year)
	31	PSD	Postal savings deposits	r_{31}	Interest rate on postal savings time deposits (1-year)
	32	CCCD	Community credit co-operatives' deposits	r_{32}	Interest rate on credit union time deposits (1-year)
	33	OTSDNFI	Other financial institutions' time and savings deposits (NFI)	r_{33}	Average interest rate at development institutions
	34	FCDNFI	Foreign currency deposits at other financial institutions	r_{34}	Interest rate on time deposits at deposit money banks (1-year or more)
	**Memo: M2B identity M2B ≡ M2A + sum of assets 18 to 34*				
OFA (Other financial assets)	**Insurance institutions**				
	35	ICR	Insurance company reserves	r_{35}	Average interest rate at other financial institutions (excluding deposits in foreign currencies and demand deposits)
	Other financial assets				
	36	DIBI	Debentures issued at BI	r_{36}	Yield on monetary stabilisation bonds (364-day)
	37	DINFI	Debentures issued at NFI	r_{37}	Yield on industrial financial debentures
	38	RPBI	RPs at monetary institutions	r_{38}	Yield on RPs at BI (91-day or more)
	39	RPNFI	RPs at other financial institutions	r_{39}	Yield on RPs at SFC* (91-day or more)

Table 9.1 (continue)

No.	Asset	Description	Rate	Rate description
40	CBS	Commercial bills sold	r_{40}	Yield on commercial bills sold (60-day or more)
		**Memo: M3 identity M3 ≡ M2 + sum of asset 18 to 40*		

Notes: 1. The data for quantities for the component of monetary assets are three-month-average data based on the month-end balances.
2. All own-rates are average quarterly data. They are after-tax rates derived by considering the types of interest payment (issuance or circulation) and tax rates. For example, suppose that the annual rate of the *i*th component is k_1 and the interest is paid on a three-month basis with tax rate t. Then the after-tax rate of return of the *i*th component is $r_i = [1 + (k_i/4)^*(1 - t)]^4 - 1$.

Korea (BOK) currently recognises as sources of monetary services in the Korean economy. According to the BOK's latest classification scheme, the narrow money measure, M1, consists of the first three assets (1–3). The M2A measure is the sum of M1 and assets 4 to 10. The current official money stock, M2, is the sum of M2A and assets 11 to 17. The M2B measure is the sum of M2A and assets 18 to 34. Finally, the broadest money measure, M3, is the sum of M2 and assets 18 to 40.

For the conduct of weak separability tests, we constructed four Divisia sub-aggregates. The four are (1) narrow money, M1; (2) short-term time- and savings deposits at banking institutions, SS; (3) long-term time- and savings deposits with terms of maturity of two years or more at banking institutions, LS; and (4) short-term highly liquid assets offered by non-bank financial institutions, HL. Certificates of deposit (CD) at banking institutions are included in the HL block. Bank trust accounts (especially, money in trust), which are handled at banking institutions but specified as non-bank trust businesses, are also included in the HL category. Money in trust is very similar in nature to time-deposits.

In constructing these Divisia aggregates (or monetary services indexes), we used the Fisher Ideal index. This decision was taken because a Divisia index, which is expressed in growth rates, is undefined when new assets are introduced; both indexes, however, perfectly satisfy Fisher's factor reversal test and can immediately reflect the introduction of new assets into the index.[5] In any event, as Diewert (1976) pointed out, the choice between these two indexes is of little importance, since the Divisia index and the Fisher Ideal index both belong to the class of Diewert-superlative index numbers and move very closely together, meaning that they are empirically indistinguishable.

Several considerations in constructing these particular Divisia monetary (sub-) aggregates are: (i) the aggregation of the component assets; (ii) the own rate of return; and (iii) the benchmark rate of return.

Aggregation

As stated above, the assets used to calculate Divisia monetary services indexes are the same as those used by the BOK to calculate the current simple-sum aggregates M1 to M3. The only major difference is that demand deposits at banking institutions are broken down into household demand deposits (DDH) and business demand deposits (DDB). The ratio for DDH is the sum of all individual demand deposits divided by the total demand deposits, whereas the ratio for DDB is one minus the DDH ratio.

In order to conduct the weak separability tests, we computed only four blocks of Divisia sub-aggregates, for M1, SS, LS and HL. The main reason we have constructed only four blocks of monetary assets is to allow the empirical implementation of separability tests. The search was limited to these groups because using more than four arguments would considerably complicate the imposition of parameter restrictions for separability tests. We assume that there exists an exact aggregator function over each sub-aggregate, based on the weak separability assumption. This separability assumption of the *a priori* existence of four exact aggregates is the maintained hypothesis in our study. The four particular groupings identified were chosen on the basis of our knowledge of institutional features of Korean financial markets.

The own rate of return

The computation of monetary services indexes requires knowledge of the user costs of the component monetary assets. These user costs are derived by using Barnett's (1978) formula. There are several special considerations in our implementation of this formula that are worthy of comment.

Various asset stocks used in monetary services index computations are not single assets, but are composite sums of several assets. For each such composite asset, the associated own-rate of interest can be calculated as the maximum of the yield-curve-adjusted rates on components of different maturities within the composite asset (Farr and Johnson, 1985). However, we cannot use this method in our study because the yield curve is not stable enough in Korea. As an alternative, we use a representative rate concept. Specifically, a representative rate based on volume size is selected among several *after-tax* rates of return for the different holding periods as the own rate of return to each composite monetary asset.[6]

We assume that households receive a zero rate of return on demand deposits and that businesses receive a non-zero rate of return. The formula for computing the rate on DDB is as follows: $r_3 = r'(1 - MMRR)$, where $MMRR$ is the maximum reserve requirement on demand deposits and r' is the rate on time-deposits with terms of maturity of three months or more.[7] As a result, the monetary services index gives more weight to the growth rates of currency and household demand deposits than does the simple-sum aggregate.

The benchmark rate

In theory, the benchmark rate of return, R, is defined as the maximum expected holding period yield of a pure store-of-value asset. This benchmark asset is specifically assumed to provide no liquidity or other monetary services and is held solely to transfer wealth intertemporally. The benchmark rate R_t, according to Barnett and Spindt (1982), is defined as follows:

$$R_t = \max[r_{bt}, r_{it}(i = 1, 2, \ldots, 40)]$$

where R_t is the benchmark rate of return for the period, t, r_{bt} is the yield of corporate bonds with a maturity of three years, and r_{it} is the own rate of the ith monetary component asset among all forty assets.[8]

9.3 Searching for admissible monetary aggregates

For the construction of consistent and meaningful monetary aggregates, admissible asset groups should first be identified. Aggregation theory is used to identify admissible (separable) component groups among monetary assets. Aggregation theory requires, in this case, weak separability of the utility function in the blocks of monetary components over which aggregation is performed. A necessary and sufficient condition for weak separability is that the marginal rate of substitution between any two assets within a group should be independent of the quantities of any assets outside the group.[9]

The model specification and data

As stated above, a monetary asset collection must be weakly separable from other assets or goods in the utility function if it is to be constructed as a consistent monetary aggregate. This necessary condition for weak separability naturally implies treating monetary assets as arguments in the utility function of the representative individual.[10]

We suppose a representative consumer's direct utility function is homothetically weakly separable, of the form:

$$u = u(c, l, f, m) \tag{9.1}$$

where c is a vector of the services of consumption goods, l is leisure time and m is a vector of the services of monetary assets.[11]

It should be noted that a two-stage budgeting decision process of the consumer is implicit in a utility tree structure of this form. In the first stage, the consumer allocates expenditures among broad categories based on price indexes for these categories; in the second stage, the consumer allocates expenditures within each category. The particular two-level structure we wish to utilise can be expressed by the following typical consumer problem:

$$\max_{m} f(m) \text{ subject } to\ \pi' m = y \tag{9.2}$$

where the utility (aggregator) function $f(m)$ is assumed to satisfy the usual regularity conditions. Total expenditure on the services of monetary assets is denoted by y, and π is a vector of user costs of monetary assets.

In what follows, the specification of the indirect utility function and the derivation of the demand system from the indirect utility function are described briefly. The demand system is derived from the following homothetic translog indirect utility function:

$$\ln V = \alpha_0 + \sum_i \alpha_i \ln v_i + (1/2) \sum_i \sum_j \beta_{ij} \ln v_i \ln v_j \tag{9.3}$$

with the restrictions imposed that $\beta_{ij} = \beta_{ji}$ and $\sum_i \beta_{ij} = 0$ for all j. V is the reciprocal indirect utility function, $v_i = \pi_i / y$, $\pi_i =$ the user cost of the ith monetary asset, $y =$ total expenditure on the services of monetary assets. Then, by the modified Roy's identity, we have the following homothetic translog expenditure system:

$$s_i = \alpha_i + \sum_j \beta_{ij} \ln v_j \tag{9.4}$$

where the normalisation $\sum_i \alpha_i = 1$ has been imposed and $s_i = \pi_i m_i / y$. The above homothetic translog model is simple to estimate, since its share equations are linear. Homotheticity, however, has very strong implications for demand behaviour, since it imposes unitary expenditure elasticities – that is, the Engel curve is linear and passes through the origin.[12] In this study, we have decided to use the homothetic translog indirect utility function and estimate the demand system as defined in Equation (9.4). This choice is primarily motivated by the empirical implementation.

Following conventional practice, we specify classical additive disturbance terms in share equations and assume that they are normally distributed with zero mean and constant covariance. Thus, we can write the stochastic version of the model as:

$$s_t = f_t(x_t, \theta) + u_t \tag{9.5}$$

where s_t is the vector of observed expenditure shares at time t, x_t is the vector of exogenous variables, θ is the vector of unknown parameters, and u_t represents a classical disturbance term with the following properties: $E(u_t) = 0$, $E(u_t, u^1{}_t) = \Omega \; \forall s, t$, where Ω is a variance – covariance matrix.

Here u_t is assumed to be a first-order autoregressive process such that:

$$u_t = Ru_{t-1} + e_t \tag{9.6}$$

where $R = [R_{ij}]$ is a matrix of unknown parameters, and e_t is the vector of a non-autocorrelated disturbance term defined as: $E(e_t) = 0$, $E(e_t, e^1{}_t) = \sum$, where $\sum$ is a symmetric and positive semi-definite covariance matrix. The disturbance term specification given above allows both contemporaneous and non-contemporaneous disturbance term to be correlated.

Since the sum of the expenditure shares equals one ($\sum_i s_i = 1$), it follows that the covariance matrix is singular because of the singularity of the system. If autocorrelation in the disturbances is absent, Barten (1969) has shown that full information maximum likelihood estimates of the parameters can be obtained by arbitrarily deleting an equation in such a system, and that the resulting estimates are invariant with respect to the equation deleted. If, however, autocorrelation is present, as assumed above, Berndt and Savin (1975) have shown that the adding-up property of a singular system imposes additional restrictions on the parameters of the autoregressive process. When these restrictions are not imposed, any estimations, and thus hypothesis tests, are conditional on the equation deleted. In this study, we assumed no autocorrelation across the equations (that is, R is diagonal). As a result, the autoregressive coefficients have been restricted to being the same for all equations.

Finally, writing Equation (9.5) for the period $t-1$, multiplying by R, and subtracting it from Equation (9.5) yields the final model to be estimated in our study:[13]

$$s_t = f_t(x_t, \theta) - Rf_{t-1}(x_{t-1}, \theta) + Rs_{t-1} + e_t \qquad (9.7)$$

The data used here consist of quarterly time series on quantities and prices (user costs) for the four composite monetary sub-aggregates discussed earlier for the period 1980–1993.

Prior to discussing our results, several other comments concerning data adjustment are in order. First, the X-11 ARIMA method is applied to the data to eliminate any seasonality that may be present. Second, each monetary sub-aggregate is divided by population to get per capita series, since our theoretical model is based on an individual decision-making problem. Next, each sub-aggregate is divided by the true cost-of-living index, p^*, to convert nominal balances to real terms. Third, the aggregate user costs corresponding to the four sub-aggregates are derived by applying Fisher's factor reversal test to data on quantities and total expenditure for each group. Finally, prior to estimation, the price indexes are all scaled to equal 1.0 in 1985.1. To ensure that the products of price and quantity indexes ($\pi_{it}m_{it}$) remain unchanged by the rescaling, the quantity series are rescaled accordingly by multiplying each one by the base period value of the corresponding price series, so that the expenditure share of each item is not changed.

Hypothesis tests on weak separability

The conventional separability tests (with Leontief separability) fall into two categories. One type is the exact test, where it is implicitly assumed that the function used exactly represents the true underlying utility function at all points of the utility surface, and the null hypothesis of separability is imposed globally for all possible values of the exogenous variables; see Berndt and Christensen (1973). Denny and Fuss (1977) used an approximate test, which is a test for local separability (only at the point of expansion). The tests we carry out for the separability conditions are based on the Denny–Fuss approximate test framework.

In order to conduct our approximate tests for weak separability, we consider the separability restrictions associated with restrictions on the functional form. Since we have four variables, there are thirteen possible asset groupings. These combinations are derived from the three possible separability patterns, and their corresponding parametric restrictions are shown in Table 9.2.[14]

The homothetic translog model of Equation (9.7) was estimated by the method of maximum likelihood.[15] Before proceeding to hypothesis testing, we checked to see whether the estimated homothetic translog model satisfied some regularity conditions – that is, non-negativity, monotonicity and quasiconvexity.[16] The estimated homothetic translog model satisfied non-negativity and monotonicity conditions at all observations. As for quasicon-

Table 9.2 Parametric restrictions for approximate weak separability tests

Separability pattern	*Parametric restrictions*	*Number of parametric restrictions*
F[G(lnQ_i, lnQ_j), lnQ_k, lnQ_l]	$\alpha_i/\alpha_j = \beta_{ik}/\beta_{jk} = \beta_{il}/\beta_{jl}$	2
F[G(lnQ_i, ln Q_j), H(lnQ_k, ln Q_l)]	$\alpha_i/\alpha_j = \beta_{ik}/\beta_{jk} = \beta_{il}/\beta_{jl}$	3
	$\alpha_k/\alpha_l = \beta_{ik}/\beta_{il} = \beta_{jk}/\beta_{jl}$	
F[G(lnQ_i, lnQ_j, lnQ_k), lnQ_l]	$\alpha_i/\alpha_j = \beta_{il}/\beta_{jl}$+ $\alpha_i/\alpha_k = \beta_{il}/\alpha_{kl}$	2
	$\alpha_j/\alpha_k = \beta_{jl}/\beta_{kl}$	

vexity, it failed to satisfy the curvature condition at some (about 30 per cent) of the observations. At the sample mean (approximation point), however, the estimated model satisfied the curvature conditions.[17]

Now we consider evidence on the existence of admissible monetary aggregates. Thirteen null hypotheses were considered. Each null hypothesis was tested using the asymptotic likelihood ratio. As is well known, the negative of twice the difference between the log of the likelihood function under the maintained hypothesis and under the null hypothesis is asymptotically distributed as a Chi-square (χ^2) with degrees of freedom equal to the number of parameter restrictions imposed under the null hypothesis.

The calculated Chi-square statistics for the hypothesis tests and selected critical values are presented in Table 9.3. Among the total of thirteen hypotheses, our testing method and data indicate only eight cases in which the admissibility of aggregation over the component monetary assets cannot be rejected at the 0.1 significance level. As mentioned above, according to the BOK's latest classification scheme, there currently exist five alternative money measures; M1, M2A, M2, M2B and M3. Therefore, the above empirical result indicates that, among five alternative money measures, at least two could be potential candidates for admissible monetary aggregates in Korea. One is Divisia M2A [(M1, SS), LS, HL], consisting of M1 (narrow money) and SS (short-term time- and savings deposits at banking institutions). The other is Divisia M2B [(M1, SS, HL), LS], which consists of M1, SS and HL (some short-term highly liquid assets offered by non-bank financial institutions). One interesting point is that the admissibility of aggregation over the M2 asset collection [(M1, SS, LS), HL] is rejected. This implies that our current official monetary aggregate, M2, may not be stable in the consumer's preference function. This may be because component assets included in the LS category are closely associated with a store-of-wealth function rather than transaction or liquidity functions.[18]

Table 9.3 Test statistics and critical values

	Log-likelihood	*Test statistics*[2]	*Degrees of freedom*	*Critical values* $X^2(0.1)$	$X^2(0.05)$	$X^2(0.01)$
Unrestricted[1]	607.540	–	–	–	–	–
[(1, 2), 3, 4]	607.167	0.746***[3]	2	4.61	5.99	9.21
[(1, 3), 2, 4]	594.614	25.852	2	4.61	5.99	9.21
[(1, 4), 2, 3]	605.222	4.636	2	4.61	5.99	9.21
[(2, 3), 1, 4]	605.187	4.706	2	4.61	5.99	9.21
[(2, 4), 1, 3]	607.045	0.990***	2	4.61	5.99	9.21
[(3, 4), 1, 2]	607.016	1.048***	2	4.61	5.99	9.21
[(1, 2),(3, 4)]	606.482	2.116***	3	6.25	7.82	11.34
[(1, 3),(2, 4)]	596.875	21.330	3	6.25	7.82	11.34
[(1, 4),(2, 3)]	605.057	4.966***	3	6.25	7.82	11.34
[(1, 2 3), 4]	601.675	11.730	2	4.61	5.99	9.21
[(2, 3 4), 1]	607.066	0.948***	2	4.61	5.99	9.21
[(1, 2 4), 3]	607.306	0.468***	2	4.61	5.99	9.21
[(1, 3 4), 2]	597.392	0.296***	2	4.61	5.99	9.21

Notes: 1. The numbers refer to asset collections described earlier. They are 1 = narrow money (M1); 2 = short-term time and savings deposits at banking institutions (SS); 3 = long-term time and savings deposits at banking institutions (LS); and 4 = highly liquid assets offered by non-bank financial institutions.

2. The test statistic is calculated as $-2 \log (L_u/L_c)$ and distributed as x^2, where L_u and L_c are the values of the unconstrained and constrained likelihood functions, respectively.

3. *** indicates statistical significance at the 0.1 level.

9.4 Performances of admissible monetary aggregates

We go on to compare the empirical performance of Divisia measures for M2A and M2B, identified above as admissible monetary aggregates based on weak separability tests, against their simple-sum equivalents. For the purpose of comparison, the current official monetary aggregate, M2, and the broadest money measure, M3, also are compared with their Divisia measures.

Historical behaviour of alternative money measures

Since the Divisia monetary aggregates are an alternative to conventional simple-sum aggregates, a brief comparison of their historical behaviour may be instructive. Comparisons of the levels, growth rates and GNP velocities of the Divisia and simple-sum aggregates for Korea are presented in Figures 9.1 to 9.8. Comparisons of the levels and velocities of Divisia and simple-sum measures are made by normalising both measures so that they equal 100 at 1985.1.

Observe from the figures that the simple-sum indexes for M2A, M2, M2B and M3 grow more rapidly than corresponding Divisia indexes, because of financial innovation and deregulation from the mid-1980s. The reason for this

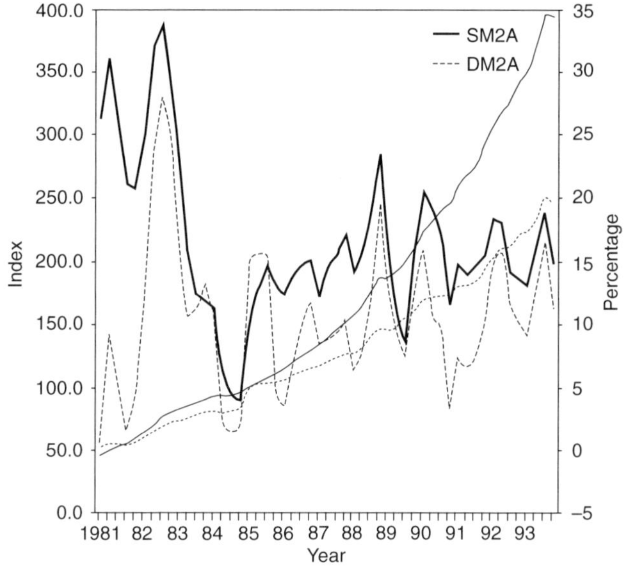

Figure 9.1 Levels and growth rates of SM2A and DM2A

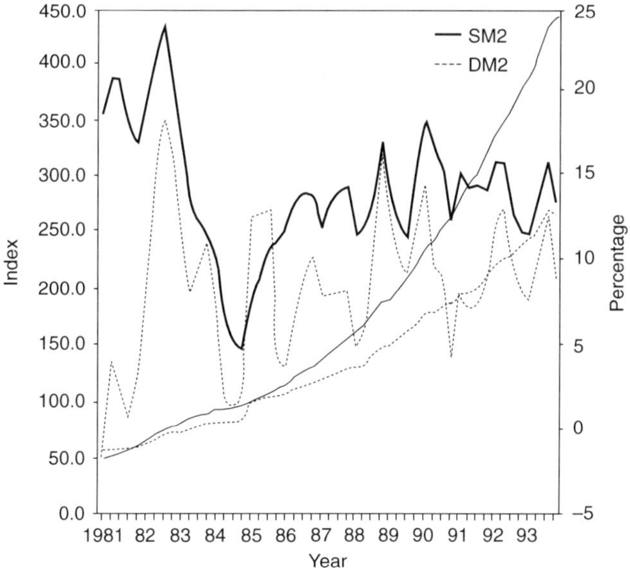

Figure 9.2 Levels and growth rates of SM2 and DM2

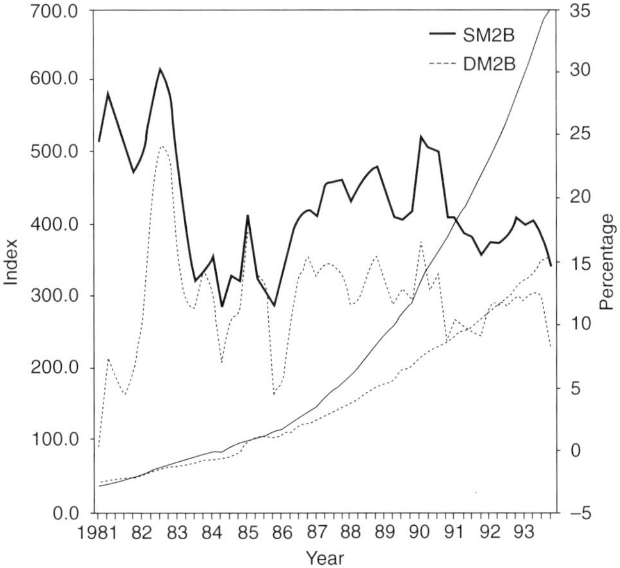

Figure 9.3 Levels and growth rates of SM2B and DM2B

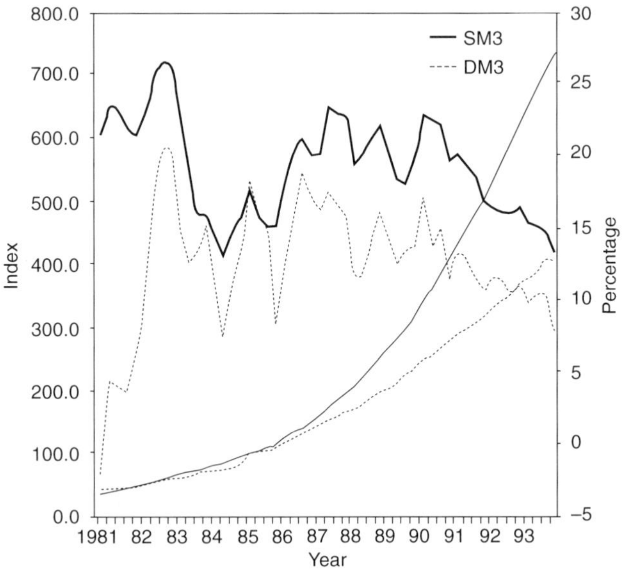

Figure 9.4 Levels and growth rates of SM3 and DM3

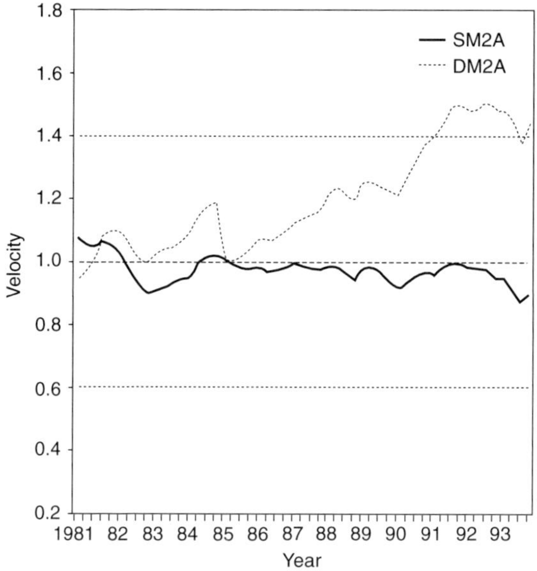

Figure 9.5 Velocities of SM2A and DM2A

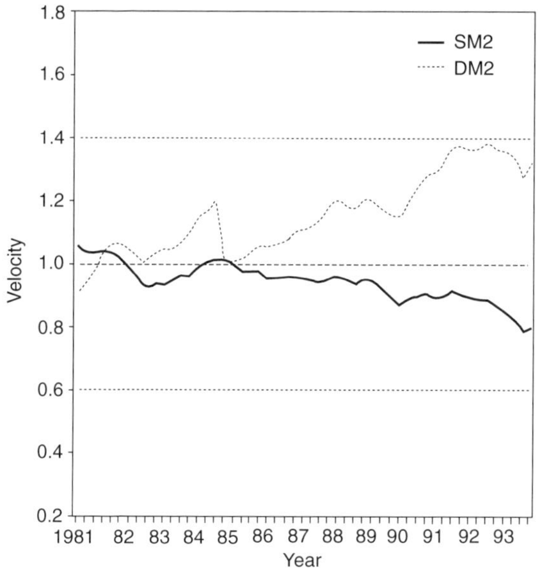

Figure 9.6 Velocities of SM2 and DM2

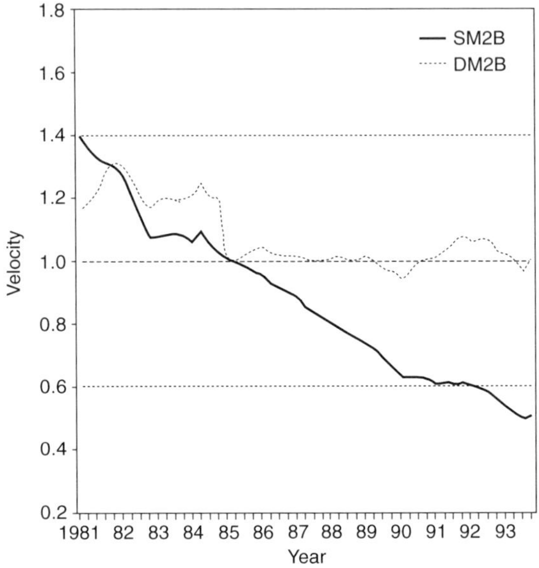

Figure 9.7 Velocities of SM2B and DM2B

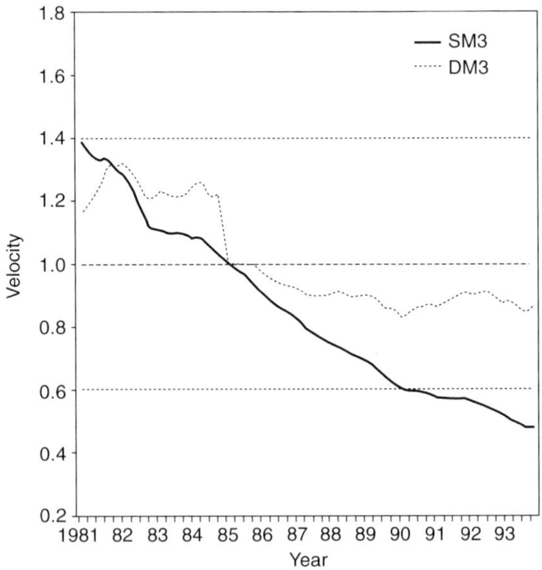

Figure 9.8 Velocities of SM3 and DM3

effect is that the simple-sum indexes give higher weights to the contributions of distant substitutes for money in aggregation than do the Divisia indexes, and these distant substitutes have been growing at a faster rate than have the more money-like components such as currency and demand deposits.

Divisia aggregation gives relatively lower weights to assets yielding higher rates of return, since a higher own-rate tends to reduce the quantity of this asset that is held and its expenditure–share weight in a Divisia index. This implies that adding successive assets with high own rates of return to those already in M2A adds little to the flow of monetary services. In this regard, the behaviour of the levels and growth rates of Divisia M2A differs little from that of Divisia M2.[19] Similarly, the behaviour of the levels and growth rates of Divisia M2B differs little from that of Divisia M3.

The behaviour of GNP velocities is depicted in Figures 9.5–9.8. While the velocities of simple-sum M2A and simple-sum M2 are apparently declining, those of Divisia M2A and Divisia M2 exhibit upward trends. While the velocities of simple-sum M2B and simple-sum M3 have shown strong downward trends, the declining trends have been relatively stable for Divisia M2B and less evident for Divisia M3. Our results suggest that the declining trends in the velocities of simple-sum measures are caused mainly by the rapid increase of distant substitutes for money. The explanation for this phenomenon is as follows. Suppose the desired level of monetary service flow is constant. A shift of one unit of M1 to other components of M2 not included in M1 (for example LS components), caused by a rise of interest rates, would lower the total flow of monetary services, since assets included in M2 but not in M1 possess a lower degree of moneyness. Therefore, in order to keep the total flow of monetary services constant, components of M2 other than those included in M1 have to grow by more than one unit. In this case, although the total flow of monetary services remained unchanged, the simple-sum M2 increases and this tends to lower M2 velocity.

It is not so clear from the figures that the velocities of Divisia money measures are more stable than those of simple-sum measures. One way to investigate the stability of velocity is to test whether its time series has a unit root (Belongia and Chalfant, 1990). As is well known, if a time series has a unit root, it is said to be non-stationary. The velocities of Divisia money measures are compared with those of simple-sum measures for M2A, M2, M2B and M3. Comparison is performed applying the Dickey–Fuller (DF) and the augmented Dickey–Fuller (ADF) tests for a unit root to each velocity series. Table 9.4 reports the DF and ADF test statistics for the log levels of each of the eight monetary velocities. In case of ADF test, the unit root hypothesis is not rejected by the test statistics for all the monetary velocities with trend and without trend, and hence no velocity measure is stationary in the log levels even after accounting for trend. On the basis of the DF tests, however, the velocities of Divisia M2, Divisia M2B and Divisia M3 are stationary in log levels at the 10 per cent level of significance after accounting for trend. Based on the

Table 9.4 Stability tests on monetary velocities (1980.1–1993.4)

Monetary variables	*Dickey–Fuller tests* *Without trends*	*With trends*	*Augmented Dickey–Fuller tests* *Without trends*	*With trends*
SM2A	– 0.93	– 1.60	– 0.02	– 2.00
SM2	– 1.98	– 2.17	– 0.54	– 1.98
SM2B	– 0.55	– 2.26	– 2.03	– 1.62
SM3	– 0.42	– 2.07	– 2.31	– 1.24
DM2A	– 1.79	– 2.48	– 0.35	– 2.70
DM2	– 2.59	– 3.19*	– 0.80	– 2.75
DM2B	– 1.40	– 3.28*	– 2.00	– 2.02
DM3	– 0.65	– 3.31*	– 1.80	– 1.53

Note: 1. An asterisk denotes statistical significance at 10 per cent level.

above results, the velocities of Divisia money measures, as a whole, may be more stable than those of simple-sum measures.

Empirical performance of alternative money measures

The empirical performance of alternative money measures and their usefulness as targets or indicators for monetary policy can be evaluated in a variety of ways. Among these, we want to focus mainly on the long-run relationships between alternative measures of money and the price level. Various methods can be used to investigate the existence of a long-run relationship between money and prices. In this study, we examine the money–price relationship by performing cointegration tests for money and price variables and then error-correction forecasts of inflation.

Cointegration tests

The quantity theory implies that the money stock and the price level are likely to have a common trend. Thus, if cointegration tests show two variables to be cointegrated, it means that there exists a long-run equilibrium relationship between the money stock and the price level.

The results from testing for cointegration between the alternative money measures and the price level are presented in Table 9.5.[20] The augmented Dickey–Fuller (ADF) tests indicate that the null hypothesis of cointegration with the price level is rejected by the test statistics for all the money measures with trend and without trend. Based on the Dickey – Fuller (DF) tests, however, the Divisia measures of M2A, M2 and M2B appear to be cointegrated with the price level in the log levels at the 10 per cent level of significance after accounting for trends over the sample period. In contrast, no simple-sum measure is cointegrated with the price level in any tests at any reasonable level of significance.

Table 9.5 Cointegration tests on relationship between price[1] level and monetary quantity index (1980.1–1993.4)

Monetary variables	*Dickey - Fuller Tests*		*Augmented Dickey - Fuller Tests*	
	Without trends	*With trends*	*Without trends*	*With trends*
SM2A	- 1.92	- 2.39	- 2.01	- 1.25
SM2	- 2.34	- 2.86	- 2.11	- 1.44
SM2B	- 2.36	- 2.82	- 2.11	- 1.51
SM3	- 2.24	- 2.71	- 2.23	- 1.46
DM2A	- 2.91	- 3.46*	- 2.14	- 1.62
DM2	- 3.36*	- 3.82*	- 2.04	- 1.70
DM2B	- 2.77	- 3.29*	- 2.08	- 1.45
DM3	- 2.72	- 3.20	- 2.19	- 1.42

Notes: 1. The price level is measured by the GNP deflator.
2. An asterisk denotes statistical significance at 10 per cent level.

Error correction forecasts of inflation

We also estimated the effect of the growth of each monetary aggregate on the inflation rate, using an error-correction model. We included uniformly four lags of inflation and money growth in each model. The results from estimating the error correction model for the period 1980.1 to 1993.4 are presented in Table 9.6. The results indicate that all the error correction coefficients, Z_t, for Divisia and simple-sum money measures are significant over all periods, even though we could not reject the absence of cointegration with the price level for the simple-sum measures. The negative coefficient on the error-correction term for all cases indicates that, when the price level is above its long-run equilibrium relationship, the rate of inflation falls in the next period.

We next forecast inflation over different periods using the error-correction models. We included the error-correction terms in all models when forecasting inflation because they were all significant. Since the relationship between money growth and inflation is thought to have changed recently, we compared out-of-sample forecasts based on each aggregate, updating the model every four quarters. That is, for the third forecast period (1991:1–1993:4), we estimated the model to 1990.4, and made forecasts for the period of 1991.1–1993.4. Then, for the second forecast period (1992:1–1993.4), we re-estimated the model to 1991.4 and made forecasts for the period of 1992.1–1993.4. Finally, for the last forecast period (1993:1–1993.4), we re-estimated the model to 1992:4 and made forecasts for the period of 1993:1–1993:4. Summary statistics comparing out-of-sample forecasts of inflation over different periods are presented in Table 9.7.[21]

As can be seen from Table 9.7, the percentage root means squared errors (%RMSE) for Divisia M2B and Divisia M3 are smaller than those of their simple-sum equivalents for all three periods, whereas Divisia M2A has lower

Table 9.6 Error correction models (dependent variable: inflation rate)

Independent variables	SM2A	SM2	SM2B	SM3	DM2A	DM2	DM2B	DM3
Constant	0.008	0.007	0.005	0.007	0.010	0.009	0.008	0.011
	(1.068)	(0.789)	(0.371)	(0.393)	(1.233)	(1.111)	(0.691)	(0.902)
Inflation (*t* – 1)	–0.031	–0.014	–0.073	–0.070	–0.111	–0.107	–0.125	–0.137
	(–0.272)	(–0.133)	(–0.662)	(–0.669)	(–1.044)	(–1.059)	(–1.218)	(–1.324)
Inflation (*t* – 2)	–0.052	–0.070	–0.091	–0.084	–0.117	–0.114	–0.101	–0.123
	(–0.484)	(–0.699)	(–0.880)	(–0.835)	(–1.131)	(–1.152)	(–0.996)	(–1.185)
Inflation (*t* – 3)	0.007	–0.011	–0.060	–0.079	–0.051	–0.056	–0.055	–0.078
	(0.066)	(–0.112)	(–0.602)	(–0.814)	(–0.486)	(–0.056)	(–0.542)	(–0.744)
Inflation (*t* – 4)	0.708	0.682	0.660	0.676	0.690	0.681	0.681	0.659
	(7.446)	(7.539)	(7.208)	(7.610)	(7.425)	(7.438)	(7.104)	(6.557)
M (*t* – 1)	–0.203	–0.371	–0.212	–0.232	–0.142	–0.145	–0.130	–0.123
	(–1.526)	(–2.042)	(–1.247)	(–0.983)	(–1.876)	(–1.757)	(–1.509)	(–1.418)
M (*t* – 2)	0.240	0.473	0.151	0.279	0.056	0.062	0.042	0.023
	(1.686)	(2.472)	(0.877)	(1.143)	(0.733)	(0.750)	(0.499)	(0.264)
M (*t* – 3)	–0.134	–0.22	–0.043	–0.395	0.024	0.042	0.082	0.047
	(–0.926)	(–1.145)	(–0.252)	(–1.600)	(0.318)	(0.508)	(0.981)	(0.546)
M (*t* – 4)	–0.020	0.049	0.135	0.340	–0.038	–0.042	–0.009	–0.005
	(–0.157)	(0.273)	(0.835)	(1.441)	(–0.524)	(–0.410)	(–0.116)	(–0.064)
Z (*t* – 1)	–0.182	–0.223	–0.204	–0.178	–0.102	–0.130	–0.108	–0.104
	(–2.390)	(–2.843)	(–2.798)	(–2.617)	(–1.915)	(–2.299)	(–2.176)	(–2.148)

Notes: Statistics in parentheses indicate *t*-ratios, the variable *Z* (*t* – 1) is the error correction term calculated from the equation (**) below, and the lagged *M* stands for the monetary aggregate denoted by each column heading.

*$\Delta \ln P_t = b_o + \sum_{i=1}^{4} b_1 \Delta \ln P_{t-i} + \sum_{i=1}^{4} b_2 \Delta \ln M_{t-i} + b_3 Z_{t-1}$.

**$Z_t = \ln P_t - a_0 - a_1 \ln M_t$.

Table 9.7 Summary statistics for error correction forecasts of inflation

Model		*SM2A*	*SM2*	*SM2B*	*SM3*	*DM2A*	*DM2*	*DM2B*	*DM3*
Forecast period	RMSE[1]	0.00625	0.00653	0.00516	0.00772	0.00602	0.00589	0.00520	0.00594
1993:1–1993:4	MEAN	0.00097	0.00096	0.00322	0.00407	0.00136	0.00210	0.00271	0.00358
	%RMSE[2]	29.1574	24.1252	66.0227	126.074	68.0958	49.7366	25.2951	23.2676
Forecast period	RMSE	0.01459	0.01292	0.01274	0.01526	0.01235	0.01231	0.01350	0.01445
1992:1–1993:4	MEAN	0.00695	0.00612	0.00603	0.00768	0.00560	0.00615	0.00645	0.00698
	%RMSE	107.995	96.275	126.980	167.113	99.1024	108.678	125.208	133.367
Forecast period	RMSE	0.02845	0.02240	0.02096	0.01720	0.01365	0.01409	0.01436	0.01384
1991:1–1993:4	MEAN	–0.02619	–0.01805	–0.01549	–0.01012	–0.00771	–0.00780	–0.00749	–0.00494
	%RMSE	249.110	151.687	112.175	84.5165	62.7525	66.5469	64.4389	76.5293

Notes: 1. $RMSE = \sqrt{\frac{1}{n}\sum_{t=1}^{n}(x_t^s - x_t^a)^2}$.

2. $\% \, RMSE = 100\sqrt{\frac{1}{n}\sum_{t=1}^{n}\left(\frac{x_t^s - x_t^a}{x_t^a}\right)^2}$.

X_t^s = simulated values; X_t^a = actual values; n = number of observations.

%RMSE than its simple-sum counterparts for only two different periods. The above results indicate that Divisia money measures apparently perform better than their simple-sum equivalents in terms of error-correction forecasts of inflation. This means that the use of the Divisia monetary aggregates should improve predictive ability substantially. Taken together, these results suggest that Divisia measures outperform their simple-sum equivalents.

However, it seems to be difficult to distinguish the best among the various alternative Divisia monetary aggregates in terms of %RMSE when we forecast inflation. For example, %RMSE ranges from 63 per cent to 99 per cent for Divisia M2A, from 50 per cent to 108 per cent for Divisia M2, from 25 per cent to 125 per cent for Divisia M2B, and from 23 per cent to 133 per cent for Divisia M3. However, when we forecast inflation from 1991.1 to 1993.4, Divisia M2A and Divisia M2B among the various alternative money measures forecast more accurately the actual inflation rate than did any other aggregates.

In sum, the most important conclusions we can derive from the above empirical results is that Divisia M2A and Divisia M2B, which are identified as admissible monetary aggregates based on aggregation theory, appeared to be the most promising candidates for targets or indicators of monetary policy in Korea.

9.5 Concluding remarks

We performed empirical tests for weak separability, as required by aggregation theory, to identify any possible candidates for admissible asset collections that could be aggregated. The results indicated that, among current alternative Korean money measures, Divisia M2A and Divisia M2B appeared to be admissible aggregates. We constructed these two admissible aggregates using the Fisher Ideal index, which is one of Diewert's superlative index numbers, and compared the empirical performance of these measures against their simple-sum equivalents. In terms of a long-run relationship between money and price, Divisia M2A, Divisia M2 and Divisia M2B appeared to perform better than their simple-sum counterparts. And, more importantly, based on the error correction forecasts of inflation, we found that Divisia M2A, Divisia M2B and Divisia M3 forecast actual inflation more accurately than did their simple-sum equivalents constructed from Korean data.

Taken together, these empirical results suggest that Divisia money measures are superior to their simple-sum equivalents. Particularly if price stability is an important objective of monetary policy, on the basis of both theoretical and empirical grounds, Divisia M2A and Divisia M2B should be the most promising candidates for alternative intermediate targets or indicator variables for the conduct of monetary policy in Korea.

Notes

1. For more detailed definitions of various measures in Korea, see Table 9.1.
2. See Belongia (this volume) for an empirical evidence that any grouping including time-deposits fails weak separability tests.
3. The measures of moneyness that we normally consider are inevitably aggregates, and any money aggregate can be conceived of as a joint product. There is ample evidence that the assets commonly combined in aggregates are not perfect substitutes. This fact gives us only two alternatives. The first is to restrict attention to a very narrow definition of money. The second is to construct an index number of monetary services which could capture the transactions services offered by a wide range of financial assets. See Barnett (1982) and Chrystal and MacDonald (1994).
4. According to Diewert, an index number is said to be superlative if it is exact for a flexible aggregator functional form, which can provide a second-order approximation to an arbitrary function. See Diewert (1976).
5. The factor-reversal tests states that the product of the values of the aggregate price and aggregate quantity indexes must be equal to total expenditure on the component assets; see Diewert (1976) and Barnett (1982).
6. The selection is based on the volume size of each component within the composite asset corresponding to the different holding periods. Also, because we computed the *after-tax* rates of return for monetary assets, marginal tax rate items have been omitted from Barnett's original user cost formula.
7. The implicit own-rate on demand deposits is estimated by Klein's (1974) formula. Ewis and Fisher (1984), Farr and Johnson (1985), and Thornton and Yue (1992) also discuss the treatment of implicit interest rates on demand deposits.
8. We also computed monetary services indexes using the curb rate in the non-official financial market as the benchmark rate R, but we found that the computed indexes are robust with respect to choice of R. Barnett and Spindt (1982) have also found their experiments with Divisia indexes to be robust with respect to choice of R.
9. Swofford and Whitney (1987), Belongia and Chalfant (1989), and Belongia and Chrystal (1991) have applied the techniques of non-parametric demand analysis suggested by Varian (1982, 1983) to test the weak separability of the alternative asset collections. The major advantages of non-parametric tests are that the results are not conditional upon a particular functional form for the utility function, and the tests can handle a relatively large number of assets or goods. The main disadvantage of this non-parametric technique is that the null hypothesis of weak separability is rejected if a single violation of consistency (generalised axiom of revealed preference (GARP)) occurs, and thus that it is apparently biased towards rejection of weak separability; see Barnett and Choi (1989). The bias arises because a sufficient, rather than necessary, characterisation of separability is used. In our study, we also tried to use non-parametric techniques but failed to test weak separability of the alternative asset groups because of a few violations of GARP at some data points. Chalfant and Alston (1988) suggest one method for inspecting these violations, and a strategy for dealing with them empirically.
10. See Hancock (1986) and Barnett and Hahm (1994) for separability tests from the perspective of a production function for monetary services.
11. The utility-tree structure defined in Equation (9.1) is treated as a maintained hypothesis in this study, although it is too restrictive, since it implies the demand for monetary services is independent of the relative prices outside the monetary group. This hypothesis is also testable, but this task is beyond the scope of this study.

12. The Gorman polar form has linear Engel curves which need not pass through the origin, but its share equations are not linear in parameters and variables. Therefore, this model is relatively difficult to estimate and conduct hypothesis testings upon. This model is often termed the quasi-homothetic translog model, and has been estimated by Manser (1976) and Serletis (1986).
13. For this work, the system has been estimated with the deletion of the first share equation. In order to check invariance of maximum likelihood parameter estimates with respect to the equation deleted we have estimated the model more than once, deleting a different equation each time.
14. For the derivation of these restrictions, see Denny and Fuss (1977). We should express the restrictions for weak separability in terms of the free parameters of the model. Under each separability type, we must be able to eliminate a number of free parameters equal to the number of independent parametric restrictions corresponding to that separability type. For the specific example for parameter restrictions, see Serletis (1986).
15. These estimates are obtained using a FIML program on the TSP econometric package at the Bank of Korea.
16. The non-negativity condition requires that the values of the fitted demand functions are non-negative. The condition simply means that all demands for aggregated monetary assets are predicted to be positive by Roy's identity, and this can easily be checked by investigation of the signs of the estimated average expenditure shares. The monotonicity condition requires that the indirect utility function is monotonically decreasing in prices (user costs), and this can also be checked by the average share. Finally, the curvature condition requires quasiconvexity of the indirect utility function, and it may be checked, provided the monotonicity condition holds, by direct computation of the Hessian matrix $\partial^2 V/\partial v_i \partial v_j$. The Hessian matrix is required to have at most one negative eigenvalue, with all others being positive or zero.
17. In this type of translog model, the curvature condition is usually violated at some sample points, since it does not satisfy global curvature conditions. Note that our separability tests are approximate in the sense that the null hypotheses are imposed only at a point of approximation rather than at every sample point. For example, those functional forms such as Fourier flexible functional forms (Gallant, 1981), Minflex Laurent functional forms (Barnett, 1985), and generalised symmetric Barnett functional forms satisfy global curvature conditions.
18. The separability tests carried out here cannot be conclusive, but rather should be viewed as a first step towards shedding some light on the issue of choosing admissible asset groupings appropriate for aggregation. Further research is clearly needed in this area. For example, since we have used the homothetic translog functional form, other flexible functional forms such as the basic translog or the generalised translog could be utilized. Or other forms could also be utilized, such as Fourier flexible functional forms (Gallant, 1981) and Minflex Laurent flexible functional forms (Barnett, 1985), which possess global properties.
19. As stated above, the M2A measure comprises M1 (currency and demand deposits) and SS (short-term time- and savings deposits) at banking institutions. On the other hand, the official monetary aggregate, M2, is the sum of M2A and LS (long-term time- and savings deposits) at banking institutions. The only difference between these two measures is these LS components, which consist of long-term time- and savings deposits at banking institutions, with terms of maturity of two years or more. These components possess explicitly fixed terms, and their explicit

own-rates of return are higher than those of transactions deposits. Apparently, these components have very low liquidity, and thus the public associates these more closely with the store-of-wealth function rather than transaction or liquidity functions. These LS components amounted to 32.4 per cent of the M2 money stock as of December 1993. On the other hand, the M1 and SS blocks amounted to 25.9 per cent and 41.7 per cent, respectively.

20. We conducted unit root tests for money and price variables and found that we could not reject the null hypothesis of a single unit root in each series of alternative money measures and the GNP deflator tested here.
21. We also performed the same analysis using nominal GNP instead of the price level in the tests. We found similar results to those shown in Table 9.7.

References

Barnett, William A. (1978) 'The User Cost of Money', *Economics Letters*, vol. 1, pp. 145–9.

Barnett, William A. (1982) 'The Optimal Level of Monetary Aggregation', *Journal of Money, Credit and Banking*, vol. 14, pp. 687–710.

Barnett, William A. (1985) 'The Minflex Laurent Translog Flexible Functional Form', *Journal of Econometrics*, vol. 30, pp. 33–4.

Barnett, William A. and Paul A. Spindt. (1982) 'Divisia Monetary Aggregates: Their Compilation, Data, and Historical Behaviour', *Federal Reserve Board Staff Study*, vol. 116 (Washington, DC: Publications Services, Federal Reserve Board)(May).

Barnett, William A. and Seungmook Choi (1989) 'A Monte Carlo Study of Tests of Blockwise Weak Separability', *Journal of Business and Economic Statistics*, vol. 7, no. 3, pp. 363–77.

Barnett, William A. and Jeong Ho Hahm (1994) 'Financial-Firm Function Approach', *Journal of Business and Economic Statistics*, vol. 12, no. 1, pp. 33–46.

Barnett, William A., Douglas Fisher and Apostolos Serletis (1992), 'Consumer Theory and the Demand for Money', *Journal of Economic Literature*, vol. 30, pp. 2086–119.

Barnett, William A., Edward K. Offenbacher and Paul A. Spindt (1984) 'The New Divisia Monetary Aggregates', *Journal of Political Economy*, vol. 92, no. 6, pp. 1049–85.

Barten, A. P. (1969) 'Maximum Likelihood Estimation of a Complete System of Demand Equation', *European Economic Review*, vol. 1 pp. 7–73.

Belongia, Michael T. (2000) 'Consequences of Money Stock Mismeasurement: Evidence from Three Countries', Chapter 13 in this volume.

Belongia, Michael T. and James A. Chalfant (1989) 'The Changing Empirical Definition of Money: Some Estimates from a Model of the Demand for Money Substitutes', *Journal of Political Economy*, vol. 97, no. 2, pp. 387–97.

Belongia, Michael T. and James A. Chalfant (1990) 'Alternative Measures of Money as Indicators of Inflation: A Survey and Some New Evidence', *Federal Reserve Bank of St Louis Review* (November/December), pp. 20–33.

Belongia, Michael T. and K. Alec Chrystal (1991) 'An Admissible Monetary Aggregate for the United Kingdom', *Review of Economics and Statistics*, vol. 73, no 3, pp. 497–502.

Berndt, E. R. and L. R. Christensen (1973) 'The Internal Structure of Functional Relationships: Separability, Substitution, and Aggregation', *Review of Economic Studies*, vol. 40, no. 3, pp. 403–10.

Berndt, E. R. and N. E. Savin (1975) 'Estimation and Hypothesis Testing in Singular Equation Systems with Autoregressive Disturbances', *Econometrica*, vol. 43, pp. 937–57.

Chalfant, James A. and Julian M. Alston (1988) 'Accounting for Changes in Tastes', *Journal of Political Economy*, vol. 96, no. 2, (April) pp. 391–410.

Chrystal, K. A. and Ronald MacDonald (1994) 'Empirical Evidence on the Recent Behaviour and Usefulness of Simple-Sum and Weighted Measures of the Money Stock', *Federal Reserve Bank of St Louis Review* (March/April) pp. 73–116.

Denny, M. and M. Fuss (1977) 'The Use of Approximation Analysis to Test for Separability and the Existence of Consistent Aggregates', *American Economic Review*, vol. 67, no. 3, pp. 404–18.

Diewert, W. E. (1976) 'Exact and Superlative Index Numbers', *Journal of Econometrics*, vol. 4, pp. 115–46.

Diewert, W. E. and T. J. Wales (1987) 'Flexible Functional Forms and Global Curvature Conditions', *Econometrica*, vol. 55, pp. 43–68.

Donovan, D. J. (1978) 'Modelling the Demand for Liquid Assets: An Application to Canada', *IMF Staff Paper*, vol. 25, pp. 676–704.

Ewis, N. A. and D. Fisher (1984) 'The Translog Utility Function and the Demand for Money in the United States': *Journal of Money, Credit and Banking*, vol. 14, no. 1, pp. 34–52.

Farr, Helen T. and Deborah Johnson (1985) 'Revisions in the Monetary Services (Divisia) Indexes of Monetary Aggregates', Board of Governors of the Federal Reserve System, *Special Studies Paper* 189.

Gallant, A. R. (1981) 'On the Bias in Flexible Functional Forms and an Essential Unbiased Form: The Fourier Flexible Form', *Journal of Econometrics*, vol. 15, pp. 211–45.

Hancock, D. (1986) 'Aggregation of Monetary Goods: A Production Model', in William A. Barnett and K. Singleton (eds), *New Approaches to Monetary Economics* (Cambridge University Press).

Klein, B. (1974) 'Competitive Interest Payment on Bank Deposits and the Long-Run Demand for Money', *American Economic Review*, vol. 64, no. 6, pp. 931–49.

Manser, M. E. (1976) 'Elasticities of Demand for Food: An Analysis using Non-Additive Utility Function allowing for Habit Formation', *Southern Economic Journal*, vol. 43, pp. 879–91.

Serletis, Apostolos (1986) 'Monetary Asset Separability Test', in William A. Barnett and K. Singleton (eds), *New Approaches to Monetary Economics* (Cambridge University Press). pp. 169–182.

Serletis, Apostolos and A. Leslie Robb (1986) 'Divisia Aggregation and Substitutability among Monetary Assets', *Journal of Money, Credit and Banking*, vol. 19, pp. 430–46.

Swofford, J. L. and G. A. Whitney (1987) 'Non-parametric Tests of Utility Maximization and Weak Separability for Consumption, Leisure, and Money', *Review of Economics and Statistics*, vol. 69, pp. 458–64.

Swofford, J. L. and G. A. Whitney (1991) 'The Composition and Construction of Monetary Aggregates', *Economic Inquiry*, vol. 24, pp. 752–61.

Thornton, Daniel L. and Piyu Yue (1992) 'An Extended Series of Divisia Monetary Aggregates', *Federal Reserve of Bank of St Louis Review* (November/December) pp. 35–52.

Varian, H. R. (1982) 'The Nonparametric Approach to Demand Analysis', *Econometrica* vol. 50, pp. 945–73.

Varian, H. R. (1983) 'Nonparametric Tests of Consumer Behaviour', *Review of Economic Studies*, vol. 50, pp. 99–110.

Yue, Piyu and Robert Fluri (1991) 'Divisia Monetary Services Indexes for Switzerland: Are They Useful for Monetary Targeting?', *Federal Reserve Bank of St Louis Review* (September/October) pp. 19–33.

10
Divisia Monetary Aggregates for Taiwan

Yen Chrystal Shih

10.1 Introduction

Taiwan has implemented major financial liberalisation measures since the late 1980s. In July 1987, trade-related foreign exchange controls were abolished and capital-flow-related foreign exchange controls greatly relaxed. The entry of new securities firms was permitted in January 1988, with the result that the number of securities firms increased from 60 to 150 within the first year. The limit on daily fluctuations in stock prices was raised from 3 to 5 per cent in 1988 and to 7 per cent in the following year. In December 1990, foreign institutional investors were allowed to invest directly in the local stock market. In respect of the banking sector, a revised Banking Law was promulgated in September 1989, leading to bank interest rates on deposits and loans being completely liberalised, and new private commercial banks were allowed to be established. As of the end of 1993, sixteen new private banks had begun operating.

Along with the process of price and entry deregulation, local financial markets expanded rapidly, and financial price variables (such as interest rates, exchange rates and stock prices) became flexible and increasingly sensitive to market conditions.[1] The resultant volatility in these financial prices in the second half of the 1980s, which was unparalleled in Taiwanese post-Second-World War history, deeply affected the portfolio behaviour of households and firms.[2] Consequently, the narrowly-defined monetary aggregate MIB, which is vulnerable to deposit-shift behaviour, fluctuated significantly. Faced with the increasing instability of money demand for MIB, in 1990 the central bank replaced MIB with the broadly-defined monetary aggregate M2 as the intermediate target variable of monetary policy. Since differing degrees of monetary services are provided by the component assets under the definition of the broad aggregate M2, this shift to M2 as a policy target has aroused concern as to whether the traditional M2, which sums the balances of component assets with equal weights, can serve as an appropriate measure of monetary service flows in society. One solution to this is to apply a Divisia weighting strategy to the component assets to create admissible monetary aggregates.

The purpose of this chapter is to provide technical details with regard to the construction of Divisia monetary aggregates for Taiwan, and to evaluate the empirical performance of such aggregates against the standards chosen for the intermediate target variable in the conduct of monetary policy.

10.2 Construction of Divisia monetary aggregates

In order to construct Divisia monetary aggregates for Taiwan, component assets based on the definition of M2 have been classified into the following eight categories:

1. Currency in circulation and checking accounts;
2. Passbook deposits;
3. Passbook savings deposits;
4. Time deposits;
5. Postal savings deposits redeposited with the central bank and other monetary institutions;
6. Foreign currency deposits;
7. Negotiable certificates of deposit and Treasury bills; and
8. Bank debentures and savings bonds.

According to the definitions of money, MlA is composed of the monetary assets listed in categories (1) and (2); MlB is composed of the monetary assets listed in categories (1), (2) and (3); and M2 includes all the monetary assets listed in the eight categories. The main characteristics of the data on monetary assets and their rates of return are briefly introduced according to category.

1. *Currency in circulation and cheque accounts*. In Taiwan, most household consumption involves cash transactions, since the majority of local stores are small in size and do not accept customers' cheques in payment for goods. The historical movements in currency in circulation exhibit a strong seasonal pattern, primarily reflecting the effect of the Chinese New Year holiday and election days. As for cheque accounts, cheques are basically a medium of exchange for large transactions among business companies. During the period between 1981 and 1991 the total share of currency in circulation and cheque accounts in M2 declined gradually, averaging 13.2 per cent over the whole period. Currency and non-interest-bearing cheque accounts are treated as having zero yield in constructing the Divisia aggregates for Taiwan.
2. *Passbook deposits*. Payments for public utilities, taxes and securities can be made against the balances of passbook deposits. As observed, passbook deposits increased significantly, between 1987 and 1989, when speculation

in the local stock market reached its historical peak. It should be noted that the Taiwan stock market is dominated by small individual investors, and passbook deposits are commonly used by such investors to settle stock transactions. Therefore, the link between the volume of stock trading and passbook deposits has always been very strong. The share of passbook deposits in M2 over the period between 1981 and 1991 averaged 8.4 per cent. The average daily interest rate on passbook deposits at the First Commercial Bank (IRPD) is adopted as the representative rate of return on passbook deposits.

3. *Passbook savings deposits*. Passbook savings deposits are very similar to passbook deposits in terms of their payment function, except that the former cannot be used to settle stock transactions.[3] Since passbook savings deposits were originally created for the purpose of promoting savings, a higher interest rate is paid on passbook savings deposits than on passbook deposits, and only individuals and non-profit institutions are allowed to open savings accounts. Passbook savings deposits are very sensitive to the gap in interest rates between time-deposits and passbook savings deposits, and are less related to transaction volume than are passbook deposits. Over the period between 1981 and 1991, passbook savings deposits on average contributed 12.6 per cent of M2. The average daily interest rate on passbook savings deposits at the First Commercial Bank (IRPSD) is used as the representative rate of return on passbook savings deposits.
4. *Time deposits*. Time deposits are the most common form of savings for the general public. Time deposits taken by banks on average accounted for 43.9 per cent of M2 over the period between 1981 and 1991. The maturities of time deposits include: one month, three months, six months, nine months, one year, two years and three years. In order to determine the representative rate of return for time deposits, a number of studies in the literature, such as Cockerline and Murray (1981), Ishida (1984), and Serletis and Robb (1986), suggested making a yield curve adjustment for interest rates in respect of time deposits with long maturities, while others, such as Yue and Fluri (1991), have simply selected short-term interest rates on time deposits to serve as the representative yield. In our case, because of lack of complete time-series data regarding interest rates on Treasury bills and government bonds of different maturities, it is technically impossible to make a yield curve adjustment for interest rates on time deposits with long maturities. Therefore short-term interest rates on time deposits have been chosen as the representative rate of return on time deposits. Since the representative rates of return on monetary assets discussed in this chapter are all based on a holding period of three months, the average daily interest rate on three-month time deposits at the First Commercial Bank (IRM3) is used as the representative rate of return on time deposits.
5. *Postal savings deposits re-deposited with the central bank and other monetary institutions*. The postal savings system is not classified as a monetary

institution. Hence only the postal savings deposits that are re-deposited with monetary institutions can be brought within the definition of M2. However, since the postal savings system is not allowed to make loans, nearly all its deposits are re-deposited with the central bank and other monetary institutions. The re-deposits accounted for 18.4 per cent of M2 over the period between 1981 and 1991, being ranked next only to bank time deposits. The postal savings system accepts three types of deposit: namely, transfer accounts; passbook savings deposits; and time savings deposits. The representative rate of return on the re-deposits (IRRPD) is measured as the weighted average of interest paid in respect of these three types of postal savings deposits, and the quantity shares of the three types of deposits in the total at each point in time are given as the weights.

6. *Foreign currency deposits.* Although some foreign currency deposits may be held as payments for future imports, in most cases the purpose in holding foreign currency deposits is to gain from the appreciation in foreign currencies. The average share of foreign currency deposits in M2 over the period 1981–91 was only 0.9 per cent. Since US-dollar deposits account for the vast bulk of foreign currency deposits, the representative rate of return in respect of foreign currency deposits (IRFCD) is measured as the interest rate on three-month US-dollar deposits plus the rate of appreciation in respect of the US dollar against the New Taiwan (NT) dollar in the corresponding three-month period, assuming that the depositors have perfect foresight regarding the appreciation.
7. *Negotiable certificates of deposit and Treasury bills.* The combined share of NCDs and Treasury bills in M2 averaged 1.9 per cent during the period 1981–91. The shortest maturity of NCDs is one month and the maturities of the rest are multiples of one month, up to one year. Treasury bills are issued by the central bank to regulate financial conditions. The maturities of Treasury bills include 91 days, 182 days, 273 days and 364 days. NCDs and Treasury bills often offer better rates of return than bank deposits with comparable maturities, since the local banking sector is dominated by a few large banks, which causes bank deposit rates to be lower than market rates. In addition, these money market instruments can easily be liquidated in the secondary market. The secondary market interest rates on NCDs are slightly higher than those on Treasury bills; however, this difference in interest rates reflects the tax-exempt status of Treasury bills rather than the higher degrees of monetary services provided by this instrument. As far as the historical data in respect of their interest rates are concerned, only the secondary market rate with regard to three-month NCDs and the weighted average of the secondary market rates with regard to NCDs with maturities of over three months are compiled and published. Hence the average daily secondary market rate in respect of three-month NCDs (IRNCD) is used as the representative rate of return for these two assets.

8. *Bank debentures and savings bonds.* Bank debentures are issued by four specialised banks to attract medium-term funds, with maturities ranging from three to five years. Savings bonds are issued by the central bank to absorb excess liquidity, and their maturities include six months, one year, two years and three years. During the period 1981–91, outstanding bank debentures and savings bonds contributed only 0.8 per cent of M2. As for the data in respect of the interest rates on these assets, no complete time-series data on the interest rates for these two assets are available. However, in practice, when banks issue bank debentures or the central bank issues savings bonds, there is often reference to interest rates on time-deposits with the same maturities. Furthermore, for these two assets, most are with maturities of one-year. Therefore the average daily interest rate in respect of one-year time deposits at the First Commercial Bank (IRYI) serves as the representative rate of return in respect of bank debentures and savings bonds.

Table 10.1 contains the names of the variables in respect of the time-series of the balances of these eight types of asset and their representative rates of return, and also summarises the key statistical characteristics of these time-series.[4] Figure 10.1 depicts the movements in the rates of return of these eight types of asset over the period 1981–91. In order to calculate the user costs (or rental prices) of these assets, it is necessary to select an asset to serve as the benchmark asset that does not provide any monetary service and whose rate of return should be no less than the rates of return of the monetary assets. Some articles in the literature, such as that by Belongia and Chalfant (1989), selected bonds as the benchmark asset, and interest rates on bonds as the benchmark interest rate. However, it might be difficult in some cases to find a single rate series that exceeds all other rates on monetary assets at each point in time. Hence, some studies, such as those by Swofford and Whitney (1986) and Serletis and Robb (1986), chose the highest interest rate of all component assets at each point in time as the benchmark rate. Other studies, such as Barnett and Spindt (1982), Ishida (1984), Farr and Johnson (1985), and Swofford and Whitney (1987), adopted the higher interest rate between bond rates and the maximum among all own rates of component assets at each point in time. In the case of Taiwan, whose bond market is not well developed, no complete sets of data regarding bond yields are available. Therefore, the maximum among all own rates at each point in time has been chosen as the benchmark rate.[5] The opportunity cost of holding each monetary asset is measured as follows:

$$P_{i,t} = (R_t - r_{i,t})/(1 + R_t)$$

where R_t represents the price of the asset i at time t; R_t represents the

Table 10.1 A taxonomy of monetary assets and variable names of component asset and interest rate series

Category	*Balance of assets*			*Interest rate on assets*		
	Variable name	*Begin at* (Yr. Mon.)	*Share in M2 (%)*	*Variable name*	*Begin at (Yr. Mon.)*	*Rate of return (%)*
Currency	CURN	1961.07		–	–	
Checking accounts	MICA	1961.07	13.2	–	–	0
Passbook deposits	MIPD	1961.07	8.4	IRPD	1961.07	2.18
Passbook savings deposits	MIPSD	1968.09	12.6	IRPSD	1968.09	4.79
Time deposits	MITD	1961.07	43.9	IRM3	1970.12	6.98
Postal savings re-deposits	MIRPD	1964.04	18.4	IRRPD	1970.12	5.67
Foreign currency deposits	MIFCD	1961.07	0.9	IRFCD	1975.01	8.32
NCDs	MINCD	1975.08	1.9	IRNCD	1980.11	7.49
Treasury bills	PTB	1987.04				
Bank debentures	PBD	1980.10	0.8	IRY1	1970.12	8.31
Savings bonds	PSD	1986.03				

Notes: 1. The data on the balance of assets are end-of-month data since daily average data are not available.
2. Both the shares of the component assets in M2 and their rates of return are calculated as the averages over a sample period from January 1981 to December 1991.
3. Data on these variables are obtained from *Financial Statistics Monthly*, Central Bank of China.

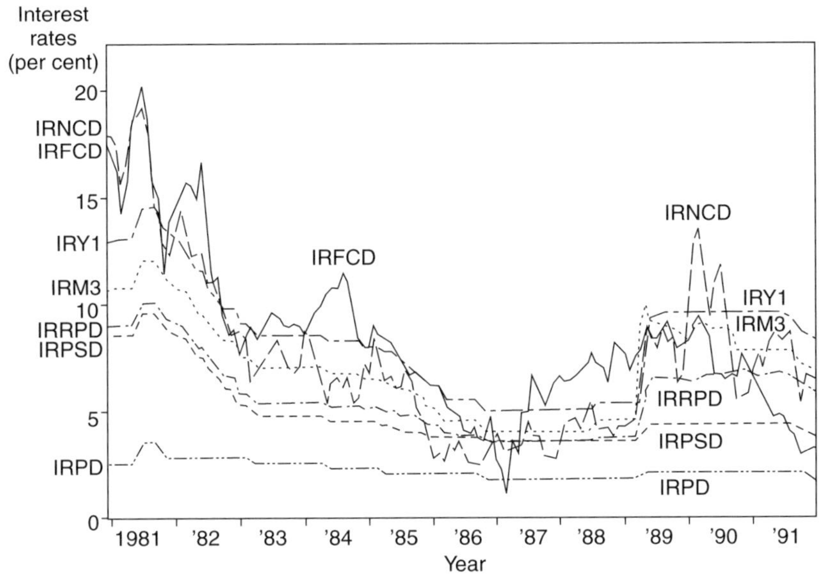

IRFCD = Interest rate on foreign currency deposits
IRNCD = Interest rate on negotiable certificates of deposit
IRY1 = Interest rate on 1-year time deposits
IRM3 = Interest rate on 3-months time deposits
IRRPD = Interest rate on re-deposits
IRPSD = Interest rate on postal savings re-deposits
IRPD = Interest rate on passbook deposits

Source: Central Bank of China, Financial Statistics Monthly.
Figure 10.1 The representative rates of return on monetary assets

benchmark rate at time *t*; and $r_{i,t}$ represents the own rate of the asset *i* at time *t*. Given the data on the prices and quantities of each monetary asset, the expenditure weight of asset *i* at time *t* ($S_{i,t}$) can be measured as follows:

$$S_{i,t} = P_{i,t} * M_{i,t} / \sum_{i=1}^{n} P_{i,t} * M_{i,t}$$

where $M_{i,t}$ represents the balance of asset *i* at time *t*. The Divisia monetary aggregates (DM_t) may then be constructed according the following formula:

$$DM_t = DM_{t-1}{}^{*}\exp\{\sum_{i=1}^{n} S'_{i,t}{}^{*}[\ln M_{i,t} - \ln M_{i,t-1}]\}$$

where $S'_{i,t}$ is the average of $S_{i,t}$ and $S_{i,t-1}$. Based on this Divisia money formula,

Table 10.2 Correlations of the growth rates of monetary aggregates

Correlation coefficient		*Simple-sum aggregates*			*Divisia aggregates*		
		M1A	*M1B*	*M2*	*M1A*	*M1B*	*M2*
Simple-sum aggregates	M1A	1.0000					
	M1B	0.9139	1.0000				
	M2	0.6327	0.6995	1.0000			
Divisia aggregates	M1A	0.9974	0.9130	0.6477	1.0000		
	M1B	0.9516	0.9912	0.6987	0.9544	1.0000	
	M2	0.8714	0.9273	0.8714	0.8804	0.9335	1.0000

the share of each component in the growth rate of a Divisia aggregate is the ratio of the expenditure on the monetary services it provides to the total expenditure on monetary services from all components in the aggregate.

Figure 10.2 depicts the movements in the growth rates of Divisia MlA, Divisia M1B and Divisia M2, in contrast to the movements in the growth rates of the corresponding simple-sum aggregates. As observed, the movements in the growth rates of narrowly-defined monetary aggregates are relatively unstable over time, when compared with those of broadly-defined monetary aggregates, regardless of the aggregation procedure adopted. As to the comparison made between the simple-sum and Divisia aggregates, the simple-sum and Divisia aggregates under the narrow definitions are highly correlated and, in the case of the broad aggregate M2, different aggregation procedures produce monetary measures that move relatively differently. The movements in Divisia M2 are in some ways similar to the movements in narrowly-defined monetary aggregates, since Divisia M2 weights the component assets within the definition of the narrowly-defined monetary aggregates more heavily than other components. Therefore, deposit shifts, which have no effect on simple-sum M2, still effect Divisia M2 through their influence on the share weights. The correlation coefficients for the growth rates of the six monetary aggregates listed in Table 10.2 also suggest that different aggregation procedures affect the broad aggregates more significantly than they do the narrow ones.

10.3 Empirical results and their interpretation

Because the ultimate goal variables of monetary policy in Taiwan (that is, the economic growth rate and the inflation rate) are not controllable directly, the

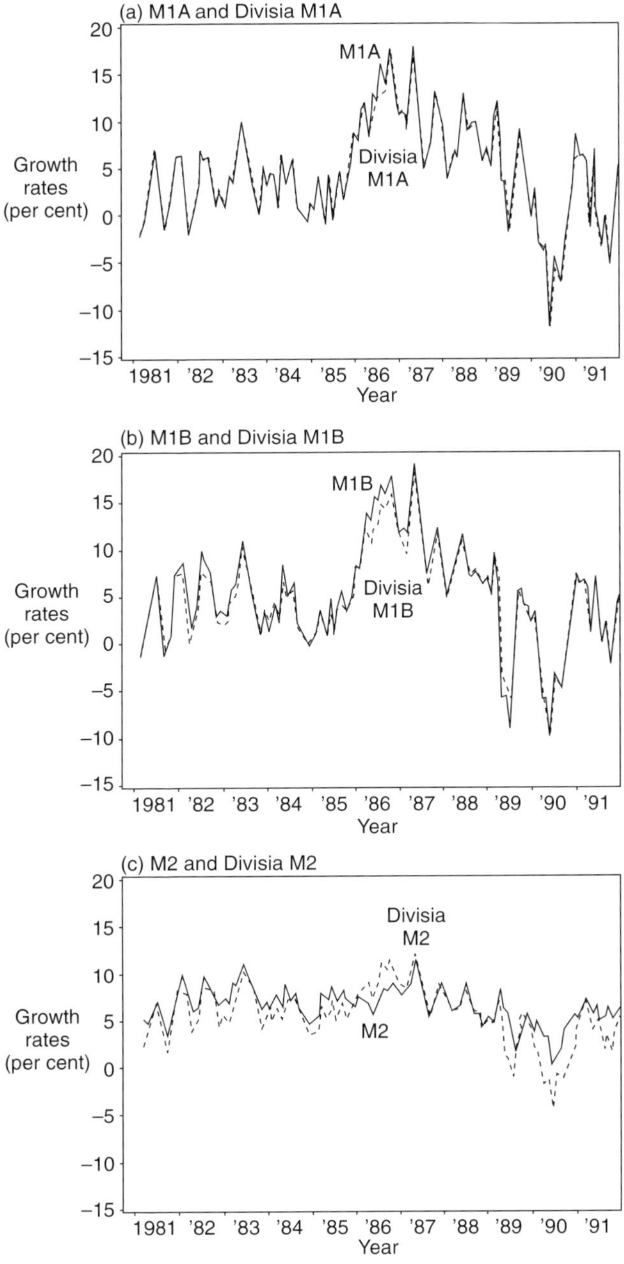

Figure 10.2 Movements in money growth

central bank usually follows an intermediate target strategy that involves a two-step process in the conduct of policy. First, the central bank determines the target level of the intermediate target variable that is most likely to correspond to the desired economic growth rate and acceptable inflation rate. The second step is to determine the levels for, or changes in operational instruments required to achieve, the intermediate target. According to this mechanism of monetary policy, an intermediate target variable should meet two qualifications. First, it shares stable and predictable relationships with economic growth and inflation. Second, it is controllable in the sense that predictable relationships exist between it and reserve money, required reserve ratios and the discount rate. The purpose of this section is to investigate whether the Divisia monetary aggregates constructed in the previous section and conventional simple-sum monetary aggregates possess these qualities.

Linkage between monetary aggregates and economic activity

In this part, the stability of velocities, the stability of money-demand functions, and the relationship between the inflation rate and money growth rates are examined carefully in order to compare the linkages between the six monetary aggregates and economic activity.

Stability of velocities

The movements in the velocities of monetary aggregates are plotted in Figure 10.3. It is apparent that a major decline in the velocities of narrow aggregates can be identified in the second half of the 1980s, when wild speculation in the securities market induced individual investors to transfer funds from time-deposits into passbook deposits. The broad aggregate M2, which internalises the deposit shifts, has relatively stable income velocity compared to the narrow aggregates.

The estimated growth trends in the GNP velocities of the six monetary

Table 10.3 Estimated trends in the velocities of GNP and standard deviations from the trends

Monetary aggregates	$\bar{R}^2$	*Estimated trend coefficient C1*	*RMSPE (%)*	
Simple sum aggregates	M1A	0.76	–0.0150	11.85
	M1B	0.88	–0.0257	11.03
	M2	0.99	–0.0137	2.30
Divisia aggregates	M1A	0.73	–0.0142	10.87
	M1B	0.83	–0.0203	10.34
	M2	0.97	–0.0126	4.57

Note: $V = C0 + C1^{*}t + C2^{*}t^2$.

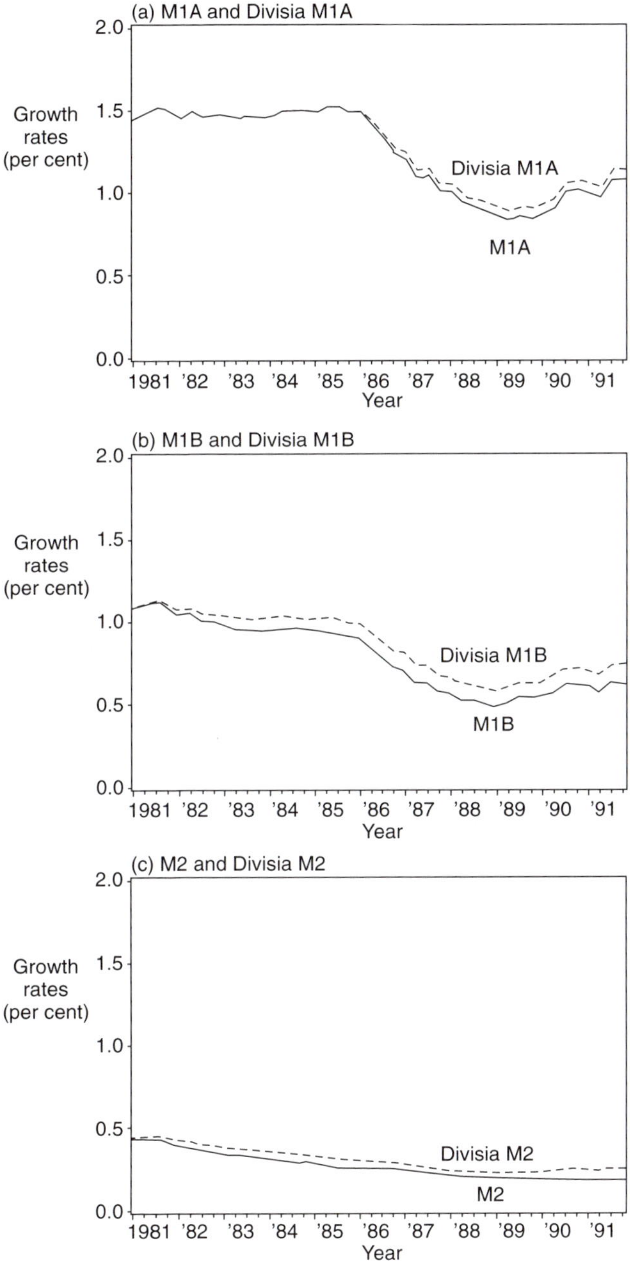

Figure 10.3 Velocities of monetary aggregates

aggregates, derived from a quadratic function, are reported in Table 10.3. The sample period extends from the first quarter of 1981 to the fourth quarter of 1991. The standard deviations from the trend (that is, the root mean squared errors) given in the table represent the percentage deviations of nominal GNP from the desired GNP levels implicit in the monetary targets, if the monetary aggregates are on target. Therefore, the standard deviations are one of the measures of the usefulness of the monetary aggregates as intermediate target variables for achieving a nominal GNP objective. The results of the estimation indicate that the velocity deviations in respect of broad aggregates are smaller than narrow aggregates no matter what kind of aggregation procedure is involved and, in the case of the narrow aggregates, the velocity deviations are slightly reduced if the simple-sum aggregates are replaced by the Divisia aggregates when measuring the velocities. The results for the broad aggregates, however, are just the opposite, in that deposit shifts affect Divisia M2 to some extent, but do not affect simple-sum M2. Hence, given the stability of velocities criterion, simple-sum M2 is preferable to other aggregates in terms of serving as an intermediate target variable.

Stability of money demand equations

The velocity deviations from trends may be questioned on the grounds of whether the trends are fixed. To improve on this point, the stability is evaluated of money demand equations that take account of real GNP, interest rates and lagged adjustments. Moreover, from the central bank's point of view, the parameter estimates of the money demand function of an intermediate target variable, based on historical data, are used to calculate the target zone of the growth of the target variable for the coming year. Therefore, the stability of the money demand equation is the most crucial requirement with regard to the central bank's practice of selecting an intermediate target variable. A short-run money demand function is specified as follows:

$$\ln (\mathrm{M}_t/\mathrm{P}_t) = a_0 + a_1^* \ln (\mathrm{GNP86}_t) + a_2^* \ln (\mathrm{CPS90}_t) + a_3^* \ln (M_{t-1}/P_{t-1}) + e_t,$$

where M_t represents monetary aggregates at time t; P_t represents the GNP_t price deflator at time t, and $\mathrm{CPS90}_t$ represents 90-day commercial paper secondary market interest rates at time t.

Prior to the estimation of the money demand equations it is necessary to test for cointegration among the variables involved in each of the equations to ensure the existence of long-term equilibrium as implied in the functions. Because candidates for inclusion in a cointegrating vector must share an identical order of integration, the augmented Dickey–Fuller tests for unit roots were applied to the natural logarithms of the series of real money stock, real GNP and interest rates. The sample period extends from the first quarter of 1981 to the fourth quarter of 1991. The results presented in Table 10.4 indicate that real GNP, interest rates, and simple-sum M2 are integrated of order one,

Table 10.4 Results of Dickey–Fuller tests for unit roots

Dickey–Fuller tests	Simple-sum aggregates (in real terms)			Divisia aggregates (in real terms)			1n (GNP86)	1n (CPS90)
	1n (RM1A)	*1n (RM1B)*	*1n (RM2)*	*1n (RM1A)*	*1n (RM1B)*	*1n (RM2)*		
Level								
U-ROOT (C, 1)	–0.7054	–0.9887	–2.2446	–0.7110	–0.8886	–1.7406	–0.0469	–2.1863
U-ROOT (T, 1)	–1.1546	–0.9117	0.2364	–1.0927	–0.9129	0.2040	–3.2148	–1.7486
1st difference								
U-ROOT (C, 1)	–2.0654	–2.1726	–3.5997*	–2.1346	–2.1842	–2.6009	–6.6695*	–4.8458*
U-ROOT (T, 1)	–2.0869	–2.3124	–4.4694*	–2.1676	–2.2930	–3.1424	–6.5872*	–5.1928*
2nd difference								
U-ROOT (C, 1)	–5.5153*	–5.6818*	–6.7476*	–5.7031**	–5.7189*	–6.3360*	–7.2407*	–8.5088*
U-ROOT (T, 1)	–5.5024*	–5.6395*	–6.6714*	–5.6822*	–5.6782*	–6.2826*	–7.1454*	–8.4054*

Notes: 1. 'C' indicates the inclusion of a constant term and 'T' indicates the inclusion of a constant term and trend.

2. MacKinnon critical values:

		1%	5%	10%
Level	U-ROOT (C, 1)	–3.5930	–2.9320	–2.6039
	U-ROOT (T, 1)	–4.1896	–3.5189	–3.1898
1st difference	U-ROOT (C, 1)	–3.5973	–2.9339	–2.6648
	U-ROOT (T, 1)	–4.1958	–3.5217	–3.1914
2nd difference	U-ROOT (C, 1)	–3.6019	–2.9358	–2.6059
	U-ROOT (T, 1)	–4.2023	–3.5247	–3.1931

3. * indicates that the null hypothesis of non-stationarity can be significantly rejected at the 5% significance level.

while simple-sum M1A, simple-sum M1B and Divisia aggregates are integrated of order two. They each differ from real GNP and interest rates in terms of their orders of integration. The results of the Engle–Granger tests for cointegration reported in Table 10.5 indicate that, among the six monetary aggregates, only simple-sum M2 is cointegrated with real GNP and interest rates.

The estimated coefficients and respective statistics are shown in Table 10.6. From this it can be seen that the estimated coefficient of real GNP in the money-demand equations of simple-sum M1A, simple-sum M1B, Divisia M1A, and Divisia M1B are all statistically insignificant at the 5 per cent significance level, while all the coefficients in the money-demand equations of simple-sum M2 and Divisia M2 are statistically significant as well as possessing correct signs. The underlying relationships for structural stability are also investigated, by means of recursive regressions. The recursive estimated coefficients of real GNP are plotted in Figure 10.4. It is apparent that, in the case of money demand for narrowly-defined monetary aggregates, there exists a structural break in the second half of the 1980s, while the recursive estimated income elasticities of the money-demand for simple-sum M2 are very stable over time. Therefore, in terms of the stability of the money-demand equations, we also tend to favour the simple-sum M2.

Relationship between inflation and money growth

As Taiwan moves from being a developing country to a developed country, price stability as a final goal of monetary policy is becoming increasingly important. It is necessary for the central bank to evaluate how much of the current inflation can be explained by past values of the growth of the six monetary aggregates. Since Taiwan is a highly open economy, its inflation is affected not only by its domestic monetary policy but also by certain external factors. In the 1980s the economy experienced a sharp appreciation of the NT dollar and a significant cut in tariff rates. These factors contributed to the decline in the prices of imported goods. Hence the inflation rate equation is specified as follows:

$$\dot{CPI}_t = a_0 + \sum_{i=0}^{m} b_i{}^* \dot{M}_{t-i} + \sum_{j=0}^{n} c_i{}^* \dot{MPI}_{t-i} + e_t$$

where CPI_t represents the annual growth rate of consumer prices at time t; M_t represents the annual growth rate of money stock at time t; and MPI_t represents the annual growth rate of prices of imported goods after adjusting for tariffs.

The results of the J-tests, as reported in Table 10.7, indicate that Divisia M1B and Divisia M1A performed best in explaining inflation in Taiwan, and that both simple-sum M2 and Divisia M2 are not ideal information indicators insofar as inflation is concerned.

Table 10.5 Results of the Engle–Granger tests for cointegration

Engle–Granger tests	*Simple-sum aggregates (in real terms)*			*Divisia aggregates (in real terms)*		
	1n (RM1A)	*1n (RM1B)*	*1n (RM2)*	*1n (RM1A)*	*1n (RM1B)*	*1n (RM2)*
U-ROOT (C, 1)	–0.8008	–1.0204	–3.2914	–0.7717	–0.9424	–1.6004
U-ROOT (C, 4)	–2.4833	–3.5347	–4.1025*	–2.5722	–3.3645	–2.9402

Notes: 1. 'C' indicates the inclusion of a constant term.
2. MacKinnon critical values:

	1%	5%	10%
U-ROOT (C, 1)	–4.6527	–3.9494	–3.6020
U-ROOT (C, 4)	–4.6822	–3.9659	–3.6137

3. * indicates that the null hypothesis of non-cointegration among the real money stock, real GNP and interest rates is rejected at the 5% significance level.

Table 10.6 Results of the estimation of money demand equations

Dependent variable		*Constant*	*Independent variables* 1n (GNP86)	*1n (CPS90)*	*Lagged dependent*	$\bar{R}^2$	*RMSE*
Simple-sum aggregates	1n (RM1A)	0.8925	–0.0600	–0.0620*	1.0074*	0.99	0.0315
		(0.9403)	(–0.5975)	(–4.5951)	(19.0586)		
	1n (RM1B)	0.0904	0.0395	–0.0644*	0.9492*	0.99	0.0289
		(0.1029)	(0.4221)	(–5.8176)	(21.6118)		
	1n (RM2)	–2.7917*	0.3527*	–0.0288*	0.8174*	0.99	0.0204
		(–2.6987)	(2.9628)	(–3.4656)	(14.7311)		
Divisia aggregates	1n (RM1A)	0.6769	–0.0377	–0.0566*	0.9963*		
		(0.7514)	(–0.3793)	(–4.3617)	(18.2870)	0.99	0.0307
	1n (RM1B)	0.1945	0.0252	–0.0586*	0.9567*		
		(0.2372)	(0.2786)	(–5.3837)	(20.4540)	0.99	0.0287
	1n (RM2)	–1.3881	0.2185*	–0.0426*	0.8569*		
		(–1.7693)	(2.3183)	(–5.2022)	(17.5066)	0.99	0.0213

Notes: 1. *t*-statistics are in parentheses.
2. * indicates that the coefficient is significantly different from zero at the 5% significance level.

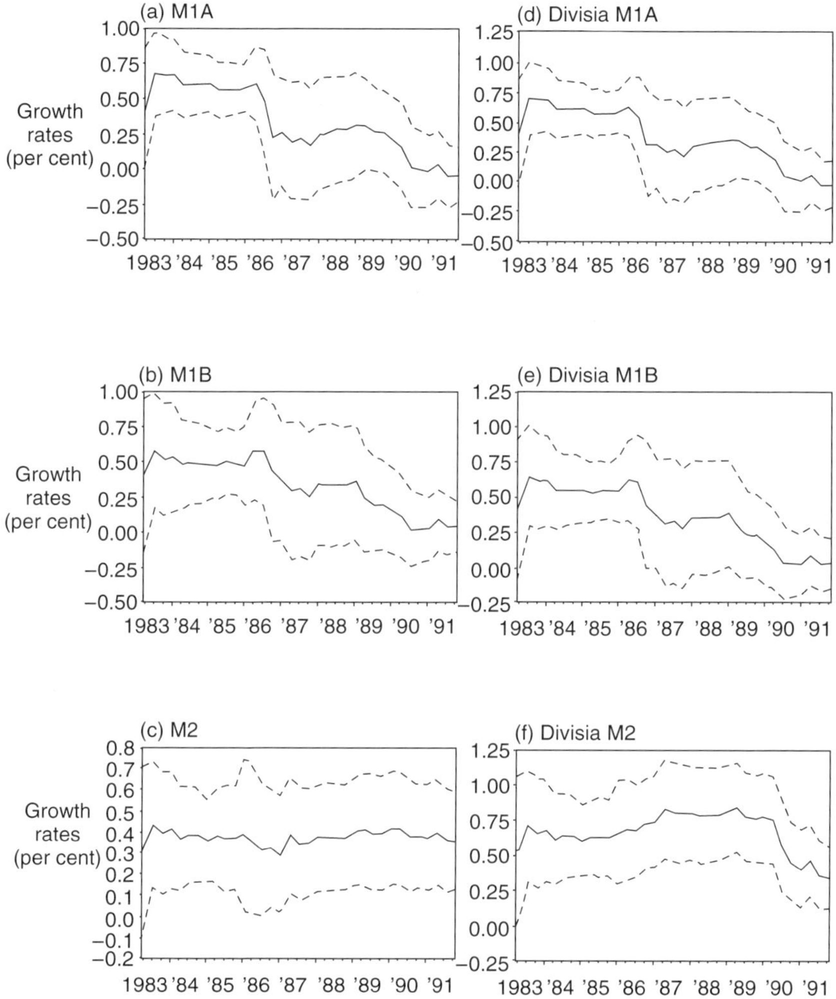

Figure 10.4 Recursive estimated coefficients of real GNP

Controlability of monetary aggregates

As noted earlier, the practical use of a monetary aggregate as an intermediate target variable also depends on its controllability. A monetary aggregate that shares a strong relationship with economic activity might be of little use as a monetary target variable if its movements cannot be controlled well by the central bank.

Table 10.7 $\overline{R}^2$ and J-tests for linkages between inflation and money growth

$\overline{R}^2$	*Simple-sum aggregates*			*Divisia aggregates*		
	M1A	M1B	M2	M1A	M1B	M2
	0.74	0.73	0.67	0.75	0.76	0.42

J-tests	Null Hypothesis H0					
	Simple-sum aggregates			*Divisia aggregates*		
	M1A	M1B	M2	M1A	M1B	M2
Alternative hypothesis H1						
Simple-sum aggregates						
M1A	–	6.4684*	33.0487*	0.9014	2.2355	30.2281*
M1B	5.5553*	–	36.6874*	5.4001*	0.0007	32.9445*
M2	42.3018*	39.5352*	–	41.6634*	41.3226*	50.9968*
Divisia aggregates						
M1A	3.2697	7.7641*	34.3943*	–	3.3181	31.0644*
M1B	4.6296*	2.9938	36.6739*	3.7906	–	34.7872*
M2	0.7442	0.3844	21.3375*	0.4361	1.6398	–

Notes: 1. The J-test, developed by Davidson and MacKinnon (1981), is used to test whether an alternative specification adds to the explanatory power of the specification under the null hypothesis H0:

H0: CPI = f(M′, MPI) + $e1$; H1: CPI = f(M″, MPI) + $e2$

2. * indicates that the alternative specification adds to the explanatory power of the specification under the null hypothesis H0 at the 5% significance level.

In practice, the central bank in Taiwan controls the growth of money through the implementation of policy instruments. It can control reserve money directly by engaging in open market operations, issuing NCDs, Treasury bills and savings bonds, accepting re-deposits from banks and the postal savings system, or by extending accommodation to banks. It can also adjust the required reserve ratios against bank deposits to influence money multipliers, and adjust the discount rate in order to induce a change in banks' operations. Hence the controllability of monetary aggregates can be tested by examining their relationships with reserve money, required reserve ratios and discount rate. The controllability equations are specified as follows:

$$\ln(M_t) = a_0 + a_1^* \ln(RM_t) + a_2^* \, rr_t + a_3^* \ln(rdis_t) + e_t$$

where M_t represents monetary aggregates; RM_t represents reserve money; rr_t represents required reserve ratios;[6] and $rdist_t$ represents the discount rate.

The empirical results, listed in Table 10.8, suggest that the central bank in Taiwan can significantly influence the movements in almost all of the six monetary aggregates by means of various operational instruments. The only exception is that Divisia M1A and simple-sum M1A appear to lack a close link with the discount rate.[7]

10.4 Conclusions

The relationship between M1B, the previous intermediate target variable of monetary policy in Taiwan, and nominal GNP has become increasingly uncertain since the late 1980s. This phenomenon has led the central bank to adopt the broader aggregate M2 as the new target variable. This chapter develops Divisia M1A, Divisia M1B and Divisia M2 by using Taiwanese data, and compares their potential usefulness as an intermediate target variable with simple-sum M1A, M1B and M2. The empirical results indicate that no significant differences exist in terms of the controllability of these six monetary aggregates. However, simple-sum M2 has a relatively strong relationship with nominal GNP in terms of the stability of velocities and the stability of money demand equations as compared with the other five aggregates and Divisia M1B is most closely related to inflation. These results favour the use of simple-sum M2 to serve as the intermediate target variable, with Divisia M1B serving as an information indicator to help predict the movements in inflation.

It seems puzzling that, in the case of Taiwan, we found no strong basis for preferring Divisia M2 to simple-sum M2. However, as noted previously, wild stock market speculation has been the major cause of deposit shifts and instability of money demand for narrow aggregates. Divisia M2, which weights the components under the definitions of narrow monetary aggregates more heavily than other components, is also unable to avoid the effect of deposit shifts. Nevertheless, this linkage between stock transactions and

Table 10.8 Controllability of monetary aggregates

Dependent		*Independent variables*				$\bar{R}^2$	*RMSE*
		Constant	*1n (RM)*	*rr*	*1n (rdis)*		
Simple-aggregates	1n (M1A)	1.6833*	0.9115*	–0.0073	–0.0629	0.98	0.0746
		(3.6383)	(20.1839)	(–0.7400)	(–0.9955)		
	1n (M1B)	0.9039*	1.0568*	–0.0285*	–0.1320*	0.99	0.0708
		(2.0581)	(24.6593)	(–2.8950)	(–2.1994)		
	1n (M2)	1.1829*	1.1316*	–0.0361*	–0.1252*	0.99	0.490
		(3.8924)	(38.1616)	(–5.2949)	(–3.0152)		
Divisia aggregates	1n (M1A)	2.2102*	0.8703*	–0.0080	–0.0635	0.98	0.0687
		(45.1915)	(20.9516)	(–0.8306)	(–1.0910)		
	1n (M1B)	1.8890*	0.9570*	–0.0218*	–0.1069	0.98	0.0664
		(24.5842)	(23.8017)	(–2.3522)	(–1.8993)		
	1n (M2)	2.9902*	0.9687*	–0.0235*	–0.2012*	0.99	0.0296
		(16.2728)	(54.0304)	(–5.7020)	(–8.0129)		

Notes: 1. *t*-statistics are in parentheses.
2. * indicates that the coefficient is statistically significantly different from zero.

deposit shifts is conditional upon the size and structure of the stock market and the level of efficiency in cash management.[8] As total issues of listed stocks in the Taiwan stock market continue to increase, and more institutional investors participate in the market, the turnover rate of listed stocks is expected to decline from the unreasonable highs of the past,[9] with the result that the local stock market will become less speculative than in the 1980s. Moreover, as cash management becomes more efficient, financial transactions will require less money to be held. These developments will gradually lessen the impact of stock market speculation on money-demand behaviour. Hence, we suggest that after these developments reach a certain stage, a re-evaluation of the usefulness of Divisia aggregates as a monetary target variable may be worthwhile.

Notes

1. For example, the exchange rate of the New Taiwan (NT) dollar against the US dollar appreciated sharply from 40.32:1 in the third quarter of 1985 to 27.65:1 in the first quarter of 1989, reflecting the huge trade surpluses and surge in capital inflows. The annual growth rates of the Taiwan stock price index exceeded 100 per cent in both 1988 and 1989, because of the excess liquidity.
2. The rapid growth in stock transactions and the increasing volatility in interest rates and foreign exchange rates have resulted in large and frequent deposit shifts between transaction deposits and time-deposits or foreign currency deposits.
3. Starting in November 1993, passbook savings deposits have also been allowed to be used to settle stock transactions.
4. Each of the time-series of the balances of the component assets is seasonly adjusted prior to aggregation.
5. Since foreign currency deposits have the highest rates of return among all component assets at all points in time, these deposits are virtually excluded from the Divisia aggregates.
6. Since the series of required reserve ratios against cheque deposits, passbook deposits, passbook savings deposits, time deposits and time savings deposits are highly correlated, the required reserve ratio against cheque deposits is used as a representative series.
7. However, the discount rate is not an important instrument in terms of controlling the growth of money, and its effect on the growth of money is indirect and relatively small.
8. Wenninger and Radecki (1986) supports this hypothesis based on the US experience.
9. The turnover rates of the listed stocks in the Taiwan market were 162.12, 267.47, 294.98, 523.52, 458.71 and 285.29 per cent in 1986, 1987, 1988, 1989, 1990 and 1991, respectively.

References

Barnett, William A. (1982) 'The Optimal Level of Monetary Aggregation', *Journal of Money, Credit and Banking*, vol. 14, no. 4 (November), part 2, pp. 687–710.

Barnett, William A. (1982) 'Recent Monetary Policy and the Divisia Monetary Aggregates', *The American Statistician*, vol. 38, no. 3, pp. 165–72.

Barnett, William, Edward Offenbacher and Paul Spindt (1981) 'New Concepts of Aggregated Money', *The Journal of Finance*, vol. 36, no. 2, pp. 497–505.
Barnett, William, Edward Offenbacher and Paul Spindt (1984). 'New Divisia Monetary Aggregates', *Journal of Political Economy*, vol. 92, no. 6, pp. 1047–85.
Belongia, Michael T. and James A. Chalfant (1989) 'The Changing Empirical Definition of Money: Some Estimates from a Model of the Demand for Money Substitutes', *Journal of Political Economy*, vol. 97, no. 2, pp. 387–97.
Belongia, Michael T. and K. Alec Chrystal (1991) 'An Admissible Monetary Aggregate for the United Kingdom', *Review of Economics and Statistics*, pp. 497–503.
Chetty, V. K. (1969) 'On Measuring the Nearness of Near-Moneys', *American Economic Review*, vol. 59, pp. 226–9.
Chou, Nan-Ting (1991) 'An Alternative Monetary Policy Target: The New Benchmark Divisia Monetary Index', *Applied Economics*, pp. 1699–75.
Davidson, Russell and James G. MacKinnon (1981) 'Several Tests for Model Specification in the Presence of Alternative Hypotheses', *Econometrica*, vol. 49, no. 3, pp. 781–93.
Farr, Helen T. and Deborah Johnson (1985) 'Revisions in the Monetary Services (Divisia) Indexes of the Monetary Aggregates', Staff Studies, Federal Reserve Board.
Gauger, Jean and Harold A. Black (1991) 'Asset Substitution and Monetary Volatility', *Journal of Money, Credit and Banking*, vol. 23, no. 4, pp. 677–91.
Ishida, Kazuhiko (1984). 'Divisia Monetary Aggregates and Demand for Money: A Japanese Case', *Bank of Japan Monetary and Economic Studies*, vol. 2, no. 1, (June), pp. 44–86.
Laumas, G. S. (1968) 'The Degree of Moneyness of Savings Deposits', *American Economic Review*, pp. 501–3.
Lee, T. H. (1966) 'Substitutability of Non-Bank Intermediary Liabilities for Money: The Empirical Evidence', *Journal of Finance*, vol. 21, pp. 441–57.
Serletis, Apostolos and A. Leslie Robb (1986) 'Divisia Aggregation and Substitutability among Monetary Assets', *Journal of Money, Credit and Banking*, vol. 18, no. 4, pp. 430–46.
Serletis, Apostolos (1987) 'Monetary Asset Separability Tests', in William A. Barnett and Kenneth J. Singleton (eds), *New Approaches to Monetary Economics Proceedings of the Second International Symposium on Economic Theory and Econometrics*, vol. 1, pp. 169–82 (Cambridge: Cambridge University Press).
Swofford, James L. and Gerald A. Whitney (1987) 'Nonparametric Tests of Utility Maximization and Weak Separability for Consumption, Leisure and Money', *The Review of Economics and Statistics*, pp. 458–64.
Timberlake, R. H. Jr and J. Fortson (1967) 'Time Deposits in the Definition of Money', *American Economic Review*, pp. 190–3.
Varian, Hal R. (1983) 'Non-parametric Tests of Consumer Behaviour', *Review of Economic Studies*, pp. 99–110.
Wenninger, John and Lawrence J. Radecki (1986) 'Financial Transactions and the Demand for M1', *Federal Reserve Bank of New York Economic Review*, no. 2, pp. 24–9.
Whitney, Gerald A. and James L. Swofford (1986) 'Flexible Functional Forms and the Utility Approach to the Demand for Money: A Non-parametric Analysis', *Journal of Money, Credit and Banking*, vol. 18, no. 3, pp. 383–9.
Yue, Piyu and Robert Fluri (1991) 'Divisia Monetary Services Indexes for Switzerland: Are They Useful for Monetary Targeting?', *Federal Reserve Bank of St Louis Review*, September/October, pp. 19–33.

11
Weighted Monetary Aggregates: Empirical Evidence for Australia*

G. C. Lim and Vance L. Martin

11.1 Introduction

December 1983 represents a watershed in the development of the Australian financial system. This point in time coincides with the floating of the Australian dollar on world financial markets, and marks the culmination of a period of rapid financial deregulation and innovation. Some of the major changes included the removal of interest-rate ceilings and quantitative controls, and the granting of licences to foreign banks.

These changes have had profound implications for the financial system: the Australian financial system is more integrated with the rest of the world, banks are progressively extending their services into traditionally non-bank activities, new banking products have been introduced, and interest rates on bank deposits are more sensitive to market forces. The characteristics of monetary assets – and bank deposits in particular – have thus been altered, and associated with this is the nature of substitution between assets; see, for example, Lim (1993). In fact, the changes to the Australian financial system have been so pronounced that the Reserve Bank of Australia abandoned its policy of monetary targeting in January 1985, because the traditional relationships between monetary aggregates such as M3 and economic activity supposedly no longer held. A check-list approach was adopted but was soon replaced with policy directed at monitoring and influencing the cash rate; see for example, Milbourne (1990, p. 235).

The main aim of this chapter is to investigate whether the basic relationship between money and income has withstood the onslaught of financial innovations over the 1980s and into the early 1990s in Australia, and whether the relationship is better modelled using weighted monetary aggregates than unweighted aggregates. In answering this broad question, it is necessary to tackle a number of ancillary questions. The first concerns whether the

* We would like to thank Michael Belongia for many helpful comments and suggestions on an earlier version of this chapter.

traditional long-run demand for money, as based on the official unweighted monetary aggregates, has broken down over the period. If it has, this may be the result of the inability of the unweighted aggregates to capture changes in the substitution between assets, and this problem may be resolved by the use of a weighted monetary aggregate. Recent techniques in time-series based on stochastic trends and cointegration are used to answer this question. The second line of inquiry is to explore empirically the possibility that new linkages between money and income have developed during the period, and whether these linkages are encapsulated by weighted monetary aggregates, or by the traditional unweighted aggregates. The identification of more complex transmission mechanisms in both the short run and the long run are investigated, using recent techniques of non-linear time-series analysis and dual-factor structure models.

The key result of this chapter is that there has been an underlying long-run demand for money, based on the official broad unweighted monetary aggregate, since the late 1980s, in Australia. But, while this provides a necessary condition for designing an effective monetary policy, both significant non-linearities and complicated short-run relationships between money and income are identified that would tend to hamper monetary policy as a short-run stabilisation mechanism. Further these complications are not resolved by the use of weighted monetary aggregates. In fact, the result show that, from a policy point of view, there is little to be gained from the adoption of weighted monetary aggregates.

The rest of the chapter proceeds as follows. A discussion of the properties of the key series used in the empirical investigation are given in Section 11.2. Alternative monetary data are used in Section 11.3 to identify whether a long-run demand for money in Australia existed during the 1980s and early 1990s. The identification of long-run non-linear structures is the subject of Section 11.4, while attention is switched in Section 11.5 to investigating the interrelationships between money and income over the business cycle. Section 11.6 provides the main conclusions and some implications for conducting monetary policy in Australia.

11.2 Data

The data are monthly and, where appropriate, seasonally adjusted. All data are derived from the database dX. In the case of the national accounts data, these series are converted from quarterly to monthly using a simple linear interpolation. The sample period chosen starts in July 1984, after the floating of the Australian dollar, and ends in December 1993, a total of 114 observations.

The Australian statistics

The data set used in the empirical analysis consists of the sub-monetary assets used to construct broad money in Australia. This set consists of currency (A_0),

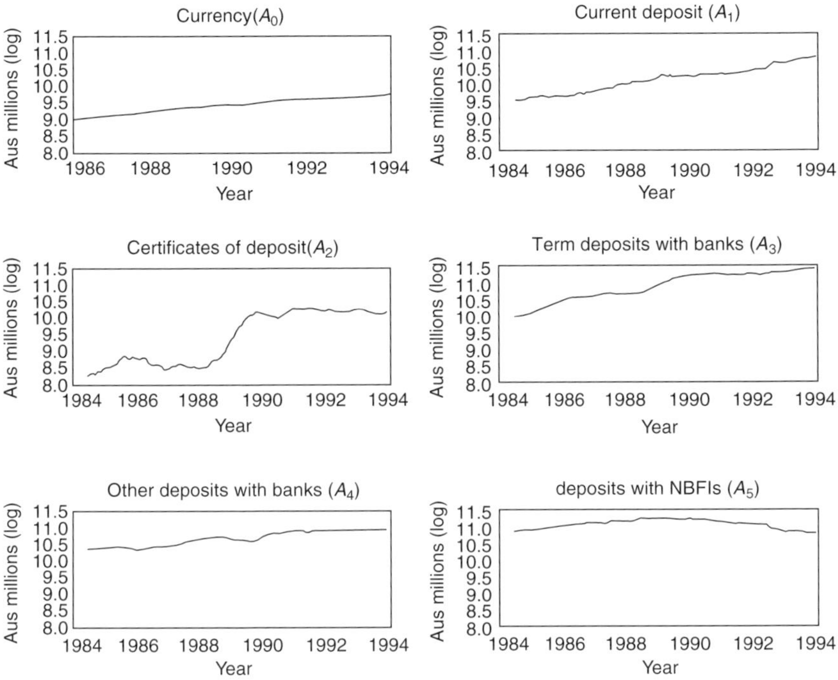

Figure 11.1 Subordinate monetary aggregates

current deposits with banks which includes both non-interest-bearing and interest-bearing deposits (A_1), certificates of deposit (A_2) (hereafter CODs), term-deposits with banks (A_3), other deposits with banks (A_4), and borrowings from the private sector by non-bank financial institutions, less currency and bank deposits by non-bank financial institutions (A_5) (hereafter NBFIs). Time-series plots of these six sub-aggregates, in logs, are given in Figure 11.1.

Three of the official unweighted monetary aggregates are presented in Figure 11.2. These range from the 'narrow' aggregate M_0, which is the money base, to the 'broader' aggregates $M_3 = A_0 + A_1 + A_2 + A_3 + A_4$, and $M_6 = M_3 + A_5$. These aggregates are standardised so that the initial observation is equal to unity for commensurability with the weighted aggregate computed below, and are expressed in logs.

The own rates of return on the six assets are denoted by R_0 to R_5. In the case of current deposits, the own rate of return is chosen as the minimum return on transaction and investment accounts holding less than \$2000. This rate was chosen because it was not possible to obtain an accurate weighted return based on all types of current deposits. The own rate of return on currency is chosen

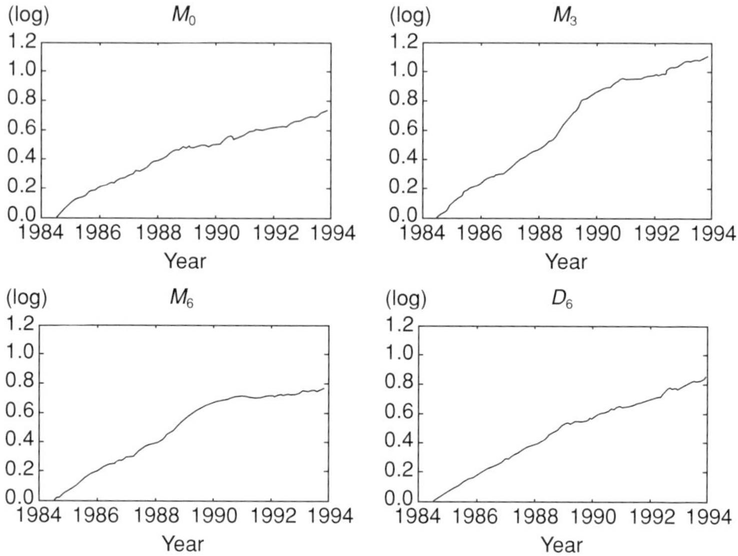

Figure 11.2 Monetary aggregates: unweighted and weighted

to be zero. In addition, the 90-day bank bill rate R_{90}, will serve as an opportunity cost variable for certain assets in the empirical analysis and will be used in the construction of the rental prices in computing the Divisia monetary aggregates.

The national accounts data used are the implicit price deflator (P) with base year 1989/90, and real GDP (Y/P). Time-series plots of velocity based on the three official unweighted monetary aggregates, M_0, M_3 and M_6, are given in Figure 11.3.

Weighted monetary aggregates

The weighted monetary aggregate investigated in this paper is based on the Divisia aggregate discussed by Barnett (1980); see also Barnett *et al.* (1992) for a recent review. The Divisia monetary aggregate analysed is constructed from all six sub-monetary assets used to construct broad money, M_6. The benchmark interest rate used in the construction of the Divisia aggregate is determined as Max (R_1, R_2, ..., R_5, R_{90}). The Divisia aggregate is identified as D_6, in keeping with the identifier used for M_6. The Divisia aggregate, in logs, is plotted over time in Figure 11.2.

Figure 11.3 shows that Divisia velocity has tended to exhibit relatively greater stability than the unweighted aggregates throughout the 1980s. Over the first part of the 1990s Divisia velocity tended to fall, as did velocity based

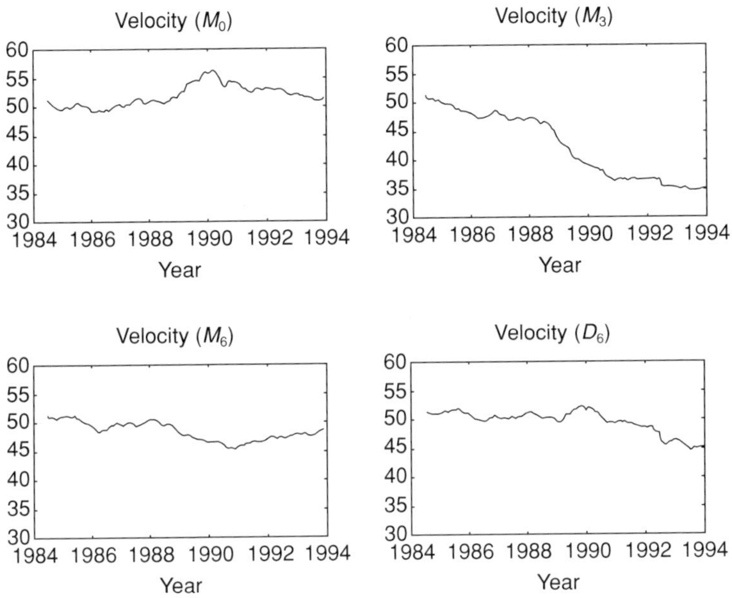

Figure 11.3 Velocity: unweighted and weighted

on M_0 and M_3, whereas the velocity of unweighted broad money, M_6, has tended to rise.

Statistical properties of the data

Some descriptive statistics of the data are given in Table 11.1. The average monthly growth rates of the monetary sub-assets are positive for A_0 to A_4, but negative for A_5. This is further highlighted in Figure 11.1, where NBFIs deposits, A_5, grew gradually during the 1980s and then fell consistently during the 1990s to a similar level to that of 1984. The most rapid average growth is for certificates of deposits, A_2.

The monetary sub-asset exhibiting the greatest volatility in its growth rate is CODs, A_2. Relative dispersion for its growth rate, as measured by the coefficient of variation, is $100(5.624/1.681) = 334.6$ per cent, which is larger than it is for the other assets. Also, the minimum and maximum values of -12.457 per cent and 18.622 per cent respectively, show that CODs have exhibited the largest monthly changes of all the assets. The large changes in CODs is highlighted in Figure 11.1, where there was a massive increase during the latter part of the 1980s, which settled down during the first part of the 1990s.

A comparison of the average growth rates of the monetary aggregates, unweighted and weighted, shows that the Divisia aggregate D_6, has a lower average growth rate than the unweighted aggregate M_3, but a higher average

Table 11.1 Descriptive statistics

Variable	*Mean*	*Std. dev.*	*Min.*	*Max.*
Δ log (A_0)	0.757	0.570	–0.774	2.535
Δ log (A_1)	1.152	2.142	–5.700	11.537
Δ log (A_2)	1.681	5.624	–12.457	18.622
Δ log (A_3)	1.254	1.646	–1.756	5.322
Δ log (A_4)	0.482	1.375	–4.495	7.823
Δ log (A_5)	–0.064	1.719	–12.190	4.334
Δ log (M_0)	0.641	0.726	–1.926	2.423
Δ log (M_3)	0.979	0.816	–0.909	3.692
Δ log (M_6)	0.691	0.631	–0.998	2.196
Δ log (D_6)	0.762	0.635	–1.048	3.628
S_0	0.297	0.078	0.190	0.621
S_1	0.248	0.085	0.098	0.411
S_2	0.007	0.009	0.000	0.036
S_3	0.137	0.523	0.017	0.236
S_4	0.151	0.070	0.000	0.292
S_5	0.160	0.071	0.030	0.326

growth rate than the money base, M_0, and the broadest unweighted monetary aggregate, M_6. The divergence in the growth rates between M_6 and D_6, is partly highlighted by the estimates of the average weights of the Divisia aggregate as given by S_j, $j = 0, 1, 2, ..., 5$, in Table 11.1. The results show that there is a relatively higher weight given to currency A_0 (an average of 0.297) and demand deposits A_1 (an average of 0.248) in the Divisia aggregate than the unweighted aggregate, where the weights are both $1/6 = 0.167$. It would seem that the relatively higher weight given to the two most liquid assets is more than compensated for by the smaller weight given in the Divisia aggregate to CODs A_2, which had the highest growth rate over the period.

11.3 The long-run demand for money

The significant movements during the 1980s and early 1990s in the Australian monetary assets identified in the previous section suggest some monetary instability in Australia. Whether this instability has been significant enough to destroy the basic determinants of the long-run Australian demand for money is investigated now using the multivariate cointegration procedures of Johansen (1991).

The basic money demand equation postulated is:

$$\log\frac{M_t}{p_t} - \phi_0 - \phi_1\log\frac{Y_t}{p_t} - \phi_2 R_t = u_t \tag{11.1}$$

where M_t/P_t is real money; Y_t/P_t is real income; R_t is the pertinent price variable; and u_t is an error term whose properties are discussed below. When M_t is chosen as the unweighted monetary aggregate, $M_{6,t,}$ the price variable is chosen as the highest own rate of return each period as this is the Leontief price dual that comes from the assumption of perfect substitutability implied by simple-sum aggregation. In the case where M_t is chosen as the Divisia aggregate, $D_{6,t,}$ the Divisia price dual is used.

The results of the Johansen maximal eigenvalue and trace tests for the number of cointegrating vectors are given in Table 11.2. The length of the lag distribution of the VAR is six months. The results show unambiguously that there is one cointegrating vector in the case of the unweighted monetary aggregates: $M_{6,t}$. For the Divisia aggregate $D_{6,t,}$ the maximal eigenvalue statistic suggests one cointegrating vector, whereas the trace statistic suggests none.

The derived long-run coefficients in Equation (11.1) for the long-run money-demand equation for alternative monetary aggregates are also given in Table 11.2. The most notable feature of these parameter estimates is that the long-run income elasticity is much higher for the unweighted aggregate than it is for the weighted aggregate.

While the results provide strong support for a long-run stable relationship between the variables in Equation (11.1), the diagnostics reported in Table 11.2 reveal evidence of significant misspecification. There is significant first-order serial correlation as given by AR, first order ARCH, and significant heteroskedasticity as given by the Breusch-Pagan test, BP. There is also evidence of nonnormality as given by the Bera-Jarque test BJ, in the residuals of the estimated cointegrating equation based on $M_{6,t}$, but not based on $D_{6,t}$, at the 5 per cent level. More importantly, both the RESET test, and the BDS test of independence by Brock *et al.* (1986), point towards significant non-linearities in the demand for money, based on either the unweighted or weighted aggregates, which have been excluded from the cointegrating relationship as encapsulated by Equation (11.1). Further, the neural network test of neglected non-linearity of Lee *et al.* (1993), as given by NEURAL, also suggests significant non-linearities at the 5 per cent level in the estimated residuals of the cointegrating equation based on $D_{6,t,}$ but not in the residuals based on the unweighted aggregate $M_{6,t}$.

11.4 Non-linear structures

An important assumption underlying the long-run model in Equation (11.1) is that it is linear. Although cointegration was found for the money-demand equations based on both the unweighted and weighted monetary aggregates, the diagnostics reported in Table 11.2 point towards significant non-linearities in both money-demand relationships. To help unmask these non-linearities, the methods of Lye and Martin (1994), and Creedy *et al.* (1994), are used.

Table 11.2 Cointegrating variables: log (M/P); log (Y/P); R

Johansen maximal eigenvalue test			
H_0, H_1	*log* (M_6/P)	*log* (D_6/P)	*95% C.V.*
$r = 0, r = 1$	30.039	23.081	22.002
$r \leq 1, r = 2$	12.734	9.188	15.672
$r \leq 2, r = 3$	5.278	2.152	9.243
Johansen trace test			
H_0, H_1	*log* (M_6/P)	*log* (D_6/P)	*95% C.V.*
$r = 0, r \geq 1$	48.051	34.421	34.910
$r \leq 1, r \geq 2$	18.012	11.340	19.964
$r \leq 2, r \geq 3$	5.278	2.152	9.243
Estimated cointegrated vectors			
log (Y/P)	1.518	0.852	
$R = R_{\text{MAX}}$	0.671		
R = Price dual		0.061	
Constant	-6.701	-9.555	
Diagnostic tests: p-values			
AR	0.000	0.000	
ARCH	0.000	0.000	
BP	0.000	0.000	
BJ	0.006	0.182	
RESET	0.000	0.000	
NEURAL	0.372	0.003	
BDS	0.000	0.000	

Notes: AR = LM test for first-order autocorrelation; ARCH = LM test for first order autoregressive conditional heteroskedasticity; BP = Breusch–Pagan LM test for heteroskedasticity; BJ = Bera–Jarque LM test for normality; RESET = Ramsey's test for functional form; NEURAL = Lee, White and Granger (1993) test for neglected non-linearity using one activation function; BDS = Brock, Dechert and Scheinkman (1986) test for independence assuming an embedding dimension of $m = 10$ and $\varepsilon = 1.25\ \sigma$

The approach is based on replacing the normality assumption of the error term, u_t, in Equation (11.1) by a distribution that is a generalisation of the normal distribution. One form of the generalised normal distribution that is convenient here is:

$$f(u_t) - \exp[\Theta_{1,t}u_t + \Theta_{2,t}u_t^2/2 + \Theta_{4,t}u_t^4/4 - \eta_t] \tag{11.2}$$

where $\Theta_{i,t}$, $i = 1, 2, 4$ are functions that control the shape of the distribution; and $\eta_t = \log \int \exp\ [\Theta_{1,t}\ u_t + \Theta_{2,t}\ u_t^2/2 + \Theta_{4,t}\ u_t^4/4]\ du_t$, is the normalising constant. This distribution contains the standard normal distribution as a special case when $\Theta_1 = \Theta_4 = 0$ and $\Theta_2 = -1.0$.

An important feature of the generalised normal distribution is that it can exhibit a range of distributional shapes including skewness, kurtosis and even bimodality. It is this last feature that is relevant here, as the occurrence of bimodality can constitute evidence of multiple equilibria; see Creedy and Martin (1994). In particular, the occurrence of bimodality can serve as a natural measure of instability as it represents the occurrence of two stable equilibria, and that there is a non-zero probability that the process can switch from one stable equilibrium to another. An alternative interpretation of bimodality is that it can represent evidence of misspecification arising from, for example, structural change.

In specifying the density, the functions $\Theta_{1,t}$ and $\Theta_{2,t}$ are assumed to be given by:

$$\Theta_{1,t} = \theta_{1,0} + \theta_{1,1}\log\frac{Y_t}{p_t} + \theta_{1,2}R_t \tag{11.3}$$

$$\Theta_{2,t} = \theta_{2,0} + \theta_{2,1}\log\frac{Y_t}{p_t} + \theta_{2,2}R_t \tag{11.4}$$

where R_t is the same price variable used to specify the long-run demand for money. The implications of this approach are twofold. First, it makes the density in Equation (11.2) time-varying; and second, it results in the relationship between the money supply and the determinants of the demand for money being non-linear; see Creedy, *et al.* (1994).

The non-linear model given by Equations (11.2) to (11.4) is estimated by maximum likelihood methods for both the unweighted and weighted monetary aggregates; for a discussion of estimation issues, see Cobb *et al.* (1983), and Lye and Martin (1993). A test for bimodality based on the statistic derived in Lim, Martin and Teo (1998), is given in Figure 11.4. This statistic is distributed asymptotically as $N(0, 1)$. Large negative values (that is, values less than –2) constitute evidence of bimodality.

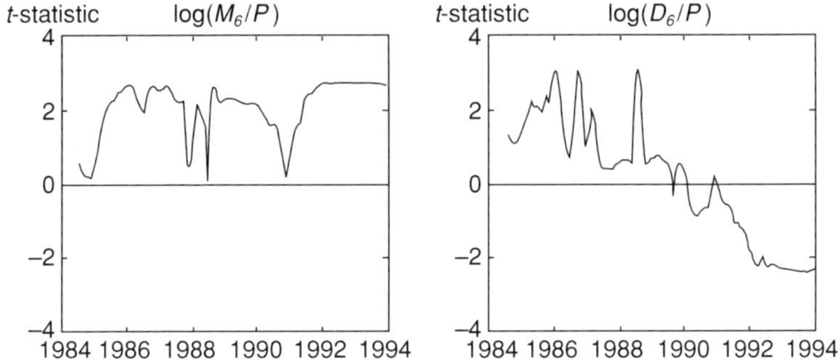

Figure 11.4 A test for bimodality

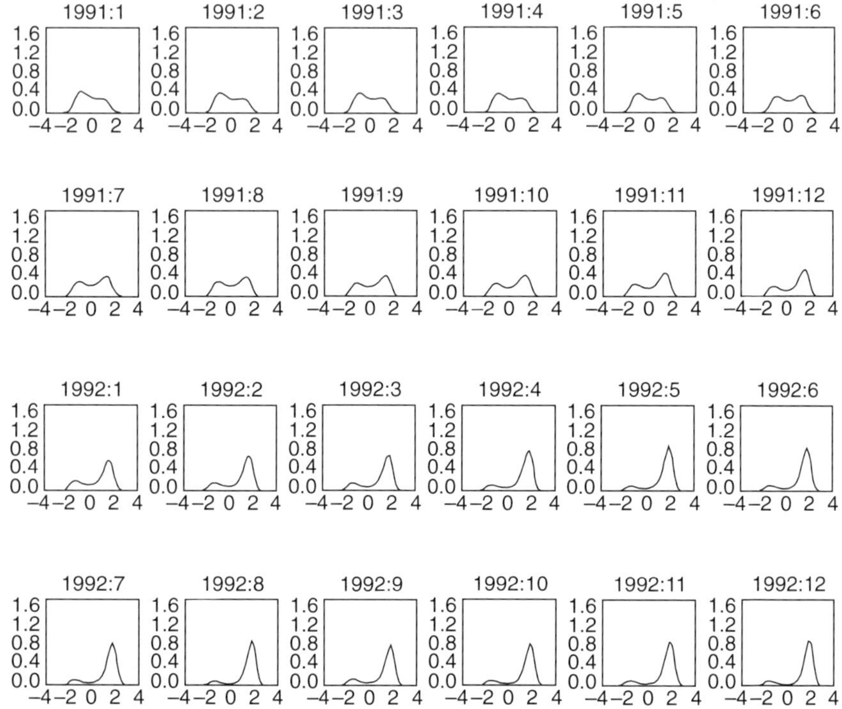

Figure 11.5 Density snapshots of log (D_6/P): 1984:7–1993:12

The most striking aspect of the results shown in Figure 11.4 is that there is no evidence of bimodality for the model based on the unweighted monetary aggregate. This contrasts with the results based on the weighted aggregate where there is evidence of a significant period of bimodality at the end of the sample period beginning in 1991. To highlight the bimodality properties of the long-run money demand model in the case of D_6/P, distributional snapshots are given in Figure 11.5 for the period 1991:1 to 1992:12. Note that the distribution at each point in time is conditional on the values of $\{\log(Y_t/P_t), R_t\}$. Hence, as these values change over time, so does the shape of the distribution. Compare this with the usual case, where only the mean changes or both the mean and the variance change. The occurrence of bimodality in the Divisia monetary aggregate distribution, but not in the distribution of the unweighted monetary aggregate, suggests that the unweighted aggregate is relatively more successful in capturing the structural changes occurring in the Australian financial markets over the period 1984 to 1993.

11.5 Business cycle behaviour

The analysis so far has tended to concentrate on identifying long-run relationships between assets and the determinants of asset demands. That is, the analysis has concentrated on zero frequency. There may also exist significant relationships between assets and the determinants of asset demands at other frequencies such as business-cycle frequencies. With deregulation of the financial system these interrelationships may have become more pronounced during the 1980s and early 1990s, leading to substitution between assets and resulting in greater coherence with the business cycle. The identification of relationships at these non-zero frequencies is particularly important if the goals of the monetary authorities are based on some short-term feedback mechanism rather than being focused on controlling an intermediate target in the long run.

A natural way to proceed to identify relationships over the business cycle is to use spectral analysis. Given the multivariate nature of the problem, the algorithms devised by Bowden and Martin (1993, 1995) (BM hereafter) are appropriate here. The BM approach is based on the principal component approach for condensing information. Letting $\Omega(w)$ be the $(n+1) \times (n+1)$ correlation matrix of the $(n+1)$ monetary assets at frequency w, this matrix is decomposed using an eigen decomposition as follows:

$$\Omega(w) = P(w)\Lambda(w)P(w)' \tag{11.5}$$

where $\Lambda(w)$ is an $(n+1) \times (n+1)$ diagonal matrix containing the eigenvalues ordered from largest to smallest at frequency w, and $P(w)$ is an $(n+1) \times (n+1)$ matrix containing the associated eigenvectors.

To determine the interrelationships between assets and income over the business cycle using the BM analysis, all variables are initially rendered stationary by expressing each series as differences of logs, and are normalised to have zero mean and unit variance. The number of ordinates chosen to estimate spectra and cross-spectra is 300, which are smoothed with a window width equal to eleven.

The results of the BM procedure for the business cycle (forty-three months) are presented in Table 11.3 for the case where the variables are all expressed in real terms, and Table 11.4 for the case where all of the variables are expressed in nominal terms. Similar results were obtained for other neighbouring business-cycle frequencies, but are not reported here to save space. The cumulative sum of the normalised eigenvalues ($\sum \lambda_i$) are given at the bottom of the table: λ_1 represents the proportion of the total variation in the assets that is explained by the first principal component; $\lambda_1 + \lambda_2$ represents the proportion explained by the first and the second principal components, and so on. The results shown in Tables 11.3 and 11.4 indicate that for both the real and nominal models, about 60 per cent of the total variation is explained by the first principal component. There is also some information contained in the

Table 11.3 BM decomposition of the series: A_0 P, A_1/P, ..., A_5/P, Y/P

(squared) coherence, 43-month cycle			
Series	*Factor 1*	*Factor 2*	*Factor 3*
A_0/P	0.566	0.060	0.210
A_1/P	0.404	0.299	0.050
A_2/P	0.665	0.052	0.216
A_3/P	0.891	0.011	0.025
A_4/P	0.700	0.261	0.028
A_5/P	0.127	0.165	0.511
Y/P	0.325	0.614	0.018
$\sum \lambda_i$	0.604	0.813	0.922

Table 11.4 BM decomposition of [A_0, A_1, ..., A_5, Y]

(squared) coherence, 43-month cycle			
Series	*Factor 1*	*Factor 2*	*Factor 3*
A_0	0.301	0.398	0.193
A_1	0.430	0.019	0.424
A_2	0.770	0.093	0.060
A_3	0.827	0.060	0.064
A_4	0320	0.617	0.047
A_5	0.344	0.325	0.256
Y	0.572	0.387	0.022
$\sum \lambda_i$	0.558	0.857	0.949

second (and even the third) principal components, with over 90 per cent of variation being explained by these three factors jointly. Thus there appear to be three latent factors operating among the six assets and income over the business cycle.

The squared coherences reported in Table 11.3 are simply squared correlations between series and factors. Inspection of this table shows that there is at best a weak relationship between the six real assets and real income over the business cycle. For example, the (squared) coherence associated with real income in the first factor is only 0.325, while real income dominates the second factor, with minimal contributions from any of the real assets. In contrast, the nominal results shown in Table 11.4 show a strong relationship between nominal income and the nominal assets, with the strongest linkage between nominal income and the nominal certificates of deposit (A_2) and term deposits (A_3).

These results help to explain to a certain extent the lack of significant causal linkages between money and income found in most empirical studies. For example, performing a simple bivariate Granger causality test (not reported in this chapter) between money and income using a VAR with six lags for the Australian data, generates no significant causal linkages. This is true if the variables are expressed in real or nominal terms. The key point is that neither the unweighted aggregate M_6, nor the weighted aggregate D_6, captures all the linkages between the subordinate assets and income, so therefore aggregation, unweighted or weighted, tends to represent a misspecification of these linkages.

11.6 Conclusions and implications for policy

This chapter has provided an empirical investigation for Australia of the relationships between alternative measures of money and income over the period 1984–93, a period following significant financial innovation. The main conclusion of the chapter is that there is an underlying long-run demand for money based on the broadest official unweighted monetary aggregate, as well as on the weighted monetary aggregate, using the weighting method suggested by Barnett (1980). However, significant non-linearities and complicated interrelationship were identified between money and income over the business cycle. These complexities were not resolved by the use of weighted monetary aggregates. These points, taken together, support the use of monetary policy for achieving long-run stability, but highlight the potential problems of pursuing short-run stabilisation policies based on controlling monetary aggregates. They also suggest that there is little to be gained from the adoption of a weighted monetary aggregate over the use of an unweighted aggregate.

A number of useful lines of future research, investigating the characteristics of the transmission mechanism between money and income, are suggested by the results of this chapter. Perhaps the most important is in uncovering the nature and form of the non-linearities between monetary assets and income. The empirical analysis detected evidence of multiple equilibria, which might have been the result of significant structural change. Another useful area for research suggested by the results on business cycles is in identifying more precisely the nature of the multi-factor interactions between income and assets.

References

Barnett, W. A. (1980) 'Economic Monetary Aggregates: An Application of Index Number and Aggregation Theory', *Journal of Econometrics*, vol. 14, pp. 11–48.

Barnett, W. A., D. Fisher and A. Serletis (1992) 'Consumer Theory and the Demand for Money', *Journal of Economic Literature* (December), pp. 2086–119.

Bowden, R. J. and Martin, V. L. (1993) 'Reference Cycles in the Time and Frequency Domains: Duality Aspects of the Business Cycle', in P. C. B. Phillips and V. B. Hall (eds), *Models, Methods and Applications in Econometrics: Essays in Honour of Rex Bergstrom* (London: Allen & Unwin), pp. 201–19.

Bowden, R. J. and Martin, V. L. (1995) 'International Business Cycles and Financial Integration', *Review of Economics and Statistics*, vol. 77, pp. 305–20.

Brock, W. A., W. D. Dechert and J. A. Scheinkman (1986) 'A Test for Independence Based on the Correlation Dimension', Discussion paper, University of Wisconsin-Madison, Department of Economics.

Cobb, L., P. Koppstein and N. H. Chen (1983) 'Estimation and Moment Recursion Relations for Multimodal Distributions of the Exponential Family', *Journal of the American Statistical Association*, vol. 78, pp. 124–30.

Creedy, J. C. and V. L. Martin (1994) 'A Model of the Distribution of Prices', *Oxford Bulletin of Economics and Statistics*, vol. 56, pp. 67–76.

Creedy, J. C., J. N. Lye and V. L. Martin (1994) 'Non-linearities and the Long-run Real Exchange Rate Distribution', in J. C. Creedy and V. L. Martin (eds), *Chaos and Non-Linear Models in Economics: Theory and Applications* (London: Edward Elgar) pp. 196–212.

Johansen, S. (1991) 'Estimation and Hypothesis Testing of Cointegration Vectors in Gaussian Vector Autoregressive Models', *Econometrica*, vol. 59, pp. 1551–80.

Lee T. H., H. White and C. W. J. Granger (1993) 'Testing for Neglected Nonlinearity in Time Series Models: A Comparison of Neural Network Methods and Alternative Tests', *Journal of Econometrics*, vol. 56, pp. 269–90.

Lim G. C. (1993) 'The Demand for the Components of Broad Money: Error-Correction and Generalized Asset Adjustment Systems', *Applied Economics*, vol. 25, pp. 995–1004.

Lim, G. C., V. L. Martin and L. E. Teo (1998) 'Endogenous Jumping and Asset Price Dynamics', *Macroeconomic Dynamics*, vol. 2, pp. 213–37.

Lye, J. N. and V. L. Martin (1993) 'Robust Estimation, Nonnormalities, and Generalized Exponential Distributions', *Journal of the American Statistical Association*, vol. 88, pp. 253–9.

Lye, J. N. and V. L. Martin (1994) 'Non-linear Time Series Modelling and Distributional Flexibility', *Journal of Time Series Analysis*, vol. 15, pp. 65–84.

Milbourne, R. (1990) 'Money and Finance', in S. Grenville (ed.), *The Australian Macroeconomy in the 1980s*, Proceedings of a Conference, Research Department, Reserve Bank of Australia, pp. 222–276.

Part IV

Evidence from North America

12
The Canadian Experience with Weighted Monetary Aggregates*

David Longworth and Joseph Atta-Mensah

12.1 Introduction

One of the alternative methods for constructing monetary aggregates that has received much attention in the literature is the method proposed by Barnett (1980), which uses statistical index number theory. His approach makes use of aggregation theory to compute indices of financial assets that reflect the total utility, relative to some base period, attributable to the monetary services obtained from these assets.

Unlike the simple summation monetary aggregates, these alternative 'superlative' weighted monetary aggregates are derived from optimisation behaviour of economic agents and thus have stronger theoretical underpinnings. However, it is unclear whether their empirical performance is superior to the summation aggregates. Poorer empirical performance could arise, for example, because of difficulties in translating the theory into empirical counterparts.

The purpose of this paper is to compare the empirical performance of Canadian weighted monetary aggregates (in particular, Fisher Ideal aggregates) and the current summation aggregates in terms of their information content and forecasting performance for prices, real output and nominal spending for the period 1971:Q1 to 1989:Q3. (The data on the Fisher Ideal aggregates end at this point.) The major aggregates to be considered are M1, M2, M3 and M2+. Additionally, we consider M3+ (which adds near-bank deposits to M3) and two liquidity aggregates, which we call LL and LL+.

Work for earlier periods by Cockerline and Murray (1981, based on data from 1968:Q2 to 1980:Q4) and Hostland *et al.* (1988, based on data from

* An earlier version of the chapter was presented at the Annual Meetings of the Canadian Economic Association, Calgary (June 1994). The authors wish to thank Robert Amano, Pierre Duguay, Charles Freedman, John Murray and Walter Engert for their useful comments and criticisms and Greg Tkacz and Gordon Lee for valuable research assistance. The views expressed in this paper are those of the authors. No responsibility for them should be attributed to the Bank of Canada.

1969:Q1 to 1986:Q4) had shown that weighted monetary aggregates rarely do better (and never do much better) than simple-sum aggregates in predicting major Canadian macroeconomic variables. This chapter examines whether the addition of data from the late 1980s changes these conclusions.

The Bank of Canada believes that it can best promote good overall economic performance by pursuing price stability. In this regard, in February 1991 the Bank and the Canadian government jointly set out a path for the reduction of inflation. The goal was to make inflation, as measured by the consumer price index (CPI), come down gradually to the midpoint of a 1 to 3 per cent band by the end of 1995. Furthermore, this target band was extended to the end of 1998 in a joint agreement with the government announced in December 1993. In the short run, the Bank concentrates on a core measure of inflation which is defined using the CPI excluding food, energy, and the effects of indirect taxes. Both before and after the adoption of the inflation-control targets, the Bank followed the growth of monetary aggregates very closely for the information they contain about the future inflation, nominal spending growth, and output growth. Although the Bank pays most attention to core inflation and overall CPI inflation, it is also concerned with the overall inflationary process. Thus it is interested in forecasts of inflation measured by the GDP deflator, as well as in what the forecasted growth of output would imply about the level of excess demand or excess supply in product markets. Given that the model used for producing the staff economic projection has no direct role for the monetary aggregates but has a direct role for the output gap in the inflationary process, it is important to have other forecasting models based on monetary aggregates that give information on both inflation and output growth. The types of indicator models discussed in this chapter play this role.

The chapter is organised as follows. Section 12.2 presents a brief literature review of the theory and empirical work on the weighted monetary aggregates, with emphasis on the Canadian evidence and the difficulties in translating theoretical concepts into empirical counterparts. Section 12.3 presents and discusses further empirical work on short-run indicator models. Section 12.4 discusses empirical results on the estimation of long-run demand-for-money equations. Section 12.5 presents causality tests between the aggregates and selected variables in a vector error-correction model (VECM). Section 12.6 summarises our conclusions.

12.2 Literature review

The monetary aggregates currently used at the Bank of Canada are constructed by the simple summation of their various component assets. However, the components of the aggregates do not have the same degree of substitutability for one another, and some are clearly less liquid than currency and demand deposits. Hence, the simple summation of the various components of the aggregates does not accord with economic theory. This is because simple summation assumes that the assets in the aggregates are perfect substitutes (infinite elasticities of substitution). The alternative methods for constructing monetary aggregates examined below address this problem by using economic theory to derive weights for components of the aggregates consistent with the monetary services they provide.

Theoretical construction of superlative monetary aggregates

Consistent with Barnett's (1980) proposal, 'superlative' monetary aggregates have been developed, based on index number theory.[1] This method defines money as a monetary quantity index. As noted by Barnett, under this approach aggregates are measured in terms of the flow of services that constitute the output of the economy's monetary transactions technology. The flow of monetary services is determined by weighting the quantity of each component asset with its unique rental cost. Second, superlative indices are exact for flexible functional forms. Thus they avoid the restrictive assumptions required to justify the linear form of the summation aggregate. Third, superlative aggregates internalise pure substitution effects of changes in user costs, such that the index will not change unless an income effect is present. Income effects are reflected in the form of utility or monetary service changes. However, changes in user costs alone can cause simple-sum aggregates to change even if the value of the underlying monetary services sub-utility function is unaffected (that is, the income effect is zero). Thus the potentially key empirical difference between the two will be changes in the simple-sum measure (akin to a shift variable in a regression) when no change in the economy's monetary service flow has occurred.

Two superlative indices used in the literature are the (Tornquist–Theil) Divisia and the (chain-linked) Fisher Ideal.[2] One advantage of the Fisher Ideal Index over the Divisia index is that, as an index measured in *levels*, it can handle the introduction of new assets and changes to the characteristics of the financial assets in the indices. The change in the Divisia index, however, is based on the changes in the logarithms of its components and, because the logarithm of zero is minus infinity, the formula for computing the Divisia index implies that the growth rate of the Divisia aggregate equals infinity when a new asset is introduced. Thus, in a period when a new monetary asset is introduced, one can use the Fisher Ideal index by setting the growth rate of the new asset to zero.

Translating theory into empirical counterparts

In recent years, financial innovations have fundamentally altered the characteristics of many monetary assets. These innovations have increased the liquidity of most of the deposit liabilities of deposit-taking institutions. Such developments are a major reason why proponents of Divisia and other superlative indices have called for new ways of defining and measuring the monetary aggregates.

Cockerline and Murray (1981) and Fisher *et al.* (1993) have argued that, despite their theoretical appeal, the superlative indices have a number of drawbacks. First, Cockerline and Murray find that rates posted on savings deposits and other monetary components can exaggerate the effective rate economic agents expect on their investments. They argue that minimum balance requirements for certain accounts, early encashment penalties on some fixed-term assets, and other service charges, all tend to reduce the measured own rates of return on monetary assets. These measurement problems are further complicated by the possibility that financial institutions cross-subsidise activities so that service fees or interest rates may vary as a customer does other business with the institution.

A second measurement problem is that calculating user costs will be complicated by aggregating across assets with different maturity dates. Cockerline and Murray explain that, if the yield curve is downward sloping (say, as a result of future inflation being expected to fall), then current short-term interest rates will be higher than long-term rates. Hence, the rental price of some of the monetary assets may be negative. However, since the rental price, $((R_{Bt}-R_{it})/(1 + R_{Bt}))$, is used in the superlative index as a measure of liquidity, it is meaningless when the rental price is negative. Cockerline and Murray address this problem by adjusting all the own-interest rates with maturity greater than one year to an effective 91-day holding period return.[3]

Third, the method of constructing the superlative indices assumes that economic agents hold the optimal values of assets in their portfolio and makes no allowance for portfolio adjustment costs. However, in practice, investors constantly readjust their portfolio holdings in response to changes in interest rates. Since the superlative method measures user cost of an asset by the difference between the rate on a benchmark asset and its own rate of interest, and the portfolio adjustment costs are not captured in the interest rates, the 'true' user cost is underestimated. Spencer (1994) suggests that a theoretical and consistent way of addressing the portfolio-adjustment-cost problem is to assume that economic agents optimise the current distribution of monetary assets, not with respect to the actual returns observed, but with respect to permanent or trend returns on each asset. Spencer defines the trend return of an asset, which is smoother than the actual return, as a weighted average of current and past returns on the asset. In order to allow for portfolio disequilibrium, Spencer recalculates the Divisia weights using the smoothed user costs derived from trend returns. When using UK data, Spencer finds that his measure of Divisia M4 aggregate to perform better empirically than its simple-sum counterpart.

Fourth, the calculation of the user cost of any asset assumes that the benchmark asset is completely illiquid. This implies that an asset traded in secondary markets does not qualify as a benchmark, because a secondary market would enable that asset to be readily converted into more liquid assets that could be used for transactions. In practice, it is difficult to come by such an asset. Also, the benchmark asset must be chosen so that the user costs are non-negative.[4] Cockerline and Murray argue that a negative user cost would imply that economic agents would be prepared to sacrifice some of the returns on a purely non-monetary asset in order not to receive monetary services.

Fifth, Fisher *et al.* (1993) mention that one reason why superlative indices have not been widely accepted is their interpretation in the short run. The weights on the component assets (that is, the expenditure shares, S_i) are very sensitive to changes in interest rates. A rise in interest rates will increase the user cost of currency and therefore lead instantaneously to a higher weight. However, as the higher interest rates cause investors to hold less cash in their portfolios, the weight for currency will fall over time. Because of this lag, current weights are not optimal, unless investors adjust their portfolios instantaneously with changes in interest rates. Furthermore, in the short run, in a situation in which the amount of currency held by economic agents grows more rapidly than the amount of interest-bearing deposits, an increase in interest rates will instantaneously increase the weight for currency and reduce that on interest-bearing assets, thereby leading to an increase in the superlative index growth rate. As a result, Fisher *et al.* (1993) note that the superlative index could be a misleading indicator of the stance of monetary policy in the short-run.

Empirical evidence for Canadian monetary aggregates

Cockerline and Murray (1981) were the first to apply Canadian data to evaluate the empirical properties of Divisia monetary aggregates. The authors compare the performance of the Divisia and the summation aggregates in terms of their information content, money – income causality and stability in money-demand equations. Their study finds that while the Divisia aggregates follow smoother time-paths than the summation aggregates, their overall performance is unclear. For example, the Divisia aggregates contain less information on contemporaneous and future levels of income than do the summation aggregates. In causality tests, the study also finds the Divisia aggregates to be inferior to their summation counterparts. However, the demand functions for the Divisia aggregates are found to be more stable than those of the summation aggregates.

After the study by Cockerline and Murray, the Bank of Canada switched to maintaining a database for the Fisher Ideal Index rather than the Divisia index. The switch was carried out because Divisia indices cannot handle the introduction of new assets.

Hostland *et al.* (1988) use Canadian data to conduct studies on the information content of the Fisher Ideal monetary aggregates. Consistent with the earlier results of Cockerline and Murray, the authors find that the Fisher Ideal monetary aggregates generally contain less information than the summation aggregates. Hostland *et al.* (1988) compare the information content of alternative monetary aggregates, of which half are summation aggregates and the other half Fisher Ideal indices of monetary services, and finds M1 to be the most informative aggregate for both nominal and real GDP.[5] Fisher Ideal M1ALD (M1 plus non-personal notice deposits at banks) is found to be the most informative for prices. Consistent with the results of Cockerline and Murray, Hostland *et al.* (1988) find that broad aggregates (M2+, M3BC and M3+) have the highest contemporaneous correlation with nominal GDP, while narrow aggregates (M1 and Fisher Ideal M1ALD) have the most leading information about nominal GDP. Hostland *et al.* (1988) also find that the superlative monetary aggregates add little information to the summation aggregates. Hence there is no significant information loss in using summation aggregation.

Serletis and King (1993) examine the empirical relationships between monetary aggregates (summation or Divisia), income and prices in Canada.[6] The study finds none of the monetary aggregates to be cointegrated with the price level or nominal income. Based on the criterion of the smallest test tail area in Granger-causality tests, Serletis and King find the growth rate of simple-sum M2+ to be the best leading indicator of inflation; the growth rates of the Divisia aggregates and simple-sum M1 appear to be more useful than the growth rates of the other simple-sum aggregates for anticipating future movements in nominal income. Simple-sum M1 and Divisia M1 are the best leading indicators of real output.

Chrystal and MacDonald (1994) compare the summation monetary aggregates to the Divisia aggregates for different countries, including Canada. Their study involved the application of non-nested testing methods to the St Louis equation to determine the relative information content of alternative monetary aggregates. Their test compares this equation, on the one hand, with simple-sum money and, on the other with Divisia indexes or the currency equivalent index derived by Rotemberg *et al.* (1995). The study shows that summation M1 has the highest information content for nominal GDP, closely followed by Divisia M2.[7] Their results also show that, although summation M2, M3 and L do not have significant information content for nominal income, all their Divisia equivalents do. (Chrystal and MacDonald (1994) do not examine the 'plus' aggregates, which include deposits in non-bank financial institutions.)

In order to carry out causality tests, Chrystal and MacDonald use the Johansen and Juselius (1990) methodology to estimate the number of cointegrating vectors in a vector autoregressive model (VAR) comprising the various measures of money, real GDP, the GDP deflator and the Treasury bill rate. They also estimate a vector error-correction model (VECM) implied by the cointegration results. The VECM is then subjected to exclusion tests on the lags of each the differenced variables and on the lagged cointegrating terms. The exclusion tests are carried out using the linear Wald statistics, which have a central chi-squared distribution.

Among the simple-sum and 'Divisia' aggregates they examined, constructed from data from Canadian-chartered banks, Chrystal and MacDonald (1994) found that (at a 5 per cent level of significance) only simple-sum M1 caused real GDP, and only simple-sum M2 caused the GDP deflator.

12.3 New empirical evidence on short-run indicator models

In this part of our study we examine empirical evidence up to 1989:Q3 (the last date available for all the Fisher Ideal aggregates) on the following:[8]

(i) the aggregates with the best fit in indicator model equations for inflation (as measured by the CPI, CPI excluding food and energy, and the GDP deflator), the growth of nominal GDP, and the growth of real GDP (Section 3.2);
(ii) the aggregates with the lowest root-mean-squared errors for one-quarter-ahead out-of-sample forecasts for the five goal variables listed in (i) above (Section 3.3); and
(iii) the aggregates with the lowest root-mean-squared errors for multi-period-ahead forecasts for the five goal variables (Section 3.4).

Definitions of the monetary aggregates

This study examines seven simple-sum aggregates and their Fisher Ideal counterparts. The seven simple-sum aggregates include the three standard chartered-bank-based aggregates (M1, M2, and M3); two deposit-taking institutions aggregates (M2+ and M3+), which add to the bank aggregates the corresponding deposits from non-bank deposit-taking institutions; and two liquidity aggregate (LL and LL+) that add to M3 and M3+, respectively, bankers acceptances, commercial paper, Canada Savings Bonds, Treasury bills held by the non-financial public and 1–3-year Government of Canada bonds held by the non-financial public. For comparability with the Fisher Ideal indices, which were constructed in the spring of 1990, these data are taken from the February 1990 issue of the *Bank of Canada Review* for the major aggregates (with the other aggregates constructed by summation). (In particular, this means that M2+ does not include money market mutual funds and individual annuities at life insurance companies, items that were subsequently added to its definition.)

The comparable Fisher Ideal indices, denoted by the suffix FI, are M1FI, M2FI, M3FI, M2+FI, M3+FI, LLFI, and LL+FI. The benchmark rate, which by construction was forced to dominate all other own interest rates, is defined as:

R_{Bt} = Max (adjusted 10-year Industrial bond rate, 90-day finance company paper rate, adjusted 3-year Canada rate).[9]

Note that the Fisher Ideal aggregates are constructed, following one standard practice in the literature, by applying a different index number to official asset collections designated as aggregates by the central bank. Some research, however, has shown that these official groupings fail tests for weak separability such that even weighted versions of them will perform poorly.[10]

Table 12.1 Mean and standard deviation of the four-quarter growth rates of the monetary aggregates

Simple-sum aggregates	*Mean*	*Standard deviation*	*Fisher ideal aggregates*	*Mean*	*Standard deviation*
M1	7.49	4.54	M1FI	7.65	4.41
M2	11.07	3.78	M2FI	8.53	3.27
M2+	11.97	3.51	M2 + FI	9.27	3.19
M3	11.12	5.87	M3FI	9.08	3.76
M3+	11.97	5.17	M3 + FI	9.74	3.56
LL	12.39	3.64	LLFI	9.83	2.89
LL+	12.73	3.48	LL + FI	10.25	2.89

Table 12.2 Mean and standard deviation of the four-quarter growth rates of the goal variables

Goal variables	*CPI*	*CPIXFE*	*GDP Deflator*	*Nominal GDP*	*Real GDP*
Mean	4.29	4.17	4.23	8.08	3.85
Standard deviation	3.30	2.79	3.19	4.13	2.83

Data and summary statistics

The data for the monetary aggregates are quarterly, and are available from the first quarter of 1968 to the third quarter of 1989. Table 12.1 and 12.2 present the mean and standard deviation of the year-on-year growth rates of the aggregates and selected macroeconomic variables. As shown in the table, with the exception of simple-sum M1, the simple-sum aggregates, on average, grew faster than their Fisher Ideal counterparts.

Also the standard deviations show that the growth rates of the simple-sum aggregates fluctuated more than their Fisher Ideal aggregates.

Plots of the four-quarter growth rates of the monetary aggregates are depicted in Figure 12.1. With exception of the M1-aggregates, the figure shows the Fisher Ideal aggregates to grow more slowly than their simple-sum counterparts.

Deregulation in Canada was largely completed by 1967. However, as noted by Freedman (1983) and Fine (1990), major financial innovations – including the introduction of new deposit accounts – took place in the early 1980s. These developments led to a move away from M1 deposits.

Information content of five goal variables

In this section we use the Akaike information criterion (AIC) to choose the best bivariate indicator models, using the growth rates of various monetary

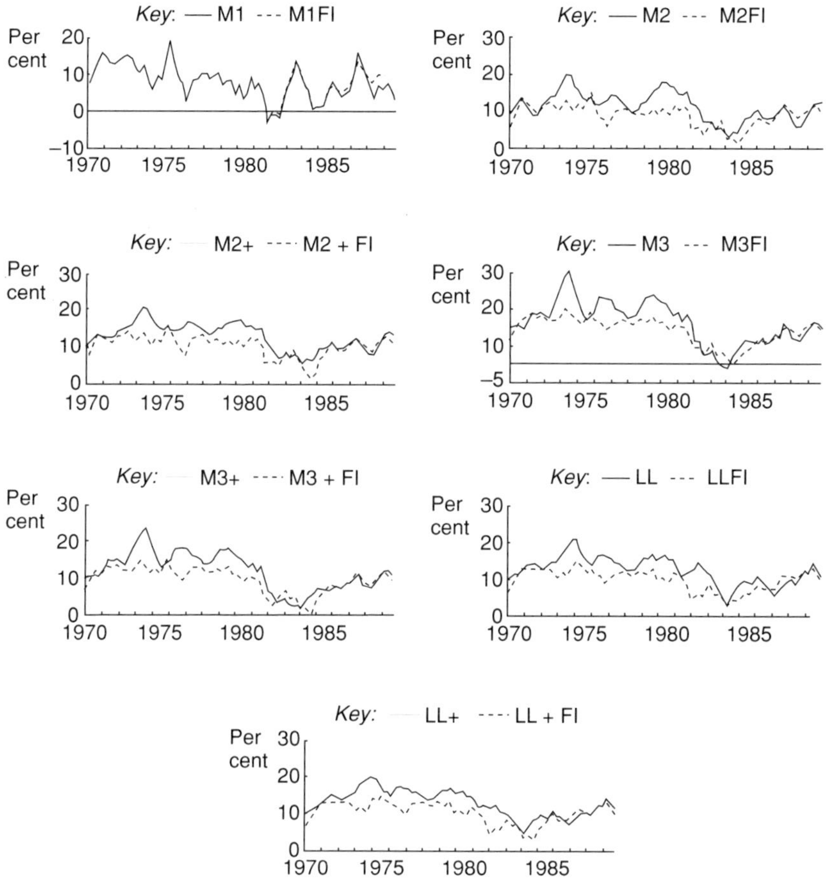

Figure 12.1 The four-quarter growth rates of the monetary aggregates

aggregates and lags on the dependent variable to explain the growth rates of five goal variables:[11] the CPI; the CPI excluding food and energy (CPIXFE); the GDP deflator; nominal GDP; and real GDP. The sample period is again 1971:Q1–1989:Q3. The general form of the indicator model is:

$$\Delta g_t = a + \sum_{i=1}^{k} \beta_i \Delta m_{t-1} + \sum_{j=1}^{h} \gamma_j \Delta g_{t-i} \tag{12.1}$$

Where g and m are the logarithms of the goal and money variables, respectively. The parameters k and h are the optimal lag-lengths, chosen over the range 0 to 12 and according to minimum AIC.

Table 12.3 The three best indicator models in estimation, based on the minimum Akaike Information Criterion (AIC)

Rank	*CPI*	*CPIXFE*	*GDP deflator*	*Nominal GDP*	*Real GDP*
1	M2+ (3.299)[a]	M2+ (2.842)	M3 + FI (5.141)	M1 (11.530)	RM1[b] (11.598)
2	M2 (3.657)	M2 (2.851)	M3FI (5.196)	M1FI (11.596)	RM1FI (12.602)
3	M3 (3.769)	M3 (2.924)	M2+ (5.218)	LL + FI (12.926)	RLL + FI (13.839)

Notes: [a] The AIC is recorded in parentheses.
[b] Note that an *R* prefix indicates that money is in real terms, using the CPI.

Based on the minimum AIC, Table 12.3 displays the three best indicator models for each of the five goal variables. The models were ranked according to AIC, to compare our results with those of Cockerline and Murray (1981) and Hostland *et al.* (1988).[12] For four of the five goal variables, a simple-summation aggregate fits the best: M2+ for the CPI and CPIXFE; and M1 for nominal GDP and (expressed in real terms) real GDP. Only in the case of the GDP deflator does a Fisher Ideal aggregate, M3 + FI, perform best.

In Table 12.4 we use Davidson and MacKinnon's (1981) J-test to determine whether the best Fisher Ideal model adds explanatory power to a specification with the best summation aggregate, and vice versa. For the three inflation models we find that neither the simple-sum model nor the Fisher Ideal model can alone explain the goal variable: both types of aggregate contain useful information. For nominal GDP, the two models appear to be so highly collinear that both models fit well and neither model adds to the other. For real GDP, the Fisher Ideal aggregate adds nothing to the simple-sum aggregate, but the simple-sum aggregate adds significantly to the specification of the Fisher Ideal model; hence the simple-sum model in this case is dominant. In the context of a St Louis equation, Chrystal and MacDonald (1994) perform similar tests and find that simple-sum M1 has the greatest informational content for nominal income, but it is closely followed by Divisia M1. Chrystal and MacDonald also find that, for broader aggregates, the Divisia measure has significant informational content for nominal income than its simple-sum equivalent.

Table 12.5 compares the results of our study with those of Cockerline and Murray (1981), Hostland *et al.* (1988)(HPS), Serletis and King (1993) (SK) and Chrystal and MacDonald (1994). The results show fairly strong similarities. Both our study and HPS find that a fairly broad Fisher Ideal monetary aggregate performs best for the GDP deflator (Fisher Ideal privately-held money supply in their case, and M3 + FI in ours), while SK found that the

Table 12.4 Davidson and MacKinnon (1981) J-tests

Goal variable	*Money*	H_0: *Goal* $= SUM\beta + \varepsilon$ H_1: *Goal* $= FI\gamma + \upsilon$ *Goal* $= (1-\alpha)\, SUM\beta + \alpha\, (FI\gamma) + \varepsilon$	H_0 *Goal* $= FI\gamma + \upsilon$ H_1: *Goal* $= SUM\beta + \varepsilon$ *Goal* $= (1-\alpha)\, FI\gamma + \alpha\, (SUM\beta) + \upsilon$	*Conclusions*
CPI	M2+ LLFI	Reject H_0 (3.04)	Reject H_0 (5.03)	Neither model provides complete specification
CPIXFE	M2+ LLFI	Reject H_0 (2.85)	Reject H_0 (3.83)	Neither model provides complete specification
GDP deflator	M2+ M3 + FI	Reject H_0 (3.02)	Reject H_0 (2.50)	Neither model provides complete specification
Nominal GDP	M1 M1FI	Do not reject H_0 (0.81)	Do not reject H_0 (1.09)	Cannot reject either specification
Real GDP	RM1 RM1FI	Do not reject H_0 (1.18)	Reject H_0 (2.23)	Summation model not rejected, but FI model is

smallest tail area in their Granger-causality tests for the deflator occurred in the case of M2+ (our preferred simple-summation aggregate). All five studies found that M1 was the aggregate that performed the best in estimation for nominal spending, although in SK M1 was ranked equally with M1FI. For real GDP, both HPS and we found that real M1 was the best aggregate, while SK, who restricted themselves to nominal aggregates, found that M1 and M1FI did equally well.

One-quarter-ahead out-of-sample forecasts for five goal variables

The models estimated above were used to generate out-of-sample forecasts in the following way. First, the models were estimated over the sample period 1971:Q1–1981:Q4 and the value for the following quarter was forecast. The model was then re-estimated with the additional quarter of data, and the next quarter was then forecast. This process was repeated for each quarter until 1989:Q3. The root-mean-squared errors were then calculated for the period 1982:Q1–1989:Q3.

For each goal variable the three best models by the root-mean-squared-error criterion are shown in Table 12.6. Again, simple-sum aggregates dominate in the majority of cases. It is the liquidity aggregates LL+ and LL that provide the

Table 12.5 Best aggregates in estimation: a comparison of various studies

Goal Variable	*Money*	*Cockerline and Murray* (1968: Q2–1980: Q4)[a]	*Hostland Poloz and Storer* (1969: Q1–1986: Q4)[b]	*Serletis and King* (1968: Q3–1989: Q3)[c]	*Chrystal and MacDonald* (1968: Q3–1987: Q1)[d]	*Longworth and Atta-Mensah* (1971: Q1–1989: Q3)
GDP Deflator	Summation	–	M2	M2+	–	M2+
	Superlative	–	PHMS-FI	M3 + FI	–	M3 + FI
	Overall	–	PHMS-FI	M2+	–	M3 + FI
Nominal GDP	Summation	M1	M1	M1	M1	M1
	Superlative	M1D	M1ALD-FI	M1FI	M1D	M1FI
	Overall	M1	M1	M1,M1FI	–	M1I
Real GDP[e]	Summation	–	RM1	M1	–	RM1
	Superlative	–	RM1ALD – FI	M1FI	–	RM1FI
	Overall	–	RM1	M1, M1FI	–	RM1

Notes: (a) Sample periods in parentheses.
(b) Note that M1ALD is defined as M1 plus non-personal notice deposits at banks. Also PHMS is defined as M2 plus non-personal fixed-term deposits at banks.
(c) Based on smallest tail area in Granger causality tests.
(d) Based on the St Louis equation.
(e) R before an aggregate indicates that it is expressed in real terms.

Table 12.6 Lowest RMSE for one-quarter-ahead forecast (annualised growth rates)

Rank	*CPI*	*CPIXFE*	*GDP deflator*	*Nominal GDP*	*Real GDP*
1	LL+ (1.630)	LL (1.178)	M2 + FI (1.889)	M1FI (2.812)	RM1 (3.199)
2	M3+ (1.670)	LL+ (1.208)	M2+ (1.903)	M1 (2.848)	AR Model (3.487)
3	M2 (1.671)	M3 (1.222)	M3 + FI (1.909)	LL + FI (2.9359)	RLL (3.499)
Best FI aggregate	M2FI (1.678)	M3FI (1.296)	–	–	RM1FI (3.517)

Table 12.7 Best aggregates in prediction: a comparison of various studies (one-quarter-ahead prediction)

Goal variable	*Money*	*Hostland Poloz and Storer (1975Q1–1986Q4)[a]*	*Longworth and Atta-Mensah (1982Q1–1989Q3)*
GDP deflator	Summation	M2	M2+
	Superlative	PHMs – FI	M2 + FI
	Overall	M2	M2 + FI
Nominal GDP	Summation	M1	M1
	Superlative	LLFI	M1FI
	Overall	M1	M1FI
Real GDP	Summation	RM1	RM1
	Superlative	Not available	Worse than autoregressive
	Overall	RM1	RM1

Note: (a) Forecasting periods are in parentheses.

best forecasts for CPI and CPIXFE, respectively, while real M1 continues to do best for real GDP. M2 + F1 is marginally better than M2+ and M3 + FI as a predictor of the GDP deflator, although the latter two variables had done better as in-sample predictors. Finally, M1FI did better than M1 in predicting nominal GDP, although the ordering had been the reverse in estimation.

Table 12.7 compares the results from Table 12.6 with those obtained by HPS. In both studies, real M1 was the best out-of-sample predictor of real output. HPS found M1 to be the best predictor of nominal spending, whereas we found that M1FI was best. Finally HPS found M2 to be the best predictor for the GDP deflator, whereas M2 + FI was preferred over our sample period.

Multi-period out-of-sample forecasts for five goal variables

We undertook further studies to find out which of the simple-sum and Fisher Ideal aggregates would do best in multi-period forecasts using bivariate vector autoregressions, with the second equation explaining the monetary aggregate by its own lags, and lags on the goal variable. The out-of-sample forecasts for 1982:Q1–1989:Q3 were performed in a way similar to that described above, except that multi-period forecasts were calculated in each case.

Table 12.8 presents the three best predictors for the 1-, 2-, 4-, 8-, and 12-quarter horizons. With the exception of inflation measured by the GDP

Table 12.8 The three best aggregates in the prediction of the annualised average growth rates of the goal variables (based on lowest RMSE)

Quarters	*Rank*	*CPI*	*CPIXFE*	*GDP deflator*	*Nominal GDP*	*Real GDP*
	1	LL+	LL	M2 + FI	M1FI	RM1[b]
		(1.6301)[a]	(1.1778)	(1.8890)	(2.8122)	(3.1988)
1	2	M3+	LL+	M2+	M1	RLL
		(1.6704)	(1.2081)	(1.9034)	(2.8482)	(3.4985)
	3	M2	M3	M3 + FI	LL + FI	RLL+
		(1.6709)	(1.2218)	(1.9089)	(2.9359)	(3.5099)
	1	M2+	LL	M3 + FI	M1FI	RM1
		(1.4607)	(1.1461)	(1.6379)	(2.9541)	(2.672)
2	2	LL+	LL+	M2 + FI	LL + FI	RM1FI
		(1.5074)	(1.1471)	(1.7052)	(2.9644)	(2.8942)
	3	M3+	M3	M2+	M3 + FI	RLL
		(1.5138)	(1.1819)	(1.7086)	(2.9841)	(3.0436)
	1	M2+	M3	M3 + FI	M3 + FI	RM1
		(1.4285)	(1.1110)	(1.7183)	(3.2171)	(2.1669)
4	2	M3+	M2+	M3FI	LL + FI	RM1FI
		(1.6165)	(1.1286)	(1.7923)	(3.2755)	(2.3404)
	3	M3	M2	LLFI	LLFI	RLL
		(1.6990)	(1.1382)	(1.7998)	(3.3285)	(2.4502)
	1	M2+	M2+	M3 + FI	M2+	RM1
		(1.8634)	(1.1770)	(2.0550)	(3.7496)	(2.0757)
8	2	M3+	M3+	M3FI	LL+	RLL
		(2.1701)	(1.3136)	(2.1360)	(3.7509)	(2.1411)
	3	M2	M3	LL + FI	M3 + FI	RLL+
		(2.1761)	(1.3279)	(2.2457)	(3.8054)	(2.1577)
	1	M2+	M2+	M3 + FI	M2+	RM1
		(2.5266)	(1.4677)	(2.7282)	(4.2628)	(2.1054)
12	2	M2	M3+	M3FI	LL+	RLL
		(2.6007)	(1.5948)	(2.7714)	(4.2877)	(2.1191)
	3	M3+	M3	LL+	M2	RLL+
		(2.7926)	(1.6164)	(2.8254)	(4.3710)	(2.1224)

Notes: (a) The RMSE is in parentheses.
(b) Note that an R prefix indicates that money is in real terms, using the CPI.

deflator, the broader simple-sum aggregates were the best predictors of inflation over the various horizons. In the case of the GDP deflator measure of inflation, M3+FI was seen as the best predictor over the forecast horizons beyond one quarter ahead.

With regard to nominal income, M1FI was the best predictor over the 1- and 2-quarter horizons; for 8- and 12-quarter horizons, M2+ was observed as the best predictor. Lastly, real M1 was found to be best predictor of real GDP for all horizons.

Following Chong and Hendry (1986), encompassing tests were conducted on the predictions of the best simple-sum and the best Fisher Ideal models. The tests were conducted by regressing the following equation:

$$g = \phi_0 + \phi_1 \hat{g}_{SS} + \phi_2 \hat{g}_{FI} + \zeta$$

where g is the observed goal variable, g_{SS} is the out-of-sample forecast of the goal variable obtained from the best simple-sum model, and $\hat{g}_{FI}$ is the prediction from the best Fisher Ideal model. The test involves checking the statistical significance of the coefficients, θ_1 and θ_2. If one of the coefficients is significant and the other is not, the model with the significant coefficient encompasses the competing model. On the other hand, if both coefficients are significant, then both models are complementary and an 'optimal' forecast could be constructed on the basis of the two models. Finally, if none of the coefficients is significant, then neither model encompasses the other.

The results reported in Table 12.9 suggest that the Fisher Ideal models encompass the simple-sum models in explaining most of the predictions for the growth rates of the GDP Deflator and the CPI. Given the lower RMSE (see Table 12.8) for the simple-sum models in the case of the CPI this most probably indicates that the Fisher Ideal projections have a greater bias. Except in a few cases, neither the Fisher Ideal nor the simple-sum model encompasses the other in predictions of the growth rates of CPI excluding food and energy, and nominal GDP. The simple-sum model typically encompasses the Fisher Ideal model in the case of real GDP.

12.4 Empirical evidence on long-run demand-for-money equations

In this section of the chapter we apply the methodology of Johansen and Juselius (1990) to examine the long-run demand-for-money equations for each aggregate. The stability of the estimated demand functions are also examined.

Identifying the cointegrating vectors

This section discusses the cointegrating vectors estimated, using the Johansen and Juselius methodology, for the simple-sum and Fisher Ideal monetary aggregates.

Table 12.9 Encompassing J-test results for the dynamic out-of-sample forecasts (annualised average growth rates) (forecast horizon: 1982Q1–1989Q3)

Goal variable	*Money*	*1Q Money*	Φ	*2Q Money*	Φ	*4Q Money*	Φ	*8Q Money*	Φ	*12Q Money*	Φ
CPI	Best SS	LL+	0.225 (1.162)	M2+	0.219 (1.128)	M2+	0.053 (0.299)	M2+	0.060 (0.623)	M2+	0.079 (0.798)
	Best FI	M2FI	0.598 (3.536)**	M2 + FI	0.553 (1.850)	M2 + FI	0.477 (2.104)*	M2 + FI	0.362 (2.493)*	M2 + FI	0.233 (2.198)*
CPIXFE	Best SS	LL	0.743 (1.141)	LL	0.835 (2.541)*	M3	0.273 (1.488)	M2+	0.051 (0.371)	M2+	–0.063 (-0.581)
	Best FI	M3FI	0.109 (0.181)	M2FI	0.004 (0.016)	LLFI	0.417 (2.572)*	LLFI	0.218 (1.326)	LLFI	0.124 (1.230)
GDP deflator	Best SS	M2+	0.333 (1.599)	M2+	0.152 (1.072)	LL+	–0.035 (–0.232)	LL+	–0.173 (–1.537)	LL+	–0.250 (–2.516)*
	Best FI	M2 + FI	0.434 (2.185)*	M3 + FI	0.564 (3.273)**	M3 + FI	0.552 (3.914)**	M3 + FI	0.511 (5.347)**	M3 + FI	0.284 (3.358)**
Nominal GDP	Best SS	M1	0.462 (1.598)	M1	0.516 (1.679)	M1	0.405 (3.036)**	M2+	–0.474 (–2.730)*	M2+	–0.216 (–1.880)
	Best FI	M1FI	0.181 (0.662)	M1FI	0.058 (0.201)	M3 + FI	0.010 (0.065)	M3 + FI	0.515 (3.488)**	M3 + FI	0.438 (3.620)**
Real GDP	Best SS	RM1	1.021 (2.378)*	RM1	0.935 (2.668)*	RM1	0.900 (1.719)	RM1	1.371 (3.050)**	RM1	0.901 (2.309)*
	Best FI	RM1FI	–0.129 (–0.300)	RM1FI	–0.088 (–0.203)	RM1FI	–0.114 (–0.263)	RM2FI	–2.566 (–4.232)**	RM2 + FI	–1.506 (–2.099)

Notes: *t*-statistics in parentheses.
* Significantly different from zero at the 5% level.
** Significantly different from zero at the 1% level.

Note that the Johansen and Juselius methodology is designed for variables that are integrated of order one. Unit-root tests were conducted on the monetary aggregates (simple-sum and Fisher Ideal), user costs, R90, real income, and the three measures of inflation. The ADF or Phillips–Perron tests suggest that all the variables used in this research are integrated of order one.

It has been argued by Fisher *et al.* (1993) that in estimating the demand-for-money function for a Fisher Ideal monetary aggregate, the user cost of the aggregate should be used in the function rather than an interest rate. The argument is that since the Fisher Ideal aggregates contain interest-bearing assets, the relevant measure of the 'opportunity cost of holding money' is the user cost rather than levels of one or more interest rates.

In this chapter, we chose not to use the user costs in estimating the demand functions because exclusion tests conducted did not find them to be statistically significant. The exclusion tests were carried out in two ways. First, for each of the Fisher Ideal aggregates, we estimated the following equation and determined the statistical significance of the rental price index:

$$\begin{aligned} A\,(L)\ \Delta\ \text{money}_t = {} & A_0 + B(L)\ \Delta\ \text{income}_t + C\,(L)\ \Delta R90_t \\ & + D(L)\ \Delta \text{infl}_t + \gamma \text{ECM}_{t-1} + E(L)\ RP_t + \varepsilon_t \end{aligned} \tag{12.2}$$

where Δ is the difference-operator, *RP* is the user cost, the last term is an error term, and money and income are in real terms. ECM is the error-correction term, which is derived from the estimated cointegrating vectors from money, income, *R*90 and inflation. If *RP* was an important variable, then *E(L)* would be statistically significant in the above equation.

The second method estimates the following alternative dynamic equation:

$$\begin{aligned} A(L)\ \Delta\text{money}_t = {} & A_0 + B(L)\ \Delta\text{income}_t + C(L)\ \Delta R90_t + D(L)\ \Delta\text{infl}_t \\ & + \alpha\text{money}_{t-1} + \beta\text{income}_{t-1} + \delta R90_{t-1} \\ & + \theta\text{infl}_{t-1} + K(L) RP_t + \varepsilon_t \end{aligned} \tag{12.3}$$

The purpose of the second method is to relax the constraint of imposing the cointegrating vectors. The importance of the *RP* depends on whether the *K(L)* terms are statistically significant. Note that, in both regressions, the Akaike information criterion was used to select the lag lengths.

The results of the exclusion tests show that, under the two scenarios outlined above, the user costs are statistically insignificant at the 1 per cent significance level. Hence the *RPs* were dropped in the estimation of the money-demand functions.

In Table 12.10 we report the cointegrating vectors that fit the characteristics of a money-demand function – that is, where the income elasticity is positive, the semi-interest elasticity is negative, and inflation is also included in the equation. (For each cointegrating vector in Table 12.10, the first term is the coefficient of money initialised to unity; the second term is the income elasticity; the third term is the semi-interest elasticity; and the fourth term is the semi-elasticity of inflation.)

Table 12.10 Estimated cointegrating vectors that fit the characteristics of a money-demand function

Money	*System including CPI*	*System including CPIXFE*	*System including the GDP deflator*
M1	[1 -0.540 0.241–0.009]	[1 -0.457 0.149 -0.031]	[1 -0.219 0.070 -0.0031]
	[1 -0.607 0.040 -0.050]	[1 -0.318 0.032 -0.052]	[1 -0.440 0.023 -0.033]
M2	[1 -1.109 0.010 0.012]	[1 -1.061 0.006 0.021]	[1 -0.719 0.035 0.042]
M2+	[1 -1.431 0.012 0.009]	[1 -1.500 0.023 0.008]	[1 -1.233 0.034 0.023]
	[1 -1.890 0.014 -0.021]		
M3	None	[1 -1.343 0.337 -0.120]	None
M3+	None	[1 -1.686 0.208 -0.072]	None
LL	None	[1 -1.750 0.009 -0.016]	[1 -1.274 0.001 0.019]
			[1 -1.608 0.003 -0.006]
LL+	[1 -1.483 0.006 0.016]	[1 -1.559 0.003 0.016]	[1 -1.374 0.009 0.018]
		[1 -1.812 0.003 -0.009]	
M1FI	[1 -0.590 0.230 -0.007]	[1 -0.516 0.150 -0.028]	[1 -0.243 0.079 0.003]
	[1 -0.675 0.041 -0.051]	[1 -0.371 0.032 -0.052]	[1 -0.489 0.025 -0.033]
M2FI	[1 -1.350 0.058 -0.060]	[1 -0.780 0.034 -0.042]	[1 -0.890 0.034 -0.032]
M2 + FI	[1 -1.739 0.066 -0.067]	[1 -1.094 0.039 -0.046]	[1 -1.192 0.040 -0.037]
M3FI	[1 -1.806 0.077 -0.098]	[1 -1.021 0.046 -0.077]	[1 -1.318 0.052 -0.068]
M3 + FI	[1 -2.015 0.078 -0.093]	[1 -1.263 0.049 -0.074]	[1 -1.487 0.053 -0.064]
LLFI	[1 -2.587 0.111 -0.119]	[1 -1.299 0.048 -0.065]	[1 -1.439 0.054 -0.053]
LL + FI	[1 -2.963 0.122 -0.132]	[1 -1.558 0.056 -0.074]	[1 -1.686 0.062 -0.061]

The Johansen and Juselius estimates obtained in this chapter suggest the existence of cointegrating relationships among the monetary aggregates (in real terms), real income, R90, and inflation. However, not all of the vectors can be interpreted as long-run money-demand functions. In general, for the vectors that could be described as money-demand functions, Table 12.10 shows that, for both the simple-sum and the Fisher Ideal aggregates, the semi-interest elasticity for the narrower aggregates is larger than that associated with the broader aggregates. As expected, we also found the income elasticities of the broader aggregates to be greater than those of the narrow aggregates.[13]

Estimating dynamic-money-demand equations

Dynamic money-demand equations for all the aggregates were estimated in two ways. The first method uses the cointegrating vectors estimated by Johansen and Juselius's methodology as an error-correction model (ECM). Thus, the following regression equation was used in estimating the demand function for all the monetary aggregates:

$$\begin{aligned} A(L)\,\Delta\text{money}_t = A_0 &+ B(L)\,\Delta\text{income}_t + C(L)\,\Delta R90_t \\ &+ D(L)\,\Delta\text{infl}_t + \gamma\text{ECM}_{t-1} + \varepsilon_t \end{aligned} \tag{12.4}$$

where Δ is the difference-operator, the last term is an error term, and money and income are in real terms. Within this framework, ECM acts as a measure of disequilibrium in any period.[14] Note that for dynamic stability of the functions, the estimated coefficients of the ECM terms must be negative. Also, if the ECM term is negative and statistically significant, then deviation of money from its long-run path (represented by the cointegrating vector) will lead to future changes in money holdings by economic agents, in order to move closer to their optimal long-run position.

In Table 12.11 we present the estimated coefficients of the ECM terms in the dynamic money-demand functions. The ECM term is generally negative and significant in the dynamic money-demand equations for the simple-sum monetary aggregates, especially in the case where the CPI is the price index that is used. In the case of the Fisher Ideal aggregates, other than M1FI, the ECM term was not very significant in the regression equations, thus casting doubt on the existence of a long-run money demand equation in level form.

Stability of the money-demand functions

A rolling Chow test was used to assess the stability of the estimated dynamic money-demand. Plots of the F-statistic for the various periods of the test are presented in Figures 12.2 and 12.3. Figure 12.2 shows that the dynamic money-demand equations for the simple-sum aggregates are very stable. However, as depicted in Figure 12.3, the demand function for the Fisher Ideal aggregates is not stable.[15]

Table 12.11 Estimated coefficients of the ECM term in the dynamic money-demand functions

Money	*System including CPI*	*System including CPIXFE*	*System including the GDP deflator*
M1	–0.021	–0.039	–0.049
	(–6.921)**	(–7.508)**	(–4.613)**
M2	–0.076	–0.026	–0.006
	(–2.857)**	(–1.808)	(–1.561)
M2+	–0.049	–0.038	–0.017
	(–3.632)**	(–3.384)**	(–3.566)**
M3	0.011	–0.003	0.002
	(3.493)**	(–1.637)	(0.820)
M3+	0.012	–0.005	0.001
	(3.790)**	(–2.262)*	(0.300)
LL	–0.096	–0.129	–0.077
	(–4.048)**	(–4.007)**	(–3.648)**
	–0.073		–0.066
	(–2.834)**		(–2.461)*
LL+	–0.088	–0.097	–0.033
	(–4.484)**	(–4.473)**	(–2.284)**
M1F1	–0.015	–0.036	–0.055
	(–5.054)**	(–7.935)**	(–6.733)**
M2FI	–0.010	–0.015	–0.004
	(–1.084)	(–0.992)	(–0.240)
M2 + FI	–0.007	–0.001	–0.001
	(–0.933)	(–0.037)	(–0.073)
M3FI	–0.007	–0.019	–0.006
	(–1.293)	(–2.378)*	(–0.776)
M3 + FI	–0.005	–0.006	–0.002
	(–1.037)	(–0.734)	(–0.291)
LLFI	–0.001	–0.013	0.001
	(–0.074)	(–1.512)	(0.107)
LL + FI	0.002	–0.019	0.003
	(0.573)	(–2.327)*	(0.441)

Notes: *t*-statistics in parentheses.
* Significantly different from zero at the 5% level.
** Significantly different from zero at the 1% level.

12.5 Short-run causality tests

In this section, we estimate a representation of a vector error-correction model (VECM) and subject it to exclusion tests on the lags of each of the first-differenced variables and on the lagged cointegrating terms. The VECM is of the form:

$$\Delta X_t = \Gamma_1 \Delta X_{t-1} + \Gamma_2 \Delta X_{t-2} + \dots + \Gamma_p \Delta X_{t-p+1} + \alpha \mathrm{ECM}_{t-p} + \varepsilon_t \qquad (12.5)$$

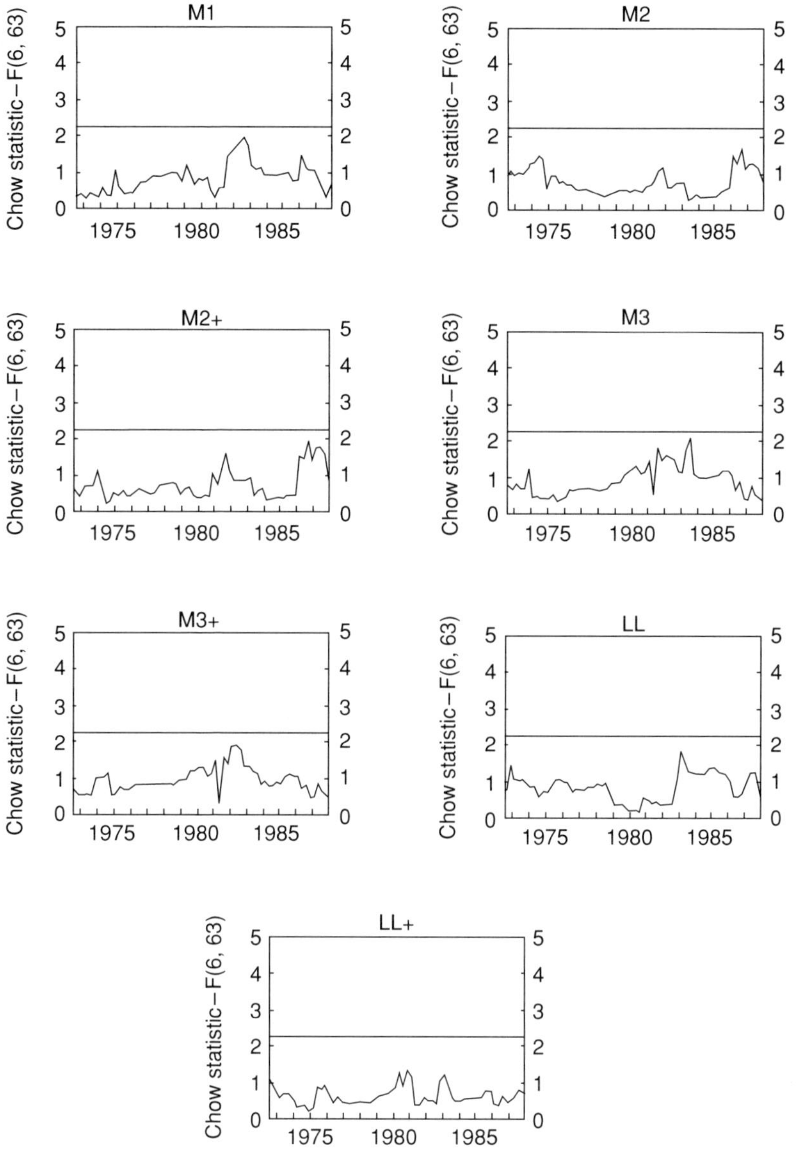

Notes: F(6, 63) at the 5% critical level = 2.246
F(7, 61) at the 5% critical level = 2.166

Figure 12.2 Rolling Chow tests for simple-sum monetary aggregates

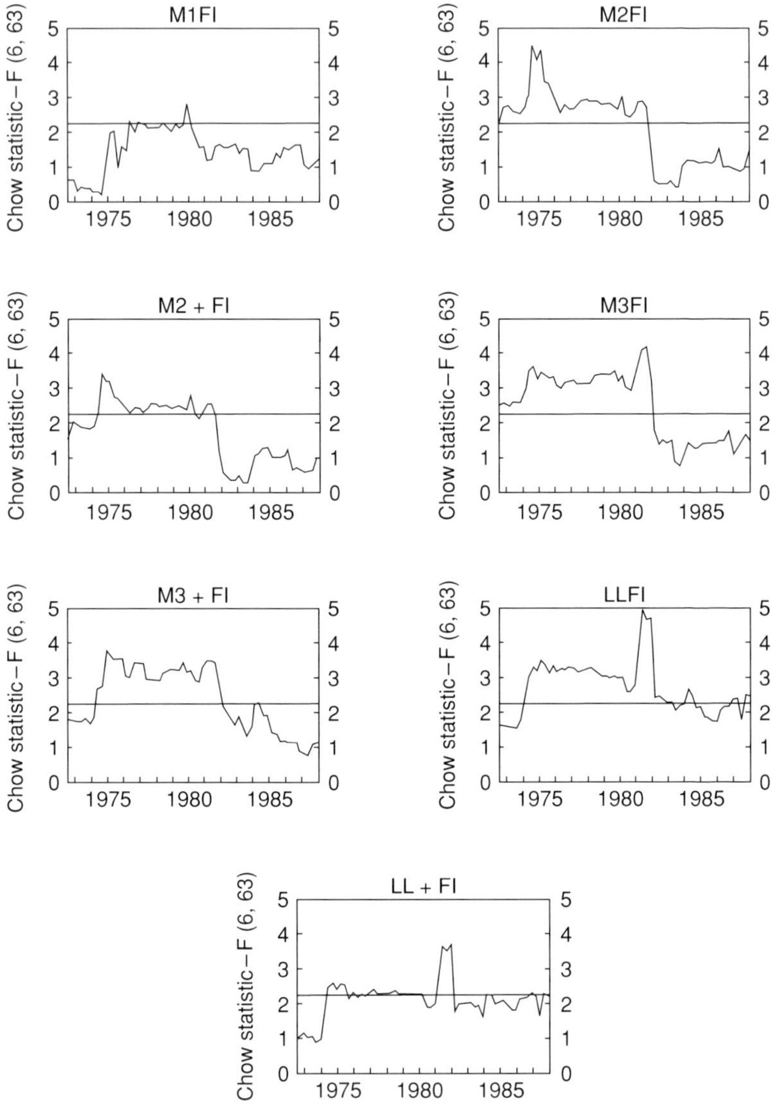

Notes: F(6, 63) at the 5% critical level = 2.246

Figure 12.3 Rolling Chow tests for Fisher Ideal monetary aggregates where

$$\text{ECM}_{t-p} = \hat{\beta}' X_{t-p} \tag{12.6}$$

and $\hat{\beta}$ denotes the statistically significant cointegrating vectors obtained by the Johansen and Juselius methodology. Note that the variables in the VECM are the same variables used in determining the cointegrating vectors. The exclusion tests are performed using F-statistics.[16]

A summary of the results is as follows:

- M1FI is the only aggregate that significantly influences real income in the short run.
- M2, M2+, M3 and M3+ are the only aggregates that significantly influence CPI in the short run.
- M3, LLFI and LL+FI are the only aggregates that significantly influence CPIXFE in the short run.
- M2+ is the only aggregate that influences the GDP deflator significantly in the short run.
- R90 influences all the Fisher Ideal aggregates significantly, M1, M2, M3, M3+ and real income in the short run.

12.6 Conclusion

In this chapter we have compared the empirical performance of Canadian weighted (Fisher Ideal) aggregates and the current summation aggregates in terms of their information content and forecasting performance for prices, real output and nominal spending for the period 1971:Q1 to 1989:Q3, at which point the data on the Fisher Ideal aggregates end. Additionally, we have examined the properties of money-demand equations for these aggregates, including, importantly, their temporal stability.

'Indicator model' equations explaining the rates of change of real output, nominal spending and prices in terms of lagged own rates of growth and the rate of growth of one of the monetary aggregates generally reaffirm the conclusions of the earlier studies that weighted monetary aggregates rarely do better than simple-sum aggregates in predicting major Canadian macro economic variables. In particular:

- In-sample estimation shows that the simple-sum aggregates M2+, M1, and real M1 provide the best explanation for the CPI (or CPI excluding food and energy), nominal spending, and real output, respectively, while Fisher Ideal M3+ provides the best explanation for the GDP deflator; and
- Out-of-sample forecasts over horizons of 1-, 2-, 4-, 8-, and 12-quarters show that broad simple-sum aggregates such as M2+, M3, LL and LL+ provide the best forecasts for the CPI and CPI excluding food and energy (although in the context of J-tests, Fisher Ideal models generally encompass simple-

sum models for the CPI); Fisher Ideal M3+ provides the best forecasts for the GDP deflator at forecast horizons greater than 1-quarter; Fisher Ideal M1 provides the best forecast for nominal spending at short horizons, while simple-sum M2+ provides the best forecast for the same variable at longer horizons; and real M1 provides the best forecasts for real GDP at all horizons.

Cointegrated money demand functions are hardly ever found for Fisher Ideal aggregates broader than Fisher Ideal M1 (the two exceptions are M3FI and LL+FI when the CPI excluding food and energy is used as the price measure). In contrast, cointegrated money-demand functions are found for all the simple-sum aggregates, in particular when the CPI is used. Rolling Chow tests almost always reject the stability of the Fisher Ideal money demand functions, while they cannot reject the stability of the simple-sum money demand functions when the CPI is used.

In the context of a vector error-correction model containing real money balances, a 90-day interest rate, inflation and real output, only broad simple-sum monetary aggregates are found to cause CPI inflation and GDP deflator inflation in the short run, while the two Fisher Ideal broad liquidity aggregates are found to cause inflation measured by the CPI excluding food and energy in the short run (as is simple-sum M3).

Overall, on the basis of in-sample fit of indicator models, out-of-sample forecasts by indicator models, the specification of money demand functions, and the temporal stability of money demand functions, one would conclude that Canadian simple-sum monetary aggregates are generally empirically superior to Fisher Ideal aggregates. In particular, broad monetary aggregates are generally best in predicting inflation, M1 works well in predicting nominal spending, and real M1 is the best predictor of real output.

Notes

1. Diewert (1976, 1978) introduced these indices to the literature. He suggests that an index is superlative if it is exact for some aggregator function. In other words, there is a close correspondence between the aggregator function and the index number formula.
2. See Barnett *et al.* (1992) for other superlative indices and the exact formula for constructing each one.
3. Barnett *et al.* (1992), Thornton and Yue (1992), and Farr and Johnson (1985) suggest other ways to avoid this problem.
4. Barnett *et al.* (1992, p. 2105, footnote 31) suggest a way to guarantee this.
5. The forty-six aggregates are: (1) currency; (2) monetary base; (3) M1; (4) M1ALD (M1 plus non-personal notice deposits at banks); (5) M13 (M1ALD plus daily interest chequing and personal savings deposits at banks); (6) M2 (M13 plus personal, fixed-term deposits at banks); (7) PHMS (M2 plus non-personal, fixed-term deposits at banks); (8) PHMSB (PHMS plus bankers' acceptances); (9)PHMSBC (PHMSB at banks); (11) M3B (M3 plus bankers' acceptances); (12) M3BC (M3B plus commercial paper); (13) LL (M3BC plus Canada Savings Bonds, Treasury bills held

by the public, and 1–3 year Government of Canada bonds); (14)–(24) M1 to LL *plus* corresponding deposits held at trust and mortgage loan companies, credit unions, and *caisses populaires* (the abbreviations for these aggregates and with a '+'); and (25)–(46) Fisher Ideal monetary indices corresponding to the same level of aggregation for M1 to LL and M1+ to LL+.

6. What Serletis and King refer to as Divisia aggregates are in fact Fisher Ideal aggregates.
7. What Chrystal and McDonald call Divisia aggregates for Canada are in fact Fisher Ideal aggregates.
8. The Bank of Canada decided to stop constructing the Fisher Ideal aggregates in mid-1990. This decision was motivated by three factors. First, the cost of constructing these aggregates, which relates to the cost of constructing some of the component parts and their rental prices, was considered to be too high. Second, the failure of any of these weighted-sum aggregates to outperform simple-sum aggregates consistently as indicators argued against their maintenance. Third, the difficulties in translating theoretical concepts into empirical counterparts was thought to reduce the potential empirical gains from superlative aggregates.
9. The ten-year Industrial Bond rate is the maturity-adjusted and liquidity-adjusted McLeod, Young, Weir index of rates on prime corporate issues, purged of any special features (for example, low coupons, retractables or convertibles).
10. Belongia and Chrystal (1991) and Belongia, Chapter 13, this volume, find this problem to exist with the official monetary aggregates of UK, USA, Japan and Germany.
11. We use the term 'goal variable' to mean a variable that the monetary authorities are interested in, whether they have targets for it or not. As explained in the introduction, the Bank of Canada has inflation-control targets, but in that context is very interested in the growth of output because of its effect on the output gap and thus on inflationary pressure.
12. Note that critical values for the differences between AICs do not exist in the literature.
13. We also tested whether the long-run income elasticity of the demand for real balances is unity. Based on the likelihood-ratio statistic, the restriction on income was not rejected for any of the aggregates in the system that uses the GDP deflator. In the system that uses CPI, the restriction on the income elasticity is rejected for LL, M2FI, M2+FI, M3FI, M3+FI, LLFI and LL+FI. In the case of the system that uses CPI excluding food and energy, the restriction on the income elasticity is rejected for LL, LL+ and all the Fisher Ideal aggregates except M1FI.
14. Note that in all cases only the cointegrating vectors that were found to be statistically significant in the regression equation were included.
15. Note that Figures 12.2 and 12.3 are based on the regression equations that use the CPI. Similar results are obtained for those involving the CPIXFE and the GDP delator.
16. We also used the VECM and recursive regressions to compute the root-mean-square errors (RMSE) for forecasts of selected macroeconomic variables at 1- to 12-quarter horizons. Based on RMSE, the results show that the narrower measures of the Fisher Ideal aggregates are best at predicting CPI at shorter horizons while, at longer horizons, the broader measures of the simple-sum aggregates are the best. Also M2 and M3+ are best at predicting CPI excluding food and energy at shorter horizons while, at longer horizons, the broader measures of the Fisher Ideal aggregates are the best. For the GDP deflator, M2+ is the best predictor. Finally, the forecast results show that broader measures of the Fisher Ideal aggregates are best at

predicting real GDP at shorter horizons; M1 is the best at eight-quarters ahead, while M3 is the best at twelve-quarters ahead. The out-of-sample results from the VECM model must be accepted with caution. Given that the money-demand functions were found to be unstable and the ECM terms insignificant for most of the Fisher Ideal aggregates, one would have had little basis for choosing these aggregates for use in VECM models.

References

Akaike, H. (1973) 'Information Theory and an Extension of the Maximum Likelihood Principle', in B. Petrov and F. Csake (eds), *Second International Symposium on Information Theory* (Budapest: Akademiai Kiado).

Barnett, W. A. (1980) 'Economic Monetary Aggregates: An Application of Index Numbers and Aggregation theory', *Journal of Econometrics*, vol. 14, pp. 11–48.

Barnett, W. A., D. Fisher and A. Serletis (1992) 'Consumer Demand Theory and the Demand for Money', *Journal of Economic Literature*, vol. 30, pp. 2086–119.

Batten, D. S. and D. L. Thornton (1985) 'Are Weighted Monetary Aggregates Better Than Simple-Sum M1?' *Federal Reserve Bank of St Louis Review*, vol. 67, pp. 29–40.

Belongia, M. T. 'Consequences of Money Stock Mismeasurement: Evidence from Three Countries', Chapter 13, this volume.

Belongia, M. T. and K. A. Chrystal (1991) 'An Admissible Monetary Aggregates for the UK', *Review of Economics and Statistics*', vol. 73, pp. 497–503.

Chong, Y. and D. Hendry (1986) 'Econometric Evaluation of Linear Macro-Economic Models', *Review of Economic Studies*, vol. 53, pp. 671–90.

Chrystal, K. A. and R. McDonald (1994) 'Empirical Evidence on the Recent Behaviour and Usefulness of Simple Sum and Weighted Measures of the Money Stock', *Federal Reserve Bank of St. Louis Review*, vol. 76 (March/April) pp. 73–109.

Cockerline, J. P. and J. Murray (1981) 'A Comparison of Alternative Methods of Monetary Aggregation: Some Preliminary Evidence', *Bank of Canada Technical Report*, vol. 28.

Davidson, R. and J. MacKinnon (1981) 'Several Tests for Model Specification in the Presence of Alternative Hypothesis', *Econometrica*, vol. 49, pp. 781–93.

Diewert W. E. (1976) 'Exact and Superlative Index Numbers', *Journal of Econometrics*, vol. 4, pp. 115–46.

Diewert, W. E. (1978) 'Superlative Index Numbers and Consistency in Aggregation', *Econometrica*, vol. 46, 883–900.

Farr, H. T. and D. Johnson (1985) 'Revisions in the Monetary Services (Divisia) Indexes of the Monetary Aggregates', *Board of Governors of the Federal Reserve System, Staff Study*, p. 147.

Fine, E. (1990) 'Institutional Developments Affecting Monetary Aggregates', *Monetary Seminar 90* (Ottawa: Bank of Canada), pp. 555–63.

Fisher, D., S. Hudson and M. Pradhan (1993) 'Divisia Indices for Money: An Appraisal of Theory and Practice', *Bank of England Working Paper Series No. 9.*

Freedman, C. (1983) 'Financial Innovation in Canada: Causes and Consequences', *American Economic Review*, vol. 73, pp. 73–109.

Hostland, D., S. Poloz and P. Storer (1988) 'An Analysis of the Information Content of Alternative Monetary Aggregates', *Bank of Canada Technical Report*, p. 48.

Johansen, S. and K. Juselius (1990) 'Maximum Likelihood Estimation and Inference on Cointegration – with Application to the 'Demand for Money', *Oxford Bulletin of Economics and Statistics*, vol. 52, pp. 169–210.

Muller, P. (1990) 'The Information Content of Financial Aggregates during the 1980s', *Monetary Seminar 90* (Ottawa: Bank of Canada), pp. 183–304.

Rotemberg, J. J., J. C. Driscoll and J. M. Poterba (1995) 'Money, Output, and Prices: Evidence from a New Monetary Aggregate', *Journal of Business and Economic Statistics*, vol. 13, pp. 67–83.

Serletis A. and M. King (1993) 'The Role of Money in Canada', *Journal of Macroeconomics*, vol. 15, pp. 91–107.

Spencer, P. (1994) 'Portfolio Disequilibrium: Implications for the Divisia Approach to Monetary Aggregation', *The Manchester School of Economics and Social Studies Journal*, vol. 62, pp. 125–50.

Thornton, D. L. and P. Yue (1992) 'An Extended Series of Divisia Monetary Aggregates', *Federal Reserve Bank of St. Louis Review*, vol. 74, (November/December) pp. 35–52.

13

Consequences of Money Stock Mismeasurement: Evidence from Three Countries

Michael T. Belongia

Central banks continue to publish simple-sum measures of the money stock and draw policy inferences from their behaviour even though it has been demonstrated conclusively that these data violate basic principles of economic and index number theory. As such, any in-sample results based on simple sum data must be spurious. Furthermore, the absence of any statistical properties in these data preclude their use in making out-of-sample forecasts.[1] Nonetheless, some research, which acknowledges the conceptual error of simple-sum measures, has defended their use on practical grounds.[2] Generally speaking, the reasoning has been that index number theory raises some interesting and *potentially* important issues for the construction and use of measures of the money stock, but that measurement has turned out to be unimportant empirically in real-world applications.

A related issue has received even less attention, even though it is logically prior to the choice of an appropriate aggregation formula. This issue is the *composition* of a monetary aggregate. Demand theory requires that a group of assets represents a weakly separable commodity block if they are to be aggregated. Although it is possible to test for the existence of weak separability, this has been done infrequently on monetary data, and the standard practice for central banks and many economists still appears to be one of using an *ad hoc* judgment about an asset's 'moneyness' as the criterion for inclusion in an aggregate.[3]

This chapter addresses both issues for three countries: the USA, Germany and Japan. After conducting tests for weak separability to identify asset groupings that are candidates for use as a monetary aggregate, Divisia measures of these groupings are compared both to the official simple-sum aggregates targeted by the central banks of these countries and the Divisia measures of the same official aggregates. By proceeding in this manner it is possible to make inferences about the implications of both asset composition and choice of index number on money stock measurement. In contrast to the benign neglect demonstrated by central banks, the results indicate that the weakly separable asset groups often are not those used as the basis for policy decisions, and that superlative measures generally offer fundamentally different answers about the relative ease or tightness of monetary policy.

13.1 Monetary aggregation: a review of the issues

Testing for admissible asset groupings

To construct a measure of a country's money stock it is necessary to choose a bundle of commodities thought to reflect the characteristics of 'money' and then to aggregate this bundle into a single index-number measure. Typically, central banks have approached the first issue by grouping assets according to subjective judgements about their characteristics ('moneyness'). Moreover, each has tended to produce a range of measures, from narrow aggregates containing only highly liquid and non-interest-bearing assets to broader measures that encompass progressively more illiquid assets, which can be converted into readily-acceptable media of exchange only at increasing cost. Thus, the representative central bank produces a measure of narrow money (M1) based on something close to pure media of exchange, a broader aggregate (M2) which adds assets (for example, savings balances) that can be converted into currency or demand deposits at relatively low cost, and a much-broader aggregate (M3) which includes assets (for example, large-denomination time-deposits) that can be converted to a spendable form at relatively high cost. Having determined these asset groupings, central banks have constructed the relevant aggregate as an unweighted sum of balances in different asset categories. These simple-sum indexes are reported as the official measures of a country's money stock, monitored as indicators of the stance of monetary policy and implemented in research to test hypotheses about the effects of money on economic activity.

Although it is possible that the asset collections used in the official definitions of various monetary aggregates are, by chance, weakly separable groups, the problem with using subjective judgements about characteristics of moneyness to define a monetary aggregate can be seen in a simple example. In the USA this approach has led to the inclusion of interest-bearing NOW accounts in M1 while excluding other interest-bearing cheque account deposits (MMDAs and money-market mutual funds (MMMFs)). Obvious questions raised by such a demarcation are why, on the one hand, an interest-bearing asset (NOWs) is included in a measure purported to represent 'pure' media of exchange and, on the other, assets (MMDAs and MMMFs) that share many characteristics in common with NOW accounts are excluded from M1. Both from a conceptual and a practical standpoint, it seems clear that measurements of, and inferences about, changes in the money stock can be wrong if the monetary aggregate excludes assets with important characteristics (or includes assets with few characteristics) of money.[4]

The conditions necessary for an admissible asset collection – a linearly homogeneous, weakly separable commodity block – implies the traditional approach of inserting money as an argument in the utility function of the representative individual. This assumes that the consumer follows a multi-step budgeting process where, in the first step, expenditures are allocated across broad commodity groups. By assuming further that the utility function is weakly separable in financial assets, it is then possible to investigate which financial assets, in the second-stage budgeting decision, are weakly separable from other (near-money) financial assets. The question now is how to test the weak separability of the alternative asset collections.

Previous work has split on this issue into parametric and non-parametric tests. In what follows, the non-parametric approach is taken because it provides information of interest without being sensitive to choice of functional form.[5] The information provided by the non-parametric test is whether, for a set of observed prices and quantities: (i) a stable utility function exits that rationalises the data; and (ii) the data are compatible with a utility function that is weakly separable in some subset of goods.

Varian (1982, 1983) demonstrated, based on earlier work by Afriat (1967), that consistency requires the data to exhibit no violations of the generalised axiom of revealed preference (GARP). GARP is equivalent to the existence of a well-behaved utility function which, when maximised subject to a budget constraint by a rational consumer, could have generated the observed data. If a subset of the goods satisfies GARP while an aggregate of these goods along with the other goods still satisfies the consistency property, the conditions for an admissible group of assets have been met: a utility function exists which both rationalises the observed data and is consistent with weak separability in these goods.

But, while avoiding irksome choices about functional form, this non-parametric test has been criticised on two grounds. First, the test finds a rejection of GARP even if its conditions are violated at a single data point; moreover, no objective criterion exists to determine whether a 'small' violation is a true rejection of the null, or is associated with measurement error in aggregate data. A second objection is that results from this test are to be interpreted a bit cautiously because it is apparently biased toward rejection of the null hypothesis.[6] This direction of the bias, however, implies that one can be confident of identifying a separable group when the test does not report a rejection. At the same time, this bias and the nature of the non-parametric test indicate that it can be important to examine the data more closely when the NONPAR algorithm indicates that GARP fails to hold only at a few data points. To this end, a procedure devised by Chalfant and Alston (1988) is used in this chapter to check the size of any violations, and qualified judgements are made about the likely source and importance of these occurrences.

Simple-sum versus superlative aggregation

At a conceptual level, index number theory shows that a simple-sum measure *must* be wrong because its attribution of equal weights to each asset category requires that the assets within the aggregate *must* be perfect substitutes. The empirical evidence on elasticities of substitution between asset pairs, however, indicates relatively low substitutability, even among such things as demand deposits and NOW accounts, and certainly offers no support for the infinite elasticities of substitution that are required for simple-sum aggregation. Thus, there is no doubt that simple-sum aggregates are 'wrong' in principle. For this chapter, however, a different question is considered: are the simple-sum measures good enough approximations to the theoretically ideal index numbers that they can be used for empirical work?

The implications of choosing a particular set of weights for measuring monetary service flows can be seen in a simple example. Suppose that the US M1 aggregate reflects all monetary assets of interest – there is no substitution between M1 assets and non-M1 assets. If interest rates on NOW accounts rise so that some people shift from non-interest-bearing demand deposits into NOWs, a simple-sum measure of M1 will be unchanged. For a superlative index, however, the change in this single interest rate will affect all relative user costs and expenditure shares of M1's components; because shares are the index's weights, M1 itself will also change. In this case, for example, the weight given to NOW accounts will change because their user cost has fallen and their quantity has risen. At the same time, the weights given to other assets will also have to adjust to satisfy the constraint that budget shares for all assets in the aggregate sum to 1. These adjustments will produce a change in a superlative measure where none occurred in a simple-sum measure.

13.2 Evidence on asset groupings

Tests for weak separability were conducted using values for real deposits in the individual asset categories used to construct each country's monetary aggregates and each asset's corresponding nominal user costs as defined above. The individual deposit categories for each country, their abbreviations and their levels and shares of various aggregates are listed in Table 13.1. Quarterly data were used over sample periods that were generally free of significant financial innovations.

Among the many problems with Varian's test already noted, several others are worth mentioning before discussing the results. First, the analysis implicitly assumes full adjustment within the periodicity of the data. Thus, for example, if a sharp change in the slope of the yield curve would normally induce people to shift money out of CDs, but the average CD maturity is six months, quarterly data are likely to reveal violations of GARP. For analogous reasons, it is difficult to use the test in periods when new assets are introduced

Table 13.1 Asset categories, abbreviations and size characteristics

	Asset	Abbreviation	Share of: M1A (%)	M1 (%)	M2 (%)
USA (92.4)	Currency	CUR	46.9	29.4	8.5
	Household demand deposits	DDCON	20.0	12.5	3.6
	Business demand deposits	DDBUS	33.1	20.7	6.0
	Other checkable deposits	OCD		37.4	10.8
	Super NOWs at commercial banks[1]	SNOWC		0.0	0.0
	Super NOWs at thrifts[1]	SNOWT		0.0	0.0
	Overnight RPs	ONRP			1.5
	Overnight eurodollars	ONED			0.6
	Money market mutual funds	MMMF			9.9
	Money market deposit accounts[2] at commercial banks	MMDAC			0.0
	Money market deposit accounts at thrifts[2]	MMDAT			0.0
	Savings deposits at commercial banks	SDCB			21.4
	Savings deposits at thrifts	SDT			12.3
	Small time deposits at commercial banks	STDCB			14.6
	Small time deposits at thrifts	STDT			10.6
			M1 (%)	M2 (%)	M3 (%)
Germany (90.1)	Currency	CUR	33.5	18.8	11.6
	Sight deposits	SD	66.5	37.2	23.1
	Time deposits	TD		44.0	27.2
	Savings deposits at statutory notice	SDSN			38.1

Table 13.1 (*continued*)

	Asset	Abbreviation	M1 (%)	Share Of: M2 + CDs (%)	M3 + CDs (%)
Japan (91.2)	Currency	CUR	29.1	6.6	4.1
	Currency deposits	CD	16.5	3.8	2.4
	Ordinary deposits	OD	45.9	10.5	6.5
	Deposits at notice	DN	8.5	1.9	1.2
	Corporate time deposits	CTD		29.2	18.2
	Personal time deposits	PTD		46.0	28.7
	Certificates of deposit	CD		1.9	1.2
	Postal savings	PS			17.4
	Money trusts	MT			4.5
	Loan trusts	LT			6.1
	Remaining M3 + CDs	REST			9.5

Notes: 1. These were eliminated as separate asset categories in April 1986 and are now part of other checkable deposits.
2. These were eliminated as separate asset categories in September 1991 and are now part of savings deposits.

because lagged adjustments – as individuals gradually move funds into the new accounts – will be reflected as violations of GARP. This is especially important because a violation at only one data point will lead to a rejection of weak separability. Moreover, as a non-parametric test, one is never certain whether a rejection was caused by a legitimate inconsistency with GARP or measurement error in aggregate data.

Finally, the test requires a great deal of prior judgement about groupings. Considering only one problem for US data alone, using 22 assets in L to test weak separability for all possible groupings of 5 assets leads to 22!/5!*17!, or 26 334 possibilities. Clearly, with M1A being composed of three assets, M1 being composed of four and M2 being composed of eleven, just testing all possible groupings of three, four and eleven assets would be an enormous problem. As in previous work in this area, the size of the problem is reduced by taking the central banks' official groupings as given and testing them in conjunction with alternative groupings suggested in other research or by financial innovations.

The results of this exercise are reported in Table 13.2. for the USA; M1A, M1 and M2 were taken as official asset collections to be tested, along with the CE grouping suggested by Rotemberg *et al.* (1995) and the MZM grouping suggested by Poole (1992).[7] In addition to testing groups suggested by previous research, two other general guidelines were followed: testing the separability of non-interest-bearing cheque account deposits from interest-bearing equivalents and of immediately-liquid deposits from time-deposits. These guidelines were especially useful in limiting the search for alternatives to the official groupings for Germany and Japan.

The results for the USA are striking in that only the CE asset grouping, which is not a reported monetary aggregate, comes close to satisfying GARP with no violations. In contrast, M1A and M1 fail to satisfy GARP at numerous data points. In between are MZM and M2, which fail at relatively small numbers of data points. As noted earlier, the bias of the non-parametric test and the absence of significance levels suggest that the data should be examined more closely when the NONPAR algorithm indicates that GARP fails to hold only at a few data points. The Φ matrix of Chalfant and Alston (1988), which is composed of elements representing expenditures on q_{it} quantities at p_j prices, allows one to check for consistency of consumer preferences by examining above- and below-diagonal elements. These ratios simply indicate whether a consumer, who *could* have bought a preferred bundle (as revealed by his behaviour in a previous period) at a later period's set of prices, in fact did so. If he did, his behaviour is consistent with GARP, and the ratio of above-to-below diagonal elements will be greater than 1.0. If the ratio is less than 1.0, however, either of two judgements is possible: GARP is rejected by a demonstration of intransitive preferences, or measurement error in the data produced an error in this ratio. As a practical matter, the question often becomes one of determining, for example, whether a ratio of 0.9997 is more likely to indicate intransitivity of consumer preferences or measurement error.

By applying this approach to data for the CE grouping, it is revealed that GARP is violated at only two data points (observations 15 and 36), where the ratios of above-to-below diagonal elements of the Φ matrix also take values greater than 0.999; MZM, which requires adjustments at more data points, still results in ratio values near 1.0. These small corrections necessary to satisfy GARP seem to be within the range of measurement error. On this basis, small adjustments were made in price or quantity values at the points where violations of GARP occurred, so that CE, M2 and MZM could be retained for further examination. Other groupings were rejected because GARP was violated at a substantially larger number of data points and by greater magnitudes. Overall, these results suggest that a decade of financial innovations seems to have rendered several of the traditional US monetary aggregates obsolete as separable groups.

The results for Germany and Japan follow a similar theme: the asset groupings behind the official aggregates targeted by the central banks generally fail weak separability at large numbers of data points, while other non-official groupings pass after modest adjustments in the raw data at only a few data points. In particular, the M3 grouping is rejected for Germany and the M2 + CDs grouping is rejected for Japan. Moreover, the narrow asset collections that do not include time-deposits seem to have better success in satisfying the restrictions of GARP. For Germany, narrow collections of currency plus sight deposits (analogous to M1-A in the USA) or currency, sight deposits and savings balances (similar to the CE in the USA) are candidates for aggregation. In Japan, several similar collections of sight-deposits and other immediately-liquid balances satisfy GARP. Overall, and despite the low power of the non-parametric test, the results are nearly uniform in suggesting one general result: *time deposits should not be part of a* ***monetary*** *aggregate*. As time deposits represent (see Table 13.1) more than 25 per cent of US M2 and German M3, and 75 per cent of Japanese M2 + CDs, the puzzle of misbehaving monetary aggregates since the mid-1980s may be explained in part by aggregates based on inadmissible asset collections.

13.3 Simple-sum versus Divisia measures: some initial evidence

Using both the official aggregates targeted by central banks and the new groupings identified by the weak separability tests reported in Table 13.2, a set of Divisia aggregates can be constructed and compared. In particular, there are two interests. The first is to evaluate the stability and performance of simple-sum and Divisia measures of the official aggregates even though they fail tests for weak separability. The point here would be to identify the influence of weighting alone on an aggregate's growth rate and other matters of interest for monetary policy. A second comparison can then be made between Divisia measures of the newly-identified asset groupings, and both simple-sum and

Table 13.2 Results of tests for weak separability

(a) USA (1983.1–1992.3) *Partitions*	*GARP*	*Consistency*	*Number of violations*
MIA	No	No	115
L – MIA	No		(2)
M1	No	No	65
L – M1	Yes		
M2	No	No	23
L – M2	Yes		
CE	Yes[1]	No	2
L – CE	Yes		
MZM	No	No	6
L – MZM	Yes		

(b) Germany (1975.1–1990.1) *Partitions*	*GARP*	*Consistency*	*Number of violations*
C + CD	Yes	No	0
TD + SAV	No		(53)
C + SD	Yes	Yes	0
TD	Yes		
SAV	Yes		
C + SD + TD	No	No	86
SAV	Yes		
C + SD + SAV	Yes	No	0
TD	Yes		

(c) Japan (1979.1–1991.1) *Partitions*	*GARP*	*Consistency*	*Number of violations*
C + CD	Yes	No	0
M3 – (C + CD)	Yes		
C + CD + OD	Yes	No	0
M3 – (C + CD + OD)	Yes		
C + CD + OD + DN	No	No	6
M3 – (C + CD + OD + DN)	Yes		
C + CD + OD + DN + PS	Yes	No	0
M3 – (C + CD + OD + DN + PS)	Yes		
M2 + CDs	No	No	2
M3 – (M2 + CDs)	No		(2)

Divisia measures of the official aggregates. In this exercise it should be possible to see the effects and asset composition together. In particular, with Divisia weights declining, and own-rates of return rising, it may be revealed that the weakest part of this exercise – the tests for weak separability – is of less practical importance when broad aggregates are constructed with Divisia weights.

These comparisons begin with Figures 13.1–13.3, each of which shows the growth rates of three measures: the simple-sum targeted aggregate, a Divisia measure of the same asset collection, and a Divisia measure of one alternative asset collection suggested by the weak separability tests. These figures, which plot the annualised growth rates of these series, each show occasions where the simple-sum and Divisia measures offered fundamentally different indications of the stance of policy. In the USA for example, simple-sum M2 revealed little change during the period from 1980 to 1986. Divisia measures of M2 and the CE asset grouping, however, exhibited marked contractions and substantially lower average growth rates over 1980–82, a pattern much more in keeping with the two recessions and substantial US disinflation during the early 1980s. A similar pronounced divergence occurred in the two years prior to the 1990–1 recession, with the Divisia measures of M2 and the CE grouping again showing sharp declines relative to simple-sum M2. Other episodes of divergence are also clear in the plot.

A similar story is also to be found for the other countries. Figure 13.2 shows that Divisia M3 for Germany exhibits marked declines in its growth rate in 1981 and 1989, while the simple-sum measure indicates little or no change in its growth rate. For Japan, shown in Figure 13.3, the Divisia measure of M2 + CDs reflects a much sharper contraction than the simple-sum measure over 1980–91 and shows a more restrictive policy in the most recent data as well. These figures, while offering no evidence on whether monetary targeting is a good or bad idea *per se*, do indicate that money stock measurement can have important implications for any attempt to monitor or target a monetary aggregate.

Differences at turning points

Although many central bankers would argue that the trend rate of money growth is the best indicator of the trend rate of inflation, the usefulness of this belief is subject to at least two caveats. First, the results produced by the cointegration literature (for example, Hallman *et al.*, 1991) indicate extraordinarily lengthy periods as the interval of full adjustment to a long-run equilibrium between money and the price level – more than twenty years in the case of their P-star model. Second, the substantial literature documenting the procyclical nature of money growth, at least for the USA, suggests that monitoring the thrust of monetary policy at business-cycle turning points will be important, both for attaining price stability and for avoiding the introduction of additional volatility to the cycle. Together, both points argue for looking at the relative degrees of monetary stimulus and their changes at important turning points. This issue is highlighted in Table 13.3.

The entries in this table are correlation coefficients for *changes* in money growth rates over the full samples for each country and one notable episode suggested by the plots in Figures 13.1 and 13.2, when simple-sum and Divisia measures moved in markedly different ways. For the USA, for example,

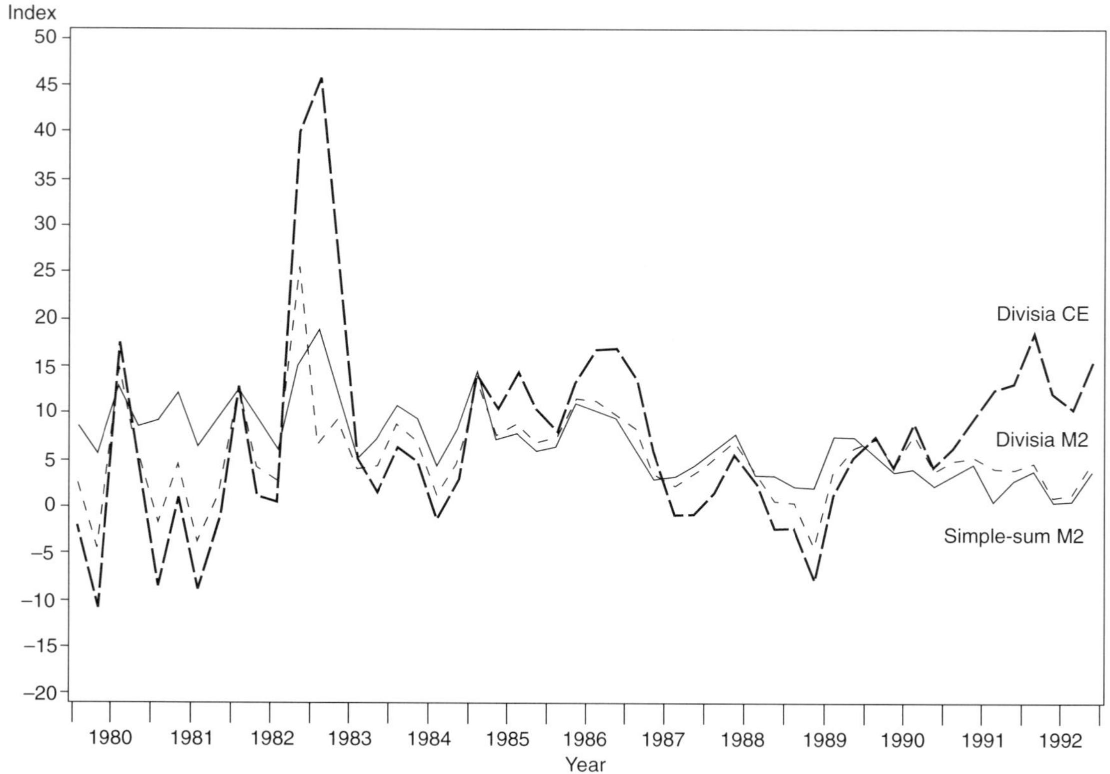

Figure 13.1 Growth of simple-sum and Divisia M2, and Divisia CE (USA: 1980Q1–1992Q4)

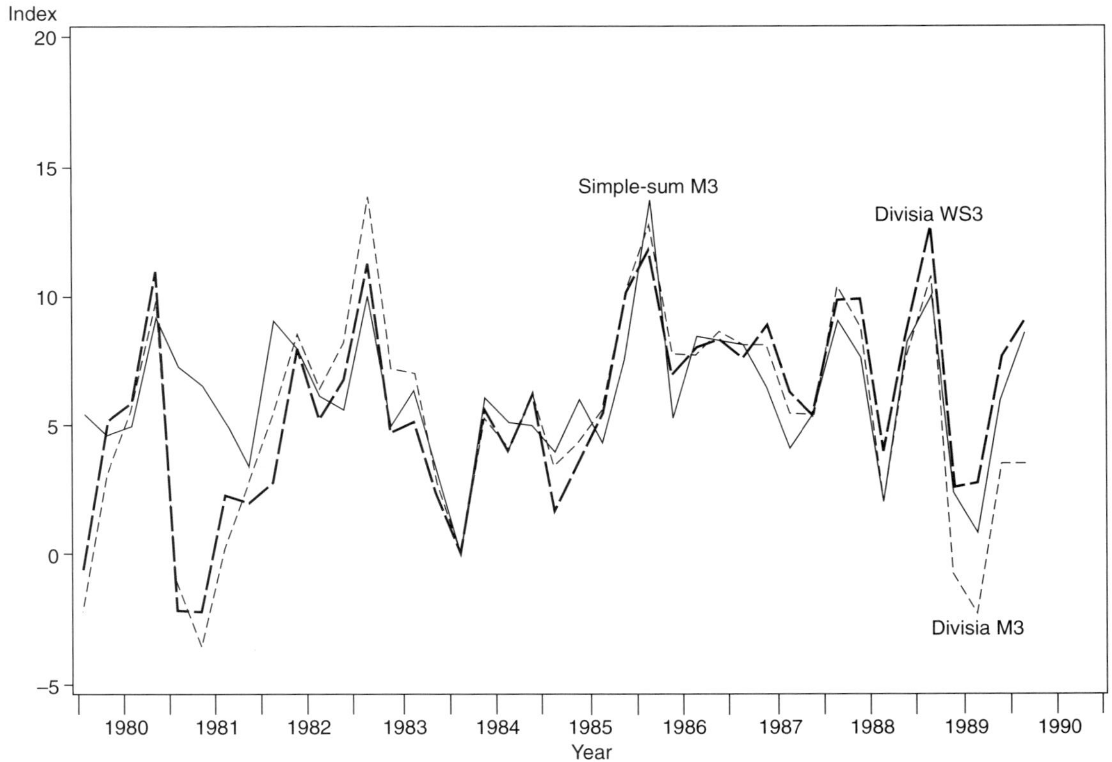

Figure 13.2 Growth of simple-sum and Divisia M3, and Divisia WS3 (Germany: 1980Q1–1990Q1)

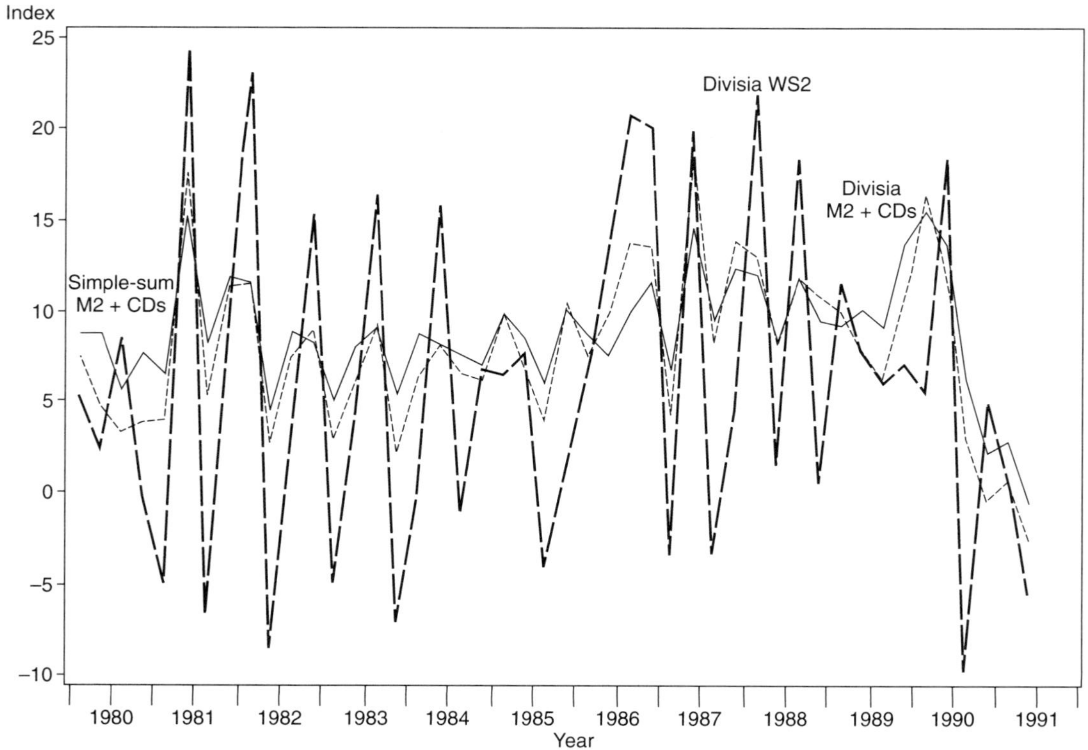

Figure 13.3 Simple-sum and Divisia M2 + CDs, and Divisia WS2 (Japan: 1980Q1–1991Q2)

Table 13.3 Correlation coefficients between changes in money growth rates

USA	Period: 1960.1–1992.4				Period: 1980.1–1982.4			
	SSM2	DM2	DCE		SSM2	DM2	DCE	
DM2	0.7051			DM2	0.6485			
DCE	0.7649	0.8121		DCE	0.8924	0.7702		
DMZM	0.7658	0.9157	0.9660	DMZM	0.8461	0.9049	0.9640	
Germany	Period: 1975.1–1990.1				Period: 1980.1–1984.4			
	SSM3	DM3	DM1		SSM3	DM3	DM1	
DM3	0.7634			DM3	0.5924			
DM1	0.3674	0.8181		DM1	0.4320	0.9402		
WD3	0.7038	0.9345	0.8210	WD3	0.5147	0.9567	0.9612	
Japan	Period: 1976.1–1991.2				Period:1985.1–1991.2			
	SSM2 + CDs	DM2 + CDs	WD2	WD3	SSM2 + CDs	DM2 + CDs	WD2	WD3
DM2 + CDs	0.9464			DM2 + CDs	0.9342			
WD2	0.7673	0.8065		WD2	0.6696	0.6744		
WD3	0.7278	0.8612	0.8383	WD3	0.5632	0.7334	0.6566	
WD5	0.9179	0.9937	0.7874	0.8664 / WD5	0.9020	0.9923	0.6406	0.7343

Definitions of non-traditional aggregates

Germany: WD3 = currency (CUR) + non-int. bearing sight deps. (SD) + savings deps. at statutory notice (SDSN)

Japan: WD2 = currency (CUR) + current deposits (CD)

WD3 = currency (CUR) + current deposits (CD) + ordinary deposits (OD)

WD5 = currency (CUR) + current deps. (CD) + ordinary deps. (OD) + deposits at notice (ON) + postal savings (PS)

USA: DCE = Divisia aggregate of M1 + SDCB + SDSL + MMDAC + MMDAT.

changes in the growth rates of simple-sum and Divisia M2 over the entire sample have a correlation coefficient of 0.7; over the 1980.1–1982.4 subperiod, when Divisia M2 growth slowed sharply relative to the simple-sum measure, this correlation coefficient falls to 0.65. Although this small decline may not demonstrate a practical problem for the implication of monetary policy in the USA, it does suggest the potential for drawing incorrect inferences if the simple-sum and Divisia measures were less closely related.

And this seems to be the case of the other countries. For Germany, for example, changes in the growth rate of simple-sum M3 and Divisia M1 (an aggregate suggested by the tests of weak separability) have a correlation coefficient of only 0.37. For Japan, the results are analogous to those of the USA – some close correlations over the entire sample, others more modest and declines in the degree of association over key subperiods. Overall, these results indicate that changes in the growth of simple-sum aggregates at key turning points can give importantly different signals about the degree of monetary stimulus or restraint.

Comparisons of longer-run trends

Central bankers and monetary economists interested in the implications of monetary actions generally agree that the long-run trend growth rate of the money stock will give a good indication of the likely course of future inflation. As noted earlier, this is the motivation behind, and primary conclusion of, the recent 'P-star' study of the relationship between US M2 growth and inflation. But if the theoretical proposition of a relationship between trend money growth and future inflation is true, what are the consequences if Divisia and simple-sum measures of the same aggregate produce substantially different trend growth rates?

Before addressing this question, Table 13.4 first presents descriptive statistics for growth rates of the selected simple-sum and Divisia aggregates. Over the entire sample periods available for each measure, the means and standard deviations indicate that, in the US case, the average growth rates of Divisia measures of M2 and MZM over the entire sample are between 1.5 and 2.0 percentage points less than their simple-sum counterparts. Moreover, as in the previous case of correlation coefficients, the average growth rates over a key subsample are markedly different: for example, over 1980.1–1982.4, simple-sum MZM grew at a 13 per cent rate while its Divisia counterpart grew at a 6.4 per cent rate! Central bankers, economists and the financial press would clearly draw different inferences about the course of monetary policy if one series were monitored instead of the other.

Although the contrasts are less striking for other countries, the general point still is important even at this basic level: if money growth and inflation move one-to-one over time, differences of only one or two percentage points in the average growth rates of simple-sum and Divisia aggregates will still produce

Table 13.4 Means and standard deviations of money growth rates

USA	Period: 1960.1–1992.4		Period:1980.1–1982.4	
	Mean	Standard Deviation	Mean	Standard Deviation
SSM2	7.87	3.65	9.54	3.66
DM2	6.03	4.32	5.47	6.84
SSMZM	7.54	8.99	12.98	19.13
DMZM	5.95	6.43	6.42	12.33
DCE	5.91	7.38	6.62	15.03
Germany	Periods: 1975.1–1990.1		Period: 1980.1–1984.4	
SSM3	7.10	3.10	5.78	2.27
DM3	6.61	4.25	4.46	4.34
DM1	7.34	5.75	4.44	5.67
WD3	6.63	4.07	4.16	3.75
Japan	Period: 1976.1–1991.2		Period: 1985.1–1991.2	
SSM2 + CDs	9.45	3.31	9.18	3.81
DM2 + CDs	8.48	4.51	8.73	5.08
WD2	6.82	9.19	6.87	8.98
WD3	7.24	7.05	7.54	6.94
WD5	7.75	5.61	8.40	6.51

Table 13.5 Unit root tests on differences between the growth rates of alternative money stock measures

Country	*Variable tested*	
	Differences in Growth Rates	*(Second Differences in Growth Rates)*
USA		
Simple-sum M2 – Divisia M2	–3.26	
Simple-sum M2 – Divisia CE	–4.48	
Simple-sum M2 – Divisia MZM	–4.03	
Simple-sum M2 – Simple-sum MZM	–5.75	
Divisia CE – Simple sum MZM	–4.02	
Germany		
Simple-sum M3 – Divisia M3	–3.55	
Simple-sum M3 – DM1	–4.19	
Simple-sum M3 – WD3	–2.16	–7.84
Japan		
Simple-sum M2 + CDs – Divisia M2 + CDs	–2.76	–10.10
Simple-sum M2 + CDs – Divisia WD2	–4.59	
Simple-sum M2 + CDs – Divisia WD3	–3.80	
Simple-sum M2 + CDs – Divisia WD5	–2.20	–9.69

inflation errors of the same magnitude for a central bank that targets a simple-sum measure.

Stronger evidence on the commonality – or lack thereof – among growth rates of the alternative aggregates is provided by unit root tests applied to differences in the growth rates between, for example, US Divisia M2 and US simple-sum M2. If these differences were shown not to be stationary, the implication would be that differences between the two series are potentially unbounded, and that watching one aggregate rather than another will offer a fundamentally different picture of the long-run trend of money growth and the likely course of future inflation. The results of this exercise are reported in Table 13.5.

The results indicate that, for Germany and Japan, the differences between the growth rates of their current simple-sum aggregate targets and one or two Divisia alternatives are not stationary. That is to say, the differences between simple-sum and Divisia German M3 and between simple-sum and Divisia Japanese M2 + CDs are likely to grow wider over time and compound the long-run inflation error created by targeting a simple-sum rather than a Divisia monetary aggregate. While these results offer stronger evidence than that suggested by Table 13.4, the apparent stationarity of the differences between the growth rates of simple-sum and Divisia M2 in the USA is not a compelling rejection of the inference implied by simple comparisons of means: the low power of the unit root test and the calculated statistic of -3.26 relative to its -2.90 critical value offers only weak evidence on stationarity for these differences. Still, recognising that the simple-sum weighting scheme *must* produce an invalid index number, one which is subject to spurious behaviour, the evidence in Tables 13.4 and 13.5 indicates that officials of at least two, and perhaps three, central banks are monitoring aggregates that are giving an incorrect signal about the long-run thrust of their monetary actions.

13.4 Conclusions

The results in this chapter leave many questions unanswered. They say nothing about the feasibility or desirability of an intermediate target strategy for the implementation of monetary policy; they say nothing about the ability of central banks to control the behaviour of various monetary aggregates; and they offer only limited evidence on the closeness or stability of relationships between various aggregates and the final goals of monetary policy. At the same time, the results indicate clearly that the construction of a monetary aggregate is affecting judgements about the conduct of monetary policy and its effects on economic activity. On the two basic questions behind the construction of monetary aggregates – that is, which assets should be included in the aggregate and how they should be aggregated – these results indicate that the measures targeted by three major central banks fail. In general, each includes time deposits that both intuition and tests of weak separability argue do not belong in a *monetary* aggregate.

Moreover, because simple-sum and Divisia measures of the same aggregate often have different trends and also have exhibited different turning points, or even moved in different directions, the evidence implies that making inferences about the relative ease of tightness of policy depends crucially on the monetary index number that is being monitored and/or targeted.

Notes

1. A repeated manifestation of this danger is the so-called 'velocity' problem. The velocity of money, which is constructed by dividing nominal GDP by the money stock, dropped sharply in the early 1980s and has behaved erratically since then. Consequences of this 'surprise', which coincided with wide adoption of interest-bearing cheque account deposits, included wildly alarmist (false) warnings about pending inflation and the abandonment of monetary targeting because this behaviour implied that the demand for money had become unstable. If, however, this derived measure of velocity merely reflects the erratic behaviour of a simple-sum measure of money, these qualitative conclusions could be rejected.
2. See, for example, Feldstein and Stock (1994). It should be noted, however, that their dismissal of superlative indexes is based on a single, unpublished 1987 paper by staff at the Board of Governors.
3. For a survey of US studies see Barnett, Fisher and Serletis (1992). For Canada, see Cockerline and Murray (1981). For Germany, see Issing *et al.* (1993). For Japan, see

Ishida (1984). For the UK see Batchelor (1987), Holtham *et al.* (1990), and Belongia and Chrystal (1991). For Australia, see Horne and Martin (1989). For Switzerland, see Yue and Fluri (1991), and Fluri (1990). Some work has also been done on Divisia aggregates for Mexico, Brazil, and Chile.

4. Intuitive arguments in favour of narrow or broad aggregates can be found in Currie (1935, pp. 10–24), and Friedman and Schwartz (1970, pp. 89–92)
5. A separable group requires that the marginal rate of substitution between any two goods within the group is independent of the quantity consumed of any good not in the group. Aggregating over a non-separable group, therefore, means that the behaviour of goods not in the separable group will act as missing 'shift' variables; indeed, apparent but unexplained shifts in the behaviour of M1 in the early 1980s and M2 in the 1990s provided the impetus for work such as Poole's MZM measure, which focuses on the asset composition of the 'misbehaving' aggregate. Another benefit of a superlative index number is, therefore, that the effects of aggregating inadmissible asset groupings will be smaller than in a simple-sum index. If, for example, a broad aggregate is constructed and its illiquid components have few characteristics of money, they will receive a small weight in a superlative index and have less influence on the aggregate's behaviour. Thus, if a more rigorous choice criterion is not employed, one strategy to monetary aggregation would be to adopt broad Divisia or Fisher Ideal measures as they would not mistakenly exclude something important or give undue weight to something superfluous. See, for example, Barnett (1982, pp. 695–701).
6. The bias arises because a sufficient, rather than necessary, characterisation of separability is used; this was noted in Varian (1983). See also Barnett and Choi (1989), and the documentation to Varian's non-parametric demand analysis program. For a discussion of the two approaches and a survey of evidence produced by each, see Barnett *et al.* (1992), pp. 2102–04.
7. The CE asset grouping used by Rotemberg *et al.* (1995) and subsequently by Belongia (1996) includes M1 plus savings deposits. The MZM grouping covers M2 less small time-deposits, plus institution-only money market mutual funds.

References

Afriat, Sidney (1967) 'The Construction of Utility Functions from Expenditure Data', *International Economic Review* (February), pp. 67–77.

Barnett, William A. (1978) 'The User Cost of Money', *Economics Letters*, vol. 1, pp. 145–9.

Barnett, William A. (1980) 'Economic Monetary Aggregates: An Application of Aggregation and Index Number Theory', *Journal of Econometrics* (September), pp. 11–48.

Barnett, William A. (1982) 'The Optimal Level of Monetary Aggregation', *Journal of Money, Credit and Banking*, pt 2 (November), pp. 687–710.

Barnett, William, Edward Offenbacher and Paul Spindt (1984) 'The New Divisia Monetary Aggregates', *Journal of Political Economy* (December), pp. 1049–85.

Barnett, William A. and Seungmook Choi (1989) 'A Monte Carlo Study of Tests of Blockwise Weak Separability', *Journal of Business and Economic Statistics* (July), pp. 363–77.

Barnett, William A., Douglas Fisher and Apostolos Serletis (1992) 'Consumer Theory and the Demand for Money', *Journal of Economic Literature* (December), pp. 2086–119.

Batchelor, Roy (1987) 'Monetary Developments', *City University Business School Economic Review* (Autumn), pp. 17–22.

Belongia, Michael T. (1996) 'Measurement Matters: Some Recent Results in Monetary Economics Re-Examined', *Journal of Political Economy* (October), pp. 1065–83.

Belongia, Michael T. and James A. Chalfant (1989) 'The Changing Empirical Definition of Money: Some Estimates from a Model of the Demand for Money Substitutes', *Journal of Political Economy* (April), pp. 387–97.

Belongia, Michael T. and K. Alec Chrystal (1991) 'An Admissible Monetary Aggregate for the United Kingdom', *The Review of Economics and Statistics* (August), pp. 497–502.

Chalfant, James A. and Julian M. Alston (1988) 'Accounting for Changes in Tastes', *Journal of Political Economy* (April), pp. 391–410.

Cockerline, J. P. and J. D. Murray (1981) 'A Comparison of Alternative Methods of Monetary Aggregation: Some Preliminary Evidence', in Bank of Canada Technical Report No. 28.

Currie, Lauchlin (1935) *The Supply and Control of Money in the United States* (Cambridge., Mass.: Harvard University Press).

Dietrich, Lynn D. and Kevin L. Kliesen (1992) 'Data Appendix', *Federal Reserve Bank of St Louis Review* (November/December), pp. 46–52.

Feldstein, Martin and James H. Stock (1994) 'The Use of a Monetary Aggregate to Target Nominal GDP', in N. G. Manniw (ed.), *Monetary Policy* (Chicago: University of Chicago Press), pp. 7–62.

Friedman, Milton and Anna J. Schwartz (1970) *Monetary Statistics of the United States* (New York: Columbia University Press).

Fluri, Robert (1990) 'Monetare Divisia-Aggregate – eine Alternative zu den traditionellen Geldmengenindikatoren?' *Geld, Wahrung und Konjunktur*, Schweizerische National Bank (December), pp. 343–54.

Hallman, Jeffrey J., Richard D. Porter and David H. Small (1991) 'Is The Price Level Tied to the M2 Monetary Aggregate in the Long Run?', *American Economic Review* (September), pp. 841–58.

Holtham, Gerald, Giles Keating and Peter Spencer (1990) 'The Demand for Liquid Assets in Germany and the U.K.', in Peter Hooper *et al.* (eds), *Financial Sectors in Open Economies: Empirical Analysis and Policy Issues* (Washington, DC: Board of Governors of the Federal Reserve System), pp. 207–62.

Horne, Jocelyn and Vance L. Martin (1989) 'Weighted Monetary Aggregates: An Empirical Study Using Australian Monetary Data, 1969–1987', *Australian Economic Papers* (December), pp. 181–200.

Ishida, Kazuhiko (1984) 'Divisia Monetary Aggregates and Demand for Money: A Japanese Case', *Bank of Japan Monetary and Economic Studies* (June), pp. 49–80.

Issing, Otmar, von Heinz Herrmann, K. H. Todter and Hans-Eggert Reimers (1993) 'Zinsgewichte Geldmengenaggregate und M3 – ein Vergleich', *Kredit und Kapital*, vol. 1, pp. 1–21.

Meltzer, Allan H. (1991) 'The Fed at Seventy-Five', in Michael T. Belongia (ed.), *Monetary Policy on the 75th Anniversary of the Federal Reserve System* (Norwell, Mass.: Kluwer).

Poole, William (1992) 'Where Do We Stand in the Battle Against Inflation?', in *Shadow Open Market Committee: Policy Statement and Position Papers, PPS 92-01*, Bradley Policy Research Center, University of Rochester, 8–9 March.

Rotemberg, Julio J., John C. Driscoll and James M. Poterba (1995) 'Money, Output and Prices: Evidence from a New Monetary Aggregate', *Journal of Business and Economic Statistics*, vol. 13, no. 1 (January), pp. 67–84.

Swofford, James L. and Gerald A. Whitney (1991) 'The Composition and Construction of Monetary Aggregates', *Economic Inquiry* (October), pp. 752–61.

Thornton, Daniel L. and Piyu Yue (1992) 'An Extended Series of Divisia Monetary Aggregates', *Federal Reserve Bank of St. Louis Review* (November/December), pp. 35–46.

Varian, Hal R. (1982) 'The Non-Parametric Approach to Demand Analysis', *Econometrica* (July), pp. 945–73.

Varian, Hal R. (1983) 'Non-Parametric Tests of Consumer Behaviour', *Review of Economic Studies* (January), pp. 99–110.

Yue, Piyu and Robert Fluri (1991) 'Divisia Monetary Services Indexes for Switzerland: Computation and Behaviour', *Federal Reserve Bank of St Louis Review* (September/October), pp. 19–33.

Index